The Making of Middle Indonesia

Verhandelingen van het Koninklijk Instituut voor Taal-, Land- en Volkenkunde

VOLUME 293

Power and Place in Southeast Asia

Edited by

Gerry van Klinken (KITLV)
Edward Aspinall (Australian National University)

VOLUME 5

The titles published in this series are listed at brill.com/vki

The Making of Middle Indonesia

Middle Classes in Kupang Town, 1930s–1980s

By

Gerry van Klinken

BRILL

LEIDEN · BOSTON
2014

The realization of this publication was made possible by the support of KITLV (Royal Netherlands Institute of Southeast Asian and Caribbean Studies).

Cover illustration: PKI provincial Deputy Secretary Samuel Piry in Waingapu, about 1964 (photo courtesy Mr. Ratu Piry, Waingapu).

Library of Congress Cataloging-in-Publication Data

Klinken, Geert Arend van.
The Making of middle Indonesia : middle classes in Kupang town, 1930s-1980s / by Gerry van Klinken.
pages cm. -- (Verhandelingen van het Koninklijk Instituut voor Taal-, Land- en Volkenkunde, ISSN 1572-1892; volume 293)
Includes bibliographical references and index.
ISBN 978-90-04-26508-0 (hardback : acid-free paper) -- ISBN 978-90-04-26542-4 (e-book)
1. Middle class--Indonesia--Kupang (Nusa Tenggara Timur) 2. City and town life--Indonesia--Kupang (Nusa Tenggara Timur) 3. Kupang (Nusa Tenggara Timur, Indonesia)--Social conditions. 4. Kupang (Nusa Tenggara Timur, Indonesia)--Economic conditions. I. Title.

HT690.I5K55 2014
305.5'50959868--dc23

2013043761

This publication has been typeset in the multilingual "Brill" typeface. With over 5,100 characters covering Latin, IPA, Greek, and Cyrillic, this typeface is especially suitable for use in the humanities. For more information, please see www.brill.com/brill-typeface.

ISSN 1572-1892
ISBN 978-90-04-26508-0 (hardback)
ISBN 978-90-04-26542-4 (e-book)

This book is printed on acid-free paper.

Power springs up between men when they act together and vanishes the moment they disperse.

(Arendt 1958:200)

CONTENTS

PREFACE

The term 'Middle Indonesia' refers to the mediational roles played by middle classes in provincial towns. Middle Indonesia is a social zone connecting extremes. This book is part of a collective writing effort about this zone. We defined Middle Indonesia in a multidimensional way as representing: 'the geographical space between village and metropolitan city, the social space between the established upper-middle classes and the urban poor, the economic and political twilight zone between formal institutions and markets (and between informal and illegal arrangements), the cultural meeting ground of global fashions and localized practices, and the generational space between child and adult.' The project was inspired by Clifford Geertz's idea that the dynamic middle between extremes of various kinds is an interesting place to examine social change. In the vast archipelagic nation's urban hierarchy there are about 200 midsized cities with populations of 50,000 to a million. They connect metropolises like Jakarta with about 70,000 villages. The social life of these towns is dominated by people who belong, on a national scale, to the middle classes. The economy there has a higher level of informality than in Jakarta. We do not argue that the provincial town is the *only* place to study the political, economic, cultural and inter-generational life of Indonesia's middle classes – there are middle classes in the metropolises. But we do agree with Geertz that 'in-between' is the provincial town's 'most outstanding characteristic' (1963c:16). This book takes only a tangential interest in the cultural life of provincial middle classes and in the life chances of middle-class youth in these provincial urban settings. The main lines of the research programme as a whole, which did extend to those questions and was essentially anthropological, are described in an edited volume (Van Klinken and Berenschot 2014).[1] The present book focuses on the political and economic history of the middle class in one particular provincial town, Kupang, on the island of Timor in the east of the archipelago. Middle-ness is, of course, in the eye of the beholder. To someone in Jakarta, Kupang looks more like a terminus than a middle – shipping and aerial lines end here. But to a farmer's son from the hills of Amanuban

[1] Other publications to come out of this project are described in the introduction to this volume. See also online documentation at www.kitlv.nl.

behind Kupang, who took days to reach Kupang on horseback, it was a place full of wonders, and perhaps a gateway to even greater wonders, if he could find the money to take a ship further west.

The collective writing effort at my institute, the Royal Netherlands Institute of Southeast Asian and Caribbean Studies (KITLV), goes back to 2002. Our primary interest was not in ethnographic studies of remote places, but in power. As Indonesia democratized and adopted decentralized forms of governance, power seemed to become less a matter for the 'commanding heights' and more a mediated affair playing out in many places around the vast archipelago. Led and inspired by my colleague Henk Schulte Nordholt, the KITLV research division has brought together many talented scholars from all over the world in the last decade to try to understand the embeddedness of Indonesian politics in local societies. 'In Search of Middle Indonesia' was the latest incarnation of that quest. About two dozen 'Middle Indonesia' researchers – PhD students, postdoctoral researchers and supervisors – met frequently throughout a five-year period. Many ideas first mooted in those meetings have found their way into this book.

The institute has been a delightful home. Countless seminars and research lunches, in room 138 overlooking Leiden's old moat, touched almost every conceivable topic in Southeast Asian studies. Its superb library, friendly staff, and understanding administrators have created the most supportive environment any researcher could wish for. Generous financing came from the Royal Netherlands Academy of Arts and Sciences (KNAW in Dutch) through the second Scientific Programme Indonesia-Netherlands (SPIN).

In the research plan, Kupang was supposed to represent an average provincial town, much like so many others in the same demographic category, in which nothing of national importance ever seems to happen yet which sustains, as they all do, its share of the diverse flows of ideas and resources that ultimately hold a country together. Its rocky landscape looks unattractive to first-time visitors arriving in the dry season. But it has grown on me over the years between 2009 and 2011 when I made sustained visits there. My colleague Chris Brown experienced the same growth of affection, and he produced a fine photographic exhibition of Kupang to prove it. It now hangs at the KITLV. More than 80 people shared their knowledge of Kupang's history with me, many of whom I interviewed multiple times. They are listed below. We ate together, and some invited me to stay; others sent materials by post or shared memories by email. The best informants are now all old. I feel privileged to have learned from them. There is not space to honour them all, but I cannot omit special mention of a few: Hendrikus Ataupah, who would tell me, 'I can give you an hour to talk,' and then give me three, at a tempo that left me parched and with a lame writing hand; Leo Nisnoni, whose hospitality and archival collection is famous throughout the (admittedly small) community of foreign researchers who have set foot in this town; and Heny Markus, who opened her heart to my wife and myself with the most intimate of family stories. And I will never forget Bobby Toebe and his friendly workers at the Maliana Hotel overlooking the beach, who served cake and coffee punctually at 3:30 p.m.; Bruder Rufinus, who made my wife and I welcome at the fine SVD library in Ende, and Stef Meo who opened the Ledolero library to us with equal kindness; Ratu Piry in Waingapu who spoke to us at length about his father Sam and his uncle Jakob Piry; F.H. Foebia in Soë who delights in books; Revs. Robert and Len Tahun who twice offered my weary wife and me unforgettable hospitality in Oinlasi – Robert passed away in 2012; and their son Rev. Yanni Tahun who with equal generosity became my guide to Kuanfatu. In Sydney, Gordon and Ruth Dicker opened their home to me, and they, as well as Colville Crowe, donated their 1950s slides of Timor to the KITLV; and Clark Cunningham rummaged through his old papers for me. To go on would please me and them, but perhaps not my readers.

If they are not always mentioned in the relevant chapters, it is because some of the topics we discussed remain sensitive even today, and they do not want their names in print. I know already that some will be delighted and proud of their contributions, while others will be frustrated that I left things out or perhaps got them wrong. My biggest worry is that I am involving some of them in a story that they think is not the one that should be told. The agonies of doing critical research among informants who have become friends in a provincial town are discussed in Chapter 3. To all I can only say, as I learned in Java: 'Beribu-ribu terima kasih, mohon maaf lahir batin, semoga bermanfaat bagi sesama.'

In June 2010 nine colleagues gathered at a roundtable to discuss an early version of the manuscript. They were Adriaan Bedner, Ben White, David Henley, Gerben Nooteboom, Henk Schulte Nordholt, John F. McCarthy, Rosanne Rutten, Suraya Afiff, and Tania Li. Their insistent questions – including the dreaded, 'What is the central question of your book?' – rang in my ears for months and inspired new fieldwork in the hills beyond Kupang. Whether or not I have now achieved greater clarity on everything they wanted to know – from peasants to barbers, from factionalism to brokerage – these nine colleagues were my most stimulating critics. The detailed comments made by two anonymous reviewers for the press helped me clarify the argument and pre-empt many errors and infelicities from reaching the printed page. Naturally, only I am responsible for all those problems that they did not detect or that I obstinately refused to correct.

If I had known how difficult this project would be I may not have started it. A chapter in the book is devoted to the obstacles facing the historian researching a postcolonial provincial town. That chapter could have become an even longer litany if I had described the whole germination process. Before this book became what it did become, it was going to be about many other things. Among the several roads that looked promising at the time, but whose discoveries will have to await development later, are a national newspaper survey on several towns for the 1950s and 1960s by my research assistant Basilius Triharyanto, a visit to Canberra for statistical work with censuses, and a wonderful season of fieldwork in Pontianak. I mention these other roads not only in the (doubtless vain) hope of eliciting some sympathy from fellow researchers who happen to read this, but also to make a point to the general reader about my underlying intention – that it was not to become the final authority on one particular provincial town, but to stimulate further work on an important social zone of which Kupang is one site.

My wife Helene van Klinken shared bone-jarring motorcycle rides and flights on some local airlines that perhaps should not have been selling tickets. She also talked the book through with me in our little Leiden flat overlooking the water. And at the end she ran a sharp eye over the entire text. A simple 'thanks' is inadequate for everyone in this preface, but particularly for her.

The narrative pacing picks up as the book develops. The impatient reader may wish to skip the first two chapters or refer to them later. The reader less familiar with overall Indonesian history will find useful timelines on the internet.[2] Some chapters started life as publications elsewhere. An earlier version of Chapter 2 appeared in the journal *Urban Geography* (Van Klinken 2009a). Chapter 3 first appeared as a chapter in a volume on biographies East and West edited by Maureen Perkins (Van Klinken 2012). Chapter 5 is based on a paper in the journal *City and Society* (Van Klinken 2013a). They have all been extensively rewritten to make the present book a coherent whole.

[2] For example, https://en.wikipedia.org/wiki/Timeline_of_Indonesian_history (accessed 27 August 2013).

The note on spelling remains obligatory. Place names are given in their modern spelling (thus Sabu, not Savu or Savoe; Rote, not Roti). Personal names are given as they were used at the time, but the region is relaxed about these things and I have not achieved total consistency.

Gerry van Klinken
Leiden, August 2013

Thanks ...

In Kupang: A.B. Doko, Adolf Michael (Mike) Lino, Eddie and Erna Barbier and family, Ben Mboi, Benjamin (Benny) Benufinit, Boetje Latuparissa, Bp. Mboeik (Lery's father), Christoffel Kana, Christoffel Kelokila, Cornelis Lay and his family, Cornelis Tapatab, Dami Herewila, Damyan Godho, the El Tari family (Gultom Tari, Benjamin Tari), Frans Rengka, Fred Benu, Frederika ('Rikka') Lani, Gustaf Dupe and his brothers Ao Johanes Dupe and Hi Hengki Dupe, Habib Gudban, Harry Therik, Hendrikus Ataupah, Hengky Malelak, Itja Frans, John and Karen Campbell-Nelson, Leo Mali, Leo Nahak, Leopold Nisnoni, Leonidus Radja Haba, Lery Mboeik, Maria ('Mia') Noach, Mery Kolimon, Munandjar Widiyatmika, Nano Malubala, Niti Susanto, Paul Doko, Piet Salasa, Piet Y. Francis and Margreta Gertruida Noelik, Pius Rengka, Robert M. ('Robby') Koroh, Ruth Heny A. Nitbani-Markus, Selvy Lay, Sjors Lie, Wely Kono, Yakob Mboeik, and Yanuaris Koli Bau.

In and around Soë: Alexander Nubatonis, Daniel Teneo, F.H. (Fredrik Hendrik) Foebia, and Levinus Selan. Elsewhere in West Timor: Bonifacius Timoneno (Buraen), Bernadus Timoneno (Buraen), Blasius Manek (Atambua), Dominikus ('Domi') J.H. Luan (Atambua), Eleanor ('Mama Ellen') Toma and Hendrikus (Hengky) Toma (Buraen), Johan Christian Sapai (Nunusunu), Robert and Len Tahun (Oinlasi), Melianus Babis (Kuanfatu), Napoleon Fa'ot (Tetaf), Salmon Neonloni (Nunusunu), Yanni Tahun (Kuanfatu), Yohanes Tusi (Kusi), Yunus Tafuli (Kuanfatu), and Yusuf Neo'laka (Kusi),

In Waingapu: Jakob (Jaap) Palikahelu, Lika Palikahelu, Ratu Piry and family, Robert Gana, Umbu Retang Nduma. Elsewhere in Sumba: Ngarabili and Yohana Bora (Lamboya), and Yusuf Ama Rajah (Waikabubak).

Elsewhere in the world: Anouk de Koning (Leiden), Basilius Triharyanto (Jakarta), Clark Cunningham (Urbana), Colin Barlow (Canberra), Colville Crowe (Sydney), David Mitchell (Melbourne), Gordon and Ruth Dicker (Sydney), Graham Brookes (Sydney), Huberto Thomas (Maumere), Jacqueline Vel (Leiden), John Prior (Maumere), Malcolm McKinnon (Wellington), Manu Toebe (Jakarta), and Mike Grant (Perth).

LIST OF FIGURES

CHAPTER ONE

SOME HIDDEN STRENGTH

[S]tate power is rooted, in part, in the micropolitics of the localities.

(Boone 1998:25)

What holds Indonesia together? The question suddenly became urgent when widespread demonstrations amidst economic crisis forced the authoritarian President Suharto to step down in May 1998. Secessionist movements were active in Papua, Aceh and East Timor. When communal violence broke out in Maluku, Central Sulawesi and parts of Kalimantan, the word 'disintegration' suddenly leapt into the public discourse in Indonesia. For a while, no country in the world had more experts wondering aloud what the decisive national glue factor was. This dark question even began to overshadow hopeful ones concerning prospects for democracy and prosperity. Many thought society was so fractious that, without a strong figure at the top, the country would Balkanize, fall into religious fundamentalism, or descend into economic chaos. One foreign journalist wrote: 'Diplomats in Jakarta sometimes debate whether it is the breakup of the Soviet Union or of the former Yugoslavia that offers the better illustration of how things could fall apart in this country.'[1] Similar fears had preoccupied foreign policy specialists in the mid-1960s as the previous strong figure, Sukarno, grew frail. Both then and more recently, some with longer experience of the country spoke more optimistically about the strength of nationalism, the common language, and about the tolerance and pluralism that have always characterized these Southeast Asian people. In between the pessimists and optimists were those who simply felt Indonesia would somehow 'muddle on.'

There was cause enough for worry – Yugoslavia really did fall apart – but on Indonesia the optimists turned out to be right. Other than having a sunny disposition, what did they know that others did not? It was my impression that they had traveled more. They experienced the nation not

[1] Cameron W. Barr, 'No borders in Spice Island clash,' The *Christian Science Monitor*, 20 January 2000.

simply as an elaboration of an exemplary centre (a *mandala*, a powerful trope of Southeast Asian statecraft – Wolters 1999), but as a myriad of personalized networks spreading across the archipelago. Thus Jakarta's recurring crises were deprived of some of their power to spook them. It perhaps even translated to a different idea of the way power works across distance. Nobody formulated it quite like that, but it seems a productive possibility, and it is the jumping-off point for this book.

This is a book about the history of Indonesia viewed not from the top but from within those personalized networks that helped to establish national power. It presents the history of middle-class actors in one particular town in order to build an argument about the way power works in Indonesia more broadly. The remainder of this introductory chapter sets out some important preliminaries. The first of its five sections describes 'two Indonesias,' the extremities – a small heartland of money, government, and big cities, and a vast rural and provincial town periphery. The second introduces Middle Indonesia as a way to understand what holds those two Indonesias together, which is less elitist than a top-down approach. An adequate history of Indonesia requires a mental horizon that spreads, not simply from the 'centre' to the 'periphery,' but from the commanding heights to that great middle that touches the bulk of ordinary Indonesians. The third and fourth sections turn to some theoretical literatures on power and class that underpin this broadened mental horizon. The fifth introduces one particular town, the object of the present study. It is located in a region of Indonesia that had so little contact with the Republic's formative experiences as to make the question 'what holds Indonesia together?' look very real. A chapter outline follows in the final section.

Two Indonesias

The common shorthand for regional differences within Indonesia contrast Java with the Outer Islands. Reality is a little more complex, but there is no question that a small number of heartland or core regions are easily distinguishable from a large peripheral zone. It is no exaggeration to speak of two Indonesias. While the heartlands are naturally prominent in the historiography – the personalities of national leaders (Friend 2003), the revolution in Java (Anderson 1972), the emergence of new forms of political community through 'print capitalism' (Anderson 1991) – a great deal of history-writing has been concerned with the problem of distance beyond the heartlands. Jean Gelman Taylor's marvelously accessible book

Indonesia traces the slow growth of connections between widely separated peoples, particularly in the nineteenth century. 'Within the archipelago's many communities there developed an overlay of shared experience,' she wrote (Taylor 2003:238). New economic networks developed after 1800 when Batavia forced the outer islands to shift their trading links from Singapore to the new colonial capital. As the state and commerce expanded together, prosperity increased in Java and also in the peripheries – even if the benefits were not equally distributed (Dick et al 2002). In short, there is plenty of evidence to support the observation Ricklefs (2008:186) made in his standard history of Indonesia, when he wrote that 'the history of twentieth-century Indonesia was shaped to a considerable degree by this distinction [between Java and the outer islands].'

What distinguishes the heartlands from the periphery? Hugo et al (1987:84–8) quoted the following checklist of features of the heartland: a modern economy predominates (industry, services, or mining or plantations); commercial and transport networks from other regions have their focus here; foreign and domestic private investment plays an important role; the central government spends a lot of its foreign exchange and development funds in the heartland on modern infrastructure and from here carries out administrative functions that affect other parts of the country; and there are proportionately more large towns with social and cultural institutions (such as good universities) that also service other parts of the country. Most of Java has fallen into this category since colonial times, but so have the regions around Medan and (to a lesser extent) Makassar. Most of the money streams through these core areas, as well as a disproportionate amount of government activity. The largest cities are all in the heartland, with their associated flows of energy. In terms of connectivity – telegraph lines, steamship routes – Java was one of Southeast Asia's economic core areas, though always overshadowed by Singapore. The many evocative maps in the book by Dick and Rimmer (2003) on the globalizing impact on Southeast Asia of technological change, economic development and politics demonstrate how much of the archipelago's economic energy flowed through the core areas, particularly Java, and by contrast how little of it passed through the hinterland of the outer islands (e.g. pp. 28, 76, 85, 94–99, 220–1, 224).

The social tensions created by the rapid growth of capitalism were also greater in the core areas than in the peripheries, and this led to earlier and more intense social movements of all kinds there. Most of the turbulent twentieth century's mobilization took place in Java and parts of Sumatra.

The sparsely-populated, poorly-connected and rural areas of the periphery, by contrast, saw little mobilizational activity. This can be easily learned by consulting Robert Cribb's *Historical atlas of Indonesian history* (2000, 2010). When the nationalist movement began in Java early in the twentieth century, the modern colonial state had put down deep roots in an island whose fertility had long provided the Netherlands with its colonial surplus. Adrian Vickers' history of modern Indonesia firmly locates that modernity in the cities (Vickers 2005:59–84). The colonial Dutch feared radicalism mainly in Java and parts of Sumatra (though South Kalimantan worried them too at times), and not without reason. The first mass movement Sarekat Islam (1912) and the Indonesian Communist Party (Partai Komunis Indonesia, PKI) (1920s) had their bases in Java. And the pattern continued after the Japanese interregnum. The economic importance of the heartlands led Java to become a battleground between republicans and the returning colonial Dutch after World War II. This is where the iconic revolution of national liberation largely played out. Communist party (PKI) votes in the 1955 election were concentrated in Java, as were votes for the populist Reformasi party PDI (Partai Demokrasi Indonesia) in 1999.[2]

However, the heartlands cover less than 15% of the territory's land area (even if Papua is excluded from the periphery, since it did not formally join the nation till 1969). In the outer island regions, an urban hierarchy of smaller towns reflects a shallower history of capitalist penetration and state formation. How did these peripheral areas of the archipelago become part of the nation? The work done on transport networks and on cities by the historical geographer Howard Dick (1998, 1986, 2003) is relevant to this question about the political and social history of Indonesia. Dick recognized the steep contours between global city space, urban space and hinterlands, and the impact this had on the growth of the

[2] Sarekat Islam, the first mass political movement in the Netherlands Indies, started in Surakarta, Java, in 1909. It won adherents throughout the colony, with some significant concentrations in southern Sumatra and eastern Borneo, but most were in Java (Cribb 2000:146). Later it split into a militant 'Red' communist movement and a moderate 'White' Islamic one. When in the late 1920s the government began arresting communists for planning insurrection, most of the resulting convictions for political crimes occurred in Java (Cribb 2000:147). The self-proclaimed Republic of Indonesia in the late 1940s was confined to parts of Java and Sumatra, while its leadership was based in Java's Yogyakarta (Cribb 2000:160). Communist party (PKI) votes in the 1955 national election were strongest in Java, whereas conservative religious parties ruled the roost in the outer islands (Cribb 2000:163–5). Nearly half a century later, the opposition party PDI-P got most of its votes in 1999 in Java, whereas the regime party Golkar, a typical patronage party, continued to do well outside Java even after Suharto's departure (Cribb 2000:189–90).

nation. Economic networks alone were not enough to tie the heartlands to the peripheries. The increasingly globalized elites in the big cities of the heartlands – previously colonial, now indigenous upper classes – did not and still do not care much about the poor periphery. Only the sheer territoriality of the state, with its national sovereignty respected by other states and its popular sovereignty exercised by citizens everywhere, saddles the national elite with a responsibility towards the rest. But they could not possibly live up to those responsibilities by themselves – they faced an 'action-at-a-distance' problem. Potential citizens were scattered over a huge area. The human diversity enclosed by the country's capacious boundaries is so extravagant that people can be forgiven for thinking of national unity as an accident of imperial history.[3] How did national power bridge distances and reach into those areas where popular feelings had been lukewarm at best? To grasp that problem they, and we, need to travel into those vast spaces beyond the heartlands, where there is very little capital yet where millions of people live.

At first only a few privileged sites – places, people and their institutions – served as bridges across these distances. Over time, these pioneering sites of mediation facilitated increasingly dense new networks of communication. The towns functioned as nodes in these networks. Seen from beyond the heartlands, the puzzle of Indonesia's existence becomes a predominantly spatial one. How was an increasingly dense web of connections ultimately built between the heartlands and the peripheries? Central elites alone could not solve this problem. Middle class actors in provincial towns spread right across the country could, since they straddled the heartlands and peripheries socially and geographically. Pursuing these actors will result in a history of state formation from the middle rather than from above.

Middle Indonesia

The central premise of this book is that the terms on which Indonesia has survived from 1945 until the present day are co-determined in the regions,

[3] Christine Drake (1989) plotted a number of integrative variables on a series of maps designed to indicate where the government needed to work harder at its 'assimilationist' strategies. They included integrative historical experiences such as revolution, shared socio-cultural characteristics such as language, religion and nation-wide organizations, transport and telecommunication, and economic interdependence. The maps show that eastern Indonesia was poorly integrated. Though such variables are too essentialist to be convincing, the maps remain suggestive.

particularly in the provincial towns. Indonesia is a work in progress with an irreducible spatiality about it. The short-hand term 'centre-periphery' does not entirely do justice to this spatiality when it implies that the periphery is homogeneous. In reality those vast regions consist of smaller centres in which people think of themselves as 'central' in relation to their own 'periphery.' The network is a better metaphor – more on this below. Top-down or radial notions of power have not been good at grasping this networked spatiality. The country's urban hierarchy implies a spatial graininess, which separates places and people who are well-connected from those rural folk who, as Tania Li has put it, are increasingly 'surplus' (Li 2009). The better-connected towns are concentrated in the central island of Java, while the sparsely settled outer islands have far fewer sizeable towns and a less developed transport hierarchy. Researchers in the project of which this book is a part invented the name 'Middle Indonesia' for the social zone comprising middle classes in provincial towns.[4] Middle Indonesia plays a primarily mediatory role, between the central state and the bulk of society.

Estimates of the number of spatially distinct, functionally urban areas in Indonesia vary widely. 'Functionally' urban means it does not just have a concentrated population but offers urban services such as banks and high schools. If we ignore the smallest towns, which are hardly functionally urban, a conservative number is 'about 200.'[5] About half the urban population lives in them. The economic and particularly the bureaucratic

---

[4] A description of this project, and of the term Middle Indonesia, can be read in the introductory chapter of Van Klinken and Berenschot 2014.

[5] The following estimates have been made at various times (not a complete list).

831 – 'spatially distinct, functionally urban areas' – 1985 – the government's National Urban Development Strategy Project (NUDS 1985:65). Of these, 508 had populations over 10,000. When neighbouring centres were agglomerated, this left 384 discrete urban centres over 10,000. Of these 85 had populations over 50,000 – 52 of them in Java.

400 – 'definite towns' or 'towns in the narrow sense' – 1987 – from a German study in the 1980s using direct field observations (not government data) and combining a 25,000 population threshold with a minimum number of 'central place facilities' such as banks, hospitals and schools (Rutz 1987:84).

270 – towns with populations in the range of 50,000 to a million – 2010 – http://www.citypopulation.de/Indonesia-CU.html#Stadt_alpha (accessed 17 August 2013), using data from Axel Pieles; apparently based on government administrative boundaries, which means that (for example) suburbs of a large city such as Medan are reported as separate towns.

170 – towns with populations in the range 50,000 to a million – 2005 projection – calculated by myself from figures in Rutz (1987). One reason for the low estimate is that some entirely new towns have appeared since Rutz did his work, among them Batam (now nearly a million!). Other towns have changed their names (e.g. Ujung Pandang became Makassar).

ties between the heartland and the peripheral areas all pass through the network of provincial towns that cover the entire country. The rapid spread of provincial towns in the periphery since late colonial times had everything to do with the establishment of a modern state in those regions (Rutz 1987:84).

The first social scientist to take a serious interest in Indonesian provincial towns was the Dutch sociologist W.F. Wertheim (1959) (but see also Logemann 1953). The towns that grew up throughout the overwhelmingly rural archipelago after the economic liberalization of 1870 and the final burst of pacification over the subsequent 40 years were western enclaves, he wrote. Europeans and Indo-Europeans dominated them despite their small numbers – less than 10% of the urban populations, fewer even than the ethnic Chinese inhabitants. The towns had a clear class structure, which was mirrored in their ethnic make-up. Moderately rich Europeans, often there only for a short-term posting, lived in beautiful open villas. Comparatively well-off middle class Indo-Europeans lived in good stone houses. Lower middle class Indonesians lived in 'decidedly bad' housing, especially in the large towns – perhaps a house in the 'better' kampong (which was still dirty), or else in very small and expensive new houses. The Chinese lower-middle class lived in overcrowded Chinese districts or in the kampong. The Indonesian poor lived in 'abominably bad' semi-rural kampongs – which were hovels and fire hazards. Town planners took no account of the poor majority, since Europeans thought Indonesians should live in a rustic traditional setting and not intrude into their town. The rising middle class, consisting of Indo-Europeans and Indonesian 'intellectuals,' were mostly officials. They maintained a nineteenth century 'mestizo' culture, while still emphasizing their own respective cultures. According to Wertheim (1959:185), these westernized urban Indonesians found themselves increasingly united across regional differences by 'cultural movements expressing social discontent.... [T]his new Indonesian culture was to be a typically urban culture. However small a percentage of Indonesians may have lived in the towns, these towns were the most dynamic element in Indonesian society, and thus assumed a very great influence on the social and political events throughout the archipelago.'[6]

---

[6] Wertheim (1987) was critical (in my view rightly) of a later study on the Indonesian town, edited by Nas (1986), for failing to understand that the town is 'an arena of social conflict.'

Since then, the town's ethnic make-up has changed radically – most Europeans and Indo-Europeans are gone. But the political dynamism and the class differences – which were always the real key to the town's urban politics (Colombijn 2010) – have remained. Robert Van Niel (1960:22, 77) in his study on Indonesia's indigenous middle class also placed its origins in the early twentieth century in the towns, where a 'semi-Westernized element of great fluidity' – lesser aristocrats and even villagers with some western education – felt drawn to the European symbols of power and authority.

The city (*kota*) has been an important site in Indonesia's literary imagination. Indonesian novels set in the 1920s depicted the city as essentially a colonial construct, structured by the school and the government office (Kato 2003). The prestige of an official appointment exceeded that of the merchant's trade. But it was also a place of freedom. Love could blossom there, free from the social constraints of the village of origin. City people called themselves 'I' (*saya*), equivalent to the democratic Dutch first person singular *ik*, rather than the servile *hamba* or the inferior *aku*. It was a place where western time was kept, punctuated by striking clocks and by a rest day on Sundays rather than at Friday prayers. Nevertheless, the middle-sized provincial town has remained almost invisible to the Indonesian reading public. Indonesian fiction appears to have no equivalent to Gogol's *Dead souls* or Updike's *Rabbit* series. Most of it is set in the iconic village or in the big city, but very little in the middle-sized provincial town. Even the observant Pramoedya Ananta Toer, whose early *Tales from Blora* are set in a provincial town, hardly seemed to notice the town as a spatial setting. This contrasts with India, for example, where small and intermediate urban centres are almost a field of research in their own right (Basile and Harriss-White 2003, Jeffrey 2010, Wessel 2001), and even has its own fiction (Mishra 2006). A new research focus on provincial towns in Indonesia is important not so much for the sake of the towns themselves but because they represent nodes of interaction in today's decentralized Indonesia. The premise underlying this book is that the 'micro-politics' (to use Catherine Boone's term) in and around provincial towns may not look very exciting, but they do continually help to constitute state power in this the world's fourth largest nation.

Unlike the term 'Middle America,' which suggests a somewhat static societal 'average,' in the middle of the bell curve, we intend the term 'Middle Indonesia' to convey the idea of a meeting place between extremes. As noted in the preface, the research proposal for the 'In Search of Middle Indonesia' project described it as a social zone that connects the metropolitan with the peripheral, along several dimensions. Along the spatial dimension, the provincial town occupies an intermediate position in the urban hierarchy, between village and metropolitan city. Along the socio-economic dimension, its middle classes are situated socially in between the very rich in their metropolitan gated communities and the urban and rural poor. Culturally, global fashions and localized practices meet in the provincial town on a more equal footing than in either the metropolis or the village. Economically, it serves as an entrepôt between an agricultural hinterland and national and global markets. Administratively, the town stands between the central state and local society – many towns are the seat of the lowest level of administrative autonomy (the district, *kabupaten*). Middle Indonesia thus occupies a halfway position along all four dimensions of the 'distance' separating the citizen from the state, in Diane Davis' (1999) helpful conceptualization. That distance is understood geographically, institutionally, and in terms of class and culture. The most excluded are those who live in small villages, have little access to institutions of power, do not belong to a class close to power, and do not share the culture of the powerful. Those in the middle are not only closer to the state than these people, but they can also mediate that closeness to them. Mediation is a social process, with both formal institutional and informal aspects. In politics as well as in the economy, the town displays a higher level of informality than does the metropolis – a high proportion of its workforce is informally employed; and politics are more personal and less institutional.

A brief historical sketch will illustrate both the problem and the crucial mediating role of Middle Indonesia in solving it. The Dutch considered most of the outer islands to hold little economic value. They had only pacified them late in the nineteenth century, mainly to keep out other imperial powers. They invested little in building a modern administrative machinery, instead leaving native authorities in charge. Cribb's historical atlas shows, for example, how much smaller the number of prisoners, military garrisons, and railway connections were in the colonial outer islands by comparison with Java (Cribb 2000:134, 136, 140). The periphery in most of eastern Indonesia, with its small towns scattered in an agrarian landscape, represents a different Indonesia to the one we normally encounter in the history textbooks. The distance that separated this other Indonesia from the heartlands of the state was certainly geographical, since the places that embodied it were physically remote from Java. But the region also had few people wealthy enough to have much influence in the heartlands, few institutions to connect with the new Indonesia, and moreover a culture (language, religion, lifestyle) that did not entirely recognize the world on the other side. The iconic national revolution of 1945–49, by which the nation would escape the accident of imperial history and assume its own identity, was in reality confined to merely a portion of the former Netherlands Indies, namely Java and parts of Sumatra (with considerable republican activity in South Sulawesi and parts of Kalimantan). These were the most populous parts of the archipelago, but covered only about 30% or so of its land area. The colonial Dutch resumed their rule over the remaining 70%. Throughout the 1950s various regional revolts tore at the fabric of the nation; worst affected were Ambon, West Java, Sulawesi, and parts of Sumatra. Several were helped along by foreign powers. All were run by provincials out of the micro-politics of their towns. Desperate poverty turned the country into the basket case of Southeast Asia. The fact that Indonesia survived at all seemed a miracle. In most accounts, the instability of the 1950s was due to weakness at the centre, leading to numerous regional rebellions. And conversely its ultimate survival was attributed to successful centralization of power in Jakarta – Sukarno's charisma and the military's repressive reach. But this is both to overestimate Jakarta's autonomous strength and to underestimate the desire for national unity in the regions. Jakarta in those early years was itself divided between rival institutions, each of which looked for support in the regions. Sukarno had to travel constantly to maintain his influence. The armed forces were too fragmented to be truly effective even for internal policing, let alone to fight a unifying external war (which they tried against Malaysia and Dutch-held New Guinea with limited military success). Jakarta hardly dared to extract personal income taxes from its citizens for fear of non-compliance. Rather than lay down the law, it negotiated. Territorial integrity was its main worry. Provincial elites, keen to be part of the nation but proud of their own resourcefulness, were its most demanding negotiating partners. The chief instrument in Jakarta's arsenal was not the means of violence but patronage – mainly the gift of the means of primitive accumulation. The ideological mantle for these exchanges was a form of state socialism with broad emancipatory appeal, but whose statism found particular favour among a rising provincial middle class.

The big turnaround in this rather decentred polity came in late 1965, when the fear of a communist takeover finally united the nation's fractious elites into supporting a centralized military counter-revolution (Slater 2011). The oil boom that fortuitously followed not much later boosted Jakarta's coffers. However, closer inspection reveals that even that centralizing regime change could only be established with support from the regions. Elites in the latter pledged their loyalty only in exchange for increased patronage. The threat of sabotage, which remained their chief weapon, operated behind closed doors throughout the New Order. It became audible to the public again as the New Order weakened in the early 1990s. In 1998 it led to an ambitious decentralization programme, which has 'structurally privileged cities' (Miller 2013). Nor had the provinces been merely divisive before 1965. The unifying message of the republican revolution in the heartlands, the trade and transport networks established in the last decades of colonial rule, and the bureaucratic structures that replaced the rule of the rajas in the countryside, all passed through a network of provincial towns. So, whether for good or ill, for national unity or against it, the future of Indonesia has been co-determined in Middle Indonesia.

Associational Power

An alternative, less elitist notion of power has been mentioned repeatedly, but what does that actually involve? A book about this by the human geographer John Allen (2003) became for me an agenda-setting work. It opens with this striking rebuke: 'We have lost the sense in which geography makes a difference to the exercise of power.' Allen's book then offered two helpful insights. One was to deploy a notion of power that took into account the problem of transmission across space. Human proximity, face to face contact, is an essential element. The common instrumental idea of power is that of 'power over' others. It moves through bureaucracies as if it was a fluid. But proximity leads to a bottom-up idea of power, 'power to' get things done together. This has been called 'associational' power. Hannah Arendt wrote about it most cogently. She believed that only legitimate power was real. Power was about empowerment, about social capital that grows through collaboration. The Indonesian national revolution is a good example. By *associating* together in movements of solidarity, Indonesians generated enough power to defeat a well-armed, well-connected western colonizer.

Allen's other key insight was that power operates in many different 'modalities.' The Indonesian revolutionaries expanded their solidarity by persuading others to join them. Sometimes they seduced them with dreams most people shared, at other times they enticed them with material rewards, or manipulated them with threats or impossible promises. Instrumental modalities of power operated alongside these associational ones. Propaganda was made, 'traitors' were imprisoned or murdered, dissidents intimidated. The revolutionary state had limited coercive capacities, however, and instrumental power was much less readily available than its leaders might have wished. Whether associational or instrumental, then, power is exercised in a wide range of modalities.

State institutions, when observed in this relational light, quickly lose the image of almost complete autonomy that their office-holders like to attribute to them, and that much scholarly analysis, particularly during the authoritarian New Order, allowed them to retain. Instead, they begin to look fragmented, contingent, and negotiated. Catherine Boone's comparative study on the history of state formation in three West African countries deployed the fertile phrase: 'state power is rooted, in part, in the micro-politics of the localities' (Boone 1998, 2003). In the period 1950–1970 these states built institutions out of the political constraints and opportunities that confronted them on the ground. Even though each West African state had the same problems – the one she examined was how to administer agricultural exports – they solved them in different ways because they met different forms of local resistance and collaboration. In those places where rural elites were in a position to challenge the state for a share of the profits, states built large and centralized bureaucracies (Ghana under Nkrumah); where rural elites were weak, states left a milder form of indirect rule (Senegal, Ivory Coast). In other words, African states are more deeply embedded in localized power relations than is generally assumed, and the same should be said for Indonesia.[7]

Rather than rigid structures in which power is immanent, a relational view of power suggests flows and mediation. Spatialized power is better understood in terms of network functions, notably brokerage. Consistent with Allen's mediated notion of power, I envisage associational power being created in the context of social networks. Indonesia's extensive geography created severe collective action problems. Michael Mann captured these problem precisely with his opening observation in his magnum opus on the nature of power: 'Societies are constituted of numerous

[7] Other recent studies of state formation in Africa have similarly situated the development of large institutions in local configurations of power. They include Gillian Hart's study of a South African township (2002) and Jeffrey Herbst's sweeping history of African states (2000). They reflect the sense of path dependency, strategic interaction, and even irrational ritual that pervades the study of institutions in the various 'new institutionalisms' since the mid-1990s (Hall and Taylor 1996). The present book moves in the same direction. We first developed these ideas in two introductory chapters for an earlier book on the socially embedded state in Indonesia (Van Klinken and Barker 2009). At the time we felt inspired by the 'state in society' ideas of Joel Migdal (2001).

overlapping and intersecting sociospatial networks of power' (1993:I, 1). Technological means to mobilize resources at a distance did exist in the late 1940s – radio, newspapers, telephony, aeroplanes, ships and, ultimately, military force. These could help the centre project its will to the regions with minimal fear of distortion. But in this poor country ruined by war, such means were often too weak and the alternatives out there too numerous for organizational or electromechanical techniques alone to be decisive. Far more important were human brokers who were able personally to connect together geographically diverse social networks around the archipelago. The places of densest brokerage were the provincial towns. Mestika Zed's (1991) dissertation on the provincial brokers who ran Palembang is a pioneering exploration of this notion, which unfortunately remains unpublished.

Urban brokers of various kinds play important roles in this book. They included quasi-intellectual activists, military officers, bureaucrat-politicians, teachers, Chinese traders, and church leaders. Robert K. Merton, who pioneered the study of brokers, would have called the individuals in the present history 'cosmopolitan influentials' (1968:447). They had high status in and around Kupang. Their social capital derived from their ability to connect two places with widely different cultures, yet their social ties with the locals were in fact rather weak and asymmetric. They themselves were hardly any longer 'locals,' whose social capital grew out of organic embeddedness in the local community and who enjoyed strong symmetric relationships within their town community. At the same time, they possessed a local knowledge that the Dutch, the Japanese, and the Javanese could never achieve. In the more refined five-part typology of Gould and Fernandez (1989), they were 'liaison brokers,' mediators who stood outside both the groups they were trying to connect.[8]

Intermediate Classes

Since Wertheim described them as 'the most dynamic element in Indonesian society,' surprisingly few social scientists have focused specifically on

---

[8] Brokers create a directed connection between two otherwise unconnected principal parties. Gould and Fernandez identified five types of brokers: 1) the coordinator (all three parties belong to the same group – internal brokerage); 2) the itinerant (broker from the outside, both principals belong to the same group – e.g. stockbroker); 3) the gatekeeper (broker belongs to the group being approached by a rival group – e.g. journal editor); 4) the representative (broker belongs to the group that is approaching a rival group – e.g. diplomat); 5) the liaison (broker comes from outside both rival groups – e.g. real estate agent).

life in the urban settlements. Actually even the large cities have seen very little work – Abeyasekere's (1989) history of Jakarta and Dick's history of Surabaya (2002) being two notable exceptions. The first intensive work on towns was done by Clifford Geertz and his MIT associates. They picked a very small town in Java in the 1950s. They found it to be essentially static, a 'hollow town,' reacting to outside stimuli in ways that were 'always defensive, reactive, evasive, and in the end .... sterile and debilitating' (C. Geertz 1965:5–7). The idea of stagnation was also strong in the work on provincial towns, such as that on Yogyakarta and Padang, by Hans Dieter Evers (1972). Later authors, however, began to see more dynamism and even conflict within the towns. Freek Colombijn's (1994) fine history of Padang found conflicts over urban space between 'strategic groups' that were in and others that were out of power. And Howard Dick, who picked the large city of Surabaya, found it to be riven by class conflicts over the urban land grabs that followed industrialization (Dick 2002:472).[9] Class, absent from mainstream Indonesian studies for many years, may be making a come-back.[10]

Class analysis is often thought to be incompatible with the more horizontal brokerage analysis of the previous section. But brokers can have interests of their own. They can impress their interests on the action-at-a-distance process by, as Marsden (1982) put it, charging 'commission.' Think of sabotage and rent-seeking. Indonesian provincial discourses of religion and ethnicity usually veil real material interests. Once provincial town politics became politicized in the 1930s, most of their actors were officials. That remains the case today. Burgeoning studies of Indonesian local politics in recent times have shown that they are capable of both modernization and exploitation.[11] As the first optimistic flush of modernization theory was passing, studies of Third World 'urban bias' began exposing the ways in which narrow urban interests were able to hijack development plans intended for the nation as a whole (Bates 2008, Lipton 1977, Mellor 1976). A version of state socialism was popular all over the Third World in the early post-World War II years. Where this ideology

---

[9] Some more examples are discussed in Chapter Two.

[10] Official pressure on the social science research agenda in Indonesia must be part of the reason (Hadiz and Dhakidae 2005). Since the fall of the Berlin wall no one any longer claims that class is the primary dimension to social life. Race, gender and nationality are also important in various contexts. But class analysis does not depend on it being the main force at work.

[11] Some of the most relevant literature is conveniently summarized in the introductory chapters to Henk Schulte Nordholt and Van Klinken (2007) and Van Klinken and Barker (2009).

placed state infrastructure development and industry above agrarian agendas it became a fig leaf for urban greed. Bates wrote of a core coalition consisting of government, industry, and organized labour – a coalition from which farmers were excluded and which resulted in deteriorating welfare for the poorest of the poor, the subsistence peasants.

A notable impulse to focus on these provincial urban coalitions, still worth reading, came from the Polish development economist Michal Kalecki (1972). Classes, whether big as in Marx or small as in much contemporary class analysis, are primarily a way of answering analytical questions about the connection between political action and material interests. Kalecki was particularly fascinated by the political action of a lower-middle class. His work on Indonesia and Egypt in the 1950s led him to notice something few after him were to do, namely that the urban hijackers were not necessarily rich or at the top of the social pyramid. The politics of many underdeveloped countries were dominated by people from the lower-middle classes and rich peasants. This should be surprising because, whereas a ruling class normally serves the interests of big business, these members of the lower-middle classes did not. Kalecki's (1972:162) core thesis was as follows.

> 'Are there any specific conditions today favouring the emergence of governments representing the interests of the lower-middle-class (including in this also the corresponding strata of the peasantry)? It would seem that such conditions do arise at the present in many underdeveloped countries:
>
> (i) At the time of achieving independence the lower-middle-class is very numerous while big business is predominantly foreign-controlled with a rather small participation by native capitalists.
> (ii) Patterns of government activities are now widespread. Apart from the obvious case of socialist countries, state economic interventionism plays an important role in developed capitalist countries.
> (iii) It is possible to obtain foreign capital also through credits granted by socialist countries.
>
> In the process of political emancipation – especially if this is not accompanied by armed struggle – representatives of the lower-middle-class rise in a way naturally to power.'

Indonesia was one of the countries in which this unusual social inversion appeared to apply. Rather than working with big capital to develop the economy in a *laissez faire* fashion, the state wished to make the investments itself. The lower-middle classes were thus protected from foreign capital. Not only socialist countries practised economic planning but those in the western sphere of influence as well. The form of state capitalism that this produced, according to Kalecki, 'leads directly to the pattern of amalgamation of the interests of the lower-middle-class with state capitalism.' Where pure market capitalism was sure to force small firms out of business in its drive to industrialize, state interventionism would see them as essential for building up the country's productive capacity. This did not make them rich in absolute terms but did guarantee they would not fall back to the level of the peasant. Kalecki observed: 'It is true that this lower-middle-class and the prosperous peasants are not really rich; in many instances their standard of living is lower than that of workers in developed countries. But in comparison to the mass of poor peasants, who also flood the cities as unemployed or badly–paid home workers, the petty bourgeois is a tycoon with a lot to lose' (Kalecki 1972:166–7). The typical petty bourgeois fascination with religion and militarism, incidentally, is the reason why 'the governments in question favour religion – even to the point of adopting an official religion – and show a tendency towards external expansion and militarism associated with it.'

The politics of these provincial lower-middle class were motivated by a desire to maintain state protection against capitalist forces for themselves, and to keep class rivals at bay. Above them were the upper middle class, whose natural alliances were with foreign capital. In Indonesia these were the Dutch, and to some extent the Chinese, since indigenous capitalists could be counted on the fingers of one hand. Above them too was the native (largely bureaucratic) aristocracy. And below them were the numerous small landowners, landless peasants and urban poor, the latter mainly migrants from the countryside looking for work. White collar workers, meanwhile, were likely to be their allies, especially when employed by state enterprises. If Kalecki had gone a step further and mapped out his 'intermediate regime' argument in spatial terms, he might have added that the provincial town was the home territory for this surprisingly dominant lower-middle class. Several other social scientists, for example Cockcroft (1998) working in Mexico and Harriss-White (2003) in India, have made use of Kalecki's insights when writing about predatory urban coalitions that thrive in the middle regions of the social spectrum by means of their political rather than their entrepreneurial skills. Harriss-White's work has been a particularly important inspiration for this book. Both are a sustained argument in support of Kalecki's observation, spatially extended.

Kalecki's intermediate class resembles Lenin's petty bourgeoisie, 'masters of the countryside,' but it does not fit neatly into the core Marxist two-class scheme of capitalists versus workers. It is neither clearly on the side of capital nor that of labour; its members have control over some means of production but they often also provide their own labour. It is not obvious who they are exploiting, if anyone. This led Harriss-White to use the term 'non-polar' for this class, an uncomfortable category on the margins of Marxist theory. Yet the reality on the ground *is* often exploitative, and there may be a better way of describing it. Instead of the now discredited labour theory of value, Aage Sørensen (2000) proposed rent-seeking as the source of inequality. Exploiters have access to assets that earn them rents, while the exploited do not.[12] 'Assets' do not have to be money but can be many other things such as knowledge (education) or official power. In the bureaucratic politics that shaped Indonesia's provincial intermediate classes, the power to extract rents from government and to deny them to others are the fundamental driving forces separating the haves from the have-nots. The political turmoil that defines Middle Indonesia for us as observers revolves, to a large extent, about access to this asset.

It is the thesis of this book that middle classes in provincial towns are involved in some of the nation's most interesting 'action at a distance' processes. It is in this dynamic sense that Middle Indonesia is somehow constitutive of the country as a whole. That Indonesia did not fall apart after 1998 (except for the independence of tiny East Timor, annexed illegally in 1976) had as much to do with some hidden strength within Middle Indonesia as with leadership in Jakarta. The most interesting historical period to reconstruct, it seemed to me, lay between the 1930s and the 1980s. If ever there was a time when recurring crises confronted central authorities with 'action at a distance' problems it was in this period of economic decline, warfare, revolution, nation-building and authoritarian developmentalism. How were these problems addressed? To find the answer, I needed to go beyond the centre to the provincial towns in the periphery, which grew in this period from colonial backwaters to bustling entrepôts. I needed to examine the class-laden politics creating new social

---

[12] Sørensen helpfully described three levels of 'theoretical ambition' among writers on class. One simply classifies the population nominally into strata according to certain criteria such as income or status. Another sees classes as observable, self-aware social groupings with identifiable boundaries (often based on occupation) and distinctive lifestyles and values. The highest level of ambition traces a fundamental antagonism between classes to structural economic inequalities between them. Exploitation, the key difference between Marxist and Weberian approaches, is a difficult concept, because the relationship between exploited and exploiter is always to some extent voluntary. However, many constraints on a perfect market have been identified, which all result in an unequal distribution of power over scarce resources.

classes in the provinces as local governments penetrated indirectly ruled areas with modern techniques, and as provincial markets grew increasingly national. In these provincial processes I expected to learn about that hidden strength of Middle Indonesia.

One Town

This study explores the mediating roles between nation and countryside played by people belonging to the middle class of one run-of-the-mill town. This section introduces that town, and then places it in a broad historical, geographical and social context. Kupang lies on the Indonesian half of the island of Timor, which lies on the southeastern edge of the archipelago (Figure 1). On the tourist map (Figure 2, this grubby sheet seemed to be the last one available anywhere) the old heart of the town lies at the top left. The left bank at the mouth of the creek is the location for the Dutch fort Concordia, still standing and today a small military base. It was built by the Portuguese and taken over by a small Dutch VOC garrison early in the seventeenth century (Farram 2004, Fox 1977, Hägerdal 2012, Leirissa et al 1984). By the early nineteenth, the township was a significant imperial outpost. It became the capital of a new province in late 1958, and began to expand rapidly in the 1970s. The old harbour now only takes small wooden boats and visiting sailing yachts – a new harbour was built at Tenau, 10 km to the west, in the mid-1960s. But the Chinese godowns are still there on the other side of the creek, supplied by trucks from Tenau. From this old core, roads radiate towards newer parts of town. One runs east along the coastal flats, and eventually into the interior towards Timor Leste. Another runs southeast up the hill towards the governor's office and then the airport. A third passes the town's busiest traffic lights before heading even further up the hill south towards the university and education department offices.

Kupang has many unique peculiarities. Yet it too exhibits the 'in-between' characteristics that Clifford Geertz, on the basis of his work in 'Modjokuto,' thought was so typical of the Indonesian provincial town (1956, 1963c, 1965). There were practical reasons for choosing this particular town.[13] It was one of five towns within the broader Middle Indonesia

[13] The original intention was to write a history based on more than one town. I was interested particularly in towns outside Java, because of their distance from Jakarta. But historical information about such towns proved so difficult to find for the crucial post-war period that one by one the other candidates dropped out, until only Kupang survived. In the 1960s, not a single provincial town outside Java had a newspaper that is archived today

Figure 1. Indonesia.

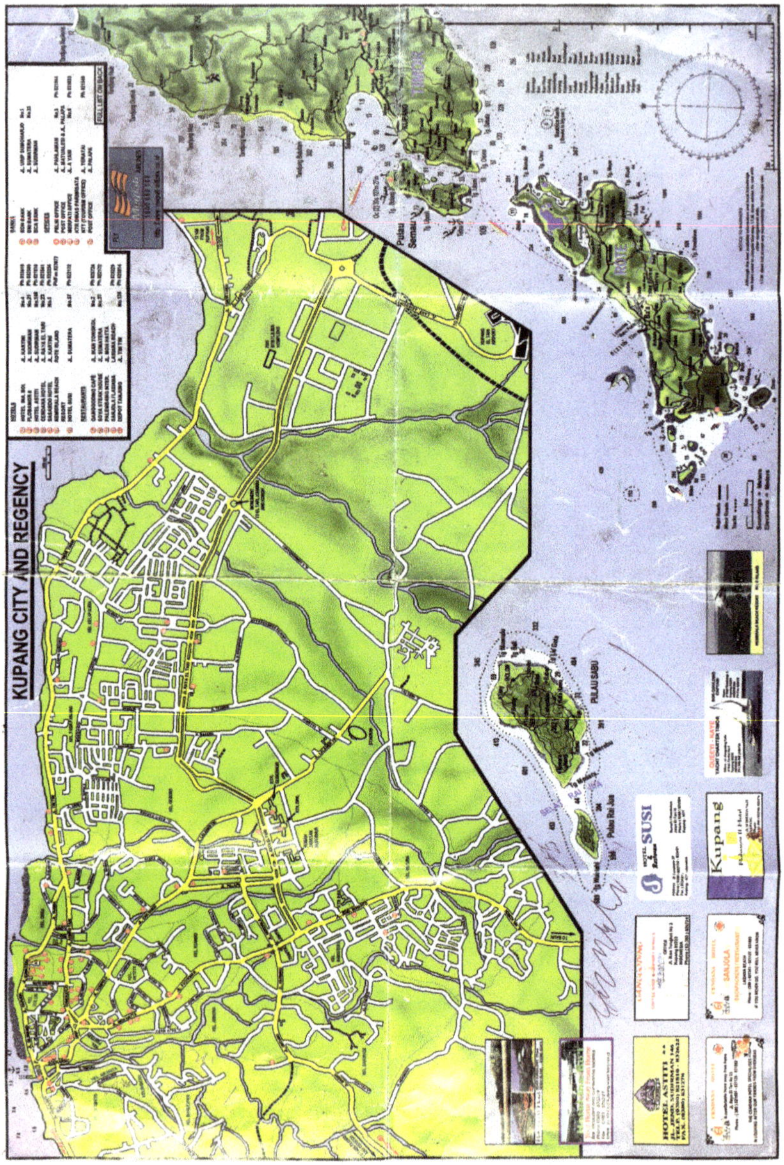

Figure 2. Tourist map of Kupang.

research programme for in-depth ethnographic work. Its economy was dominated by the state; others in the programme had more market-driven economies. A student in the Middle Indonesia programme, Sylvia Tidey, was writing an ethnographic dissertation on it (Tidey 2012), and one of our Indonesian colleagues wrote perceptively about his youth there in the 1970s (Lay 2014). The more one learns to know and love a town the less 'typical' it appears to be, and indeed there are clearly many distinctions to be made between towns (Nas 1981). But the intention, to restate it once again, has always been to look for generalizable processes of mediation along the several dimensions connecting the state with society that Diane Davis (1999) identified.

In 1930 Kupang had a population of 7,000. By contrast, the leading city of Batavia at this time had 533,000 inhabitants, Makassar 85,000, and Ambon about 17,000 (Hugo et al 1987:101–2). Kupang was a colonial outpost in a poor subsistence economy. It lay at the end of the colonial shipping network whose main nodes were Makassar, Surabaya, Batavia, and then Singapore further west (Dick and Rimmer 2003:94, 96). All the small towns around the vast archipelago were run by a handful of Dutch officials, and had only a tiny indigenous elite interested in issues beyond the town. Most of these 7,000 were (descendants of) migrants from nearby islands. They lived in semi-rural wooden houses and talked about local affairs. In 2010 the town had a population of about 340,000 (BPS Kota Kupang 2011:47) – nearly 50 times larger. Its hinterland was and remains thinly populated and largely rural. We have no exact information on the town's evolving class structure. In general the increase of modern education throughout the twentieth century went hand-in-hand with urbanization.[14] Even today Kupang still has no industry to speak of. The only

in the Indonesian National Library in Jakarta, and only Medan and Padang have substantial newspaper archives surviving from the 1950s (Hardjoprakoso 1977). These two cities are now too large to qualify as Middle Indonesian towns. Pontianak, a market-oriented town with a population today of half a million, gave up some of its secrets to me during several visits, but inter-ethnic suspicion made it difficult to dig deeper in the oral history; I hope to revisit this town in the future.

14 Along with urbanization, literacy was extremely low everywhere in the colonial Netherlands Indies – under 20% for male adults (with a few exceptions) in 1920, with female literacy far below that (Cribb 2000:38–41). Education participation rates for children were minimal – around 10% as late as 1935 (Cribb 2000:144). Agriculture remained the main occupation in 1930, though at slightly lower levels in Java (55%) than outside it (where it ranged up to 75%, not counting plantations) (Departement van Economische Zaken 1936:33–5). All these indicators experienced steady development throughout the twentieth century, especially in the New Order after 1966. Urbanization and middle class formation went hand in hand with increased literacy. Today, the United Nations lists Indonesia as a 'middle income' country. Its middle class, based on generously low consumption

exception is a large state-owned cement plant opened in 1980, but it was mothballed after going bankrupt in 2008.[15] Yet it has a substantial, confident middle class, culturally Indonesian and engaged in modern politics, which looks largely to the state for its income.

We set the lower bound of a typical Middle Indonesian town at 50,000. Many human geographers take this as the size beyond which a town becomes 'urban,' meaning it has grown beyond a small agricultural service centre and begins to host higher order services, such as government administration, education, health and commerce.[16] The political scientist Robert Dahl (1967) once proffered that 50,000 may also be the minimal size for a town to host an effective urban civil society. Any smaller and its associational life was likely to dissolve into factional strife. In a postcolonial country, the town is more likely than the countryside to host the largely literate, non-agricultural, mobile, urban and reasonably prosperous society that, ever since Karl Deutsch (1961), is regarded as capable of generating modern institutional politics. That the sociality of cities is different – more competitive, more technological, more heterogeneous and above all more impersonal – has been a basic assertion since the inception of urban studies (Wirth 1938). But we still have little idea how politics in a postcolonial intermediate town differs from that in a large city or for that matter from that in a village. It is important to find out, because enormous numbers of people live in such towns. In between the small town and the metropolitan city of over a million, the intermediate town houses nearly a quarter of the country's population. Intermediate towns play mediating roles that reach perhaps 80% of the population.[17] If these predictions about the varied social consequences of the population of a postcolonial town growing beyond the 50,000 threshold are correct then Middle Indonesia was made in Kupang somewhere in the half-century after 1930. By that last year the population had grown to 70,000, of whom the vast majority was literate. All other things being equal, this is

levels, has recently been estimated at 43% (ADB 2010). Literacy rates topped 80% by 1990, urbanization rates reached 45% by 2004, and more than half the working population said they worked mainly outside agriculture by the mid-1990s.

15 'Berharap asap pabrik semen Kupang mengepul lagi,' *Antara*, 26 July 2009.

16 Rondinelli (1983:48–9) defines the secondary city in a developing country, which performs essential urban functions, as any centre over 100,000. Hardoy and Satterthwaite (1986:13–5) adopt a lower limit for the urban, defining the small town as 5,000–20,000, with the intermediate urban centre as 20,000–100,000.

17 Hardoy and Satterthwaite (1986:6) quote a UN figure showing that 80% of Third World populations generally live in or within the sphere of influence of intermediate towns.

when it was able to sustain the dynamism of which Wertheim had written. Over this period we therefore expect to see some sort of urban civil society emerge – it is the *making* of Middle Indonesia that is of interest in this book.

Substantial towns are rare in Indonesia's periphery. Table 1 shows the distribution of towns counting at least 50,000 inhabitants throughout the archipelago between 1905 and 1980. With only 7% of the total land area, Java's population density has given it a much higher density of substantial towns than the rest of the archipelago. The level of urbanization has always been similar in Java and the outer island,[18] but substantial towns outside Java are widely scattered, leaving most people, particularly in eastern Indonesia, living in the vicinity of much smaller towns. In 1905 the Netherlands Indies was truly rural. Only four towns exceeded 50,000, and three of them were in Java. By 1930 the number had grown to just 17, of which 12 lay in Java, including the colonial capital Batavia. All the Javanese towns were moreover within such easy reach of each other by means of frequent trains, such that the distinction between village and city began to diminish (Dick and Rimmer 2003:133). Fifty years later, at the height of the developmentalist New Order, the human geographer Terry McGee

Table 1. Number of towns with populations exceeding 50,000 (Milone 1966:108–21, 129–53); 1980 column from Rutz (1987:265–82).

	1905	1920	1930	1956	1961	1980
JAVA	3	7	12	18	30	57
OUTER ISLANDS	1	2	5	11	19	55
Sumatra	1	1	3	No data		32
Kalimantan	0	0	1	No data		6
Sulawesi/ Maluku/ Bali/ Nusa Tenggara	0	1	1	No data		17
Kupang pop.		5,792	7,171	No data	29,831	91,633

18 In the Netherlands Indies in 1930, 92.6% of natives were rural in Java and 95.9% in the outer islands (Departement van Economische Zaken 1936:2–6). The number of large towns per unit population is also the same: Java had 69% of the country's total population in 1930, and the same proportion of substantial towns. The population proportion has declined to 58% today, and with it Java's proportion of large towns.

suggested that it was no longer analytically relevant to make the distinction, since villages had now become quasi-urban (creating a *desakota* – village-city) (McGee 1991). The remaining five towns in 1930, meanwhile, were scattered over such a wide area of the far more poorly interconnected outer islands that, until today, no one has been tempted to abandon the distinction between village and city. In 1930, Kupang was not yet one of those significant towns. How it became one, and what role it played in the integration of Indonesia's heartlands with that other, more rural Indonesia in the periphery, is the burden of the chapters that follow.

Chapter Outline

The book opts for a conventional chronological chapter development, tracing the transition in Kupang from small colonial outpost in the 1930s to the large town that it became in the mid-1970s. To capture the complexity of the themes discussed above, the approach mixes institutional and biographical narratives, at times approaching a social history (inasmuch as it is still possible to reconstruct it at this distance). Rather than simply recounting a story, however, each chapter aims to solve a problem. The historical arguments they attempt to build are best explained by outlining each subsequent chapter.

Chapter Two, 'A historical synthesis,' looks to history for an explanation for the politics of localism, ethnic identity, and bureaucratic careerism that typified Indonesian provincial town arenas after 1998. It is a synthetic, programmatic sketch of the intertwined histories of Indonesia's provincial towns, the central state, and the bureaucratic intermediate classes that dominate them. The networked dynamic of power gave provincial middle classes considerable room to manoeuvre. It turned them into assertive yet socially conservative political actors on the national stage, who at the same time uneasily manage their poorer citizens through webs of patronage.

Chapter Three, 'A researcher's notes,' focuses reflexively on the challenge of doing historical research in a provincial town in the global south. It is the first to zoom in on Kupang. The problems are severe, and help explain why Indonesian town histories are so rare. Paper archives are scarce. A greater obstacle is that a history of national political violence has created many taboos on local public discourse. The most interesting stories circulate only in private versions that 'must not be written.' The chapter also introduces some of Kupang's key mediating personalities, who will reappear in subsequent chapters.

Chapter Four, 'Betting on the rajas,' explores the relations between the town and its hinterland. The problem of Middle Indonesia is not simply the conventional one of centre versus periphery. The town is itself a centre with a periphery. The intense struggles that took place in this regional arena in the 1950s and 1960s were not simply re-enactments of national ones. They were the outcome of oppressive power relations that had crystalized in the countryside beyond Kupang in the 1930s. The Dutch were 'betting on the strong' when they invented a cheap system of indirect rule based on neo-traditional myths. Within the town, however, insulated from the rajas by 'the square mile' of Dutch sovereignty, a quiet town life, punctuated by rituals of church, sport and the harbour, was slowly taking in hints of distant worlds.

Chapter Five, 'Elite brokers,' examines the ways in which resource-rich agencies in cities far away – Makassar in Sulawesi, Singaraja in Bali, and Jakarta in Java – attempted to mobilize people in Kupang in the volatile period from 1934 to 1950 that spanned the Pacific War. Brokerage is the central mechanism. Most of the first local brokers were the sons of peasants who were educated as teachers and civil servants in Java before the Pacific War. At times of violent regime change, dictated far away – 1942, 1945, and 1949 – it fell to them to become the highly mobile interlocutors between the distant capital and their societies. This was a small town community, too small for any significant civil society. Starting out as the willing or unwilling tools of oppression in the hands of alien regimes, broker elites were to grow into an indigenous middle class with clear interests of their own.

Chapter Six, 'Authority,' examines struggles to establish new forms of authority within the Kupang region in the two decades after independence. Relations between the town and its countryside once more come to the fore. As the corps of people working for a government anxious to bring change grew between 1945 and 1973, and as the town as a whole grew with it, the problem of persuading country dwellers to accept the town's authority became increasingly acute. This chapter examines the communicative strategies regional elites deployed through two rather top-down institutions, the church and the military. Why was the relatively poorly resourced Protestant church so much more successful at this than the military? The answer is that associational power is more effective than centrally 'projected' instrumental power.

Chapter Seven, 'The seductress,' explores a communicative strategy that was by contrast quite successful. Political parties in and beyond the town in that innocent period following independence did generate associational power. Cross-class coalitions formed between middle class teachers and political party townsfolk, on the one hand, and rural peasants on the other. As the message of Indonesian republicanism began to resonate among a rural population exploited by the rajas, the store of social capital was enlarged, generating power to change things.

In Chapter Eight, 'The gatekeeper,' the contradictions that lay hidden in the various cross-class coalitions discussed in the previous two chapters begin to wreak themselves. Inequalities grew as senior brokers discovered they had the capacity to control the flow of resources passing through the town. The exploitative dynamics are illustrated by examining two small, local state-backed businesses. The communist party mobilized on the uneasiness this unfairness produced. Chapter Nine, 'The making of Middle Indonesia,' sees these incipient class tensions in and around the town erupt into full-scale violence, in step with the violence being deployed by central state institutions from late 1965. Using a contentious politics analysis, it highlights the importance of local class tensions in what is usually seen only as a fight between the major players in Jakarta. The outcome was in many ways constitutive of Middle Indonesia as we know it today. Chapter Ten, 'A killing town,' tests the localist conclusions of the previous chapter by examining the ways in which the anti-communist pogroms were organized. Many local middle class actors were willing collaborators with the centrally coordinated military, driven by a mixture of national ideology and immediate material considerations.

Finally, Chapter Eleven, 'Consolidating Middle Indonesia,' examines the social strategies the winners of this local class conflict adopted to entrench their privileges. The conservative character of the town establishment has its origins as much in this local history as in the national political or economic regime or even the regional economy. At the same time, this chapter highlights the mutuality between Jakarta and these local establishments, which ensures that Indonesia holds together as a nation. A closing section in this chapter sums up what the book has learned about Middle Indonesia.

CHAPTER TWO

A HISTORICAL SYNTHESIS

> [V]ested interests in lavish and lax government expenditures have become entrenched in the political system.
>
> (Mackie 1971:62)

When democracy came to the towns of Indonesia's Lampung province in southern Sumatra in 1998, it acquired a strong ethnic colouring. The national regime change manifested itself in the two main towns – Bandar Lampung, population about 800,000, and Metro, 130,000 – through menacing demonstrations of power by the native Lampung ethnic organization Lampung Sai. 'Javanese' had been running the place for too long, was their argument. World Bank experts wrote a report warning of possible ethnic violence (Barron and Madden 2003, Diprose 2002). The ethnic trouble was part of manoeuvring over bureaucratic appointments. Emotions were stirred because government is an important source of jobs for educated people in town. The Minister for Utilization of State Apparatus (Men-PAN) in May 2003 personally chided Metro for creating too many useless government jobs. Ideally, he said, district level government should have 11 to 14 provincial offices (*dinas*) plus statutory authorities:

> But if there are 17 or more organizations, that's just wasteful and ineffective. There are districts and towns that have an office of marine affairs and fisheries, even though they are not on the coast. Metro Town in Lampung Province is an example. How appropriate is that for their region, that's what needs to be thought through, and if not it shouldn't be necessary.[1]

These two characteristics, localist politics combined with a careerist approach to expanding the bureaucracy, are today found in the hundreds of intermediate towns that make up Middle Indonesia. The purpose of this chapter is to develop a synthetic, historical account of the origins of this behaviour.

---

[1] 'Menneg PAN M Feisal Tamin: 53 persen PNS "makan" gaji buta,' *Kompas*, 17 May 2003.

Indonesia has about 200 provincial towns with populations between 50,000 and a million, yet, as stated earlier, they have attracted far less scholarly attention than the nation's few large cities. In these towns, recent democratization and decentralization have brought to light patterns of communal and localist electoral mobilization that have not been seen since the 1950s and early 1960s. Provincial towns have talked back to the centre in ways that belie their supposed passivity as expressed in the once popular term 'urban involution' (Evers 1972). This chapter builds a synthetic and historical explanation for these patterns by examining the social and spatial embeddedness of the state in the provincial town. Most of Indonesia's towns, particularly outside the heartlands in Java and parts of Sumatra, became urban only as a result of the growth of the modern colonial state after the mid-to-late nineteenth century. After decolonization in 1945, the expanding but chronically underfunded bureaucracy became an arena for contestation among emerging middle classes in these towns, which mostly lacked manufacturing since most were located outside the heartlands. The new provincial classes were politically significant because of their numbers and their mobilizational skills rather than their wealth. They successfully seized the state at the local level. Central state actors, anxious to establish political stability over a vast area with limited means, appeased them with substantial political transfer rents, particularly during the oil boom years of the early to mid-New Order, but continuing to the present day.

Wertheim (1959:185) may have called provincial towns 'the most dynamic element in Indonesian society,' but the more influential stereotype of the town has been that of 'urban involution.' The geographers Warwick Armstrong and Terry McGee (1968) coined this term to indicate the town's enormous capacity to absorb poor migrating peasants into its informal 'bazaar' economy. This dulled the revolutionary social changes that usually accompany urbanization. They borrowed the term from Clifford Geertz's (1963a) fecund, though later much criticized, notion of 'agricultural involution,' which similarly conveyed the idea that 'shared poverty' made revolution unlikely. Hans-Dieter Evers (1972, 2007) then picked up the term and made it his own throughout his many writings on the Indonesian provincial town. It encapsulated for him the lack of modernization and functional differentiation in the Indonesian intermediate town. He also highlighted a new element, namely the dominant but stultifying role of the government bureaucracy. The term has not found much acceptance in urban studies – which probably indicates both that the discipline has neglected the provincial town, and that the conceptual apparatus appropriate for studying the provincial town remains underdeveloped.[2]

The term 'urban involution' suggested that Indonesian towns need not follow the Chicago pathway to modernity. Globalization is today the major force shaping the world's big cities, also in Asia (Dick and Rimmer 2003). One central question facing students of the intermediate city is to what extent it is shaped by these same globalizing processes. A recent study by Malcolm McKinnon (2011) addressed this question by comparing three Asian megacities with three nearby provincial ones. Indonesia's Jakarta and Semarang were one of the three pairs. The economies of the megacities were indeed markedly globalized, but those of provincial cities turned out to be determined by much more local processes. Provincial economies were not stagnant, but their growth was shaped by processes familiar in the West from the nineteenth century: nation-building and urbanization. In today's Europe and North America these have run their course, but industrial revolutions and nationalist movements are still young in Asia. The labour pool that feeds them is national, not global. People move in response to wage differences between rural and urban areas, not directly to global conditions. They acquire national identities in town, not global ones. Towns like Bandar Lampung are not highly globalized, and we should not assume they will ever become as globalized as towns in the OECD core nations.

The present chapter draws on existing case studies to investigate the historical trajectory of the average provincial town in Indonesia. Subsequent chapters then test these ideas by zooming in on one particular town. Rather than adopting an essentially ecological perspective that enquires about quasi-natural growth processes, as was normal in earlier studies, this chapter takes an interest in political struggle – as advocated by the (once) 'new' urban sociology (Gottdiener and Feagin 1988). It investigates the interplay between state patronage and local social forces that have shaped today's provincial towns. The chapter consists of three parts. The first shows how new most provincial towns are and how closely their growth paralleled that of the modern state. The second focuses on the historical sociology of the bureaucracy that links the state to the town. The third examines how the social forces that emerged in these provincial

[2] In a curious twist, Mike Davis (2004) deployed the term 'urban involution' again recently, to highlight the potentially revolutionary rapid growth of informal labour in third world urban slums around the globe. This usage has no connection with the existing literature either on cities or on the informal economy.

towns under state patronage, particularly in the years after the watershed decolonization of the late 1940s, help us understand the characteristics identified in the opening paragraphs.

Towns

While megacities dominate urban studies, 52% of the world's urban population lives in settlements of less than half a million people (UNFPA 2007:9–10). Yet urban studies agendas (for example, Savage et al 2003) continue to overlook these intermediate cities, especially if they are located in the developing world. Indonesia has hundreds of such provincial towns, and they cannot be understood through the lens of the discipline's foundational studies of Chicago or Los Angeles. Rather than being transformed by the penetration of capital, as is the regnant theme in the urban sociology of Castells and Lefebvre, these towns continue to revolve around small trade and the government bureaucracy (see further discussion below). Yet they are not static, nor should they be viewed as oversized villages whose residents retain pre-urban patterns of sociation. The most striking feature of provincial town life is not alienation and individuation, but vigorous organizational life, which combines themes of 'traditional' family-like ethnic or religious community with modern techniques of mobilization and a great interest in capturing the institutions of the state. Low levels of wealth and absent mass markets make politics indispensable to getting ahead. By situating politicized ethnicity in the geography and political economy of intermediate towns, and by doing this historically, we gain insight into some key driving forces in Indonesia's current phase of democratization and decentralization.

The extent of urbanization in the Indonesian archipelago before Dutch colonization has been a matter of controversy. Anthony Reid claimed on the basis of travellers' accounts that '[i]n relation to its population, then, Southeast Asia in this [pre-colonial] period must have been one of the most urbanized areas in the world' (Reid 1980:239). Indeed, he believed European interference actually reversed this urbanizing trend. Unlike the fortified cities of the Mediterranean, however, those of maritime Southeast Asia were open to the countryside, and their inhabitants did not enjoy special rights and responsibilities. But how urban were these 'cities'? Jan Wisseman Christie, using pre-colonial written charters from Java as well as travellers' narratives, concluded soberly: 'Although Reid's suggestion may be a valid one in the case of coastal trading states whose port cities suffered under colonial rule, there is no evidence that Java was significantly urbanized before the arrival of the Dutch' (Wisseman Christie 1991:24). The most highly developed pre-colonial states were in Java, but, she argued, they were 'states without cities' – as the provocative title of her paper put it. They were decentralized and personalized. The royal court moved readily in response to wars and disasters and was only ever surrounded by villages, which also were quite mobile. 'Most of the towns and cities of modern Java owe their size, and many their very existence, to Dutch intervention,' she concluded (1991). Rutz' baseline study of Indonesia's cities and towns (1987), when projected to 2005, shows that Indonesia would now have around 170 towns like Bandar Lampung and Metro with populations between 50,000 and a million, and this is highly conservative. Nearly half of them are located outside Java.[3] By far the greatest number originated in the 19th and 20th centuries. A colour-coded map (Map II, see also pp. 62, 64) illustrates the history of these towns. Adopting a generous lower limit for the urban, Rutz traces a few back to the Hindu period before 1400 CE. Most of these (11 out of 16) are located in Java. Java also dominates those towns established in the Islamic and early colonial period between 1400 and 1700 CE (42 out of 73), such as Banten and Semarang. But this pattern changes in the next period. Between 1700 and 1900, the number of newly urban centres rises dramatically, and the trend is towards the outer islands. Eighty-nine out of 133 new towns, coloured blue on Rutz' map, are located there. Most date to the mid- and late-nineteenth century and are the direct result of Dutch imperial conquest. A swathe of blue dots pops up on the map in the Minangkabau area of West Sumatra after the Padri Wars of the 1820s and '30s. The same happened in the Palembang hinterland (southern Sumatra) after Dutch troops suppressed indigenous resistance in 1848, in the plains north of Banjarmasin (southern Kalimantan) after the war of 1859, and on the west coast of Sulawesi following the Bone Wars that sputtered for decades after 1835. Some were entirely new places, others had been settlements with a tributary relationship to a sultan. By the end of the nineteenth century only those parts of the archipelago far from the heartlands remained without towns – the interiors of Sumatra, Borneo and Sulawesi, and most of the eastern regions of Maluku, Nusa Tenggara (Lesser Sunda Islands),

[3] Rutz deployed a functional concept of the urban that results in different urban population values than that arising from the administrative boundary concept used by the Indonesian Central Bureau of Statistics (see footnote 5 in chapter 1 above). A similar functional definition was earlier adopted by an Indonesian government project on provincial towns (NUDS 1985:62).

and New Guinea. With the last serious resistance in Aceh crushed by 1904 (fighting was still to take place in Toraja in 1905 and Flores in 1907–08), and the Netherlands, committed by its 1901 'ethical policy' to expanding its presence into many new social and geographic spaces, a period of intensive state-building commenced. This was the context in which all the remaining blank areas of Rutz' map became evenly sprinkled with black dots throughout the twentieth century. Ninety-seven of the 106 new towns are located outside Java. Metro was one of them. The map of new towns is thus at the same time an historical atlas of Dutch imperialism and colonial state formation. The town and the state grew together.

Once the state had given birth to these new towns it continued to impress itself upon them in various ways (The Siauw Giap 1959). Sometimes this was indirect. Protected by a Pax Neerlandica established by superior arms, capital moved into the frontier areas in order to extract resources, so that the state's role in the birth had been that of midwife rather than mother. The tobacco plantations of North Sumatra spawned new towns in the late nineteenth century, such as Pematang Siantar and Tebingtinggi. Oil towns like Pekanbaru in Sumatra, Cepu in Java, and Balikpapan and Tarakan on the coast of Kalimantan sprang up at about the same time, again mostly in blank areas. Coal and base metal mining towns appeared in other places. But many other towns served little purpose beyond the needs of the burgeoning state. Milone (1966:73) observed that Indonesia developed more administrative towns than other Southeast Asian nations, because it has historically been administered by a greater number of administrative levels. Whereas Thailand and Malaysia have known three levels, and Burma, the Philippines and Vietnam four, Indonesia had six.[4] As roads were constructed into inaccessible areas, administrative towns and military cantonment centres grew along them, like mushrooms after rain as Indonesians say. Manufacturing played some role in Surabaya and to a lesser extent in Batavia and Semarang, but was insignificant elsewhere. Until the 1930s, the Dutch were mainly interested in the extractive possibilities of their large colony, not in stimulating competition for manufacturers at home (Dick et al 2002).

The process of state-sponsored urbanization continued throughout the twentieth century, though at varying rates. After a hiatus caused by foreign invasion, independence, revolution and political instability, the developmentalist New Order of President Suharto built new roads in the

---

[4] Centre, governor, resident, *bupati*, *wedana*, and *camat* – the residency and wedana were later abolished.

1970s and '80s. These encouraged small-town urbanization in previously remote areas all over the outer islands (beyond densely populated Java) – particularly in the islands of Nusa Tenggara, Kalimantan, Sulawesi, Maluku and Papua. Rapidly expanding educational opportunities further stimulated urban desires. The bureaucratic politics so typical of Middle Indonesia have stimulated the birth of more new towns. With the decentralization moves that followed the end of the New Order in 1998, many new districts and some new provinces were carved out of existing ones, in a process of administrative involution Indonesians called *pemekaran,* or 'flowering.' Each new district/ province required a new capital. The number of districts and their administrative equivalents has more than doubled from 246 in 1980 to over 500 in 2013.[5] Sometimes these were already administrative centres, such as Ternate, which was upgraded from a district to a provincial capital, but others were mere villages, such as Maba in North Maluku, which is now the capital of a new district. Doubtless visitors to Maba in ten years' time will find a thriving town built around the already crumbling offices of the district head. *Pemekaran* has continued throughout the twentieth century, sometimes rapidly such as after the transfer of sovereignty in late 1949, sometimes slowly such as during the early New Order. Most often it has taken place in the outer islands. In 1980, district capitals ranged in size from 25,000 to 100,000 (Rutz 1987). Growth since then has about doubled their average size.

The towns may have been new, but at first they were small and sleepy. Urbanization was slow until the New Order period (1966–98). As late as 1920 only 5.8% of the Netherlands Indies' population lived in urban areas, justifying the exotic image of serene rusticity the Dutch projected about their colony. By 1945 this figure had risen to 10% (Hugo 1996:150). Only in the late 1960s and 1970s did urbanization rates begin to pick up. Today almost 45% of the population is urban, though even this is still below the global average of just over 50% (Firman 2004:423).[6] The strongest growth in the period 1971–1980, according to Gavin Jones (1988), took place in provincial capitals with populations in the range 200,000–500,000, not in the biggest cities. A large internationally funded study of Indonesia's intermediate cities confirmed this discovery, thought it was a good thing, and

---

[5] http://id.wikipedia.org/wiki/Daftar_kabupaten_dan_kota_di_Indonesia (accessed 3 August 2013).

[6] Precise growth rates of provincial towns are difficult to establish. Definitions of what is urban vary between authorities and over time. The 1930 and 1961 censuses cover a large number of towns, with sparser data for other years before 1961. Since 1961 data has become more abundant.

recommended that the government support it (NUDS 1985). Nevertheless, governance in the towns remained poor and self-help was the norm. In the mid-1980s piped water did not reach 60–70% of urban households in Indonesia, electricity did not reach 36–54%, and housing was 'temporary' for 41–89% of households (Jones 1988:152). In every case the figures grew worse for smaller cities. The stereo-typical image of peasants who migrate to town but retain their semi-rural living conditions while eking out a living in the bazaar are, in this respect, not far wide of the mark.

As in the late colonial Netherlands Indies, so in New Order Indonesia, provincial towns are the footprints of an imperial, modernizing state marching into ever remoter places. Rutz (1987:123) described the growth of provincial towns outside Java mainly as being 'a result of the establishment of an administration and the development of transportation systems' (see supporting data in Dürr 1982). Private investment was a significant growth factor in some timber-, mineral- and oil and gas-rich provinces such as Aceh, East Kalimantan and Irian Jaya already in the 1970s (Rietveld 1988).[7] But enclaves such as Lhokseumawe, Balikpapan, and later Timika were exceptions to the rule. Whereas the growth of industry during the New Order, in a pattern reminiscent of the West, had stimulated towns in Java (Rutz 1987:124–5), that was more rarely the case outside Java. A meticulous process of counting central service facilities such as banks and government offices all over the country led Rutz (1987:141, 148) to distinguish towns according to whether private or state services were dominant. Large cities such as Jakarta or Medan were dominated by private commercial facilities, but smaller ones, particularly places outside Java like Kendari, Bengkulu, Palangkaraya, Kupang, Palu or Mataram, had a greater proportion of official facilities. While Rutz' survey is now three decades old and dates from the early years of Indonesia's New Order industrialization, it remains the best of its kind, and its gross outlines probably remain applicable. Today's visitor sees row upon row of government offices lining the major streets of towns that otherwise lack a shopping mall or a decent bookshop. Official services in many remote district capitals make up more than a third and up to half of all central services in the town. They are the legacy of New Order state investments of oil boom revenues in infrastructure for administration and general economic development.

---

[7] Rietveld combined the NUDS data with data on large domestic and foreign investment approvals. He did not investigate state investment in the provinces, and acknowledged that private investment approvals were not always realized.

The observed pattern of provincial growth was to a significant extent the result of deliberate New Order strategy. In keeping with the regime's militarism, political stability appears to have been uppermost in planners' minds. Gavin Jones (1988) wrote that the government worried about the constant flow of potentially insurrectionary rural poor into Jakarta's teeming slums. Building provincial towns was a way of keeping the pressure off the metropolis. At the same time the anti-communist national government chose to stimulate the provinces by building loyal towns rather than risk disloyalty in the countryside by means of land reform. The risk with building far-away towns is that it involved a degree of decentralization that might also stimulate regionalist sentiment. A history of regional revolts in the 1950s had taught Jakarta the price it had to pay for loyalty in the regions. Most strategic natural resources lay in the regions beyond Java. That is why the towns were made dependent on flows of politically easy cash from the oil-flushed national capital. Personal taxation rates were kept low. Local cash-raising abilities were restricted – few taxation powers were vested in the regions, and Jakarta kept most industrialists within handy negotiating distance of the national capital by means of a forest of regulations. Hans Antlöv (2003:143) put the matter boldly: not performance but loyalty determined central government funding for local governments.

> A massive patronage system was created in which the central government awarded local governments with budget allocation in exchange for loyalty. Budget allocations were not based on performance or need, but rather on how close local governments were with the central government, and how well local elites could lobby decisions-makers in Jakarta. The resulting rent-seeking system was effective in rapidly building the economy, but was not transparent or sustainable and created great regional dissatisfactions (there are demands for independence from all the above-mentioned resource-rich provinces).

Case studies of several towns conducted during the New Order underline the importance of government in their economies. Colombijn (1994:15) writes in his study of Padang, the capital of West Sumatra province: 'The city has lived most of the twentieth century on the export of smallholders cash crops and state expenditure, and not on big capitalist enterprises. The most important means of production, the cement factory, has not been owned by private entrepreneurs but by the state (since 1958).' The twin pillars of small trade and the bureaucracy typify the economy of smaller towns to an even greater extent. They make up roughly similar proportions of both the urban GDP and the workforce. But it is the bureaucrats who occupy the dominant social positions, and nearly all the educated workers are bureaucrats. A study of three small towns in Central Java with populations in the range 20,000–30,000 in the 1990s concluded that 'due to the discriminatory allocation of development projects, the concentration of civil servant salaries and the construction of public sector facilities, the research towns receive a disproportionate share of the government funds. This definitely has a positive impact on the towns economies, although it may be detrimental to their rural hinterland development in the long run' (Wouden 1997:157) (see also Titus and Wouden 1998, and a similar conclusion for small towns in East Java, Franck 1993).

Bureaucracy

Thus far the growth of provincial towns has been portrayed as if it was a unilateral process dictated by the central state, peaking when it was strongest in the late colonial and especially the New Order periods. Reality was messier. Unplanned processes such as rural-urban migration also played a role. More important for the argument here is that those interactions between state and society, which so dominated the history of the provincial towns particularly outside the heartlands, were not one way but dialectic. Case studies of it in provincial towns reveal that state institutions are embedded much more deeply in urban societies than the first section suggested. Evers (1987) has documented quantitatively how bureaucratization progressed in several Southeast Asian countries from the late nineteenth century until 1980. In the first big thrust in the late nineteenth century, opportunities for bureaucratic employment opened up even for commoners. Officials enjoyed being part of an apparatus with power far beyond those of any traditional ruler. Nevertheless, the number of bureaucrats in the Netherlands Indies remained small in proportion to the population, also when compared with Thailand and Malaysia. This began to change around the moment of decolonization. This moment was *the* watershed in the twentieth century history of Middle Indonesia. In 1950, according to Evers, there were three times as many civil servants in Indonesia as there had been in 1930 (most of the increase coming after 1945), a much bigger jump than in the other two countries. They were concentrated in the towns, which were still small in comparison with the rural population and experienced great changes as a result. The new state had to establish its control over a vast territory after years of debilitating revolutionary violence; it had to make good on the promise that independence would bring welfare for all; and it had to reward the huge numbers of fighters who had put their lives on the line for the new republic. Particularly the notion of reward – a payoff to prevent rebellion, to put it in Machiavellian terms – helped turn the bureaucracy into a massive job creation scheme in which, as observers were to note, the average clerk had hardly any real work to do.[8]

For those who qualified, exciting opportunities for upward mobility within post-colonial Middle Indonesia now opened up. The European elite who had occupied the top administrative and business layers in the towns disappeared. So did most of the Indo-Europeans who had occupied the second rung. Though some lingered as managers in large undertakings until the mid-1950s, the executive positions they had once held in government had already passed to indigenous Indonesians upon the Japanese victory of March 1942 (Feith 2007 [1962], Mackie 1971). The substantial proportion of ethnic Chinese in most provincial towns (as seen in the 1930 census, Milone 1966:122–8), most of them in retail and services, were excluded from the opportunity for social mobility because the nationalist movement had overwhelmingly portrayed them as alien, rich, and pro-Dutch. Thus it was indigenous Indonesians, often lesser aristocrats as well as commoners with a nationalist record, who moved into positions of control. For them the town had always been essentially a place of government, and they were determined to keep it that way (Milone 1966:33).

The expanded post-colonial bureaucracy did not come with expanded budgets. What the Pacific War had failed to wreck after three years (1942–45), Dutch-Indonesian fighting in heavily populated Java finished off over the next four years (1945–49). Like many newly independent nations, Indonesia adopted its own version of state socialism (Mackie 1967, Paauw 1960). The independent state promised more than the colonial one had ever done, but it could deliver less. The state expanded its economic ambitions, but no longer had the capacity to exert its will regardless of social forces. Self-funding was to a greater or lesser degree the rule for all government departments. The loss of discipline within government had less to do with Indonesian cultural failings than with structural constraints arising from the expectations raised by democracy amidst economic collapse. Indonesia became an archetypical 'soft state' (Myrdal 1968:895–900). The politicization of the bureaucracy that followed, and the corruption that

---

8 '...the Indonesian civil service should be regarded *inter alia* as a major pool of skilled and semi-skilled manpower, much of it un- or under-employed, waiting to be siphoned off by a more dynamic private sector' (Gray 1979:113).

soon disillusioned so many Indonesians who had supported the anti-colonial struggle, set its mark also upon life in provincial towns. Most political parties used government departments as patronage bases (the communist party PKI was an exception). Their generally statist ideologies arose as much from their own practices of primitive accumulation as from popular demands for welfare. Paralyzed by factionalism, the bureaucracy tip-toed around policy issues rather than dealing with them.

Small though the bureaucracy was in relation to the population as a whole, within the town it was well embedded. Donald Fagg's 1958 dissertation on the bureaucracy in the small town of 'Modjokuto,' actually Pare in East Java, administrative seat of a sub-district dominated by plantations, is a case study in a rapidly changing social hierarchy. The authority of the sub-district chief owed almost nothing to his routine bureaucratic powers and everything to his cultural skill in living up to the image of seniority and modernity now expected of him by the town's complex constituency. Pare's population was just 15,700 in the early 1950s (Fagg 1958:259). About a third of them depended on trade. About 1,000, or well over 10% of the working population, were bureaucrats, including teachers. Towns higher up the administrative scale had more officials. Civil servants made up the town's top social layer. 'Free professionals' did not exist in Modjokuto. From doctors to bankers, they all worked for the government. It is no wonder, Fagg concluded (1958:562–3), that local government had become the focus for social stratification.

The military who took over in Jakarta from early 1966 quickly shut down the political mobilization that had been so much entwined with bureaucratic factionalism till then. At first the civil service actually shrank, as communist sympathizers were purged, particularly from the agricultural and rural development bureaucracy (though the Department of Religion actually burgeoned in the period 1967–71, Emmerson 1978:95). But when, in 1974, the oil boom began to give the government the fiscal elbow room to recommence serious development programmes, thereby earning it much-needed performance legitimation, a third burst of bureaucratization ensued (Booth 1992). In this phase the absolute number of civil servants quadrupled in only ten years. Logsdon (1998) has shown how the number continued to grow between 1974 and 1994. Civil servants made up a quarter to a third of the (largely urban) non-agricultural working population in many outer island provinces in 1990, as compared with a national average of 12%. More worked indirectly for the state as contractors (Van Klinken 2007:41). Particularly the educated middle class overlapped to a great extent with the bureaucracy. A survey in

Yogyakarta and Padang showed that 85% of government employees in the sample fell into the middle class category, while 63% of the middle class members in the sample consisted of government servants (Evers and Gerke 1994). A zero-growth policy on civil servant numbers, instituted in 1994 due to falling oil prices, has caused them to level off since then. The bureaucracy was certainly not entirely dysfunctional and antisocial. The increase under the New Order was due to the rapid expansion of services like education and health. By 1994 fully 46% of all civil servants were teachers. The number employed in state-owned corporations, meanwhile, had dwindled to insignificant levels.

Nevertheless, self-funding remained a widespread practice. Understandably, in view of the employment situation in many provincial towns, this ensured that, behind closed doors, bureaucratic factionalism remained fierce throughout the New Order. A 1970s study of the newly empowered health department in the city of Makassar analyzed this factionalism anthropologically (Conkling 1975, 1979). Officials spent an inordinate amount of time cultivating relations through 'support cliques,' usually an ethnic, family or friendship group. A clique either supported a superior for promotion or planned a revolt over their abuses (Conkling 1975:96–155). Mutual suspicion was the norm. Everyone simply assumed that government contracts were awarded on the basis of favouritism, even though that was by no means always the case (Conkling 1984). Another study on the life histories of civil servants in Bandung a little earlier showed that, from high to low, most spent a considerable proportion of their time and energy on commercial business activities in order to compensate for inadequate salaries (Oostingh 1970). Although the older ones, who remembered the rather more Weberian standards in the colonial bureaucracy, were embarrassed by the 'unsuitable' commercial activities they now practised, the younger generation was less troubled by the un-Weberian favouritism that resulted from their plugging into urban commercial networks while activating networks of patrimonial obligation (p173). The civil servant-cum-entrepreneur was the key characteristic of what Riggs (1964:267–71) had called a 'sala' bureaucracy. Here the office merged into the drawing room, which paid lip service to new values while retaining powerful older ones of personal deference and showed a large discrepancy between norms and realities. Bureaucratic involvement in business ('bureaucratic capitalism' – Riggs 1966, Robison 1978) was the economic backdrop to a paralyzing factionalism. Later case studies showed how this continued to work at the provincial town level throughout the New Order. Nicole Niessen's superb study of municipal government in Bandung (1999) described in detail such practices as nepotism in civil service recruitment and contract tendering, the creaming off of project money to supplement low salaries, the use of blank receipts and dummy corporations to mask illegal cash transfers, and the influence of substantial third parties on secretive town planning practices at the expense of the poor. Sylvia Tidey (2012) has mapped the social networks tied by mutual obligations that underlie these practices in Kupang.

Social Forces

Behind the bureaucratic politics that dominate provincial towns lies a complex of social forces that deserves analysis in its own right. This section develops a synthetic account of those forces. The state is not an autonomous actor, able to impose its will freely on the population. The pattern of state patronage reflects past and present power struggles. These have sometimes led to unintended consequences that in turn change the way the state will work in the future. Mushtaq Khan in his study of rents and rent-seeking in Asia ascribes a key role to the birth in the twentieth century of an 'urban petty-bourgeoisie, the rich peasantry and other emerging middle classes,' who have the organizational abilities to assert themselves against the central government (Khan 2000:35–40). The conventionally assumed autonomy of elites at the pinnacle of the state and economy is thus limited by less well-endowed but much more numerous and at the same time highly political groups further down the social pyramid. One of the first to point out the importance of these new classes for Asian studies was the economist Barbara Harriss-White in her fine study of small town India. She used the term 'intermediate class': 'Outside India's metropolitan cities the economy is dominated by the intermediate classes, a loose coalition of the small-scale capitalist class, agrarian and local agribusiness elites, and local state officials' (Harriss-White 2003:44, 241). The overwhelming informality of the economy at this level, regulated as it is by non-market social mechanisms, such as patriarchy, ethnic and religious solidarity, and the threat of violence, makes it difficult for the central government to establish its authority. Conversely it gives the intermediate classes, who are masters of informality, the ability to sabotage government policy and manipulate subsidies in their favour. Governments of developing countries, writes Khan, seek to ensure political stability by awarding these political intermediaries substantial 'transfer rents' in the form of state subsidies. The image of emerging (lower) middle classes who pressure governments not by their economic power but by their mobilizational skills helps explain the observations quoted above by Antlöv (2003) and Jones (1988), on the reasons behind Indonesian state subsidies for provincial urbanization during the New Order.

At first, foreign academics studying Indonesia in the 1950s and '60s looked for the modernizing, individuating professionals and entrepreneurs that Dan Lerner (1964) had described so influentially in the Middle East. When Clifford Geertz researched the small town of 'Modjokuto' in the mid-1950s (the same one Fagg had investigated) he caught glimpses of Weber's Protestant Ethic in the outlooks of the Islamic traders (C. Geertz 1963c:49). But he found a lot of communal organizing besides, which he called *aliran* politics and which became a classic concept for Indonesianists. 'This provisional, in-between, "no man's land" quality of Modjokuto social life,' he wrote (C. Geertz 1963c:16), 'is, in fact, its most outstanding characteristic.' Traditional loyalties had not 'wholly dissolved,' while more modern ones had not 'wholly crystallized.' Thus arose the image of the socially and economically stagnant Indonesian provincial town.

In hindsight it is clear that Geertz overlooked two important features of town life in the 1950s. One was the fluidity of these 'traditional loyalties,' the other was the state. Other observers realized that ethnic and religious loyalties were not pre-modern vestiges but new urban inventions. Edward Bruner (1961) noticed that Batak 'traditions' grew stronger in the city of Medan than they had ever been in the countryside. The anthropologist Douglas Miles heard in the 1960s from a small-town Kalimantan Dayak politician named Mahir Mahar how he and his committee had toured the rural upriver Dayak communities before the war in order to stimulate his rural cousins' ethnic awareness. The colonial Dutch were encouraging the ethnicization of provincial politics in order to keep 'communists' at bay, and Mahar needed to create a constituency for himself.[9] Clifford Geertz himself (1963b:270) even wrote once, but without elaborating, that 'it is the very process of the formation of a sovereign civil state that [...] stimulates sentiments of parochialism, communalism, racialism [...] because it introduced into society a valuable new prize over which to fight and a frightening new force with which to contend.'

[9] 'He and his political associates acted on the assumption that in an administrative unit where Ngadju [Dayak] were a majority, ethnic loyalties of the hinterland population would keep their leaders in power against Banjarese-Malay rivalry. However, a campaign to bolster awareness of common traditional values and interests among people of various *utus* [dialect group] identity would be a necessary preliminary to the establishment of an autonomous administrative entity' (Miles 1976:126).

Two decades later, 'neo-patrimonialism' had become an important theme in studies of Indonesian national politics (Crouch 1979, Jackson 1980, King 1982). It was used to explain the sultanistic behaviour of presidents, political factionalism in Jakarta, communalistic voter behaviour, the regionalist revolts of the 1950s, and corruption generally. These analyses were focused on Jakarta, but the same behaviour is being recognized in post-New Order studies of the regions today. Vigorous communal organizing returned when democratization and decentralization came to the provinces after 1998. Though only occasionally violent, it was always part of competition for control of the local state (Henk Schulte Nordholt and van Klinken 2007). Communal organizing was not only about internal competition but also about the provinces striking back at the metropolitan capital Jakarta. One of the most popular localist battle cries was that top local bureaucratic positions and business favours should be reserved for 'regional sons' (*putra daerah*).

Communal organizing has thus repeatedly been a mobilizational technique used by well-embedded provincial elites to pressure their collective rivals, people who, in other respects (money, official status), ought to be their superiors. Their ability to rally masses of ordinary citizens with ties to family-like solidarities, whether nationalist, regionalist, ethnic or religious, gave provincial political entrepreneurs considerable bargaining powers with national political party apparatchiks, senior technocrats, and even captains of industry. They readily invoked their powers to sabotage policies designed in far-away places by, for example, threatening to revolt or (after 1998) even to secede. Even though their rhetoric often exceeded their deeds, it had been their ability to make the archipelago ungovernable that drove the Dutch to despair of reasserting their authority after World War II. After independence their agitation forced the new government to abandon the market-oriented economic policies that might have saved the country from economic collapse.

The second feature of town life Geertz tended to overlook was the state. This is strange. The 1945 Revolution had played out just a few years earlier, also in Modjokuto. The revolution aimed to radically transform the state and it overshadowed all of national politics while Geertz did his research (Feith 1958). One reason for the neglect could have been Geertz's choice of research location. Modjokuto (Pare) was a sub-district town (*kecamatan*), while civil servants were present in 'stupefying' numbers (C. Geertz 1963c:12) only in the district capital (*kabupaten*). Another reason was Geertz' methodological lack of interest in the state, something he shared with American social science generally in the early 1950s. It was to be three decades before some of them were to 'bring the state back in.' One contemporary researcher who did not share in this neglect was Herbert Feith. In his definitive study of politics in the post-revolutionary period, he estimated the national 'political public' at approximately 1–1½ million by equating it with the number of newspaper readers (Feith 2007 [1962]:109–13). This rapidly growing group consisted of 'persons in white-collar occupations and their status equivalents,' people who had largely lost touch with their rural and traditional roots and 'saw themselves as capable of taking action which could affect national government or politics.' Most of the nation's nearly half million civil servants belonged to the political public, as did religious functionaries, labour leaders, middle-size traders and revolutionary veterans. Although only a small percentage of the total population of around 80 million at the time, their overwhelmingly urban residence in a country only just over 10% urban made them a major force in town. It was this political public that provided the constituency for the political entrepreneurs Feith called 'solidarity makers' (by contrast with the elite 'administrators'). Gerald Maryanov, one of the few students of Indonesian provincial politics in the 1950s, thought that some measure of education was the primary marker of the political public. It was they, he believed, who set the tone: 'The definition of problems takes place within this group, and it sets the climate of opinion in which problems are discussed and solved. We would further suggest that the desirability or acceptability of particular policies will be entirely determined here' (Maryanov 1959:63).

Since about the 1930s, those problems had been defined almost entirely in statist terms. So few indigenous Indonesians were successful private entrepreneurs before independence that all political parties, from socialist to religious, were in favour of extensive state supervision if not outright state ownership of the economy (Sutter 1959:I, 114f). During the national war of liberation of 1945–49, Prime Minister Hatta, a Dutch-educated economist, led attempts to nationalize everything from sugar and textile production to rice distribution and land titles. Dutch and Chinese capital was the source of evil for all Indonesian politicians. The belief that private enterprise was dishonourable and the government should protect people from it was widespread (Sutter 1959:I, 692–3).

Once independence was achieved, provincial town notables continued to favour a large state sector, since their towns rarely had any industry to speak of. Laissez fair capitalism had not been restored since the turn towards protectionism by the Dutch colonizers in the 1930s (Dick et al 2002). Jan Luiten van Zanden and Daan Marks (2012) characterize this period in Indonesia's economic history as inward-looking. Central state agencies had poor capacities to exert their will, doing little to collect taxes and spending much of their time worrying about security. As told by Jamie Mackie (1971), the nationalization of Dutch industrial, trading and plantation concerns from December 1957 was the point when Indonesia turned away from laissez faire capitalism to what was soon called 'socialisme à la Indonesia.' The actual transformation of the economy fell short of its rhetoric condemning 'free fight capitalism.' Unlike in India, the Indonesian government did not regulate expenditures in the private sector, and no attempt was made to collectivize agriculture. But the central government was unable to put a halt to spiralling state expenditure in the face of demands from what Mackie called the 'political class.' Personal taxation largely disappeared, and the state drew an inadequate income mainly from highly complicated import taxation. This deficit spending led to runaway inflation by 1961–62. Yet townsfolk (at least in Java) actually benefited from the mayhem by urban middle class control of scarce imports. They also persuaded the government to launch one welfare scheme after another for their benefit. Each one broke on the rocks of the rent-seeking practices that dominated the over-swollen towns with their extensive populations of the disguised unemployed. The first of the Five Year Plans, in 1956, envisaged large investments in the public sector. Demobilized soldiers were assisted with sawmilling businesses, a Small Scale Industrialization Plan made loans for home industry, the 'Induks' scheme aimed to help indigenous merchants bypass the Chinese, the 'Benteng' system aimed to Indonesianize import licenses. Most of these efforts failed due to 'poor administration' (Mackie 1971:47). In another study Mackie quoted the reason for Indonesia's disastrous inflation: '[the nation's leaders] are restricted because of the existence of a great number of small power centres, each in a position to veto some types of government action' (Mackie 1967:10). The American economist Hans Schmitt (1962) wrote in a despairing tone that the political radicalism of the period was due to the fact that Indonesia was run by a political elite with no real interest in capital accumulation, since the biggest enterprises (even after December 1957) remained in foreign hands.

The mobilizational skills of the political public, or we may say the provincial intermediate class, was constantly on display in the 1950s and early 1960s. Overcoming tremendous logistical challenges in an archipelago of thousands of inhabited islands, its members created political party branches in the smallest towns, and ensured a nationwide election participation rate of 92% in 1955 (Feith 2007 [1962]:249). The government's inability to resist special pleading by importers was matched by more appeasement when others protested. In late 1956, areas that felt disadvantaged by Jakarta's economic policies (mainly Sumatra and Sulawesi) launched armed revolts (PRRI/ Permesta) (Harvey 1977). Though desperately poor, Jakarta responded by awarding new provinces, with generous accompanying infrastructure budgets, in all the rebellious areas.[10] Effectively gifts of the means of primitive accumulation, these new provinces are the perfect example of the political 'transfer rent' for the sake of stability that Khan was later to describe. Similar provincial threats to 'secede' following democratization in 1998 produced another wave of new provinces and districts in recent years, despite technical advice that the new administrative machinery was unlikely to improve governance.

The reason why this intermediate class activism is so effective is that, unlike the consumerist, often apolitical 'middle classes' that fascinated social scientists in the late New Order (Dick 1985, Pinches 1999, Tanter and Young 1990), these less privileged intermediate classes are culturally not so far removed from their social inferiors. They arose after 1945 from the same run-down semi-rural *kampongs* as the urban poor. We do not have good data on provincial inequalities in the 1950s, but around 1990 they were not high by global standards. Indonesia's Gini index of 0.34 is about the same as India's of 0.33, and lower than the USA's of 0.41 (Cameron 2002). Outer island inequalities – whether measured within urban areas or between urban and rural areas – are actually slightly lower than in Java. This is due to the absence of industry and the dominance of agriculture, trade and bureaucracy in those areas (Akita and Lukman 1999). The neo-patrimonial relations between intermediate class members and their poorer dependents are simply unequal friendships – they exist between people who are not separated from each other by light years on the social spectrum. This reflects the 'shared poverty' that Armstrong and McGee identified as the key characteristic of Indonesia's towns. But these towns and cities have not been politically quiescent. It is true that they have not proven to be incubators of lower class revolution. Their activism has been of the darker, more conservative kind – Metro, Lampung, in 1998 is a good example – reflecting the interests of their careerist intermediate classes.

---

10 New provinces created in the late 1950s following regional revolts in Sumatra, Sulawesi, Kalimantan and (earlier) in Maluku were these: South-, Central-, Southeast- and North Sulawesi, Jambi, West Sumatra, Riau, West-, Central- and East Kalimantan, Bali, West Nusa Tenggara, and East Nusa Tenggara. Maluku was changed from an 'administrative' to an 'autonomous' province (Legge 1961:66–8).

The locus for this activism is the informal economy – unregulated, and therefore untaxed and excluded from official statistics (Portes et al 1989 :12). Informality, some of it criminal, figures largely in the economies of provincial towns all over the world (Datta 1990). As in the 1950s so today the informal economy employs huge numbers in Indonesia. Almost two-thirds of the labour force today works in the unregistered (though not necessarily poor) informal economy. Most of this occurs in agriculture, but also in urban areas; slightly more people now work in the informal than in the formal sector, and the gap appears to be growing steadily (Angelini and Hirose 2004:6–9). Trade is almost wholly informal. Patterns of circular migration and commuting that link the town to its surrounding countryside pass substantially through the informal sector. Generally better-educated young people find a job first in the urban informal sector by using ethnic networks, before moving later into the formal sector, preferably the government (Costello et al 1987, Hugo 1996).

Where many studies have portrayed the informal economy as a valuable sponge for excess labour, which creates a buffer against revolutionary forces, others have highlighted its exploitative, Mafia-like nature. It is the cross-over between the informal sector and predation by underfunded state officials that transforms key parts of the provincial town's stereotypical bazaar economy for the 'little people' into a black economy. Local elites benefit from this economy too. More open conditions after 1998 have permitted more research into this delicate arena than was previously possible. Jun Honna (2006:78–9), for example, describes post-1998 military garrison commanders in provincial Java who sought to supplement their plummeting extra-budgetary incomes after the bankruptcy of 'regular' military businesses (such as airline and taxi cooperatives) by getting into the protection of illegal logging, human trafficking, the illicit drug trade, and stolen vehicles. The highly competitive, ethnicized and sometimes violent post-1998 election of district heads in provincial West Kalimantan, meanwhile, appears to be fuelled by a trade in illegal timber that is about as large as that in legal logs (Van Klinken 2008). Numerous other examples of lucrative shadow-state activities could be mentioned, ranging from prostitution, through illegal fishing, scams involving land, labour migration and the religious *haj* to illegal tin- and gold mining. Much of this plays out in provincial towns, where it provides the hidden context for the intra-elite struggles that do reach the newspapers. The theft of public resources these activities represent exacerbates the problems of service delivery that the central government faces and should be seen as another example of the hijacking of the state by members of Khan's 'emerging middle classes.'

The Town Today

Those emerging classes have grown enormously since the 1950s, whether one attempts to measure their size by political awareness (Feith's newspaper reading public), white-collar occupations (another of Feith's criteria), a combination of self-employed small businesspeople and local officials (Harriss-White's criterion), or a high school education (Maryanov's criterion). Rather than being distinguishable by 'objective' income or occupational criteria, however, they are known by their political action. The typical features of Middle Indonesian towns – including the localism, the communitarianism, the primitive accumulation and the manipulation of government subsidies – should be traced to the interests of these emerging intermediate classes. These differ markedly from the bourgeois concerns of those who live in the corporate, formal economy, a group that has enjoyed a lot of attention as the creators of Indonesia's 'miracle' economic boom after 1965. The argument here – which the subsequent chapters develop and which I hope others will examine with better data and sharper analytical skills than I could muster– is simply that the middle class has not only grown at its top but even more so at its bottom end. An Asian Development Bank study of consumption patterns, for example, concluded that the Asian 'middle class' had grown from 25% to 43% in the ten years from 1999 to 2009 (ADB 2010:11–2). The figure was so high because anybody not in absolute poverty was assigned to the middle class – the per-capita household expenditure threshold had been reduced to a very low US$ 2 a day. People at the bottom of the middle class have a different outlook on life from those near the top. It is the people of the lower middle class who dominate the countryside outside the heartlands through the towns of Middle Indonesia (see also the introduction to Van Klinken and Berenschot 2014). Their control of the nodes in the vast territorial network that constitutes the state has given them a national voice out of proportion to their wealth. It is their political entrepreneurship, rather than the stagnation of off-farm workers sharing their poverty in town, that sets the tone in the hundreds of towns of Middle Indonesia.

CHAPTER THREE

A RESEARCHER'S NOTES

> Don't write this, but I was forced to witness five mass executions. It was horrifying. I will never forget it.
>
> (Interview in Kupang, 2009)

In the dim coolness of his lounge room he had talked animatedly about many interesting topics in Kupang's modern history – Chinese shops in the 1950s, schools, newspapers, social rankings in town, civil servants, the Japanese occupation. As I stood up to leave and put away my notebook, the conversation suddenly turned to death. He started speaking of what he had seen in 1966 and 1967, as the military suppression of the Indonesian Communist Party, PKI, reached its height all over Indonesia. 'Don't write this,' he said. Then he told me: 'I was forced to witness five mass executions. PKI members and activists were taken out of town at night. Each time, tens of people were shot, each time with the proclamation: "Now you can see what happens to members of the PKI." It was horrifying. I will never forget it.' It was one of my first interviews in Kupang, and already I had a dilemma. How could I write history and *not* 'write this'?

This chapter seeks to reconstruct the biographies of some key actors in Kupang, people who will keep recurring throughout the book. A biographical approach is not only more interesting than a strictly institutional one, but it will also help uncover the formal and (especially) the informal connections by which power is generated in a provincial town. The growth of nationalism in a 'peripheral' area, whose analysis is the burden of this book, is a contentious political process aimed at seizing the state (Breuilly 1982). So, unlike those studies of it that begin with notions of identity or psychological needs, the focus here is on actors, organizations, and the mobilizational techniques they deploy to cross social and geographical distances. In the next chapter the actors introduced in this one will begin their work, but before we go there it is worthwhile to pause at the researcher's process of reconstruction itself.

It did not take me long to discover that critical historical research in a postcolonial provincial town confronts the researcher with daunting challenges. The painful interview quoted above exposed just part of the problem. Written sources, never abundant in such a town, are scarcer for the tumultuous 1950s and '60s than they are for the 1930s. Those written and oral sources that do exist tend to be privately controlled by a small number of intellectual gatekeepers, who represent the town's historical establishment. These people are survivors and often collaborators of multiple and violent regime changes. They share a strong commitment to a sanitized version of the town's history that covers agonizing events with silence. Some will talk about these events, but only on the understanding that they remain unwritten. The historian must become a kind of guerrilla, interrogating sources against the grain, and occasionally forced to dissemble. This chapter describes one historian's guerrilla campaign, in the face of such obstacles, to reconstruct the lives of four provincial elite actors, two winners and two losers in the social struggles of the time.

Biographers frequently perceive their task in a different light than do the gatekeepers of sources upon which they must rely. The gatekeeper has in mind a pleasing portrait, the biographer looks for possibly unflattering social and psychological processes. One feels responsibility to the subject; the other considers mainly the subject's responsibility to the world. The gap becomes a dilemma if the gatekeeper holds nearly all the available information on the subject, which is often the case in the Indonesian provinces of the 1950s. The dilemma grows if the gatekeeper invests this knowledge with the honour of their family, their town, their class, or perhaps their entire nation. If the biographer comes from the old colonial country the problem only gets bigger. Happy are those who reach an agreement to satisfy scholarship. In my case, although those who spoke to me knew the outline of my project, there was no explicit agreement about how their information would be used. They may be surprised by what they finally read.[1]

Over three northern summers between 2009 and 2011 I spent a total of three months in and around Kupang. I wanted to learn about the rise of an indigenous provincial middle class outside the central island of Java. I expected to see its members helping to hold the country together by their participation in complex mediation processes. If the birth of this

[1] I have done my best to deal ethically with what they told me by (a) not repeating information given in confidence if it can be traced to a particular person; (b) quoting the same information from a public source even if I first heard it confidentially; (c) anonymizing information given in confidence if it illustrates a broader trend already identified from publicly identifiable sources; but (d) always prioritizing my responsibility to a broad readership, even if my informants have become friends.

new middle class took place in the 1930s, when Kupang was a sleepy town of 7,000, and it reached adulthood at the height of the developmentalist New Order in the 1980s (population 91,000 – Leirissa et al 1984:53), then its formative childhood years were the 1950s and '60s. I decided to focus on the lives of several individuals that, to my social science mind, more or less reflected the most important social struggles in Kupang in the 1950s and '60s.

Preliminary reading led me to think of several social struggles in this town over the period between 1930 and 1975. Similar struggles were won and lost in many other provincial towns at about this time (Reid 1974, Ricklefs 2008:181–343, Sutherland 1979). I decided to highlight two groups who had done well in these struggles, and two who came out poorly. One group of winners were Indonesian republicans (mostly commoner bureaucrats). They rose at the expense of traditional aristocrats. Left-wing organizers looked for a while like winners, but they turned into losers when they were wiped out by yet another group, namely the military. The struggles of republicans, aristocrats, communists, and soldiers were linked to each other, and their overall context was multi-dimensional. Important contextual elements are discussed at greater length elsewhere but they include increased connectedness due to cheaper sea and air transport. The freer flow of people, movies and magazines reduced distances and stimulated everything from political centralization to new gender roles, from new church dress codes to new dances and buzz words. The absence of a national revolution in the eastern archipelago, and the surrounding subsistence agriculture, made it easier to maintain elitist and technocratic styles of government.

Who would become my subjects? History belongs to the victors, so identifying representatives of the rising forces was fairly easy. I.H. Doko (1913–1985) was in 2006 proclaimed the province's second National Hero (*pahlawan nasional*). The perfect republican. Moreover this educator and politician wrote prolifically, also about himself. As for the military, who so thoroughly dominated government throughout the New Order (1966–1998), no one could represent them as well as the flamboyant Elyas ('El') Tari (1926–1978), provincial governor for 12 years from 1966. The losers were more difficult to bring to light, as they had largely disappeared from the public record. I chose Alfons Nisnoni (1907–1987), the last king of Kupang, as my declining aristocrat. Michael Marcus (1906–1966), a Kupang politician who from 1960 headed up a successful district branch of the communist-affiliated Indonesian Farmers Union (Barisan Tani Indonesia, BTI), became my representative leftist.

Where could I learn more about these four individuals? None were nationally significant, so they are practically absent from standard history books and national Who's Who collections, such as Roeder (1971). Indeed, little of national moment ever happened in this town. Perusing the national daily *Merdeka* from 1946–1959, my research assistant Basilius Triharyanto found only a single reference to Kupang, namely when President Sukarno visited in May 1954.[2] Like those Dutch officials who filled the colonial archives with their own anxieties tied to the metropolis (Stoler 2009), the Indonesian authors of most of the small number of books we have about the provinces treat them purely as supporting acts for dramas at the centre. If they gave the centre no trouble, as apparently Kupang did not, then it was not worth writing about them. Many locals today share the blank feeling. Hearing about my interest, one Kupang student responded with a puzzled look: 'Does Kupang have a history?' The mere fact that the town exists, evidently without controversy that would make it special among the hundreds of other towns, makes it an excellent case study site for Middle Indonesia.

Nevertheless, Kupang is a literate society, and it has plenty of written local history. The provincial office of the Education Department has produced a stack of history textbooks for use in schools in East Nusa Tenggara (Nusa Tenggara Timur, NTT). These are available at the downtown state library, which I found always full of students writing their assignments. Prominents such as Doko wrote memoirs late in life. Many of the city's streets are graced with the names of local luminaries like Tom Pello, E.R. Herewila, Herman Johannes and of course El Tari and Doko. There are a startling number of statues. An enterprising journalist compiled a 300-page biographical encyclopaedia of NTT personalities with about 1000 entries (Passar 2005). Passar's encyclopaedia is by far the most comprehensive Who's Who, but several other NTT collections also contain biographical sketches or interviews (Adam et al 1997, Leirissa et al 1984, Liliweri et al 1984, Widiyatmika 1983). In short, Kupang's middle class love writing and reading about their own prominents. However, this knowledge circulates in rather personalized ways. Passar's extremely useful encyclopaedia can only be bought at the author's home in a dusty backstreet, after office hours, over tea. The memoirs, too, disappear off the shelves of the town's only decent bookstore, Gramedia, within six months of publication. The reader is advised to visit the author at home to obtain a copy.

---

2 'Presiden ke Kupang,' *Merdeka*, 17 May 1954.

Needless to say, my 'social forces' and 'political struggles' interest these local historians little if at all. Their template is still the national hero, who resists the colonial Dutch, brings Kupang into the Indonesian nation, and helps build religion and the economy. After noting in his preface the 'colossal and monumental' scope of his magnum opus, Passar wrote that he and his committee chose as their subjects all those who 'had spread the sweet aroma of the greatness, the nobility as well as the success and the esteem of Nusa Tenggara Timur as a part of Indonesia's civilized future' (p. ii). In his foreword, Professor Alo Liliweri praised the compilers' creativity, and only feared some readers might find cause to ask: 'Is this person important, is this person a prominent, is this person a leader, did this person make a positive contribution, is this person a successful human being, etc' (p. v).

A massive bust of Doko stands in the vast grounds of the provincial Education Department, which he founded in 1959. It was raised by contributions from the thousands of teachers whose careers he made possible. His political achievements on behalf of the Republic are told in one of his own books (Doko 1975, new edition Doko 1981b). As Governor El Tari wrote in a foreword, the book proved 'that Nusa Tenggara Timur has never been absent in the struggle for national RIGHTS' [emphasis in the original] – a veiled rejection of the feeling in Jakarta that poor, peripheral, Christian NTT had only been dragged into the republic by forces beyond its passive, not to say backward, self. Doko belonged to a small Kupang elite, most educated in Java, that rose to prominence under the Japanese (1942–45). Afterwards, Indonesian republicans in Java proclaimed an independent republic, but at first it controlled only most of Java and parts of Sumatra (it was also active in South Sulawesi and parts of Kalimantan). By contrast with the sustained fighting in Java, the Dutch had much less trouble reasserting control outside Java. They sought to satisfy moderate nationalists by creating a number of autonomous states within a federation that in turn was federatively associated with the Netherlands (the idea was inspired by French Indochina). Timor belonged to the most successful and most democratic of these federal states, the State of Eastern Indonesia (Negara Indonesia Timur, NIT), whose capital was Makassar. Trained before the war as a school teacher, Doko belonged to a nationalist faction. His bright personality and speaking talents led him to be appointed first Assistant Minister for Information in 1947, then full Information Minister two years later, and finally Education Minister in 1950 (Figure 3). Doko himself figures prominently in his well-told story of the decolonization of this part of the archipelago. His narrative is

Figure 3. NIT Information Minister I.H. Doko visiting the Raja of Kupang, probably 1949 (NIT Information Ministry photo; courtesy Mr. Leopold Nisnoni).

punctuated by mobilizational rallies in Kupang, whose frequency belied the town's passivity, alternating with elite conferences in Sulawesi and Java. The nationalist cause travels with Doko, backwards and forwards between the centre and the islands. Thanks to a multitude of such efforts by the young nation's educated elite, republicanism had triumphed over colonialism even in the remotest islands by 1950. His version of history has since then become unassailable. It is retold with little variation in all the provincial history textbooks (e.g. Djeki 1980, Koehuan et al 1982, Soh and Indrayana 2008, Widiyatmika 2007). Doko's books also remain a major source for western-trained historians (Ardhana 2000, Farram 2004).

If Kupang's teachers are proud of their Doko statue, the town boasts no less than three of former NTT governor, Brigadier-General (posthumously promoted to Major-General) El Tari. All are in good repair. He is one of a gigantic threesome on a roundabout at the eastern end of El Tari Road.[3]

[3] The Tirosa Statue stands on the 'PLN' roundabout. The acronym Tirosa stands for the three main islands in the colonial *afdeeling* of Timor and Islands – Timor, Rote, and Sabu. These gave rise to today's three main rival ethnic groups in Kupang's local politics. Timor is represented by Raja H.A. Koror, Rote by Prof. Herman Johannes, and Sabu by Maj.-Gen. El Tari.

Figure 4. El Tari (painting at El Tari's family home in Fontein, Kupang; artist unknown).

Another one decorates the driveway into El Tari Airport outside Kupang. And he stands two metres tall in front of the Agriculture Department office, arm outstretched in a commanding posture, instructing the peasants to 'plant, plant, plant, and plant again' (*tanam, tanam, tanam, sekali lagi tanam* – Passar 2005:272).[4] (I discovered afterwards that this tree-planting scheme to combat soil erosion failed completely, Liliweri et al 1984:112–3). His successor as governor, the soldier and medical doctor Ben Mboi, now retired but still energetic, frequently urges student audiences to become 'young El Taris' (Mboi 2009:84). The man's paternalistic good humour and frequent tours to inspire the poor to better their lot are still held to be exemplary.

[4] An even larger statue of him, in a similar pose, stands in the up-country town of Soë.

Thus Kupang honours its emancipators. What did surprise me was that even these heroes are so little understood. The rather detailed entry on Doko in Passar's encyclopaedia is mis-filed under his middle name 'Huru,' so I did not discover it till much later. It does not report his death date, 20 years before publication. To learn more, I had to go to the home of the Kupang historian who wrote the bio of him that accompanied the National Hero application. Indonesia now has 156 official national heroes, and the bureaucratic procedure that produces them is complex but well-oiled.[5] As often happens, Doko's process was initiated and financed by his son. Paultje Doko is a retired banker in Jakarta. He asked the Kupang academic Munandjar Widiyatmika to do the research. Later he paid a well-known national author to write a full-scale biography, with the intention of distributing it free of charge at a special provincial ceremony (Manafe 2009). The book was not in the Kupang bookshop; Paul Doko gave me a copy when I met him in his father's house in Kupang. Until then I had relied on a biographical sketch in the newspaper clipping on Doko's hero-hood from 2006 (Malehere and Krenak 2006), and on a rather confusing little biography written years earlier by an Education Department staff member (Boenga et al 1996). Finding the latter again entailed a visit to the author, who still worked at the department, to borrow his last copy for photocopying. My visit was enlivened by half an hour's banter with all the other office workers, for whom I was welcome relief from boredom in the stifling heat.

El Tari may have been the province's most adulated governor, but he turned out to be even more difficult to pin down on paper than Doko. Orphaned as a child, he has no surviving relatives literate enough to ensure immortality by ordering a biography. Only one obscure source mentions a birth date: 18 April 1926 (Nahak et al 2009). The one apparently fact-laden paragraph in the long El Tari entry in Passar's encyclopaedia, containing a list of his military appointments from 1945 until his death in 1978, is unsourced and full of outdated military acronyms that the editor had not understood. I later discovered that the source for this paragraph was the official obituary distributed at his funeral (Setwilda 1978). Unfortunately this document, too, was marred by errors and omissions. Military acronyms common in 1978 were backdated anachronistically to

[5] 'Pahlawan nasional,' id.wikipedia.org (accessed 20 January 2010). Doko was the second from NTT. First was Dr W.Z. Johannes in 1968. Doko was followed in 2009 by Prof. Dr. Ir. Herman Johannes, cousin to W.Z. Johannes. A number of others, such as E.R. Herewila and J.W. Amalo, have the lesser status of Pioneer of Independence (*perintis kemerdekaan*).

the 1950s, or misspelled unrecognizably. Informal revolutionary militias of the late 1940s are presented as full-scale regiments, which are then puzzlingly absent when I go to cross-check them in the national registers. Military campaigns in which he had taken part were omitted. I recovered them laboriously from the list of his medals (themselves in military shorthand) appended to the obituary.

If this is how it is with victors, how much deeper is the ignorance surrounding losers. At least Alfons Nisnoni, the last raja of Kupang, has an entry in Passar's encyclopaedia. It details his civil service career, but not the role rajas played under Dutch colonialism to control the peasant population, nor the republican challenge that led to their decline in the 1950s. Michael Marcus, the communist BTI leader in Soë, 110 km from Kupang, does not occur in the encyclopaedia at all, nor do most other leftists (an exception is the inimitable Christian Pandie of the 1920s). Aristocrats in decline, and activists championing losing causes, are clearly not 'successful human beings.' For more information on both I had to resort to guerrilla tactics – fragments in obscure books, newspaper clippings, personal archives, and especially oral history.

Sources

This is when I learned what a wasteland the Indonesian provinces of the 1950s and '60s are for the historian. It is easier to write about a medieval European town than Kupang in the 1950s. Up to 1942 the situation is not too bad. Kupang's long colonial history can be deciphered from archives preserved in the Netherlands and Jakarta (Ardhana 2000, Farram 2004, Fox 1977, Hägerdal 2012, Leirissa et al 1984). Two centuries after small VOC beginnings in the early seventeenth century, the township grew into a significant imperial outpost by the nineteenth, acquiring municipal boundaries in 1886. By the 1930s the town had no fewer than nine regular (if slim) newspapers, some mailed out to Kupang folk scattered throughout the archipelago's colonial civil service. Submarines and aircraft paused at Kupang on their way to Australia. World events punished Kupang harshly after 1942. Allied bombing during World War II left the town in ruins. The Chinese shops by the harbour, the imposing official home of the Resident, the *societeit* overlooking Fort Concordia where elite Dutch and the Europeanized aristocracy had played bridge and billiards – all were gone.

Fire, impoverishment, bureaucratic inertia, and especially repeated and violent regime change played havoc with historical records after 1942.

Today there are only three towns outside Java that have a continuous newspaper record for the 1950s, and none have any for the crisis-ridden 1960s.[6] Just when Kupang had been rebuilt, increasingly shrill politics in Jakarta caused the economic and institutional fabric to fray around the country. Only four short-lived newspapers appeared in Kupang during the half-century between 1942 and 1992, and of these only one, the wartime broadsheet *Timoer-Sjoeho*, survives in a Dutch library, where it is searchable online.[7] The colonial discipline that once required every provincial newspaper to submit an archival copy of each edition to the state secretariat apparently broke down after 1942. Politics have been more brutal than bombs. To my knowledge, no one in Kupang dared to keep their copies of the communist broadsheet *Pelopor* after the government banned it in October 1965. A photo (Figure 5) in the post-1965 Catholic magazine *Dian* (published in Ende) shows how the new regime regarded the past. A man is burning communist papers, over the caption: '...so they will not be read by those who don't have the right.'[8] Just before *Pos Kupang* finally restarted on a sound footing in 1992, NTT was one of only six provinces (out of 28) without its own daily. The only regional news journal that occasionally covered Kupang in the 1950s was the Catholic fortnightly *Bentara*, published in Ende. Significant parts survive in Catholic libraries in Ende and Maumere, but apparently nowhere else.

Disasters have done their share of damage. The town's archives, once containing material going back to VOC times, were lost when the temporary wooden building in which they were housed burned down in 1964 (arson is alleged, part of the political tensions in town at the time). What was left was flooded, then apparently burned again in 1982. Today Kupang, in keeping with its regional status, has a state library and no less than three official archives – provincial, district, and municipal. They contain abundant government publications ('grey matter') starting from the 1980s, but nothing from the 1950s and '60s. Yet few of the generous staff resources at these institutions are devoted to recovering those years. A relaxed atmosphere of chatting and newspaper-reading prevails in them. One is directed by a former harbour official who claimed to 'know nothing' as he had 'only been here eighteen months.' Another only allows non-official

[6] Medan, Padang and Ende have papers for the full 1950s. Makassar, Banjarmasin, and Palembang have papers for the early 1950s. Data from Santoso 1984.

[7] http://niod.x-cago.com/maleise_kranten/papers.do (accessed 17 August 2013). See also Kleden, Banda and Putra (2007).

[8] 'Warta berita,' *Dian*, 24 September 1976, p8.

Figure 5. '... so they will not be read by those who don't have the right': burning politically suspect papers, probably in Flores, sometime after the 1966 regime change (from the 24 September 1976 edition of *Dian* magazine, p. 8; photographer unknown).

visitors to peruse documents after they have been personally approved in an interview with the busy director. A dedicated young archivist at another, and an enormously helpful librarian at the State Library, by their contrast with the norm, merely underscored the tremendous theft of public resources that occurs in most provincial government offices.

Scarcity makes knowledge a valuable resource and its gatekeepers all the more powerful. Beyond the flimsy official texts and the statues, knowledge of the past is not public property, but a private hobby for the town's elite. Personal archives have a higher standing among those in the know than state collections. A visiting researcher soon learns that former governor Ben Mboi, for example, possesses the best library in town, although I also learned, after a good dinner that included imported red wine at the table of this gigantic man, that his library does not cover my period. Leo Nisnoni, son of Alfons Nisnoni, a retired civil servant who now makes a modest living as a tennis coach, keeps a large and well-indexed collection in his bedroom. He will dig into this with unfailing generosity for anyone interested, producing photographs, clippings, books and papers. But some personal collections too have suffered from fire: Doko's considerable personal library had been preserved by his son Paultje, but the house burned down in 2002. The neighbour's house burned down as well, containing a reportedly excellent photographic collection made by a Mr. Lobo. Some personal archives are still waiting to be re-discovered. My biggest find in Kupang was the personal library of El Tari – 26 meters of books and official reports, still sitting on their original shelves in his house three decades after his death. The house was occupied by two sons of a man whom El Tari (whose marriage was childless) had 'adopted' as his younger brother. Both are private security guards and seemed practically illiterate, but they were determined to preserve the library in memory of the great man. They had refused to surrender it to the State Library, as the law requires of its retiring top officials. El Tari's Mercedes still stood in the garage, deliberately looking neglected so rivals in the family (which seemed seriously divided against itself) would not come to claim this expensive vehicle. The good-natured men let me spend hours perusing the library. Beyond that, leads to several old people in and around Kupang who were said to possess enormous archives turned up little. 'People borrow things and do not return them,' was the usual stoic explanation.

Establishment

After thus circulating around Kupang on my little rented motorcycle for some weeks, calling often on acquaintances who possessed books and memories, my next discovery was that I had passed from free-floating researcher to a friend of the town's historical establishment. Every provincial town has such a loose network, just a handful of people, whose knowledge is widely recognized as authoritative. The privatized nature of the best archives makes them real intellectual gatekeepers. In Kupang in 2009 it certainly included Leo Nisnoni, Munandjar Widiyatmika, and Hendrik Ataupah, the latter a retired professor at Nusa Cendana University. They do not agree on everything, but lives lived as government advisers, speakers, and columnists have given them all a sense of decorum. I have not yet met a truly knowledgeable historical dissident in the provinces; the town would not tolerate them. When the rare foreign researcher comes to Kupang, these local historians feel a responsibility to be helpful but also to ensure that no dangerous impressions arise that might discredit the town. Every researcher is familiar with the generous but stifling host who offers to arrange all contacts. The answer is to diversify sources. Once it becomes clear that one has a broad range of contacts, pressure eases and respect grows.

The history of Kupang for my period, such as it is, was written by this little establishment. Most of its members are survivors of (and in some measure collaborators with) the anti-communist purges of 1965–1966. Beginning in 1966 and lasting well into the 1970s, the rector of Nusa Cendana University, Mr. Muhammad Syah (whose family came from West Sumatra), hosted a weekly gathering at his home open to all interested in the history of NTT. Alfons Nisnoni was there, so were Munandjar Widiyatmika as a young lecturer new to Kupang, the anthropologist Hendrik Ataupah, not long back from a Master's in the US, the bookish retired civil servant J.J. Detaq, two priests interested in physical anthropology and prehistory – Verschuren and Darius Ngawa, the young female historian Mia Patty Noach, just back from studies in Central Java, and two people about whom I know nothing more – I. Toto and Teddens. Like a benign shadow over the group, but too busy to attend, was I.H. Doko, who had started the history department at the university not long before that. Several of these people later wrote historical books about Kupang. Mia Noach told me they talked about uncontroversial topics. She remembers the legends of the rajas, the graves of Dutch missionaries, colonial regulations, and the books on Timor by H.G. Schulte Nordholt (1971) and Ormeling (1956). The meeting did not debate, but 'exchanged information.'

Politeness on some topics was matched by silence on others. No one was interested in the 1950s ('there was nothing here then') or even in World War II. Also never verbalized, though so recently seared into everyone's consciousness, was the anti-communist bloodbath of 1965–1966, in which thousands died in NTT. Munandjar Widiyatmika recalled to me, with some self-accusing agitation, that they did not even discuss the destruction of tradition that occurred as droves of communist peasants flocked into the church for fear of being labelled 'atheists,' surely a topic of great interest to this predominantly anthropological seminar. Thus the most terrible event ever to have happened in Kupang, the purges against communists following the military takeover in Jakarta, was left unspoken, a gaping hole from which one looks away. These things 'had never existed,' as Gabriel Garcia Marquez put it in *A Hundred Years of Solitude*.[9] The few

[9] 'Those fickle tricks of memory were even more critical when the killing of the workers was brought up. Every time that Aureliano mentioned the matter, not only the proprietress but some people older than she would repudiate the myth of the workers hemmed in at the station and the train with two hundred cars loaded with dead people, and they would even insist that, after all, everything had been set forth in judicial documents and in

foreign scholars who *have* tried to write about these events ended confessing they were hardly able to penetrate the prevailing silence wrapped in blatant falsehoods (Farram 2002, Webb 1986).

Don't Write This

Then I learned another lesson. The theatricality of public historical discourse in Kupang has limits. Out of the public view, beyond the cardboard cut-out heroes without birth dates, other biographies circulated in private. Here, losers condemned to obliteration by the town's establishment once more stirred to life, and even winners were seen to be human after all. Here, lives did not run predictably along tracks laid down by the invincible force of nationalism, but zigzagged hazardously among the contingent shoals of regime changes and personal rivalries.

Leo Nisnoni told me how his father, a tall heavy-set and kindly-looking man, realized in the 1950s that the 'good old times' at the *societeit* were over (Figure 6). The 'clerks' who had stood only just above peasants on the colonial social ladder now ran the show. Like the Balinese princes in Clifford Geertz's *Peddlers and Princes* (1963c), Nisnoni went into business with some wealthy Chinese he knew. Taking advantage of government assistance, he oversaw the construction of the town's first factory. It was a small meat-canning plant, built on his royal lands on the edge of town. It drew on the cattle that are Timor's only significant export. He told his children to be thrifty, 'like the Chinese.' But the family never had to go hungry. Republicanism in Timor did not extend to seizing aristocratic land (though there were some half-hearted attempts in that direction). There was enough money for this son to play basketball with the rich kids in town, and to be in Holland for high school throughout the 1950s. Leo and I spoke Dutch together; he learned Indonesian only in 1963. He remembered how his mother loved the silks at Toko Baru, the best Chinese store in Kupang. Less playful stories emerged too. He remembers how his father made fateful choices in uncertain times. When national politics polarized in the early 1960s, and the PKI stepped up its 'anti-feudal' rhetoric, Alfons Nisnoni joined the military-backed party IPKI.[10] 'It was for protection; a good strategy,' the son told me;

primary-school textbooks: that the banana company had never existed' (Marquez 1970 [orig. Spanish 1967]:396).

[10] Ikatan Pendukung Kemerdekaan Indonesia (IPKI) – League of Supporters of Indonesian Independence.

Figure 6. Alfons Nisnoni with family, at his silver wedding anniversary in 1960 (photo courtesy Mr. Leopold Nisnoni).

'otherwise our life could have been very different after 1965.' We had reached the dark heart of Kupang's history.

A Protestant reverend in Kupang, whose own father had been detained briefly in 1965, drew me further into this dark history. He put me in touch with a parishioner who was the daughter of Michael Marcus, the BTI leader. She agreed to talk about her father, at first reluctantly because she had never before talked of this man whom the civil servant in her regarded as a sinner, then in a flood of tears as the daughter in her remembered the father she had last seen through the bars of Kupang's old colonial jail early in 1966. She showed me photographs of a family man standing next to his neatly dressed wife named Loisa Nenobais. He had met her at the home of a Dutch missionary in Camplong, near Soë, married her in 1929, and they had ten children. Other photos showed an active churchgoer posing with the congregational council after worship; a white-shirted 1950s politician in a delegation lined up before a banner during a visit to Jakarta. Like Doko, Michael Marcus was the son of a farmer on another island, Rote (Figure 7). Like him, he trained as a teacher, probably at the church-run teacher's college in Rote. He taught in rural church primary schools around Timor for years. When the Japanese came and the schools closed down, he appears to have fed his family with a small business that later

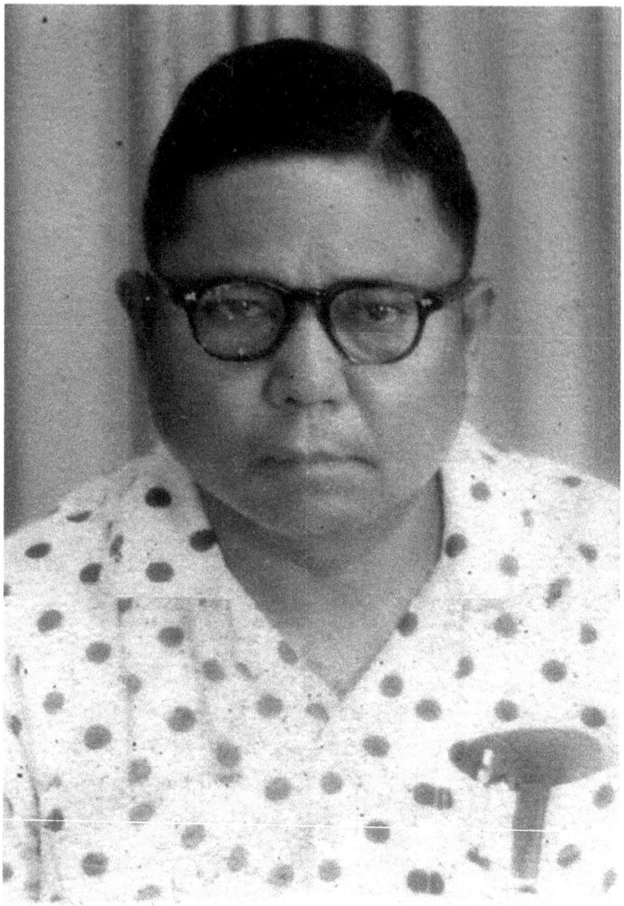

Figure 7. Michael Marcus, 1961 (photo courtesy Dra. Ruth Heny A. Nitbani-Markus).

involved a truck. Real upward mobility came with independence. Like so many teachers, he was asked to fill a political position in Kupang – first as member of the assembly for Timor and its nearby islands. This was a highly prestigious moment, but also a risky one.

In the Timor assembly he was close to the assembly speaker, E.R. Herewila, the same age as Michael Marcus and also a strong modernizer with a distaste for the rajas. Herewila introduced him to the secular nationalist party, the Indonesian Nationalist Party (Partai Nasional Indonesia, PNI) ahead of the 1955 elections. PNI was strong among bureaucrats in Java, but in Timor it was badly outpolled by the Protestant

Figure 8. Michael Marcus and family, 1952 (photo courtesy Dra. Ruth Heny A. Nitbani-Markus).

and Catholic parties. Recriminations flew. Michael's truck was supposed to have been used for smuggling to Portuguese Timor (quite possible), and he spent three months in detention before Herewila negotiated his release. From then on he worked in various executive positions in local government in Kupang (education, health) and, at some time in the late 1950s, in Soë, a few hours' drive from Kupang in good weather (the district finance department). His wife's family, the Nenobais, were influential in the district of South Central Timor of which Soë was the central town. Some of them were interested in leftist ideas, others in religious ones. In the late 1950s the communist party PKI launched a major drive to increase its presence and legitimacy in the provinces. It aimed not at revolution but, like the Italian communists, at a gradual shift in the balance of forces. The president gave it the support of his magnificent oratory. The farmers union BTI was its most impressive achievement (Pauker 1964). The organization was effective at recruiting local talent. Michael Marcus became a part-time but committed BTI organizer in Soë in July 1960. Mainly because of abuses by the local raja, who remained powerful, more farmers joined BTI here than in any other district of NTT. Soon Marcus had become a competent public speaker on land issues. His daughter remembers him engaged in serious conversation with a lawyer friend about legal technicalities, and at other times with peasants on his veranda talking in the local dialect Dawan, which he had learned. The peasants spat blood-red betel nut juice on the ground, but he was too middle class to chew.

Then the fates intervened again. Some months after the dramatic events in Jakarta on 1 October 1965, of which Marcus knew nothing, the military organized a bloody purge of communists throughout the country. Officers arrested him at his home, took him to Kupang's overcrowded little colonial jail, where he languished for weeks. One night, some time after mid-February 1966, they took him away and he was never seen again. The daughter has no idea where he is buried. He was 60 years old. She lost her oldest brother the same way. An older sister had joined the left-wing women's movement Gerwani, but she survived with a jail sentence. All this was told me through a veil of tears. Others in the family prefer to remain silent. The sister, who was still alive in 2009 and knew more, sent word she refused to speak with me, adding 'I have forgiven everyone.' Another brother, now passed away, had been an activist with the Protestant political party Parkindo in 1965. He had strongly opposed his father's communist links, and did not dare visit him in jail in 1966, not even after his father sent him his own watch as a keepsake via his sister.

Others told me similar stories of disaster striking unsuspecting families – of uncle so-and-so whom no one ever mentioned again after his death in 1966; of grandfather, a policeman who had felt quietly guilty his entire life because he was forced to execute a pious neighbour; of motorists who still today honk their horns when passing a mass burial site to ask the spirits not to disable their engines. Near Ende, in Flores, I found the site at which a prominent local communist named John Timu had been burned alive in a public execution. It was still marked with a cairn of stones laid by the village community. Even young locals could tell me how he had died, holding out his arms in the flames 'like Jesus.' Older people told me their memories of having heard military trucks pass by at night that they presumed were carrying prisoners to their executions (from a student in a dormitory at the time); of having been forced to dig a mass grave (from a farmer in a village, who was afterwards sleepless with horror for weeks); of having repeatedly witnessed mass executions (from a party activist at the time, who appeared quite cool about it now – the communists had been 'neatly cleaned up'). Near the village of Buraen, southeast of Kupang, a Christian teacher took me to see an overgrown mass grave in a forest, suggested a moment's silence, then prayed simply: 'Dear God, we are visiting this place to learn about man's inhumanity to man. Help us to find the truth of this incident.'

These older people often told me their stories in a changed voice, whispering so I had to crane forward to catch them. The discordant fragments would pop out at the close of a conversation about other things, just as the notebook had been put away. 'People were taken away at night, stabbed to death and cut to pieces, and the parts thrown into the dry riverbed. It was terrifying. People were not supposed to know and must never mention it, yet everyone knew it was the military,' one aged man in Atambua told me. Else the person would say, 'Don't write this,' and proceed to tell me a horror story that was never supposed to see the light of day. Where the source of their stories is easily identifiable, and cannot be quoted from any publicly available source, I have felt obliged to keep them secret. The alternative would be ethical betrayal. Thus I too became complicit in the silence.

Once alerted to these jarring slivers of an alternative history, other little facts, hidden among the surviving paperwork, yielded fresh significance. For all their autocracy, NTT governments in the 1950s, '60s and '70s were diligent in their reporting. When tracked down to the unlikely crevices where the tides of history had deposited them, I found in them detailed lists. Some were of government property, even including the chairs and typewriters. Others reproduced all the public committees (political party organizers, government information campaign members, etc.) down to the district level, for multiple years. From these one could reconstruct an alternative history of a provincial political class at work. The PKI had a strikingly routine presence in these lists. New Order ideology portrays the party in demonic terms, as atheists who sowed dissatisfaction among the ignorant while undermining legitimate government by intrigue and assassination. Even today, the plots that the PKI was said to have hatched to murder Christians, 'revealed' by the military late in 1965 to terrorize the elite into collaborating with the anti-communist pogroms, are still recounted as fact. Yet in these pre-1965 lists, PKI representatives sit on the same parliamentary committees, party advisory boards, land reform committees, and bureaucratic reform commissions as the other political party representatives in those democratic years. The BTI was doing 'truly constructive' modernizing work among peasants, the governor noted in a 1957 report (Reksodihardjo 1960 [1957]:37). Michael Marcus crops up repeatedly in these lists, moving from one official appointment to another, like every other busy member of the rising bureaucratic petit bourgeoisie of that time. By 1965 he was nearing retirement.

Such buried lists sometimes also revealed more about the victors than today's establishment discourse cares to admit. The list of medals attached to El Tari's obituary (omitted from the Passar encyclopaedia, and preserved only in the library of Leo Nisnoni because he used to work at the state printer that produced it) made it clear that this jovial man's life before becoming NTT governor in 1966 had been filled with fighting against fellow Indonesians. The adopted son of a well-to-do tradesman in Kupang, Elyas Tari was sent to Java for a Dutch-language primary schooling before the war. He was at a trade school for sailors when the Japanese invaded. After the Pacific War, in his early twenties, he found himself with the revolutionary republican army, fighting the colonial forces. A mortar wound left him with a scar on his jaw (he later met and punched up the ethnic Indonesian soldier who had fired this mortar…). After that the army was engaged continually in putting down insurrections. Tari received medals for being part of republican battles against the following internal foes: communist rebels in republican Madiun, East Java, in 1948; a military insurrection (Perang Ratu Adil) in republican West Java stimulated by the Dutch intelligence officer Westerling in 1950; a revolt by Ambonese ex-colonial soldiers (RMS) in the early 1950s; the Islamic rebel movement Darul Islam in South Sulawesi in the mid-1950s; and the North Sulawesi-based rebel movement Permesta in the late 1950s (Setwilda 1978).

In 1962 the battle-hardened 36-year old major was assigned to territorial duties in his home town of Kupang. To face the growing power of the communist party at this time, the military began cultivating anti-communist political forces. The civilian governor, W.J. Lalamentik, was too much the bureaucrat to engage in politics, so to help stem the growing left-wing tide within the civil service the increasingly militarized central government appointed their man El Tari deputy governor in May 1965. Tari also controlled the militarized civil defence force (pertahanan sipil, hansip). In July 1966, after the territorial command had completed its grisly programme of murder and arbitrary arrest, Tari rose to provincial governor. His first task was to cleanse the civil service of communist sympathizers, and to reward with official appointments those civilians who had collaborated in the suppression. This last crumb of information I found, after the usual circuitous expeditions to locate a copy, in the detailed report Governor El Tari's staff produced under his name at the end of his first term of office (Tari 1972). An obituary in a Catholic magazine in Flores, which the ravages had overlooked because it was hidden in a monastery, even restored some appealing signs of human frailty to the victorious El Tari. Flores had never quite forgiven Protestant Timor for running away with the new province in 1958. The paper's editorial upon the governor's death expressed its disappointment at his legacy: so many of the roads and schools had been badly built, put up willy-nilly and without public consultation, by workers who had been forced to neglect their farming to build them.[11]

Even my own institute the KITLV turned up a little gem. In the archive belonging to a colonial official I found his lengthy interrogation of Doko immediately after the Japanese occupation. He had been the Timorese face of the Japanese regime, running education, propaganda, and labour recruitment projects on their behalf. Here he explained in detail what he had done to help the Japanese, who, he wrote, were too ignorant and often too drunk to do without local help. But he had committed no war crime, and was not prosecuted by the Netherlands Indies 'temporary court

Figure 9. Brigadier-General El Tari, as Governor of East Nusa Tenggara province, meeting unknown Indonesian military officers (photo courtesy of the El Tari family, Kupang).

[11] 'Sejemput harapan untuk gubernur baru,' *Dian,* 10 July 1978, p3. The next edition, a special on El Tari's death, contained a photograph showing a medal being pinned posthumously on the chest of the dead soldier (*Dian,* 24 July 1978 p8).

martial' in Kupang (Locher 1945).[12] According to historian James Fox, fears that their collaborationist past might haunt them under the Dutch was one reason for the Timorese elite to choose the republican cause after 1945 (Fox 1977:180).

Mobility at a Price

Thus, slowly, the outline of a set of biographies began to emerge. They contained almost no psychological insight, for lack of sources. But at least they gave some social insight into a dynamic provincial society, full of struggles won and lost. Contrary to the situation in Java before World War II (Sutherland 1979), the new middle class in Kupang were not the fortunate children of traditional aristocrats but of underprivileged subsistence peasants (Doko, Marcus) or of urban tradesmen (Tari). History offered them mobility beyond their wildest dreams, but at a price. As the town grew, it became increasingly estranged from the rural environs that had nurtured it. Its newly privileged middle class looked more readily for its livelihood to dispensations from far-away powers. These were engaged in their own distant struggles, which favoured now one set of clients and now another. After Timor had joined in Indonesia's independence in late 1949, republicanism began to spread, and the aristocrat whose lineage was rooted in the soil became dispensable. As militarism spread in the mid-1960s, the same fate met the communist organizer who had promised to bring modern emancipation also to the peasants. Their place was taken by the urban bureaucrat and by the soldier, both lowly born, both on the rise thanks to their far-away patrons. Gratefully blotting out their own impoverished past, both drew their strength from the modern state's impressive capacity to generate money, coordination, and violence.

Again unlike Java (Anderson 1972), the non-aristocrats among these prominents did not win their spurs by their own deeds of revolutionary heroism, but by adroit, pragmatic demonstrations of loyalty to greater powers elsewhere. In the 1930s the higher powers had been the Dutch; during World War II they were the Japanese; afterwards, the Allies and then the Dutch again; later again, they were political party bosses,

[12] Twenty-four defendants were tried for war crimes in Kupang. Over a thousand individuals were tried at twelve such tribunals held by the Netherlands Indies. A quarter were sentenced to death and only 5% acquitted. Australia held some tribunals of its own in Indonesian territory as well but not in Kupang (Post et al 2010:407–21).

bureaucratic chiefs, and military commanders in Java who were themselves often at loggerheads with each other. Contingent events marked provincial elite lives to an extraordinary degree. As one regime violently succeeded another, first in 1942, then again in 1945, in 1950, and in 1965, their survival often depended more on others than on themselves.

This combination of thrusting upward mobility and extreme contingency inevitably brought with it moral compromises. The process deposited numerous skeletons in the cupboards of the survivors, and unending pain in the hearts of those losers who got off with their lives, to say nothing of the dead. The loss of innocence that struck them all helps explain why establishment accounts of the past are so shallow, so full of taboos. It explains the gap that yawns between the schematized, historicist public accounts of lives as they *are* written, on the one hand, and the dramatic contingency of the private accounts that the biographer 'must not write,' on the other.

The biographer who decides to incorporate the forbidden accounts into a wider story anyway might be taking a gamble on relationships with his or her friends. I trust I have not betrayed confidences. But even a strict adherence to ethical principles cannot completely prevent a feeling of discomfort, which is practically inherent in the procedure I had to adopt. Since there are almost no written documents about what I considered to be the dark heart of Kupang's political history, and since so few leftists or even their relatives survive who are able and willing to tell their side of the story, I was forced to amplify the whispered stories of those who were on the militarist side of the political spectrum. These are people who have something to lose by telling them openly. I suspect that the problem I have described applies to writing the history of any Indonesian provincial town for this fraught period, and it is not wholly open to resolution. Of course, I am not writing only for my friends in Kupang but for any world citizen interested in the lives of townsfolk in a developing country. As for my friends, the best that can happen is that what they read might help loosen the bonds of a tyrannous past and open up the possibility of redemption through compassionate knowing.[13]

---

[13] I never told them – it would have been impossible anyway – what I considered the most beautiful expression of this Schopenhauerian thought. It is Amfortas' line in *Parsifal*: '*Durch Mitleid wissend, der reine Thor* (Through compassion, knowing – the pure fool).' Schopenhauer drew his inspiration from Asia, and I dare to think the thought itself is not strange to my Asian friends.

CHAPTER FOUR

BETTING ON THE RAJAS (1930S)

> In the self-ruling lands, justice is dispensed by a traditional council. Its powers are unlimited and no appeal is possible. The raja sits at its head, and its members are district chiefs and the *controleur*. ... No wonder the accused invariably feels unconvinced and dissatisfied.
>
> (*Tjinta Kebenaran*, 20 November 1935)

Insignificant among the cities of Asia, Kupang in the 1930s seemed like a metropolis in the quiet rurality of Timor. Its little newspapers sat in judgment on the rajas out there and opened a window on the world to its indigenous readers, most of them clerks. Like most colonial towns in the archipelago, Kupang was shaped by external forces rather than by a gradual elaboration of internal ones.[1] It was a settler town with tenuous and ambiguous links to its hinterland. It exacerbated the exploitative authoritarianism of the rajas, but it also offered the only available escape from those rajas. Unlike some sultans further west, whose palaces still conveyed splendid memories of a sovereign past, these rajas were more like very local 'men of prowess' (Wolters 1982:18). But the Dutch who ran Kupang did give them a lot of room to move in the interior. The Dutch were, as Wertheim (1964) once put it, 'betting on the strong' in the interior, propping up forms of governance that Kupang's journalists and international observers alike saw as archaic.[2]

However, the town itself was excised from the rajas' domains. This setting allowed it to mediate between the soil of Timor and the larger world beyond. It would become a spring of new forms of associational power *à la* Hannah Arendt. In this chapter that spring is only just beginning to

---

[1] Redfield (1954) called this type of town 'heterogenetic,' and the other 'orthogenetic.'

[2] The American observer Rupert Emerson wrote in 1937 that persistence of the native states into the future 'is not to be regarded as either probable or desirable in most instances inasmuch as they are too small for effective survival in the great society which is engulfing them, and in their institutions and aristocracies they represent an era which is rapidly passing, if it has not already passed... [F]or the British and the Dutch indirect rule has been so sharply associated with the maintenance of the prestige and the fiction of the power of the traditional chiefs and rulers that it is difficult to see how the new society can break

bubble. To understand the passions that were to flow in the 1950s and 1960s we must begin with the disempowering rural situation in the last years before the Second World War. The problems to which the cross-class, urban-rural coalitions of the 1950s attempted to create answers were a result of the colonial practice of 'betting on the strong.' Describing them takes up the first half of the chapter. The second half reconstructs, as much as the slim historical pickings allow, the contrasting situation in the tiny town of Kupang. The beginnings of a civil society are becoming visible amid the boredom of life in a small colonial settlement. The underlying assertion of this chapter is that Middle Indonesia lies truly in the middle. It is not one end of a bipolar centre-periphery relation, as is often thought, but the mediating centre between a remote metropolis and a hinterland that was geographically proximate but socially just as remote.

The Land

Timor lies in the driest region of Indonesia. No part receives more than 1500mm a year, less than half that which is normal elsewhere in the tropical archipelago. Its dry season extends for six to seven months of the year, compared with less than three months in Sumatra and Kalimantan. Savanna (created by human burning over the centuries) is the most common vegetation, and subsistence farming still dominates agriculture today. However, in some places the local climate is benevolent. Mount Mutin in the interior catches more rain than the plains, as does the hilly southern coast of the island. Whereas most areas permit just a single annual crop, the southern coast has two. On the flats of southern Belu district, near the eastern border with Portuguese Timor, irrigated rice fields are possible. The island nowhere supports a dense population. The old kingdoms of Amanuban, Amanatun, and Belu along the south coast (Figure 12) are the densest because of their good food supply. Tubers are the original subsistence staple, but beans are also old, and maize, rice, and sorghum arrived here in the seventeenth century. Rice was traditionally eaten only on festive occasions. Total dependency on a short growing season, combined with the difficulty of keeping food stores away from pests through the long dry season, ensured that even normal rainfall years had their weeks of 'normal hunger' (Ormeling 1956).

through the artificially petrified crust of the old traditions without violent conflict.' (Emerson 1979 [1937]:464, 518–9).

The population originally lived in family clans of 50–60 people in fortified hilltop settlements known as *suku*. Land was not owned individually, but was assigned by local village elders, the *pah tuaf*. The suku seemed to have been relatively egalitarian, and political control above the hamlet level was loose. A small number of chiefs – notably the Wehali (also spelled Waihale) king of Belu – exerted spiritual authority over much of Timor, but secular authority was exercised by rajas over smaller areas. The rajas were assisted and controlled by lesser nobles known as *fetor*, and by elders and warriors (H.G. Schulte Nordholt 1971). Timor was a significant destination for slavers between the seventeenth and early nineteenth centuries. Semi-feudal rajas bartered their lowest ranked subjects for firearms, which they needed for their tribal wars.

By the 1930s the Dutch had been in Kupang for three centuries, but for most of that period they had merely occupied a toehold. From its beginnings at the Concordia fort in the seventeenth century, it had been a settler town planted on Timor's landscape. The Dutch United East Indies Company (Vereenigde Oost-Indische Compagnie, VOC) first came to the island in 1613 to prevent the Portuguese from establishing a monopoly on the sandalwood trade. In 1653 they took over the little fort the Portuguese missionary Frei Jacinthe had built eight years earlier. For the first century, the armed Dutch trading company was unable to operate freely beyond its fort for fear of trouble with the Portuguese-speaking mestizo traders known as 'Topasses.' Its local allies were fewer and weaker than those of the Portuguese. Neighbouring princes who had thrown in their lot with them faced constant reprisals from others, who enjoyed the backing of the Topasses. Allied villagers fled repeatedly into the fort for shelter (Hägerdal 2012).

Not till the second half of the eighteenth century had the Dutch and Portuguese spheres of influence separated sufficiently in Timor to allow the Dutch some room to breathe (Fox 1977:66). By the early nineteenth, the town, now no longer controlled by a commercial corporation but by the beginnings of a modern bureaucratic state, was a safe imperial outpost capable of impressing its will on the surrounding countryside. As its elbow room expanded, it began to develop a sense of mission. It could choose to adopt an activist and modernizing stance, or keep its hands off in the manner that came to be called indirect rule. Activism was close to the heart of the visionary and Kupang-born early Resident, J.A. Hazaart (1773–1848). The objectives he set out were to remain a mantra for a century or more: '... to end native unrest and rebellion on the islands, to foster the spread of Christianity, and to promote the economic development of

Timor' (Fox 1977:128). Hazaart's plan entailed a mediating play with distance typical of outposts of activist empires. Kupang had to be socially remote enough from the surrounding Timorese societies to 'end native unrest' on behalf of far-away Batavia, remote enough too from its subsistence economy to be attractive to adventurous capital pursuing economic development (not much of that has ever happened), yet close enough culturally to 'foster the spread of Christianity.' Hazaart's approach to developing imperial power was to mix modalities of domination (to end unrest) with modalities of inducement or even seduction (religion).

The population grew fastest after pacification early in the twentieth century, not only because endemic warfare and slave-trading had ended but because epidemics had too. Smallpox vaccinations were introduced in Kupang in the early nineteenth century by Resident Hazaart, and in the interior in 1843. The last epidemic of a disease that once claimed thousands occurred in 1898–99. The numbers are imprecise, since even the 1930 census, the best ever conducted in colonial times, was here somewhat unreliable. The population of Indonesian Timor (minus the nearby islands of Rote and Sabu) is thought to have trebled from 150,000 to 441,000 in the century up to 1950. It grew fastest in the fertile southern coastal areas (Ormeling 1956:183).

However, local administrator activism was frequently trumped by Batavia, which had few resources to pay for ambitious projects beyond Kupang. Trade never yielded a profit, nor was Timor of strategic importance. Until the 1870s the Dutch state officially maintained a policy of political 'abstention' (*onthouding*) in the outer islands. Throughout the nineteenth century those rajas close to Kupang who had made alliances with it continued to suffer intermittent raids from hostile kingdoms further away. Not till 1905–1915 did the Dutch launch a thorough pacification campaign in this part of the archipelago. The military Governor-General J.B. van Heutsz (1904–1909) presided over the final conquests, and when the campaign was at end end the colony's boundaries were practically those of present-day Indonesia. The Dutch had had so little presence in the interior before this that the administrator-anthropologist H.G. Schulte Nordholt (1971:185) considered the 'colonial' period proper to begin only in 1915. Even after that date, indirect rule hands-off prevailed. But, as we shall see in more detail below, it adopted a more ideological form than before. Indirect rule was now no longer a practical solution to a lack of capacity on the part of the colonial state, but a politically regressive choice. Where the smallpox vaccination campaign was an example of enlightened policy that intended to improve welfare for all Timorese, the political system the Dutch now imposed exacerbated existing inequalities. This is the development policy in the late Netherlands Indies that Wertheim (1964) summed up with the phrase 'betting on the strong.'

The heart of Kupang itself lay in the nominal 'square mile' (*vierkante paal*), a precisely bounded piece of territory carved out of traditionally ruled lands in 1886 to be administered directly by a Dutch assistant resident (Leirissa et al 1984:24–8).[3] (The small harbour of Atapupu near Portuguese Timor was also directly ruled). It was the seat of government for the Residency of Timor and Dependencies (Timor en Onderhorigheden), which consisted of Timor, Flores, Sumba and Sumbawa, and the small islands near Timor of Rote, Sabu and Alor. Beyond this tiny realm of small-town modernity the Dutch left the rajas to rule the subsistence farmers whose simple homes were thinly scattered in the interior. Initially justified as a 'humane' tolerance for local ways in the overwhelmingly rural Indies, the policy hardened into determined conservatism in the 1930s to face down rising nationalism. Rupert Emerson wrote perceptively about this retraditionalization in 1937: '[it] is to be explained less in terms of a concern for the spiritual and material ease of their people than in terms of Dutch dread of Indonesian communism and nationalism' (1979 [1937]:464).[4] Yet its greater attraction was cost. Indirect rule was

---

3 The Javanese *paal* used in Timor had a length of 1506.9 metres. The Dutch frequently demanded a *vierkante paal* for themselves when establishing a new settlement in the Indies. In Kupang, however, the legal history of this area is ambiguous. Some decrees speak of a larger coastal strip that ran right around Kupang Bay, nominally six *paal* (9km) in length and probably ceded to the Company in the early seventeenth century and originally used for farming (Ormeling 1956:117). Later the town spread into the six *paal* area too. When the Dutch formalized their possession of the town in 1886 they included the six *paal* coastal strip, but did not explicitly say whether any of it was to be directly ruled government land (*gouvernementsgebied*) (Bongenaar 2005:185). A decree of 1893 did confirm all of it as government land, but a 1907 official publication only referred to the 'so-called' government land along Kupang Bay. In 1911 the traditional ruler acknowledged that the entire six *paal* strip belonged to the central government, but in 1942 the government almanac only listed the *vierkante paal* as government land, thus apparently excluding most of the six *paal* strip. In 1949 the town became an urban shire (*gemeente*). However, that was dissolved once more in 1951 in favour of the Raja of Kupang, who now also inherited the *vierkante paal*. In 1969 the entire town became a subdistrict of the central state (*kecamatan*). Not till 1978 was this subdistrict (which could in principle be urban or rural) upgraded to an Administrative City (*Kota Administratif*) (Leirissa et al 1984:109).

4 Similarly, Benda (1966:601–2) later wrote about the mid-1930s: 'The new reforms were unmistakably moving in the opposite direction [that is, to the earlier aim of rapid modernization], the plan being to build henceforth from the bottom up rather than from the top down. The principle of systematic territorial decentralization was implicitly abandoned in favour of a new form of indirect rule in which the ethnic groups, styled the *groepsgemeenschap* (group community) in the bill of 1936, was to become the main administrative unit, and also – in the original plan – the only quasi-autonomous corporate cell within the three

cheaper than building a modern system in which citizens had rights. Until well into the 1960s, government in Timor's arid hills remained limited to what the rajas could supply, albeit increasingly supplemented by Christian mission schools, and by some central state services such as agricultural credit, road-building and vaccination.

A Dutch diplomat had claimed in 1756 there were 27 rajas in Wehali alone, in the interior of Timor (Fox 2000). In 1917 the Dutch had simplified their total number to 84 in all of Dutch-held Timor by means of forced amalgamation, and by 1938 to 48 (Ormeling 1956:79). Despite constantly manipulating the rajas, they maintained the fiction of traditional 'self-rule.' To compensate for the absence of a single raja in the immediate vicinity of the town, they created the Kingdom of Kupang and placed the compliant Nicolaas Nisnoni on the throne in 1919 (Farram 2004:115). His hunting grounds and (later) horse racing circuit provided a welcome diversion for the European menfolk (Figure 10). With headhunting a thing

Figure 10. Raja Nisnoni's horse-racing field outside Kupang, circa 1927 (KITLV image nr. 11515).

overarching island governments. Instead of creating new entities for training in modern self-government, these were the most basic old units now clad in a spurious new garb. And where the original reforms had sought to circumscribe officialdom's authority through conciliar bodies, the new reforms envisaged it as unhampered by such interference, a "brooding omnipresence" controlling, rather than guided by, traditional polities.'

of the past, the rajas lost their warrior status. They were kept on a short leash by rules and a modest salary. But they did continue to dispense their own customary (*adat*) justice.

'Traditional' Rule

Proponents claimed that indirect rule was traditional, but in practice it was a modern system. It radically altered Timor's social landscape. It was much more centralized and authoritarian than any Timor had ever known. In order to enhance control, the Dutch moved the small genealogical *suku* from the mountaintops into larger villages near military supply routes. The original villages were sometimes burned to prevent return. These larger villages were no longer genealogical communities, and the village chiefs or *temukung* the Dutch appointed over them were often arbitrarily selected (Ormeling 1956:226–7).

Rajas became the hinge on which the system turned. Their magical powers had always inspired respect among the people, but many other local influentials had ensured they did not monopolize power. Among them were the raja's *fetor*, elders, and warrior chiefs, who all provided him with manpower. Ritual lords were able to impose religious sanctions. Neighbouring chiefs could threaten violence. Now all these checks were domesticated or removed. Only the raja received a steady salary. *Fetor* became his bureaucratic inferiors. None of the local elders had a place in the new scheme. If any of them protested, the raja could ask the Dutch to arrest them. The end of warfare meant warrior chiefs and threatening rival rajas, too, lost their powers. The Christian mission, part of the colonial establishment, soon began to undermine the awe in which the ritual lords had been held (Cunningham 1962:190–7). The Dutch trusted that their continual fiddling with the raja system – now replacing one for incompetency, then fusing several domains to promote efficiency – would not reduce their standing among the population, and for a while they were right.

The rajas found the transition from lord to vassal painful but ultimately profitable. The most vigorous act of resistance came from 'Keizer' (Emperor) Bil Nope, near today's inland town of Soë. When the extent of his loss of sovereignty to the Dutch became clear he supported a revolt led by his son, and did not yield in the face of superior force. The 'Niki Niki war' of 1910 ended when fire engulfed him and his entourage in their underground fortification (Farram 2004:90–8). In its horror the event resembled the 1906 *puputan* in Bali, when nobles dressed in white walked slowly with their families into a hail of Dutch bullets. These battles for sovereignty are still celebrated in Indonesian history textbooks today (Koehuan et al 1982), but survivors in the Nope clan soon adapted to the new regime. Their appointment as 'traditional rulers' over Amanuban theoretically reduced their independence, but it also offered new benefits. It gave them sole rights over the entire territory, displacing the historical claims of other families over certain parts. They filled the space by appointing their relatives to rule over two lower levels of administration, positions known as *fetor* and *temukung* respectively. In case of trouble they would engineer a political marriage to co-opt a rival. Indirect rule knew no separation of powers – for all except the worst crimes, the rajas imposed their own judicial verdicts.[5] In extreme cases they could call on the Dutch to deal with a troublemaker. They enjoyed a fixed salary, a good house, and the right to collect taxes. And they had first pick of development projects intended for the territory as a whole. They demanded that the new road through the interior run past their front door and that Chinese be invited to settle there, thus creating a new centre for mercantilist trading in Niki Niki. They were the first to receive government credit for a cattle scheme introduced soon after pacification. In order to improve the local diet, and stimulate an export industry to Java, the government in 1912 brought the first shipment of cattle to an island that had not known them before (Ormeling 1956:122). The raja soon owned huge herds. When the raja's final authority over the usage of land throughout Amanuban was added to this, it was clear he had become a feudal ruler with power his war-prone forebears could only have dreamt of (McWilliam 1999).

These material powers sustained cultural ones. A constant stream of peasants, from each village in his realm on a rotating basis, came to his palace in Niki Niki to bring tribute. If serfdom was perhaps too severe a term to describe their obligations to the rajas in pre-colonial times, it became increasingly appropriate in the final decades of colonial rule. The great scholar of agrarian Timor, F. J. Ormeling (1956:78–80, 161–3), did not hesitate to call the system 'feudal.' Labour in the fields was known as *etu,* and in the household as *abeat. Fetor* and *temukung* could exercise similar claims. Although the labour amounted to no more than about 14 days a year for both men and women, tribute in kind and in labour is thought to have yielded a quarter to a fifth of the total rice and maize production in

5 Adat courts in Timor were finally disbanded in 1954.

Figure 11. Raja Pa'e Nope of Amanuban with entourage, circa 1927 (KITLV image nr. 11528).

Timor – much more than colonial officials generally understood (Ormeling 1956:80–1). Even the raja's own sons had to approach in a crouched position, with their hands before their faces, and back away in the same attitude after the audience. Pa'e Nope (ruled 1923–46) (Figure 11) was said to have had 42 wives. His tall western-educated son Koesa Nope had only four. Rarely spoken of in public were the seigneurial sexual rights they both had beyond their marriages. Stories are still whispered today of how the Nope kings, on tour through their realm, would spend the night in a village and ask their hosts for a 'blanket,' a 'sleeping mat' or a 'massage.' The sexual appetite of Victor Koroh, son of H.A. Koroh and the last raja of Amarasi, was similarly prodigious, though in his case it was dressed in the sunglasses and rock music of the times. According to one informant, villagers were proud to have been permitted to supply a daughter for the raja in a custom known as *atusit.*[6] Though similar stories come to us from prerevolutionary France, it seems difficult to believe that the feeling was deeply rooted in Timor. In any case, the same informant went on to say, it

[6] Interview with Pdt. Yanni Tahun, Kuanfatu, 21 July 2011. Elsewhere in Timor I have only seen this term with the meaning 'traditional midwife.'

was this custom that peasants came to regard with the greatest distaste once the rajas' powers began to wane in the late 1950s. Similar stories are told for Tua Sonbai, the old raja of Mollo, though other rajas appear to have practised more bourgeois sexual restraint.

The feudal lords became pioneers in the cattle business. Raja Koesa Nope was by the early 1960s thought to be the richest indigenous person in all East Nusa Tenggara province (Cooley 1976:348). Preferential agrarian credit went to the strongest figures, who were thought likely to repay and to be an example to innovation-averse peasants. As Ormeling put it: 'All innovations, building of schools, encouragement to visit policlinics, recruiting of workers for the execution of public works, application of new methods of cultivation, introduction of new crops or intensification of reforestation, fails or succeeds according to their [the leaders'] cooperation' (1956:79). Raja H.A. Koroh of Amarasi was held up as the best example of how successful betting on the strong could be. He ran an effective administration, persuaded people to build healthier houses, built schools and new villages closer to the main road, and planted coconut trees (whose copra he marketed himself).[7]

Commoners' tribute in forced labour and foodstuffs was available for both colonial infrastructure projects and for the rajas own lifestyle. The raja could demand up to 30 days of corvee labour a year on behalf of the state (*herendiensten*), in addition to that in the name of *adat*. Some peasant-serfs found it onerous enough to escape to a neighbouring jurisdiction to reduce it. Both women and men were liable – only 'foreigners' were exempt, including people from Rote and Sabu. However, tribute declined slowly over time. The Dutch replaced corvee labour with a cash tax just before the Pacific War, and the first act by the new parliament of Timor set up after independence in late 1949 was to forbid household services to the aristocrats.[8] Tribute practices continued informally for some years as a form of homage, partly compensated with food or payment (Ormeling 1956:82). Some people in South Central Timor told me that lingering resentment about tribute and (rarely spoken of) the *droit de seigneur*, was a factor in the peasant mobilization of the early 1960s, while others denied it.

Far greater sources of inequality than tribute were two colonial innovations. One was the introduction of cattle, the other changes in the rules

[7] *Tjinta Kebenaran*, 10 November 1936; *Tjinta Kebenaran*, 20–28 February 1937.

[8] This initiative, taken by the nationalist parliamentary speaker E.R. Herewila, is described in Chapter 7.

for allocating land usufruct. Both greatly exacerbated the gap between rajas and commoners in the half century up to at least the 1970s. When the government brought the first cattle to Timor they made them available only to the rajas, who were thought to be credit-worthy. In the 1930s the offer was extended to *fetor* and *temukung*. This was colonial betting on the strong. Although the cattle tended to die of thirst in the dry season, and anthrax was soon endemic on the island, they bred quickly. Cattle did change hands to other social groups. Common Timorese sometimes received them from the rajas in exchange for herding them. But the perpetually indebted peasants then often lost them again to Chinese creditors. The Chinese also ran the trade in cattle. By the early 1950s it was estimated that 40% of the cattle stock was owned by rajas/ *fetor*/ *temukung*, another 40% by Chinese traders, and 20% by common Timorese. The total stock of cattle was estimated at 108,000 in 1952 (Ormeling 1956:156).

The largest herds always remained in the hands of the small group of rulers. Inequality was worse in the most densely populated rural areas. Whereas the ownership pattern was reasonably egalitarian on the remote slopes of Mount Mutin, that was far from the case in the densely populated areas of southern Belu, and in the savanna lands of Mollo and northern Amanuban. There cattle numbers were high while the number of owners was low. Some individuals owned tens of thousands, with the raja of Amanuban the biggest owner of all. In the brief period between World War II and Indonesian sovereignty, a reformist Dutch administration began to reverse the preference for the rajas and to give commoners credit for cattle as well. But even then some rajas managed to get it anyway by using the names of village folk (Ormeling 1956:189, 198). Cattle possession brought benefits to the owner – mainly prestige, since cattle export from this remote territory always struggled to make a profit. But non-owners found them a nuisance. After early attempts to keep them penned failed, cattle were permitted to roam freely over the island. Subsistence peasants spent a lot of time fencing off their gardens from the raja's cattle. According to one estimate, a farmer opening up a new field for cultivation had to spend a quarter of his time on building a strong fence around it (Ormeling 1956:199).

Effective ownership of land also became increasingly concentrated in the rajas' hands. Subsistence agriculture requires a lot of land because most of it lies fallow at any moment. As early as the mid-1950s there were fears of land shortages in Timor. Ormeling calculated that, with a 12-year fallow period, the arable land in Timor was only capable of supporting an

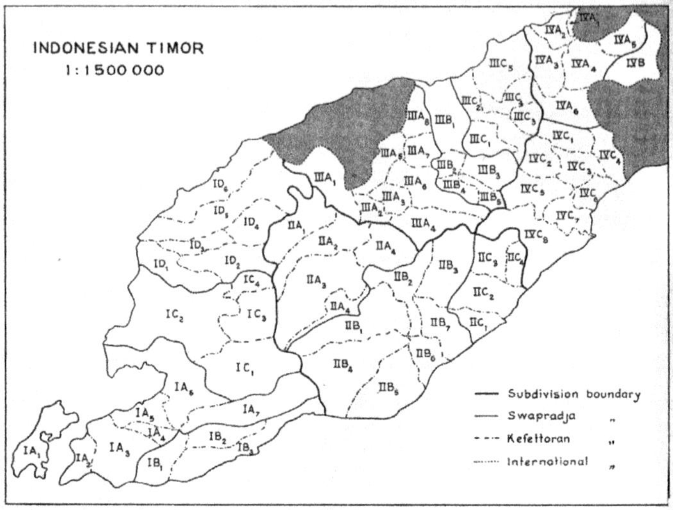

Fig. 3. Administrative units.
The units designated by the letters and figures are as follows:

SUBDIVISION	SWAPRADJA	KEFETTORAN
I. KUPANG:	A. KUPANG:	I A 1. Semau
		I A 2. Fonai.
		I A 3. Sonbait Ketjil
		I A 4. Tabenu
		I A 4. Amabi
		I A 6. Babau
		I A 7. Amabi-Oëfeto
	B. AMARASI:	I B 1. Baun
		I B 2. Oëkabiti
		I B 3. Buraën
	C. FATULEU:	I C 1. Manubait
		I C 2. Takaeb
		I C 3. Tefnai
		I C 4. Kauniki
	D. AMFOAN:	I D 1. Mosu
		I D 2. Lelogama
		I D 3. Leloboko
		I D 4. Bioba
		I D 5. Honuk
		I D 6. Naikliu
II. S. C. TIMOR [1]	A. MOLO:	II A 1. Mutis
		II A 2. Nunbena
		II A 3. Netpala
		II A 4. Bidjeli I, II.
	B. AMANUBAN:	II B 1. Noëmeto
		II B 2. Noëliu
		II B 3. Noëbunu
		II B 4. Noëbebak
		II B 5. Noëmuke
		II B 6. Noësiu
		II B 7. Noëhonbet
	C. AMANATUN:	II C 1. Noëbone
		II C 2. Noëbana
		II C 3. Noëmanumuti
		II C 4. Noëbokong
III. N. C. TIMOR [2]	A. MIUMAFO:	III A 1. Aplal
		III A 2. Noiltoko
		III A 3. Naktimu
		III A 4. Noëmuti
		III A 5. Nilulat
		III A 6. Bikomi
		III A 7. Tunbaba
		III A 8. Manamas
	B. INSANA:	III B 1. Fafinesu
		III B 2. Maubesi
		III B 3. Oëlolok
		III B 4. Subun
		III B 5. Ainan
	C. BEBOKI:	III C 1. Ustetu
		III C 2. Oëtase
		III C 3. Bukifan
		III C 4. Taitoh
		III C 5. Harneno
IV. BELU	A. TASIFETO:	IV A 1. Silawan
		IV A 2. Djenilu
		IV A 3. Lidak
		IV A 4. Bauho
		IV A 5. Lasiolat
		IV A 6. Naitimu
	B. LAMAKNEN	
	C. MALAKA:	IV C 1. Mandeu
		IV C 2. Kusa
		IV C 3. Dirma
		IV C 4. Alas
		IV C 5. Fatuaruin
		IV C 6. Lakekun
		IV C 7. Waihale
		IV C 8. Waiwiku

1. Southern Central Timor. 2. Northern Central Timor.

Figure 12. The kingdoms of Indonesian Timor in the 1950s (Ormeling 1956:10) (reprinted with permission).

agrarian population of 280,000 (Ormeling 1956:186). He believed a crisis was at hand, because the population was then already much more than that, and 12 years was thought to be too short to be sustainable except in the wet areas along the south coast. Moreover 23% of the arable land had been enclosed as forest reserves in the 1920s, and perhaps another 37% was required for livestock. Thus Ormeling identified soil deterioration as the core of 'the Timor problem.' Subsistence agriculture normally knows no private ownership of land but only usufruct of land determined by the community on the basis of customary law (*adat*). Hendrikus Ataupah, one of my key informants in Kupang, rejected the term 'feudal' for Timor's agrarian economy on these grounds.[9] Indeed, before pacification usufruct was allocated locally and democratically by the community *pah tuaf*. But later this function was increasingly taken over by the raja, at least in certain areas, and there the raja effectively did own the land. Ormeling noted that in Belu district, in Mollo (South Central Timor district) and in Amarasi (Kupang district) the raja had become the 'sole master of the soil' (Ormeling 1956:86).

These areas of South Central Timor and Belu were also the most densely populated districts, and the districts with the highest livestock inequality, as we saw. Dutch surveys in 1950 indicated that social differentiation had progressed furthest precisely in these densely populated areas, blessed as they were by both nature and colonial development policy (Ormeling 1956:189). A later observer on land use patterns in Timor, while lamenting a shortage of quality data, also noted that conflicts over land tended to occur in areas that had converted to settled, irrigated agriculture. Moreover the conflict was exacerbated by the demands of cattle-owning rajas for a 50% share of the crop in exchange for the use of their cattle to trample the fields (since the plough had never become accepted in Timor) (Sidik et al 1968:72–5). The south coast of Timor, the Belu plains, and the Babao plain outside Kupang town, were such areas.

Precisely these districts saw the greatest communist mobilization among peasants in the early 1960s. This suggests that the protests had a material basis, and subsequent chapters will bear this out. Other historians have seen in them only rural messianism or patrimonial politics. These were present as well, but any analysis that ignores the material factors overlooks something fundamental.

The Town

Colonial Kupang offered its elite inhabitants the great advantage of being on the other side of the policy of betting on the strong. At the same time its remoteness gave them a certain discretion in relation to this

---

9 Hendrikus Ataupah (1995:47) argued in a feasibility study for an agribusiness project on the slopes of Mount Mutin that farmers and cattle owners were not concerned about land ownership because it was communally owned.

policy from the centre. As the introductory Chapter 1 has argued, the town was the crucial node in the mediated transmission of political power. In the 1930s that function remained embryonic in this sleepy place. But it was becoming its own small town community, whose potential for change lay in its geographical position – in touch with both the feudal hinterland and the wider world over the horizon of the Sabu Sea.

The rajas had no say in Kupang's inner kampongs. Justice was delivered by a colonial magistrate, instead of by the raja-dominated *Landraad* responsible for justice elsewhere. Kupang's relations with its hinterland were always slightly hostile. The Indo-European Hazaart thought the local Timorese were unreliable. Better to settle the area around the fort with farmers brought from the nearby island of Rote. Rote did not rely on swidden agriculture but on the *lontar* palm. Its inhabitants were culturally closer to the Dutch – they had been begging Batavia for Dutch schools for a century, they knew about wet-rice farming, and they were open to Christianity (Fox 1977). Other settler groups arrived too – the flotsam of early colonial mobility. Many were the descendants of soldiers, some of them emancipated slaves, who had served the Dutch in various campaigns around Asia. They came from as far away as the Philippines (the so-called Papangers, Muslims), and from the closer-by islands of Solor (also Muslims) and Sabu (many of them pagans). A few hundred Chinese were encouraged to settle in order to stimulate (taxable) trade. Thus Kupang became a motley town that mainly served the needs of a colonial administration, since big capital never found much of interest. It occupied a strip of land along the coast, spreading beyond Fort Concordia's 'square mile' (see Footnote 3). Within the square mile the law of the Netherlands Indies government was in force, also in the kampongs – although, like kampongs practically everywhere in the Netherlands Indies, the kampongs of Kupang were autonomous (Colombijn 2010:186). Rotenese initially worked as farmers and lontar-tappers, but as government increased its scope of activities early in the twentieth century many of them became government clerks because they were more highly educated than other locals (Figure 13). By the 1950s the government bureaucracy in Kupang was overwhelmingly Rotenese (Ormeling 1956:223). They and the Sabunese (from the tiny island of Sabu) have kept alive Hazaart's stereotype. The lovely Sabunese wife of Raja Alfons Nisnoni (who was himself Timorese) was heard to say to her Dutch guests over dinner at their home, in perfect Dutch: 'Ah, those stupid Timorese don't understand anything' (Versluys [n.d. – circa 1960]:51). It remains a strangely anachronistic commonplace in Kupang today (Tidey 2012).

Figure 13. Government clerks await office hours in front of the Resident's official home in 1927. Most are from Rote and Sabu (KITLV image nr. 11190).

Yet the town's very compactness made it look outwards. The trade and state investment that has always dominated Kupang's economy was in those days less interested in the town than in the large hinterland. Mobility was low in its agrarian hinterland – the 200-kilometre long half-island was covered in a network of walking and horse trails. Inserted into this landscape, Kupang became a node of movement in a skein of colonial routes stretching across the archipelago and the world. Thin lines of control, communication and capital rolled out over the quiet landscape of grass and open forest along the unsealed, single-lane spinal road into the interior, which was completed in 1923 (Farram 2004:105) (Figure 14). A statue to the engineer who built it, S.E. Asmussen, stood at an intersection just east of Kupang's town centre. The rajas' rural seats became new townships along the road – which swung from side to side across the island to accommodate their wishes. A junior government official settled in each township as *controleur* to check tax collection and to write economic development plans. A government-contracted steamship from Makassar called by every fortnight, and another from Batavia via Surabaya once a

Figure 14. Official opening of (unsealed) Kupang-Atambua road, 1923 (KITLV image nr. 11147).

month.[10] An airport built on a plateau near Kupang became famous on 24 October 1934 when the 'Uiver,' the Dutch KLM's DC-2 aeroplane trialling a commercial route from London to Sydney, landed there to refuel.[11] Flights from Surabaya to Darwin of the Royal Netherlands Indies Airways (Koninklijke Nederlandsch-Indische Luchtvaart Maatschappij, KNILM) landed at Kupang airport, while Australian Qantas seaplanes heading for Singapore sometimes landed in Kupang Bay.

Kupang was a meeting point between a declining traditional order and an ascendant modernity. Such confrontations and the rapid social change they bring about have been the focus of research on towns ever since the one that started it all, the Middletown studies by the Lynds (1929, 1937) in

[10] These were respectively Line 24 (mainly picking up sandalwood and skins from Kupang) and Line 25 (cattle and passengers). From the sea Kupang in the 1930s looked like 'a small place with its white cottages and red roofs one right next to the other looking like a little Dutch town by the sea' (Boer and Westermann 1941:280) (with thanks to Howard Dick for this reference).

[11] The diary of a passenger is available at http://www.avsim.com/hangar/flight/dc2uiver/race/Domenie_Diary_dutch.htm (accessed 28 April 2010); see also http://www.environment.gov.au/heritage/ahc/publications/commission/books/linking-a-nation/chapter-8.html (accessed 6 August 2013).

the United States before World War II. The study of the small town of Springdale in upstate New York that Arthur Vidich and Joseph Bensman conducted in the 1950s (2000 [1958]) was among those the Lynds inspired. In Indonesia the Middletown books stimulated the 'Modjokuto' studies in Java done by Clifford Geertz and his Massachusetts Institute of Technology colleagues in the 1950s. In both Indonesia and the United States, most people did not live in big cities in this period. In both, an increasingly centralized bureaucracy and new mass media brought the capital city closer. But whereas in America this went together with the advent of the giant corporation, in the towns of late colonial Netherlands Indies and early independent Indonesia it was signalled by a growing awareness of the central state. The ascendant modernity for both Springdale and Modjokuto came from outside, and in both it triggered conservative reactions. As these changes penetrated the small towns, local cultural styles and patterns eroded. Some accepted the changes, while others did not, making the towns social and cultural hybrids. The present retrospective study of Kupang cannot hope to simulate what a contemporary ethnographic study might have revealed. However, the little we can reconstruct here does not suggest the overwhelming passivity in relation to national affairs that Geertz thought he observed in Modjokuto (actually Pare) ('always defensive, reactive, evasive, and in the end .... sterile and debilitating' C. Geertz 1965:7). Instead, as we shall see in a moment, the impression of Kupang just before World War II is that at least the rising indigenous lower-middle class, who left traces in surviving newspaper collections, overwhelmingly welcomed the future.

Kupang's layout in the late colonial and early independence period resembled that of dozens of similar nodes in the network of territorial control (McTaggart 1982) (see Figure 16, and compare with the recent map in Figure 2). Class – which in the Indies largely coincided with ethnicity – was the overriding differentiator. By the 1970s, a building boom had vastly expanded this walkable town up onto the karst slopes towards the south and east, yet the basic structure remained as it had been for a hundred years. The three elements were a busy Chinese trade zone, middle–class European and Chinese villas with fine sea views along the main roads (Figure 18), and wooden indigenous kampong houses in the spaces between the roads. A passenger arriving in Kupang Bay on the steamship in the 1930s would have been set down at the new pier by a launch (an improvement from the beach landing below Fort Concordia before that). Emerging at the top of the seawall in the blazing sun she could find refreshments by turning left into a shopping street that looked sleepy to a visitor from Batavia but hectic to the visiting villager (Figure 19, Figure 16). It was overwhelmingly Chinese. Almost anything available in Singapore was also for sale here, from imported rice to silks. Of Kupang's 7,000 inhabitants, 13% were ethnic Chinese in 1930 – nearly three times the European population of just 5% (Milone 1966:128, taken from 1930 census). Towns outside Java tended to have proportionately more Chinese than those in Java – Milone's tables show that 50% was by no means unusual. Kupang's most famous entrepreneur just before World War II was Tjiong Koen Siong. His art deco movie theatre called Sunlie (later the Royal, and after independence the Raya) still stands today, downgraded to a dealership for lubricating oil. It showed films only on the rare occasions that the steamship brought a new one, but it also hosted live theatre, dances, and political meetings. His Minerva ice factory next door was the stuff of poetry in the local newspapers – one newspaper suggested he should get a queen's medal for it, and when it broke down in 42 degrees Celsius heat citizens expressed worries about their health.[12] His petrol bowser served the few motor vehicles in town. In 1937 he opened an electricity generating plant to much acclaim. Koen Siong (as he is still known) also owned a lemonade factory, and ran the weekly mail truck along the pioneering road into the interior.[13]

If our visitor had turned right instead of left upon landing, she would have come upon the spacious homes and offices of top Dutch officials, ranged around the Resident's villa in an area locals knew as Fatufeto or more graphically Kampong Belanda. Nearby was the imposing Protestant church, while a Catholic church and a mosque stood a little way off. The jail, the European school, and offices for post, telegraph, telephone, taxation and other functions occupied the same area. Across the stream and up the hill, just opposite Fort Concordia's military barracks, stood the modest community hall (*societeit*), where the town's tiny European elite met over 'a little glass of liqueur, or good Portuguese port from Timor Dili, sherry' (perhaps the gin – *jenever* – universally consumed by European men in the Indies at that time was too obvious to list here too) (Versluys [n.d. – circa 1960]:17) (Figure 15). It had just 45 members in 1938. They played bridge and swapped gossip. The amusing account of their daily life in 1939 left by Mick Versluys, wife of a Dutch official, suggests that none were on intimate terms with any indigenous or ethnic Chinese person.

---

12 *Tjinta Kebenaran,* 10 October 1935; *Obor Masjarakat,* January 1939.

13 On the electricity plant: *Tjinta Kebenaran,* 10 September 1936 (also on lemonade), 20 January 1937; *Pewarta Timoer,* 6 December 1939, reports feared blackouts after his Dutch engineer leaves town suddenly. On the mail truck: *Tjinta Kebenaran,* 20–30 October 1936.

Figure 15. Societeit 'Volharding,' on Concordia square, Kupang, circa 1927 (KITLV image nr. 11442).

All these buildings hardly made the town 'urban.' In between the main roads, unmarked on any map and hidden beneath a canopy of fruit-bearing trees, were the semi-rural kampong (*negorij*) where the 79% of the population who were classified as indigenous lived (Milone 1966:128) (Figure 17). The 40% of the town's houses not made of stone were all in these neighbourhoods (Kementerian Penerangan Sunda Ketjil 1953:226). These were governed by appointed kampong heads. Chinese and Arabs also had their own ethnic heads, as was common practice across the Netherlands Indies. Better-off kampong dwellers worked in the government offices in town. Most were originally from the nearby islands of Rote, Sabu, and Southeast Maluku. It was from among them that the civil servants, teachers and politicians were to arise who had by 1950 taken over the town. Already in the 1930s the little local newspapers they read avidly were reflecting a nascent civil society.

For a small town, Kupang was well supplied with locally produced Malay-language papers. They quoted major newspapers elsewhere in the colony and even carried international news. A report of November 1933 lists no fewer than nine. Only some copies survive today.[14] All these

[14] A list of nine occurs in *Fadjar*, November 1933: 'Pewarta, Oetoesan, Sahabat, Pelita, Sedar, Fadjar, Tjermin, Warta Berita dan Taman Masehi.' Of these, only some have

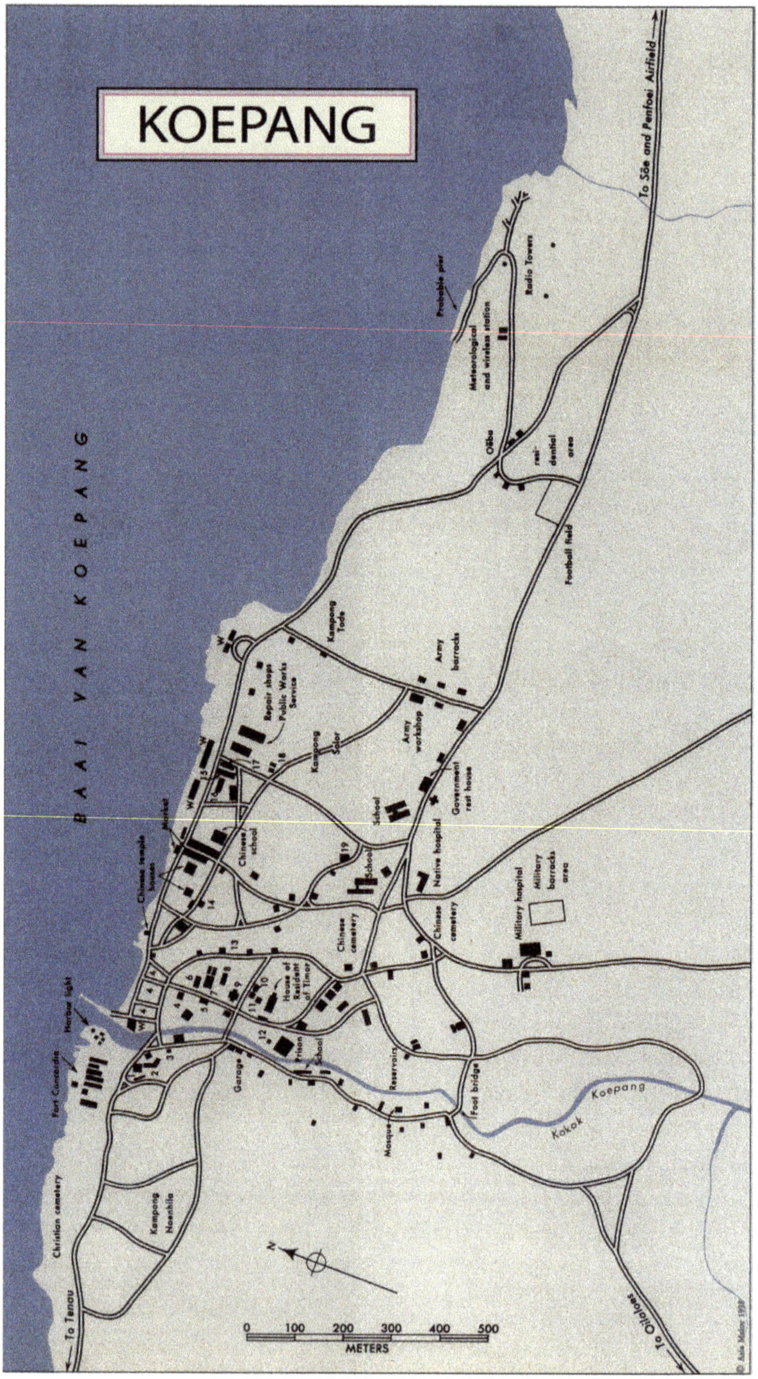

Figure 16. Kupang, May 1945 (American map based on earlier Dutch maps) (Diessen and Voskuil 1998:135) (reprinted with permission).

simple four-page broadsheets were printed either at Hermien, or at the apparently somewhat cheaper Boemi Poetra Timoer, which however demanded cash payment. Both were located in the Chinese commercial neighbourhood. Print runs were small – they appeared monthly or a little more often, sustained by advertising from the Chinese shops. They told readers what they wanted to know – football matches, bicycle accidents, break-ins, visits by theatre troupes and high officials, insults in the market, the electricity supply, passing aerial adventurers en route to Sydney. But they also carried investigative reports on the economies of small towns on other islands, international news, and lots of local political intrigue. Their pages confirmed, in a good-natured small town way, that the social hierarchy ran much as follows. The town's establishment before the war consisted of Dutch officials and soldiers, indigenous rajas, Indo-European and indigenous officials, church ministers, and teachers. Next came the Chinese traders, the richest of whom helped set tastes and provided the town with entertainment and luxuries. Below that was an indigenous mass of small traders, small service providers, farmers and fishers. Below that again, until the institution disappeared in the early twentieth century, used to come the slaves (Leirissa et al 1984:29–30).

The papers were vehicles for an up-and-coming generation of Indo-European and indigenous intellectuals. The best was the long-running *Pewarta Timoer* (News of the East), which had subscribers all over the archipelago. It catered to the first generation of native-born Kupang people to move around the vast network of colonial administrative oversight, whose nodes were the archipelago's towns. As elsewhere (Van Niel 1960, Sutherland 1979), these were Indo-Europeans and the sons of rajas (who were to be 'modernized' while retaining their aristocratic privileges). But by the 1930s they were being overtaken by a new peasant-born generation, often teachers. Some biographies of these upwardly mobile lower-middle-class people will appear in the next chapter. It was they who ran the other little newspapers in town that competed with *Pewarta Timoer*. They were rebellious and convinced they knew Timor better than their elders. *Obor Masjarakat* wrote that *Pewarta Timoer* was excessively 'sweet' on the government because its

---

survived, none completely (surviving years indicated in brackets). They are in the National Library of Indonesia in Jakarta, where most have not yet been filmed: *Tjermin Timoer* (monthly, 1931–32); *Taman Masehi* (monthly, 1932); *Oetoesan Timoer* (twice monthly, 1932–34); *Fadjar* (monthly, 1933–34); *Tjinta Kebenaran* (thrice monthly, 1935–38); *Masehi Timoer* (twice monthly, 1935–37); *Obor Masjarakat* (monthly, 1938–39); *Pewarta Timoer* (twice monthly, 1940); Timorese in Makassar published *Soeara Timoer* (monthly, 1935–36). During the Japanese occupation there was only *Timoer Sjoeho* (1942–44). Another to which reference is made is *Seroean Kita* (1939–40, now lost). During the late 1940s there was *Timoer Sedar* (revived from before the war), and *Kepanduan Timor* (both now lost).

owner W.H. Ladoex de Fretes was too 'European' to understand 'the land and people of Indonesia' (*nusa dan bangsa Indonesia*).[15]

Rival broadsheets cranked up the polemical volume in order to attract readers. Today's reader finds it impossible to reconstruct the fights the data-free *Tjermin Timoer* (Mirror of the East) engaged in with such abandon in those days. A gift for mordancy was unfortunately not sufficient to pay the bills, and most papers ran at a loss.[16] The town was too small to permit anonymous politics. A motor vehicle driver, whose occupation enjoyed considerable prestige in those days, came in to punch up the *Pewarta Timoer* editor for writing that he drove too fast.[17] *Pewarta Timoer* responded to attacks from rival newspapers with counter-accusations sometimes containing the grossest libel. It let fly in late 1935 with the suggestion that the mother of F. Djami, the young editor of rival newspaper *Tjinta Kebenaran* (Love of Truth, which also built up an archipelagic subscriber base), was an adulteress. Djami replied that he was proud of his Sabunese mother, because she had provided for her family. Her money had allowed him to live in a 'house of stone... Out of poverty we have been made rich.'[18]

The few Europeans in town did not read these local journals, and did not have one of their own. One morning late in 1938 *aspirant controleur* Dick Versluys came to his office to find one of his middle-aged Indo-European clerks bursting into a storm of indignation over an insult he had suffered in the pages of *Timoer Sedar* (The East Awakes). Versluys had no idea this paper even existed and asked his superior about it. The latter admonished him for not knowing what was going on, then explained what it was: 'Oh, you know, that little scrap of paper that is delivered every Saturday and reports all the local scandals' (Versluys [n.d. – circa 1960]:52). The clerk, a church-going man named Van Tiel who belonged to one of the old Indo-European Kupang families, had read a salacious story about his sixteen-year old daughter Melina in the paper. 'But she is still completely closed down below,' he protested, to the sniggers of his office audience, who had seen how this girl could stop work at every desk when she minced into the office. Versluys's superior the *controleur* put the libellous gossip item down to a dispute over land between Van Tiel and Pereira, the *Timoer Sedar* editor.

---

15 *Obor Masjarakat*, July 1938.
16 *Fadjar*, December 1933.
17 *Obor Masjarakat*, January 1939.
18 *Tjinta Kebenaran*, 30 November 1935.

For the most part the Dutch elite had little cause to worry about sedition in the indigenous papers. Its readers were as happy as they to take part in the rituals of sport and political loyalty the establishment organized for them. The Dutch queen's birthday on 31 August was normally the occasion for several days of games. In 1933 they were preceded by a fund-raising dancing competition in the Kupang cinema two weeks earlier. Watched by hundreds, ten dapper competitors, mainly military men and several ladies, danced the Charleston and the rumba starting at 8 p.m. The Charleston craze had been sweeping the world since its invention in America in the 1920s. Sports were the main attraction on 30 August – running races, football, and the new game of tennis. Sportsmen from Dili in Portuguese Timor acquitted themselves well against the local teams, which were made up along ethnic and professional lines (prominently featuring Arabs, Chinese, and the military). Local dignitaries Mr. C. Frans and Mr. Pello entertained the Dili visitors with food. Huge crowds came to listen to the bamboo flute orchestra on 31 August, and then went to church for thanksgiving services in Dutch or Malay. The town's notables gathered at the Resident's official home to renew their pledge of loyalty, while the children held dances elsewhere. In the afternoon another football game took place, and in the evening a ball at the societeit, where the ladies showed off their finest dresses.[19]

All the same, the police kept a close watch on the press. They were particularly irritated by the persistent criticism of corrupt or incompetent colonial officials and rajas in rural areas. The Timorsch Verbond, an association of educated and politically interested young people with a Timor connection, had been putting a lot of energy into these exposés since 1923. The criticisms were part of its campaign for membership in the proto-parliament, the Volksraad. And they were sometimes effective. A Dutch *controleur* in Sumba and an indigenous official in Sabu were sent for trial in Makassar in that year and both were found guilty of tax collection abuses. These were campaigns for good governance linked to embryonic experiments in colonial democracy. They raised hackles among senior officials, and increased membership of the Timorsch Verbond, but did not necessarily empower peasants.[20] Late in 1936 the police threatened F. Djami (editor of *Tjinta Kebenaran*) with jail for alleging malpractice in

---

19 *Fadjar*, September 1933. In honour of the occasion, the entire edition was in poetry. Another Kupang queen's birthday description is in *Tjermin Timoer*, 15 October 1931.

20 Detailed accounts of these campaigns can be found in Farram (2004) and Ardhana (2005). The Timorsch Verbond is discussed again in Chapter 5.

the justice department. His paper reported that people passing by the police station during the interrogation could hear 'a sound as of thunder and lightning, as if the police station was being broken apart.' It then added phlegmatically: 'How sad is the lot of us journalists.'[21] A couple of years later he did get three months jail, for his reporting on a raja.[22] It was to be the last gasp of militancy for Djami, though not of his political involvement (Farram 2004:128–35).

However, even without police surveillance it seems unlikely the chattering classes in Kupang would have taken an interest in fomenting revolution among the poor. It takes an eagle eye to learn from the papers that many residents in the semi-rural kampong, those without the luxury of a steady salary and who only ate from their own food gardens, suffered 'savage hunger' in the yearly September dry season.[23] Impoverished peasants who came to town from beyond the *vierkante paal* to look for work sometimes stole blankets, chickens and other readily saleable items.[24] But the level of criminality did not require a large security presence in Kupang. Just five policemen on duty at any one time were enough.

The nearest thing to an urban revolt among the poor had occurred a decade before the rise of the new generation of intellectuals. If the newspaper-reading clerks of the 1930s remembered it they did not care about it enough to write about it. Christian Pandie (1903–1950), born in Rote, had travelled to Java where he became a convinced communist. Back in the Lesser Sundas he became an itinerant barefoot lawyer (*pokrol bamboe*), telling the poor about their rights and recruiting them for the PKI's People Union (*Sarekat Rakjat*). Middle-class fellow residents in Kupang's Fatufeto suburb where he lived only listened politely in 1924 and 1925. But his words incited a revolt against feudal taxes among peasants in rural areas around Kupang including Amarasi and the island of Semau, and then also against modern taxes in Kupang's own Kampong Solor, a poor neighbourhood inhabited by Muslims. He and several fellow activists were quickly arrested and exiled to various remote places in 1926 (Ardhana 2005:281–6).[25] A three-year stint in Cipinang prison in Batavia mellowed Pandie

---

21 *Tjinta Kebenaran* 10 November 1936. Earlier that year a Kupang magistrate had fined him 50 guilders for another press violation (*Tjinta Kebenaran*, 20–30 April 1936).

22 *Obor Masjarakat*, January 1939. Even the *Pewarta Timoer* editor got three months the next year after a conflict with another local paper, *Seroean Kita* (*Pewarta Timoer*, 10 August 1940).

23 *Tjinta Kebenaran*, 30 September 1936.

24 *Pewarta Timoer*, 27 January 1940, 17 February 1940.

25 Useful details can also be read in Farram 2002. The year 1925 was a good one for agitprop. Kampung Solor also had a branch of an Islamic communist organization (which was

into an apolitical religious activist. The militancy he had triggered was long remembered among the poor in various eastern islands, and popped up again in the 1950s, but no intellectuals were involved with them again (see Chapter 7).

Discontent among these lower-middle-class intellectuals, by contrast, was hardly audible in the 1930s. They complained about little irritations. The better-off residents in Oeba, on the eastern edge of town, grumbled that the kampong folk washing their clothes and bathing at the spring made too much noise. Those near Kampong Belanda felt the jail was improperly close to the villa of His Excellency the Resident and to the monument for the birth of Princess Beatrix.[26] People at Fontein complained that the new swimming pool was causing a loss of water pressure in the kampong hydrant.[27]

Figure 17. Wooden house in Kampong Kissar, Kupang, circa 1927 (KITLV image nr. 11496).

---

quite possible in those days) called Sarikat Oesaha Solor. The Islamic communists Natar Zainuddin and Haji Datuk Batuah, exiled to the eastern region from Padang, brought radicalism to Kalabahi in Alor and Kefamenanu in Timor in the same year. And Serikat Rakjat members were also active in Adonara island east of Flores in 1925 (see also Dietrich 1989:234). Once the government had removed the instigators, however, the revolts did not spread. When radical nationalist Sukarno was exiled to Ende in Flores in 1930–31 he did not engage in political mobilization and just discussed religion.

26 *Pewarta Timoer*, 17 February 1940.

27 *Pewarta Timoer*, 9 March 1940.

Figure 18. Middle class villa on the river seen from Voorstraatbrug, now Airmata, Kupang, circa 1927 (KITLV image nr. 11459).

Figure 19. Pantjoeran Street, Kupang, circa 1927 (now the minibus terminal by the old pier) (KITLV image nr. 11449).

In any case, life in town was improving even without agitation. Not so fast as to threaten the sense of small-town decorum, but just fast enough to reduce boredom. A bicycle, made accessible by cheap Japanese imports in the 1930s, gave its young possessor a delicious means of terrorizing the quiet streets. In a community where everyone knew everyone else, a collision was not merely an accident but an attack on the very moral fabric of the community, a disruption of its hierarchies. It gave the editor of the local newspaper an opportunity to wag a moralizing finger in support of old 'strong ties' so characteristic of a local community (Granovetter 1973):

> *Bicycle Rider Lacks Concern for People.* Bai Besa Klas, who ran down the child of Mister Sampelan only the other day, has now run down the child of Mister Parinoessa. Even though this second child to be run down, whether it was the child's fault or not, suffered no harm, yet we remind the gentleman on the bicycle, do not point your face up in the air as you ride. Have a care to look out for your fellow human beings on the road.[28]

The main topics for public discussion were religion, the theatre, movies, and sport. They all brought an enticing greater world to Kupang, and none had any relation to the soil of Timor. Catholic Flores and Protestant Timor belong to a largely Christian eastern arc in an archipelago that was predominantly Islamic. Catholicism in Flores went back to Portuguese times. An equally long history of Christianity in Rote (see Chapter 6) ensured that the Protestant church was Kupang's main religious institution, although in the 1930s the church's impact in Timor's interior remained minimal. The church belonged to the state-run Indische Kerk. The local press liked to gently lampoon its bureaucratic character. A public meeting of the church council to discuss the future of the Protestant church in Timor deserved a half page in 1940. Why was it that the Bataks in Sumatra, who only 'entered religion' 50 years ago, now had an independent church, the earnest correspondent asked himself, whereas in Timor the church was still run by the state? The problem lay not with the sheep but with the shepherd, he concluded:

> 'If they don't get paid, of course there will be some among our leaders who don't like to work. Look at the other religions; how they strive to grow the kingdom of God without subsidy and without a salary, but just from the gifts of their congregation. We hear that every month paying for these gentlemen, the Timor Protestant spiritual shepherds, costs the government thousands of rupiah. And still the goal is not achieved. Our religion uses up an extraordinary amount of money compared with other religions. ... Half of the ministers do not care if no one turns up to church; so long as the service is held. What a regrettable opinion. Last week when Reverend van de Wallen preached for the first time in the Dutch church he was astonished to see so few worshippers. People will come if they understand the language, and if

[28] *Tjinta Kebenaran*, 20 February 1936.

> they are spiritually thirsty. On the other hand, if they often do not understand and then they hear things that disagree with their hearts, then surely they will choose a different way of satisfying their spiritual thirst.'[29]

Perhaps the 'different way' our ecclesiastical correspondent had in mind was Koen Seong's Sunlie cinema. There people shouted at the screen to warn the actor of danger, and 'troubled hearts were made happy.'[30] And every few months – not nearly as often as in Surabaya, to be sure – a visiting theatre troupe performed to large crowds. Manila Opera played from time to time in a godown by the harbour, among others performing Putra Genovev (Genoveva of Brabant).[31] In July 1934, the local Opera Jong Timoer, though not rated as highly as Manila Opera, performed the hilarious Arab comedy Bibi Djalik to an audience of 200 at the Sunlie cinema. The touching star was a nine-year old girl.[32] We know the complete repertoire for eight days performances by the Constantinople Company (Gezelschap Constantinopel) in Bima in 1936. All were of Malay or Middle Eastern origin, many inspired by 1001 Arabian Nights. The company played to great acclaim in a godown, but too often the impecunious audiences stayed outside trying to hear without paying, leaving the hall empty, and this led the troupe to cut short its intended month-long stay.[33] The repertoire carried on the hybrid tradition pioneered by the Indo-European Auguste Mahieu in Surabaya in the 1890s and known as stambul, a bastardization of Istanbul. By their use of pan-local Malay, the brash multi-ethnicity of their stage types, and the sheer hybridity of their stories, stambul was creating a 'shared structure of feeling' (Cohen 2006:3) that was perhaps even more cosmopolitan and 'Indonesian' than the rhetoric of the idealistic young intellectuals. The genre did not survive World War II, but by then it had done its subtle work of helping to bind Kupang into the network of towns that created a new nation.

---

[29] *Pewarta Timoer,* 9 March 1940.

[30] ('hati soesah djadi senang'); *Tjinta Kebenaran,* 30 September 1936.

[31] Opera Manila played in March 1934 and November 1936 (*Fadjar,* 19 March 1934; *Tjinta Kebenaran,* 10 November 1936).

[32] *Fadjar,* July 1934. The story was well-known in the Netherlands Indies (Klinkert 1913:181–91).

[33] They included Stevens Dalima De Amboneesche Hocus Pocus (described earlier by Manusama 1917 as Stephan de Lima, de Amboneesche toovenaar); Laila (which could be one of many plays containing that name, perhaps the popular romance Layla and Majnun, or Laela Mendara, Laila Surmana, or Laela Candra – see Cohen (2006:385–6). Other plays in the list were Njai Aminah, Tjotjok Marbah, Bajangan Maud, and Soeltan Harun al Rasjid (none of which I could identify) (*Tjinta Kebenaran,* 20 May 1936).

More than the European elite, the Chinese were brokers for this cultural hybridity. Such as it was, practically all the trade into and out of the island, from guns, beeswax and sandalwood in the past to clothing and cattle by the 1930s, passed through their hands. Many Chinese in town were well-off shopkeepers, who could afford to support their own recreational facilities. At the Lok Seng Hwe community hall in Kupang members played billiards, bridge, dominoes, chess or just read the newspapers.[34] They followed the news from China closely. In 1936, for the first time, they celebrated the anniversary of the Sun Yat-sen republic by closing all their shops and listening to speeches in praise of Chinese independence at the Chinese school.[35] They could not escape the strict bounds of their identity in the marketplace. In one remarkable effort at breaking through the barrier, a man named Tan Djing Long converted to Islam. During the fasting month observant Muslims do not even swallow their spittle. As he was walking around the market constantly spitting it out ('remember, a new convert,' the newspaper wrote sympathetically), people scolded the poor man.[36]

The Chinese were generous when entertaining the general public. For the Chinese New Year, Mr. Tjiong Koen Siong 'spared no expense, despite the economic crisis,' to hold games for all at his ice factory.[37] What were these games? Perhaps they were similar to those played at the opening of a new tennis club in Ba'a, on Rote, for which we have a list. Masses of locals came to applaud the stunts performed by the game's elite local stars – hand stands on the bicycle, 'the stupid thief,' the fishing game, 'selling cakes,' followed by the clowns Dato and Giok.[38] As with stambul, these public games were cultural hybrids. We never read here of the 'traditional' games that archaizing education department scholars in Kupang were to catalogue in the 1980s (Kopong et al 1981). The only people who seemed interested in tradition were a group of American tourists who visited Kupang in 1934. They were taken to the *societeit* to admire the music of the stringed *sasongko* and the Timorese gong, dances from Rote, and traditional warrior (*meo*) clothes. Locals in turn turned out in great numbers to watch the Americans, noting that they didn't buy very much.[39]

---

34 *Pewarta Timoer,* 17 February 1940.
35 *Tjinta Kebenaran,* 10 January 1936.
36 *Tjinta Kebenaran,* 30 November 1935.
37 *Tjinta Kebenaran,* 31 January 1936.
38 *Tjinta Kebenaran,* 29 February 1936.
39 *Fadjar,* 19 March 1934.

A Setting for Change

Protests from below against the colonial 'betting on the strong' were intermittent in the pre-war period. They are evidence that the new techniques of rule were producing real grievances among the poor. But lacking resources and opportunities they were easily suppressed. The ability to mobilize resources successfully when the opportunity presents itself nearly always requires a cross-class, urban-rural alliance. And this did happen in the 1950s and early 1960s, as later chapters will describe. In the 1930s Kupang was too small to bring social forces to bear, nor were there opportunities to do so. But the rise of a new semi-educated lower-middle class intelligentsia with a cosmopolitan outlook, living in a town that enjoyed institutionalized modern rule in a world of autocratic rajas, provided the setting for change. Their interest in the poor was limited to the abuses that they thought incompetent rajas and colonial officials were committing against them. That interest was motivated more by their desire to rule than by any feeling of solidarity. Yet at the same time the desire stimulated a sense just below the surface that real power could only be developed by crossing boundaries.

CHAPTER FIVE

ELITE BROKERS (1934–1950)

> I was the translator, the advisor, the spokesperson, the people's leader, the lottery drawer, the announcer, the teacher of Malay and Japanese language, the organizer, the leader of Seinendan, the letter composer, etc. etc.
>
> (I.H. Doko explaining his role under the Japanese to Dutch officials after WWII, Locher 1945:4).

Indonesia's grand myth of national becoming is that the Revolution of 1945 welded together a disparate colonial patchwork. The actual history of national integration across space was much more uneven. Chapter 1 introduced two Indonesias: a central Indonesian heartland – Java, parts of Sumatra and southern Sulawesi – that owned the revolution and much other mobilizational activity before and since, and many islands in a large periphery that heard about these things from afar and were otherwise preoccupied with their own affairs. Yet Indonesia is united. How did this happen? The same chapter also began to explore the idea of mediation, and in particular of brokerage, that might lead to an answer. This chapter takes up those ideas and applies them to one particular site. The brokers who brought eastern Indonesia into the new nation came from small towns in the region. The chapter traces the biography of one of the main nationalist organizers in one small provincial town in eastern Indonesia at the time when the nation was born. He and his fellows opened doors for people wanting to pass in both directions – central government officials needing access to the region, and fellow locals wanting jobs with the new government. But rather than becoming midwives to popular democracy, they remained a small group of local elites. The politics they bequeathed to the town were factional and bureaucratic, little troubled by demands from any broader civil society.

The national myth is that the 1945 revolution worked its exhilarating magic equally everywhere. Foreigners who have read only Benedict Anderson's famous book on this episode (1972) tend to forget that he was explicitly writing only about Java. However, others have grappled with spatial heterogeneities. Audrey Kahin (1985) edited a volume exploring the differences in local leadership in towns all over the archipelago during the national revolution. Local variation in the history of colonial governance was among the most important explanatory factors, she concluded. More recently, Rudolf Mrázek (2010) has recorded the highly evocative words of aging urban intellectuals in Jakarta. All of them had been engaged with the revolution when they were young, but they spoke to Mrázek mainly about the intimate spaces of their youth. This chapter, too, wishes to contribute to widening the historical terrains and challenging the assumptions of a Java-centric historiography.

In 1949 Kupang's population was just 11,000. Like many towns in this region, Kupang's economy revolved around trade and state investment. Beyond the town lay a subsistence agricultural economy. A passing car was a rarity – most people walked, a few had bicycles, and there was the occasional truck-bus heading out of town. Lower-middle class readers of the Chinese-supported broadsheets read about local incidents, agricultural statistics from neighbouring islands, and world news. Yet when the proclamation of the Republic of Indonesia in Jakarta on 17 August 1945 triggered armed youth insurrections in Java's major cities of Surabaya and Bandung, it went unremarked in Kupang. There were immediate historical reasons for this disconnect – war disasters had stunned Kupang, and Australian Allied troops took control more quickly than in Java[1] – but it also had deeper roots. Kupang was part of a different Indonesia.

The indigenous local leaders who emerged in the tumultuous years spanning World War II were typically educated individuals with some organization behind them. Like the 'marginals' described by Eric Wolf (1956) in Mexico, who rose to become the ideal 'brokers' between their rural communities and the Revolutionary government via new political organizations, they learned to operate in the manipulative environment of short-term friendships and the shifting opportunities of the early independent state. The resources that they were able to deploy varied with the character of their 'home' milieu. In central Indonesia, they tended to be professional political mobilizers. Sukarno was the supreme example. In eastern Indonesia, by contrast, they came from within the colonial state, where they worked as civil servants or teachers at state schools. Popular movements occasionally emerged in eastern Indonesia too, but colonial authorities quickly suppressed them, leaving room only for local elites

[1] They accepted the Japanese surrender in Timor on a warship in Kupang Bay on 11 September 1945, and afterwards faced no military problems to assuming total control. Civilian authority was in the hands of the Netherlands Indies Civil Administration (NICA) from the start. Australian soldiers were ordered to have no contact with the indigenous population, and were withdrawn on 18 March 1946 (Farram 2004:216–22).

whose main resources came from the faraway centre, with which they collaborated. Their local politics tended to be factional rather than mobilizational. They looked to bureaucratic superiors rather than to mass constituents. From the associative form that brought it to life in and around the cities of central Indonesia, national power acquired an instrumental, even imperial form once a small collaborating elite had introduced it to the small towns of eastern Indonesia and their subsistence hinterlands. Their modalities were those of a patrimonial authority achieved by operating through the bureaucracy.

The number of indigenous government clerks rose quickly once the colonial government began to raise its developmental ambitions after the turn of the century. As elsewhere, the first native-born Kupang people to move around the vast network of modern colonial administrative oversight and social uplift were the sons of the rajas (Van Niel 1960, Sutherland 1979). They travelled along the modern shipping routes from Kupang, first to get an education – probably at the school for administrators in Makassar (Opleiding School Voor Inlandsche Ambtenaren, OSVIA, since 1910), or to various kinds of high schools in Surabaya, Yogyakarta or Batavia, and then from one colonial office to another all over the archipelago. At first most had only lower primary schooling, but the level rose as government grew more complex. Government scholarships also went to children of farmers from the early 1930s. When some of these returned to Kupang as young teachers, they positioned themselves as a new generation of local leaders. The little newspapers some of them started were vigorous in style, full of advice for advancing the colonial modernization agenda. Their politics were factional rather than mobilizational.

Elites looked to bureaucratic superiors rather than to mass constituents. Popular movements had emerged in Kupang too. But the architectural draftsman and bush lawyer Chris Pandie never recovered his zeal for tax revolts after three years in a Batavia prison in the late 1920s (Chapter 4), and the next generation of 'intellectuals' took no more interest in them. Izaak Huru Doko (1913–1985) was one of them. He was declared a national hero (*pahlawan nasional*) in 2006 for his contribution to the independence of a united Indonesia. He was 'one of the most consistent and steadfast of the political organizers on Timor' (Fox 1977:182). But there is irony in this notion of Doko as national hero. His generation prided itself on its local roots. They were brokers who, like the town they called their own, mediated between their local compatriots and people in distant centres. His career reflects the Faustian choices confronting the whole political class in Kupang in this transitional period.

Dressing Nicely

Doko was born in Ledemanu village on the small island of Sabu, on 12 November 1913 (Malehere and Krenak 2006), the eighth of nine children in a subsistence household. Sabu was Christianized later than many other islands in this region (Fox 1977:160–169). His father's Sabunese name was Kitu Huru and his mother's Loni (Malehere and Krenak 2006). They were probably first generation Christians. Father was baptized with the name Benjamin, the mother's we do not know. They never left Sabu their entire lives.[2] The first to enter the modern state complex was his eldest brother Paul. Although only educated at the three-year village school in Sabu, Paul's Dutch was good enough to become a government clerk. When Izaak showed promise too, Paul paid for him to continue his schooling in Kupang.[3] Most of the native students there were raja's children. In 1928 he and a couple of others received government scholarships to the junior high school in Ambon (Mulo-B). In 1934, aged 21, he was among just 30 out of 300 selected to continue to the teachers college (kweekschool) at Bandung, in West Java (Boenga et al 1996). On the way he passed through that great city he had seen only in pictures – Batavia. Doko was about to become an educated, Java-experienced intellectual.

Bandung and Batavia were still abuzz with the birth of the nationalist movement a few years earlier. The outer island students picked up the buzz, but not the rebelliousness. Doko belonged to that moderate group for whom the most important thing was 'not a nation, but a lifestyle' (Henk Schulte Nordholt 2011). At the group's first public rally back in Kupang four years later, a friend named Tiboeloedji (later spelled Tibuludji) explained how Bandung had politicized them. At the student hostel for the teachers college were 208 young people from all over the archipelago. They all belonged to one of their own ethnic youth associations. 'But the Timorese did not have one, nor were they well regarded by their friends. When they realized this, they felt ashamed. They simply had to set up their own association, even if they were just two people in the hostel.' They called it 'Timorsche Jongeren,' Timorese Youth. Their purpose was to improve their Dutch by writing magazine articles, and to

2 Interview with I.H. Doko's younger brother, A.B. Doko, Kupang, 18 June 2009.

3 Paul H. Doko was killed by the Japanese in 1944 while posted in Bajawa, Flores. He was betrayed for talking too fondly about the Dutch, taken to Ende and executed. In 1948 his body was reburied in a Netherlands Indies state ceremony ('Pemakaman kembali bestuurs-assistent Doko,' *Pandji Ra'jat,* 12 October 1948).

bring advancement to the people of their island. This modest dream, born from shame, was leagues removed from the radically non-ethnic, defiantly socialist youth ideals Sukarno had proclaimed in that same town in 1926, eight years before Doko arrived. It was not even nationalism. It was a way of being middle class that was both modern and provincial, and moreover a practical choice. Sukarno was at that moment in internal exile in Flores, a large island near Timor. The young students were grateful to the government for their scholarships and looked forward to satisfying careers under its beneficence.[4]

By 1937 Doko was standing in front of classes at the best school in Kupang, the Schakelschool. His decade abroad had made him a big fish in a small pond. He overflowed with zeal to improve this hot, sleepy town, and soon became known as a dashing speaker. On 7 November 1938 he married Miss Dorkas Toepoe, his assistant at a political association he had started. They were to have four sons. The activism of these ambitious young people followed the path established in Kupang by Hazaart. Like Hazaart, they too were a self-appointed avant-garde with a civilizing mission in Timor, and like him, they showed little understanding of indigenous lives. Their parents' stony yam gardens were a distant memory. Surrounded by an impoverished rural society, the elitism of the modern bureaucrat became the core value for these urban modernizers. Not for them submission to tradition and heredity.

The new graduates were welcomed back to Kupang by the first generation of politically active Timorese, all bureaucrats with experience outside Timor who had been asserting themselves since the 1920s through their Timorsch Verbond (sketches of them are in Ardhana 2005, and Kementerian Penerangan Sunda Ketjil 1953). Their Java-educated status elevated them into Kupang's better circles, while distancing them from their parents within the poor majority. The novel element for these civil servants was that they had become part-time politicians. To the claim of technical expertise, they added a political claim – that they could broker the unique culture of the locals to the metropolis, and the uplifting

[4] The 3 July 1938 meeting brought together two rival Timorese organizations: (1) Doko's group of young activists called Perserikatan Kebangsaan Timor (outgrowth of Timorsche Jongeren and ideologically aligned with the older but now defunct nationalist organization Timorsch Verbond) and (2) a government-sponsored, pro-church breakaway group from the Timorsch Verbond called Perserikatan Timor led by the government clerk Christian Frans. The younger ones wanted the Raja of Amarasi, H.A. Koroh, for the Volksraad. The local government eventually agreed to sponsor the more 'cooperative' C. Frans, but nothing further had been done when the Japanese intervened (see the excellent institutional account in Ardhana 2005:259–79).

mission of the metropolis to the locals. The latter claim did not erupt from an outraged sense of social injustice, but expressed their proud appropriation of a colonial vision of citizenship in any future independent Netherlands Indies – which was that it would be essentially ethnic.

The association Timorsch Verbond, run by the older generation, long enjoyed financial support from the expansive Tjiong Koen Siong and other Chinese businesspeople. The latter no doubt hoped they were nurturing a new middle class with purchasing power. When visiting Kupang in June 1932, for example, Timorsch Verbond members from the big cities further west – Makassar, Surabaya, Bandung, Batavia – were careful to maintain their distance from the kampong. They stayed in the Chinese clan house Lok Seng Hwe, drove around in a car supplied by Tjiong Koen Siong instead of walking like everyone else, and held a public meeting to raise support in his downtown movie theatre. Beneath the chummy stylishness, rivalry between various elite Timorese factions was often bitter. Each clique had its organization and its local gossip newspaper. *Tjermin Timoer* ('Mirror of Timor') let fly at the Doko crowd (associated with *Tjinta Kebenaran,* 'Love of Truth') by revealing the elite connections mentioned above. The wider public cared no more for them than they for it, the paper went on sarcastically. Ordinary Kupang folk got more excited about the visit of a warship, submarine, airplane, or the Governor-General than about the Timorsch Verbond. Any complaints these young elites had about the situation in Timor were those of outsiders, it added as the final stab.[5]

Theirs, indeed, were the politics of the ambitious official. They exposed abuses, corruption, inefficiency, and special privileges, but built no social movements. They took no political risks. When the Resident banned his civil servants from joining the Timorsch Verbond in 1930, the organization quickly sagged (Ardhana 2005:273–4). In 1938, however, Batavia once more opened the door a crack to local politics by agreeing to increase the number of native delegates to the colonial proto-parliament, the Volksraad. Kupang wanted to raise a constituency for a member from Timor. The 25-year old Doko told a well-attended meeting in Tjiong Koen Siong's movie theatre on 3 July 1938 that 'tomorrow' belonged to the youth. The first essential task for the younger generation was to establish localist credentials. Their claims of belonging were self-conscious to the point of artificiality. A.Z. Palindih, the young editor of one of the local newspapers,

---

[5] *Tjermin Timoer,* June-August 1932.

whose father, judging by his name, was West Sumatran, introduced himself as 'a Timorese young person because my mother is from Timor.'[6] He said he felt moved by the native *sasongko* music played during the interval. Palindih became chair of the committee to lobby for the Volksraad seat. All the candidates they had in mind were in government service. But the young ones felt the older guard, such as the aristocrat J.W. Amalo (who worked at the state oil company in Surabaya) and C. Frans (an official at the Resident's office), had 'already become European' and had moreover spent too much of their lives in Java to be credible in Timor.

However, the younger generation, too, had developed good dress sense in Java. Fashionable suits and shirts made of 'gabardine, palmbeach or poplin' or even of Parisian silk could be ordered from the tailor at Yong Sen's shop on Pantjoeran Street (this establishment also took quality photographic portraits, and sold patent medicines – Figure 20). Clothing expressed their new identities – modern, urban, and as far removed from the Timorese sarong as possible. Maybe they had even tried the expensive Portuguese wine imported through Dili, best enjoyed with genuine Dutch cheese, both available at Koepang Stores. Gramophones and other 'modern goods' – the desirable symbols of upward social mobility – were sold at Toko Bombaij Koepang.

None of this made it easy to claim they represented the common good. Yet they desperately wanted to be intellectuals with a serious mission. 'So many youths still think this is all about dressing nicely,' the same Palindih warned gravely at the July rally. A common enthusiasm for progress would, he hoped, bridge the social chasm that now separated them from the poor. Participants called on each other to be inspired (*semangat*), to build schools and cooperatives all over the Timor residency. Like the New Order engineers who were later to transform the technical wizardry of the Palapa satellite system into a top-down discourse of nation-building (Barker 2005), these young enthusiasts gave a political meaning to the organizational techniques they were bringing to Kupang. But the *mission civilisatrice* was lonely work. Palindih observed soon afterwards in an op-ed piece in his paper that in Timor the labouring poor showed a regrettable lack of interest in the improvement plans laid before them by the intellectuals (something *Tjermin Timoer* had already noted before him):

[6] 'KT mengadakan openbare vergadering,' *Tjinta Kebenaran*, July 1938. Palindih was editor at *Obor Masjarakat*, and previously at *Pewarta Timoer* in 1936. After the war he became a journalist in Bandung.

Figure 20. Advertisement in Fadjar (Kupang), May 1933.

> When we speak of intellectuals here we mean firstly those among us with a Western education and secondly those who have [native] intelligence. … Ordinary folk come to these intellectuals to tell them things and then go home to tell others about it. The intellectuals give leadership to the impoverished people or the masses. Meanwhile the masses with the strength of their bodies, with their work, give sustenance to the intellectuals. … If we now observe society in Timor, we can see that there is no such relationship between intellectuals and people. The intellectuals have not the slightest interest in their own people; indeed they sometimes despise them. Similarly the people sometimes do not give the intellectuals a thought. This situation is not good! … There is so much we should be doing for the people, such as eliminating illiteracy, health training, education, and so on, and all of this can be done together with the government. … It is crystal clear that a deep and wide chasm separates the two.[7]

The emerging elite's disconnect with any popular constituency came back to haunt it soon afterwards. Feeling little pressure to act, the government dragged its feet on appointing Frans to the Volksraad. Soon the money from local elites dried up, and the association's energy ebbed away. Doko continued to teach. He and the other young Rotenese and Sabunese intellectuals went back to paying deference to their 'already European' elder Christian Frans, who occasionally pushed some money their way. Doko wrote articles for the church newspaper *Soeloeh Indjil,* run by a Dutch reverend, and for *Pemimpin Raiat,* the official Residency broadsheet led by Frans (Locher 1945).

The gap Palindih worried about was real. Kupang's better broadsheets often reported on the benighted lot of peasants in the town's hinterland, who were served justice by ignorant rajas instead of professional magistrates and who were unable to understand proceedings because they had no Malay.[8] But this was for these intellectuals a social problem, not a political one. On the whole their small town papers breathed colonial tranquillity. The state apparatus to them was strict but benevolent. Kupang's rituals of church, office gossip, and occasional dances at weddings were comfortable. Their papers convey no nostalgia for their ancestors' villages.

Golden Boy

As for so many of his generation all over Indonesia, the Japanese occupation gave Doko his first experience of real politics, and of blood. The

---

[7] *Obor Masjarakat,* November 1938.

[8] E.g. *Tjinta Kebenaran,* 20 November 1935, quoted at the head of Chapter 4, and *Pewarta Timoer,* 6 December 1939.

consequences of earlier choices now came into sharp focus. He was 28 years old in 1942, and had a 'bright personality' (Locher 1945). The town's airport had made Kupang an international transit point since 1940; it now became a strategic asset for the Japanese. When war broke out, Doko helped out at the Red Cross emergency hospital set up in Naikoten, Raja Kupang's home south of the town. Soon afterwards he evacuated to Tabun, a village just west of Kupang, where his wife was already.[9] Allied troops had landed to halt the Japanese advance, but they were forced to retreat and made a desperate last stand at Babao about 30 km outside Kupang in February 1942 (Farram 2004:167–9). The Japanese used Penfui as their base for continuing the bombing raids on Darwin that they had first launched from aircraft carriers. Kupang's residents feared retaliatory bombs and fled to the safety of the hills. The economy came to a halt. Doko went often to Kupang to barter for daily necessities and attend church.

The Japanese were ignorant and under-resourced in the vast archipelago. Whereas Sumatra and Java – the heartlands – were occupied by armies (respectively the 25th Army and the 16th Army), the periphery was administered by the Imperial Japanese Navy. By contrast with the mobilizational military regimes in the heartlands, the aim in the (in parts) resource-rich but population-poor islands from Kalimantan to the Sunda Islands was to annex the region permanently while avoiding political mobilization. Japanese civilian bureaucrats were brought in, who tried as much as possible to make use of native administrators (Post et al 2010:72–86). They needed loyal local allies to be their eyes and hands without triggering revolts. The Japanese doctor who had come to live in the Dutch reverend's house befriended Doko and introduced him to the new regime. With their coercive resources kept largely behind their backs, they exercised power in manipulative and even seductive ways. The young Timorese intellectuals were ambitious, experts in organization, and good public speakers. In return for their support, the Japanese offered these invaluable brokers a status leap over the Dutch and the aristocrats, unprecedented public exposure, and escape from the inevitable shortages to come.

They made Doko editor of a weekly propaganda newspaper called *Timoer-Sjoeho*. In June 1942, his paper began telling people it was safe to come back to Kupang and urging them to do so. Darwin, the feared source of long-range bombers, was a long way away and being hammered every

[9] Locher 1945. There had earlier been an emergency hospital in the Societeit (Soh and Indrayana 2008:95).

day.[10] In August the tone became threatening – those who refused to return to the markets were hoping America would win the war.[11] People were told to turn in furniture, clothing, office equipment and of course guns the Dutch may have left behind. They should plant cotton for Japanese uniforms. But Doko's persuasive powers had their limits. In September the town was still deserted, and in November 1942 residents were being urged to seek shelter from bombing raids now coming from Darwin. Many hungry children were arrested in December for stealing food. *Timoer-Sjoeho* revealed how quickly shortages had become serious when it reported a year after the invasion that 5,000 people had turned up hoping to buy one of the 1,200 pieces of cloth in a special sale in the Chinese shops by the beach. In September 1943, lucky people with ration cards had one day to replace one of their bicycle tires with a new one. Another one-day sale of rationed cloth, shoes, and umbrellas in three designated places followed in January 1944.[12] Government offices had been evacuated to temporary accommodation in Bakunase, in the hills four kilometres south of town. The authorities squeezed the Chinese traders for money and war contributions in kind (leather; donations at feasts). Kupang was reported to have 'contributed' 400,000 Dutch guilders to the Japanese war effort by April 1945.[13] But the Japanese also needed the Chinese to keep the economy turning over, and there was money to be made from scarcity. In March 1944 Tjoei Tek Giok won a contract valued at 89 rupiahs a month – a substantial amount even in inflationary times – to be the town's sole supplier of palm wine for a year (Pak Laru).[14]

C. Frans, Doko's immediate superior and one of Kupang's best-known personalities, was the Timorese face on the Japanese occupation. He had long been an admirer of Germany's energy, though not of Hitler, and he became an enthusiastic collaborator with Germany's Asian ally (Locher 1945). In January 1943 his office started showing Japanese war propaganda films in the very movie theatre where a few years earlier he and Doko had debated who should be the Timorese Volksraad candidate. However, factionalism was rife. This was partly a consequence of the poor quality of the Japanese staff, who in the area controlled by the navy turned out to be

10 'Djangan koeatir bom kapal terbang,' *Timoer-Sjoeho*, 18 June 1942.
11 'Sadarlah!' *Timoer Sjoeho*, 6 August 1942.
12 *Timoer-Sjoeho*, 27 January 1944.
13 *Borneo Shimboen*, 18 April 1945. The figures seem incredible.
14 *Timoer Sjoeho*, 9 March 1944. This is possibly a mis-spelled reference to Tjioe Tek Giok, who was to become the first ethnic Chinese Christian in Kupang in the 1950s (see Chapter 11).

'inefficient, incompetent, and unprofessional.' It was even more a consequence of naval dissatisfaction with the supremacy civilian politicians in Japan nominally enjoyed over navy affairs (Post et al 2010:86, 78). Each Timorese staff member had his Japanese patron. In May 1943, Frans was murdered by a branch of the Japanese intelligence service.[15] The problem went back to pre-war rivalries, between the Timorsch Verbond and a 1924 breakaway known as Perserikatan Timor. Allegations from other Timorese that Frans had been less than loyal appear to have played a role. Frans had been badmouthed to the Japanese by Frans Djami, the radical journalist of the late 1930s (see Chapter 4). Soon afterwards Djami was in turn tortured to death during interrogations by the Japanese police over the Frans murder (Farram 2004:194). Frans' murder was a huge shock to the collaborating elite. Apparently not even the most pro-Japanese of Timorese was safe. Doko later told Dutch interrogators he had been subject to similar intrigues, and he mentioned several names (Locher 1945).

Doko now replaced Frans as head of the Social Information Department, in charge of propaganda. Manipulating affections was core business in a wide range of activities. Besides the newspaper, which had moved to Bakunase (Djeki 1980:35–6), there were propaganda films showing in Tjiong Koen Siong's cinema, and he was in charge of education, religious affairs, and health. He organized the churches into a state-controlled ecumenical body chaired by the Raja of Kupang, Nicolaas Nisnoni (Locher 1945:9). He turned church schools into state ones (Locher 1945:9), and replaced Dutch in them with Malay (Ardhana 2005:321). But few schools were running – the first primary school in Kupang did not reopen until September 1942, in a private home. Nevertheless, the patronage he had at his disposal made him popular among other educated people in Kupang needing a job. Like the father (*bapak*) who provided the idiom for Javanese leadership roles from the schoolteacher through the military commander to the president (Shiraishi 1997), Doko became a patron particularly for the Sabunese.

The Japanese rewarded him handsomely for his services. He was named 'People's Leader' (*Pemimpin Raiat*) and appointed to the provincial council, on a generous annual salary equivalent to 1,200 Netherlands guilders. They gave him 'envelopes' and packets of cigarettes for organizing feasts, sports competitions, night markets, theatre performances (the latter

[15] Its name was said to be Otori (Farram 2004:194), but no such service is mentioned in Post et al (2010). Was Otori perhaps the name of an intelligence officer in the shadowy agency Hana Kikan?

producing sometimes hilarious local scripts). The Minseibu were bad organizers, Doko said afterwards. They partied nearly every night at their base at Airnona south of the town centre, and had little idea of what was going on in Timor (Locher 1945:17, appendix). He told Dutch interrogators that his Japanese boss at Minseibu, Captain Yuasa, regarded him as his 'golden child' (*anak emas*). He was a 'jack-of-all-trades' (*manusje van alles*):

> [I was] the translator, the advisor, the spokesperson, the people's leader, the lottery drawer, the announcer, the teacher of Malay and Japanese language, the organizer, the leader of Seinendan, the letter composer, etc. etc. (Locher 1945:4).

Public rituals were central to the Japanese effort at building power. Allied air attacks escalated with a huge raid on 10 April 1943, followed by another big one on 15 June 1943. This one led the Japanese to evacuate their offices in Kupang town to join the refugees already at Bakunase. Doko organized frequent all-day rallies on a parade ground the Japanese had cleared at Bakunase. A little larger than a tennis court, it was located at Airnona, next to Raja Nisnoni's royal well. Today it is built over by housing. This was the beginning of the popular mobilization that continued into the post-war period. They were compulsory for all civil servants and school children, much as such rituals had been under the Dutch and as they remain today. His first major appearance was at the Meiji Emperor's birthday celebration on 3 November 1943.[16] On the dais decorated with flowers, the rajas of southern Timor sat in their *ikat* finery next to Japanese navy officers in white. Most prominent of the rajas was the energetic H.A. Koroh, Raja of Amarasi just south of Kupang (1904–1951) (Doko 1981a). He had been invested acting raja of Kupang as well, because the incumbent, Nicolaas Nisnoni, was too old and pro-Dutch to be useful (Ardhana 2005:320). The programme for these rallies varied little. Bow to the flag, then sing the Japanese national anthem Kimigayo: 'May your reign/ Continue for a thousand, eight thousand generations/ Until the pebbles/ Grow into boulders/ Lush with moss.' Speeches follow by the local deputy head of government, the Ken Kanrikan, equivalent to the Dutch Assistant Resident), and by Doko.[17] Doko expressed gratitude to the heroic Japanese

---

[16] 'IH Doko, Pidato Pemboekaan Oepatjara Meizi Setsu,' *Timoer-Sjoeho*, 4 November 1943.

[17] The Ken Kanrikan was Kokobun Tojozo until January 1944, when he was replaced by Tomida Hikoziro (*Timoer-Sjoeho*, 27 January 1944).

and urged people to work hard for a prosperous Greater East Asia.[18] Primary school children sing Japanese martial songs ending in a rowdy 'Banzai!' – then games and sports, exactly as for the Dutch queen's birthday celebrations earlier. Football might pit old against young civil servants, followed by young locals against outsiders. Food is served to the invited civil servants between matches – including eggs and fruit courtesy of the raja's rural subjects. Prizes and medals follow for deserving people, and on at least one occasion the drawing of a government lottery. More speeches of gratitude and admonition, then another flag ceremony plus mournful Kimigayo, and some time after dark the little field was deserted.[19]

Recruiting bodies for the occupier's war effort was another part of the broker's role. On 11 February 1944, at the celebration of Japanese national foundation day (Kigen-setsu), Doko announced a new youth organization, Seinendan. This multi-purpose work force came late to Timor – it had been operating elsewhere for nearly a year – but soon branches were formed also in the smaller up-country towns of Timor, and in Ende on Flores (which also had a women's Seinendan). Doko was *ex officio* second in command in Kupang, under a navy *daidanco* named Tonita (Widiyatmika 2007:342). One of their most important functions was to bury the increasing number of dead from Allied bombing raids that were now targeting every large and small town of eastern Indonesia. Doko travelled all over Timor to train them (Ardhana 2005:322).[20] The ageing raja Koroh was an enthusiastic recruiter for Heiho units, more militarized than Seinendan but still unarmed. Women joined Heiho too, and more recruits were brought from Java. The raja also recruited *romusha* forced labourers. They dug defence ditches to prepare for the Allied invasion that the military feared (Ardhana 2005:320, Widiyatmika 2007:342).[21] In the first half of April 1944 wave after wave of Mitchell bombers struck all over Timor and caused big fires in Kupang.[22] In June Doko travelled to his

---

18 Similar speeches followed on 8 December 1943, to commemorate the formation of Greater East Asia, and on 20 February 1944 in honour of the Japanese soldiers who had landed on Timor's coast exactly two years earlier ('Perajaan 8 Desember 2603, Hari Pembentoekan Asia Timoer Raja,' *Timoer-Sjoeho*, 18 December 1943; *Timoer-Sjoeho*, 24 February 1944).

19 *Timoer-Sjoeho*, 17 February 1944; 24 February 1944.

20 He later claimed it only ever had 180 members and did mainly sports and a weekly military exercise with wooden bayonets (Locher 1945:3–4).

21 Widiyatmiko is incorrect to date the formation of the local Seinendan to April 1943.

22 *Oetoesan Penjoeloeh*, 11 April 1944. More bombardments of Kupang and other towns in Timor are mentioned in this Allied newspaper: *Oetoesan Penjoeloeh*, 2 June 1944 and *Penjoeloeh*, 13 October 1944.

native island Sabu to recruit forced labour for an agricultural project south of Kupang. Earlier, Koroh had begun supplying 'comfort women' to the thousands of Japanese soldiers stationed in Timor (Doko 1981a:62). Shocked locals renamed the Bakunase area 'Sodom and Gomorrah' for its brothels (Netti and Itta 1997:80). Hotel staff and restaurant waiters often received food in exchange for sexual favours (Netti and Itta 1997:81). By 1944 the war was going badly. An Allied blockade stopped food supplies from Java. The town had grown too large to live off the land, and anyway the Japanese requisitioned all surplus agricultural production (Locher 1945). Kupang residents later recalled the hungry end of 1944 as 'the year of tears' (Netti and Itta 1997:81).

In 1945 the town became symbolically Indonesian through the raising of the red-and-white flag. Where central authorities in Japan had ordered the 16th Army in the Javanese heartlands to respond to political pressure with promises of independence, they had never felt moved to give similar instructions to the Imperial Japanese Navy running eastern Indonesia. But by July 1945 Japan was nearly on its knees and ready to make belated concessions even in remote areas. At the ceremony on 8 July it did insist on the Japanese flag flying next to the Indonesian one. Doko and Raja Koroh were prominent guests.[23] In any case, as Doko later told his Dutch interrogator, he had no intention of subjecting Timor to Java. When the Japanese, thinking they were yielding to Indonesian national pride, offered to sponsor a commemoration in Kupang in honour of Diponegoro, hero of the Java War of 1825–1830, Doko told them 'the Timorese people do not know who Diponegoro is' (Locher 1945:10).

When at last it was all over and the Japanese were required to maintain the peace for the few weeks it took the Allies to land in Kupang, they put Doko in charge of the town, together with two other local prominents named Tom Pello and the medical doctor A. Gabeler (Ardhana 2005:347–8). The Allies arrived on 11 September and relieved local worries that the Japanese might engage in irrational murder in the interval (Netti and Itta 1997:84). No one worried about a nationalist youth uprising, and there was none. The first correspondent to walk around Kupang after the Allied landing, six weeks after war's end, was shocked at the destruction. The heart of town lay in ruins, its population evacuated to the Bakunase

23 Doko later claimed the flag-raising took place on 29 April 1945 (Doko 1981b:81–3). The correct date is in Doko's interrogation report of November 1945, with his speech (Locher 1945) (see also Netti 1997:83). Perhaps Doko had also been present at the first flag-raising in Makassar on 29 April 1945 (Post et al 2010:85).

coconut plantations, where even 'aristocrats and the rich' lived in little huts and ate only what they could grow. Even a year later a visitor from Ambon said the town was worse off than his own bombed-out city: 'the place where Kupang town used to be now looks just like a jungle.' Here and there people had built houses and offices from temporary materials. [24] Allied soldiers brought in loads of coins to restart the economy. They could find no beer, and no spare light bulb for the film projector. Many bridges remained unrepaired for over a decade.

More shocking to the first correspondent (identified only as 'K. K.') was the readiness of the elite to collaborate with the occupier. Seeing this representative of the new master, people sitting passively along the road told him or her what it had been like during the Japanese interregnum: 'Timor Kupang folk forgot their own people, so long as they were given as good a position as possible.'[25] K.K. was especially upset to hear of the factional betrayals, and the spying for money that claimed so many lives.

More Regime Changes

When the Allies landed, Doko was nearly 33 and already facing his second regime change. Two more were to follow – in 1950 and 1966 – and he navigated each with consummate skill. Provincial politicians with ambitions learn to be survivors. He was one of many the Dutch arrested for possible crimes committed as collaborators. But Allied intelligence cleared him of war crimes and, to avoid 'embittering' a gifted man (who had moreover received many letters of support from educated Sabunese), they put him to work organizing the repatriation of displaced persons in Timor (Locher 1945). There were large numbers of Javanese evacuees but no transport back to Java. These former forced labourers and prisoners of war had in the meantime to be fed and housed.

The returning Dutch administrators reported in April 1946 that they had no concerns about security in Kupang, but hoped shortages would not lead to dissatisfaction (Wal 1982:IV, 82–85). The revolutionary Republic of Indonesia largely controlled the Javanese heartland of the archipelago and parts of Sumatra. The Dutch Lieutenant Governor General Van Mook began seeking out local elites in the regions once more under Dutch

---

[24] 'Perdjalanan ke Ambon,' *Soeloeh Ra'jat,* 7 September 1946.

[25] '[B]angsa T Koepang sendiri loepa akan mengingatkan bangsanja sendiri asal sadja mereka itoe dikasih kedoedoekan sepenoeh-penoehnja' ('Riwajat Pendoedoek Koepang dibawah Tindasan Djepang,' by K.K, *Penjoeloeh,* 22 November 1945).

control, hoping to form a government with some traditional legitimacy. He did this by elaborating the federal structure inherent in the neo-traditionalist indirect rule approach from before the war (Yong Mun Cheong 1982). A well-supported conference of local rajas and others from the periphery, which he sponsored in the Sulawesi town of Malino in July 1946, established what was to become the most successful of the federal units, the State of East Indonesia (Negara Indonesia Timor, NIT).

However, those elites in eastern Indonesia who had invested the most prestige in the Japanese now feared downward mobility; they looked instead to the Republic. Doko formed a cautiously pro-Republican little group in Kupang with some links to Jakarta, called Partai Demokrasi Indonesia (Timor). It claimed to be the party of the 'intellectuals who are Indonesians in Timor… and can be taken as the voice of all the people of Timor.'[26] Someone in a visiting Dutch delegation thought several of its members held 'fascist' views (Ardhana 2005:356). Sensitive to the violent image the Republic had outside Java, his party told a Makassar newspaper it was 'not anti-nationalism,' but it was 'anti-banditism.' They didn't like being called 'black Dutchmen or natives,' but were 'Indonesians.' They favoured an independent Indonesia based on federalism.[27] In reality, though, the party's immediate aim was largely factional. As before the war, the differences revolved around claims of local authenticity. Bureaucrats resident in Kupang tried to pre-empt a group of Timorese resident in far-away Jakarta from representing Timor in the embryonic NIT.[28] The rajas of Timor appointed an island parliament in October 1946 (without elections), and Doko became the member for Kupang. He travelled to Denpasar in December 1946 to take part in another conference called by Van Mook, whose purpose was to make NIT a reality.[29] NIT was organized fairly consultatively into a loose, complex structure, a federation within a federation. The Dutch still ruled Timor, itself another federation, through the rajas.

By the end of 1947 Doko had become a member of the NIT parliament in Makassar, in the nationalist fraction.[30] From now on he only made

---

26 '[G]olongan tjendekiawan (intellectueel) bangsa Indonesia di Timoer… dapat dianggap sebagai soeara ra'jat Timor segenapnja' ('Mosi,' *Soember Penerangan*, 15 July 1946).

27 'Bekerdja bersama-sama,' *Soember Penerangan*, 2 July 1946.

28 'Pendirian,' *Pandji Ra'jat* 16–7-1946; *Pandji Ra'jat*, 23 July 1946.

29 Netti and Itta 1997:88–9; *Pandji Ra'jat*, 6 December 1946, 10 December 1946, 18 December 1946. They stayed in Denpasar for months (*Pandji Ra'jat*, 4 February 1947).

30 *Pelita Rakjat*, 27 November 1947, quotes Doko as a member of NIT parliament, in the fraksi nasional, urging federation by 1 January 1949. The other fractions were labelled 'democratic' and 'progressive.'

visits to Kupang. Soon afterwards he was in the NIT cabinet, as Junior Minister for Information. Early in 1949 he reached the peak of his career as Information Minister (Figure 21). He now belonged to Indonesia's busy and highly mobile political elite, flying on DC-3 airliners across the archipelago. The vital action took place far from Kupang, at a whirl of meetings in more important towns to the west, in the United Nations, and even in the Netherlands. Doko's book *History of the Independence Struggle in East Nusa Tenggara* (1981b), standard fare for history students in Timor even today, is in reality his travel diary along the network of modern transport used by the nation's highly mobile elites. His peasant-born generation of bureaucrat-politicians had displaced the Dutch administrators and the rajas as the official interlocutors for the backward east. But whereas politicians from the heartlands of Indonesia were vocal at these meetings and could claim to speak on behalf of a public brought together through associational forms of power, those from the periphery could hardly claim to carry a message from any popular constituency. They kept a low profile, realizing they were there mainly to pass the message back to their regions once all had been decided.

Doko's politics had not succeeded in stirring much grassroots feeling in Kupang. Elite rivals, judging the Dutch to be back for good, took up the sponsored Airnona rally he had invented and turned it against him. The

Figure 21. I.H. Doko as NIT cabinet minister (photo courtesy Mr. Leopold Nisnoni).

first post-war rally occurred on 23 March 1947. Indo-European civil servants, ex-soldiers from Ambon and elsewhere who had been prisoners of war in Timor, and some rajas, livened up by a bamboo flute orchestra, loudly rejected the Republic. Doko had been a 'leading propagandist under the Japanese,' they said.[31] The Dutch resident C.W. Schuller gladly paid the bill (Ardhana 2005:379). His secretary Willem Versluys wrote in January 1947 that the Timorese feared the spread of Javanese, Islamic influence to Timor (Farram 2004:229). Indeed, few people wore the Indonesian national red-and-white even though there was no ban on it.

Now based hundreds of kilometres away in NIT's capital Makassar, Doko sent his comrade E.R. Herewila to open an Information office in Kupang in February 1948. The establishment of NIT did not preclude republican subversion, and Doko was by no means the only senior NIT official to play both sides. Herewila organized a counter-rally at the Airnona field on 23 December 1948, to protest against Dutch military aggression in the Republic (Doko 1981b:162, Netti and Itta 1997:93). But like the pro-Dutch rally of March 1947, this one too seemed to attract more outsiders than native Kupang denizens. Javanese ex-Heiho and ex-forced labourers who were still waiting for transport home found it interesting. The only locals to organize some republican events were a nationalist student group and some members of the Muslim minority. Anyway, the occasional rally on the small field at Airnona on the southern outskirts of town hardly constituted politics of the kind that stirred Java during this era. The Dutch authorities in April 1946 reported to their superiors that the political situation in Kupang was 'without problems,' and Kupang hardly occurs in the Dutch reporting again after that (Wal 1982:IV, 82–85). The first Indonesian governor of the Lesser Sunda Islands summed up the Japanese occupation and revolutionary period in the eastern archipelago in the words: 'the political scene had been quiet' (Reksodihardjo 1960 [1957]:31). The brokers of Doko's generation had been unable to make a success of any of the top-down attempts to generate associational power in Kupang from afar, whether sponsored by the Japanese, the Dutch, or the Republic.

On 29 September 1949, the Resident solemnly handed over some of his powers to a Timorese council of rajas under Raja Koroh. In October and

[31] Pro-Dutch rajas in South Sulawesi later also protested against him ('Pengangkatan I H Doko Diperotes,' *Pelita Rakjat,* 27 January 1948; *Pelita Rakjat,* 28 January 1948; 'Protes dari Radja2 di Soelawesi Selatan,' *Pelita Rakjat,* 29 January 1949). But Doko never pushed the political envelope. In May 1948 he resigned from the nationalist organization Gabungan Perdjuangan Kemerdekaan Indonesia (GAPKI) because it rejected NIT's federalist standpoint (*Pelita Rakjat,* 25 May 1948).

November 1949 a Timorese parliament was chosen through local elections, and on 27 December, as elsewhere around the region, the Dutch flag was lowered in Kupang.

That Timor still did not belong to the Republic even after the flag had been raised was evident from the cool reactions to the Indonesian military operation soon afterwards that brought troops to the island. All the federal territories under Dutch control had units of the colonial but largely indigenous armed forces KNIL. A revolt against the Republic from among KNIL troops in Ambon early in 1950 threatened to spread to Kupang. The dispatch of troops is the most basic and instrumental form of power-at-a-distance, but as the Japanese had also found, Indonesia could achieve little with armed force alone. The Indonesian army approached Kupang cautiously. Doko's Information Department in Makassar facilitated a preliminary visit by two officers to size up the situation and address a sceptical public. Captain Andi Jusuf, one of the two, then travelled into the interior of Timor as far as the Portuguese Timor border. In May 1950 another military delegation, led by Captain C. Kodiowa, addressed a public meeting at Kupang's famous cinema (Netti and Itta 1997:96–9). When the first ships arrived on 25 May 1950, they pulled in at night. On board were shock troops from two battalions of the Siliwangi division in West Java, commanded respectively by Major Soekendro and Lt. Col. R.A. Kosasih (Farram 2004:285, Tari 1972:I, 32). The next day they held a public parade at Kupang's military base at Oeba, together with those KNIL troops, under Lt. Y.D. Faah, who were prepared to transfer to the republican armed forces APRIS (Netti and Itta 1997:99).[32] No violence erupted during this handover, but months of tension ensued with Kupang's local population. Allegations of misbehaviour by the Indonesian troops survived in Indonesian print even into the New Order (Doko 1981a:61). The newly recruited Timorese troops, a company under (by then) Captain Faah and under the overall command of Siliwangi officer R.A. Kosasih, were later that year deployed against their former KNIL comrades in Ambon, some of whom were also from Timor.[33] Among Faah's men was the future governor of East Nusa Tenggara, Lt El Tari (who had, however, been with the republican forces since the 1940s).[34]

[32] APRIS were the Armed Forces of the United States of Indonesia (Angkatan Perang Republik Indonesia Serikat).

[33] Interview Hendrikus Ataupah, Kupang, 11 June 2009; Buli et al 1977–78:133.

[34] APRIS troops spread out over the large neighbouring island of Flores at the same time. Something of the atmosphere surrounding this military occupation is found in the

Doko had gone on to become Education Minister within NIT in March 1950, but the federation's days were numbered. NIT dissolved itself into the United States of Indonesia on 17 August 1950, as had been Doko's desire. His remaining career was spent building up the education system in his part of the country. Yet most of Kupang's elite had never had a particular problem with Dutch colonialism. After the Japanese interlude, schools went back to teaching in Dutch, until the late 1950s. Leo Nisnoni, grandson of Raja Nicolaas Nisnoni, only forced himself to learn Indonesian at the age of 27, when he became a civil servant in 1963. He always spoke Dutch with his family.[35]

Liaison Brokers

In the first part of the period spanning decolonization, between the 1930s and the early 1950s, Kupang was a quiet little town that mainly serviced its agricultural hinterland in the eastern part of the archipelago. Far away from the nearest major city, Makassar, it was a typical Middle Indonesian small town. By contrast with the vigorous modern social movements in the heartlands that emerged from a dense network of substantial cities, politics in Kupang were confined to the factional fights among a handful of Java-educated civil servants. The resources these bureaucrats were able to deploy in order to develop power within the town were limited by an elitist lifestyle that set them apart from the great majority of the kampong poor, and by their professional obligations to government service. At the same time, the access they had to decision-making processes in the metropolis was equally limited by the insignificance of the constituency they could bring to the table.

Catholic mission journal *Ende-Post*. Just before they arrived, the editor warned his clerical readers not to imperil the mission by an ill-chosen word or a 'condescending attitude' (*dedaine houding*) towards the new authorities. A priest named Van Dijk failed to heed the warning. Coming on his horse upon a band of young Islamic men enthusiastically waving red-and-white flags, he shouted at them in his usual manner for blocking the road. The youths claimed to be 'soldiers'; this was an insult to the new nation. They man-handled the priest, threatened to kill him, and days later handed him over to a military officer in uniform, who released him. Even a year later the mission thought it necessary to repeat its warning against the use of colonial-sounding expressions to describe themselves such as 'native sister' (*inlandsche zuster*), 'New Guinea,' 'Batavia,' 'natives' (*inlanders*), or 'sir' (*tuan*) ('Aanpassing,' *Ende-Post* no. 27, March 1950, p. 3; 'P. v. Dijk schrijft over zijn molestering op 22 juni,' *Ende-Post* no. 30, July 1950 pp. 2–3; 'Pedanda Bali,' *Ende-Post* no. 36, March 1951, pp 1–2).

35 Interview with Leopold Nisnoni, Kupang, 27 May 2009.

Their resources were those of the 'liaison broker' (Gould and Fernandez 1989), who stands largely outside both the groups they are trying to connect, indeed whose prestige derives from the fact that the communication between them is limited to that which the broker conveys (see Chapter 1). This made them patrons to the tiny indigenous middle class in Kupang, a bringer of jobs, scholarships, and perhaps some protection for their upwardly mobile young people. For metropolitan interests needing to extract resources from the town and its surrounding hinterland (such as taxes, or at least an agreement not to revolt), they offered to translate demands downwards and explain problems upwards. As a side benefit, they earned substantial commissions.

Elitist politics like these seem to have been common in all the small towns of Middle Indonesia. They were those of a small, factionalized clique of liaison brokers. Middle classes were too tiny and culturally remote from the metropolis to make their own demands clear. All over Indonesia, national power came to the regions in mediated ways. Audrey Kahin once observed that the national leadership only provided the 'idea' of an independent Indonesia.[36] Actors on the ground everywhere created realities that were essentially local affairs (Kahin 1985:281). This was true in Kupang as well. But whereas Padang in West Sumatra, a town of around 80,000 with a strong political structure, managed for two years to prevent the Dutch from re-establishing control after World War II and developed a vibrant local democracy that also delivered many national leaders (Asnan 2007, Colombijn 1994:48), Kupang was at this time too small to do more than look on warily as distant powers sent garrison troops to ensure quiescence. Every central state in the twentieth century has relied on this small group of technical experts to manage the provinces. President Suharto's authoritarian New Order (1966–1998) was no different. His political party Golkar continues to do well in provincial Indonesia by dispensing patronage to locally influential bureaucrats, while doing its best to depoliticize the rest (which in the past often involved coercive threats). In the more democratic times that prevailed before and after the New Order, bureaucratic brokers were able to build up local resources that they could deploy against the centre to squeeze out concessions. This helps explain the emergence of more or less chauvinist localist movements in the towns at these times. Both Indonesia's ramshackle authoritarianism and its communalism have their origins in the spatiality of power.

---

[36] What that 'idea' was has been well described by Elson (2008).

As we shall see in subsequent chapters, there is more to Middle Indonesia than small town factionalism and the arrogance of technical elites. Over time, the flow of resources between the region and the metropolis via the town increased so as to reduce the role for 'gatekeeper' liaison brokers. Leftist movements from the metropolis in the early 1960s encouraged and protected emancipatory movements that built cross-class, urban-rural alliances. On the right, New Order economic development caused the town and its middle class to outgrow the need for brokers. Kupang's eastern Indonesia and Jakarta's central Indonesia have grown closer. The rising number of substantial towns in eastern Indonesia confirms this observation (see Table 1 in Chapter 1). A similar slow growth of national networks at the expense of local ones was recorded by, for example, Washbrook (1976) in his careful history of the emergence of provincial politics in Madras between 1870 and 1920. Within Indonesia, Mestika Zed (1991) observed a similar process in the history of Palembang, a town in southern Sumatra. Here we have confined ourselves to the beginnings of this story, which lay with that tiny number of well-dressed local brokers. These unheroic 'jacks of all trades' made their little towns legible to their confused and technically challenged metropolitan masters, and brought new ideas, money and jobs to their educated fellow townsfolk. But they left their own poor powerless.

CHAPTER SIX

AUTHORITY (1950S–1970S)

> Important officials always sat in the front seats at church. Some helped out as "elders," who arranged the Sunday service and circulated the black collection bag. Everyone wore the very best and newest clothes they owned. Officials who made gifts sometimes did it anonymously but more often by name. One of the elders read out the amount collected over the previous week, complete with names.
>
> (Lay 2014:164–5)

In the four and a half decades between 1930 and 1975 the population of Kupang grew ten times. A small, quiet colonial outpost in a feudal agrarian setting expanded into a bustling, bureaucratic, and above all Indonesian town, yet one that remained as determined as ever to set its stamp on what it tended to see as a benighted hinterland. The town grew primarily because the central state needed to exert its authority in a part of the country that Jakarta regarded as remote. But, as previous chapters have shown, power cannot be 'projected' seamlessly from one place to another far away. It must be generated locally, through face-to-face interaction, making use of the resources that are available.

This chapter begins with the spatiality of the resources made possible by the new state. It focuses on the new office buildings, churches, roads, and sports facilities springing up around the town and into the interior, and on the rituals that came to be associated with them. The money the central state invested in Kupang was insignificant on the national scale, but to the locals it was extravagant. People still today recall the construction of the new sports stadium in 1962/63 by Lt. Col. Paikun and the large Protestant GMIT church at Oeba around the same time. All that new concrete added functionality to the town. More importantly, it framed a new spatiality of power. The facilities were imbued with new rituals and manners that changed the lives of people already living in the town, and attracted many from beyond its boundaries. Roger Barker found that behavioural codes were, as it were, written into the walls of the store in Oskaloosa, the small Kansas village that he observed intensively in the early 1950s (Schoggen 1989). In the same way the large churches that were being refurbished or built anew in the 1950s became novel 'behavioural settings' for Kupang's youth and its elders alike, as the quote heading up this chapter illustrates. The new urban space, in other words, facilitated fresh modalities of power. These ranged from coercion and authority to the more attractive modalities of inducement and even seduction.

Having explored the construction of new urban spaces in the period to the early 1970s, the chapter then asks how middle class members of two urban institutions deployed those resources to build particular types of authority, in the town but especially in the countryside beyond it. It chooses two that were rather top-down, namely the military and the church. To be effective, Max Weber showed, power must be legitimate, and this involves building relations of trust. Authority differs from domination in that it has obtained the assent of those to whom it is directed. Even the most coercive of institutions could only develop power by deploying its resources in a network of relationships. The town was one of the most important places where such relationships could grow in the provinces.

Both the military and the church adopted bureaucratic organizational techniques to reach large populations. Both promoted new ideas of corporeal and social order that rose above loyalty to feudal lords. Both preached obedience to a higher authority – one a bit higher than the other. Both spoke at first mainly to an urban audience, but then also tried to reach an overwhelmingly rural population from their urban base. State administration expanded rapidly in the 1950s and particularly the 1960s, starting from a low base, and these two institutions lent authority to that expansion. Rather than focusing on the details of their organizations, this chapter looks at the way these institutions built associational power through face-to-face interaction.

Maps

The map Allied pilots had on their knees as they repeatedly dropped bombs on Kupang from 1943 onwards (Figure 16) shows a small town that could be crossed on foot in a quarter of an hour. All the buildings one expects in a colonial outpost of this size were there, on paper still pristine: Chinese shops and godowns along the shore, the large Chinese cemetery up the slope behind them, their community hall and, up the slope behind that, offices and the Resident's villa. Schools, the jail, two hospitals, churches and a mosque, and, out along the coastal road towards the northeast, the military barracks completed the picture. Native houses that occupied most of the town area were invisible on this map. Set among such tall trees that from the sea Kupang looked like a forest, these wooden houses filled the colonial interstices and spread into the countryside where the town's edges merged into the raja's domains.

One native who recalled the town's layout as it had been in the 1940s highlighted the indigenous features that were to him most authentic (Figure 22): just east of the Chinese shops, a teak plantation; on the hills to the south at Bakunase, a coconut plantation; in between, a recreational nature reserve, with large trees whose names were signposted in several languages, and concrete picnic benches set underneath them – in the wet season the town's aspect was green; and set among the greenery, three houses of rajas known as *sonaf*. The resident's house did not even deserve a mention on this map. The *sonaf* belonged to the Tabenu, Nisnoni and Funay families – aristocrats who upheld the social order. Kupang town was carved out of the much larger Kupang kingdom ruled by Raja Nisnoni. At one time grandiosely called an 'empire,' the Dutch put the Kupang kingdom together out of a series of smaller principalities. Each of these smaller entities retained its identity and was run by a *fetor*, a position inferior to the raja that was also hereditary. The heads of the Tabenu and Funay families were *fetor*.[1]

A map from 1973 illustrates the scale of the transformation (Figure 23). This is just the central portion of a 35-page street directory. Whereas in colonial times the streets had been named after natural features, places, fruits, or even social classes,[2] after 1949 they were named after political heroes. At first these tended to be local nationalist heroes such as I.H. Doko, later extended to Indonesian heroes such as Sukarno and Imam Bonjol. After 1966 several were renamed for military heroes such as Ahmad Yani. Thus successive central governments imposed their ideology upon the urban streetscape. Army and police facilities are now located in the heart of town, no longer simply on the margins. The number and type of government offices has proliferated. We see a livestock inspectorate, an immigration office, a government pawn shop, a provincial 'logistics depot' (Dolog, holding subsidized rice). Restaurants and apothecaries seem to be everywhere, and there is a second movie theatre, the Kupang Theatre.

---

[1] Kupang kingdom was instituted by the Dutch in 1919 to reduce the bother of dealing with the previously existing village-sized principalities of: Semau, Tabenu, Ambi, Funay, Little Sonbait and Amabi Oefetto (Farram 2004:115).

[2] Some examples: Pantjoeranstraat – Spring Street; Boomstraat – Tree Street; Zeestraat – Sea Street; Voorstraatbrug – Front Street Bridge; Kasteelstraatbrug – Castle Street Bridge; Heerenstraat – Gentlemen Street.

Most scars of the Allied bombing have been built over. A bus terminal occupies a bombed-out area near the harbour that was never rebuilt. Hundreds of minibuses swarm in and out of it each day – noise levels rise as once deserted streets become positively dangerous. The Chinese cemetery still appears on this map, but the dead in this piece of prime real estate are about to be evicted in favour of a state bank (Doko 1982:30–1). The rajas have disappeared from the map altogether.

The town has expanded south beyond its colonial municipal boundaries (see Footnote 3 in Chapter 4). A swathe of new government buildings arose in the 1970s on the rice fields and the jail food gardens at Oebobo, above the former Chinese cemetery. A new university, education department offices, governor's office, and a gigantic church had been built even further up the hill at Oepura, previously a peri-urban village. The aristocratic Funay family who claimed to own this land grew rich out of the transformation. The city got its first town plan (Samiarsa et al 1969). Public transport used to consist of a single wheezing and dusty bus. After a couple of false starts with government, and then police-owned public buses that ended in bankruptcy, Governor El Tari licensed Chinese entrepreneurs to run private services. Soon numerous Mitsubishi Colt minibuses plied the newly asphalted streets. Urban growth produced severe shortages of drinking water. The old spring at Oeba near the coast was busier than ever with bathers and men filling drums to sell to the Chinese, but the new suburb of Oepura had found its own spring in the hills. Where in the 1930s Tjiong Koen Siong's generator had lit up the town for a few hours in the evening on a government contract, since 1974 a state-owned electricity plant in the kampong west of town had been keeping lights burning all night. Other state-run enterprises stood as monuments to bad planning or worse. Both the sandalwood factories built by Governor El Tari on Raja Nisnoni's peri-urban lands in 1973 and 1974 were idle. Timor had almost no sandalwood trees left – a fact that was known when they were built. The meat canning factory built by Raja Nisnoni in 1952 had already closed in 1963 because, equally predictably, it could not compete with Balinese and foreign canned meat.

The map has blown out because the urban population has more than quintupled since 1945 (Figure 24) (some of this increase is due to incorporation of populations by expanding urban boundaries). Most of the increase came in the late 1960s, as New Order development money began to flow. In 1959 Kupang became capital of the new province of East Nusa Tenggara (the region had previously been run from Bali). Many observers have noted the crucial role of the state to Kupang's rapid growth (Rutz

1987:148, Samiarsa et al 1969), but we still do not have good insight into the demographics of the migrants who flooded into town. The bureaucracy is a mobile zone and recruited so many educated people from all over the province and indeed Indonesia that they no longer constituted a tiny elite in Kupang, as they had done in the 1930s, but a new class. But many poor people also came to town, to escape poverty and boredom in the village and to seek new opportunities in petty trade or unskilled labour. The removal of colonial travel restrictions was one factor in this growth. People must have been driven to move by the misery in the countryside, where hunger was normal and preventable malaria and respiratory ailments headed the list of reported diseases (36% and 23% respectively, Pemda NTT 1973:92). Class differences between this semi-literate 'urban proletariat… only a step away in terms of sophistication and skills and non-labour resources from the countryside in which most of them were not long ago born' (H. Geertz 1963:34) and the new middle class of Chinese traders and indigenous civil servants were growing.

Most provincial towns in Indonesia passed through many troubles in the immediate post-war years. Evidence of a 'soft' state was everywhere. This was true of towns in the heartlands affected by the revolution, but also of those in the periphery not directly affected by it. A survey of newspaper reports concerning eight towns throughout the 1950s shows

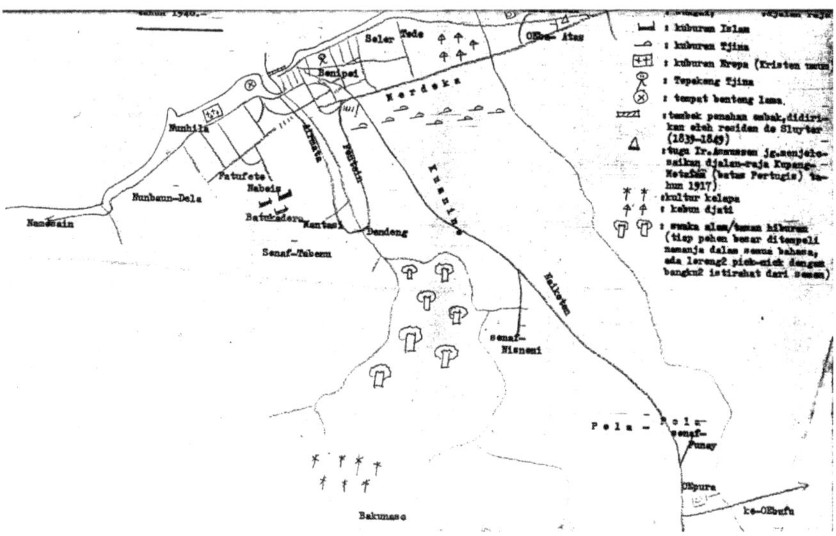

Figure 22. Kupang, 1946 (Parera 1969).

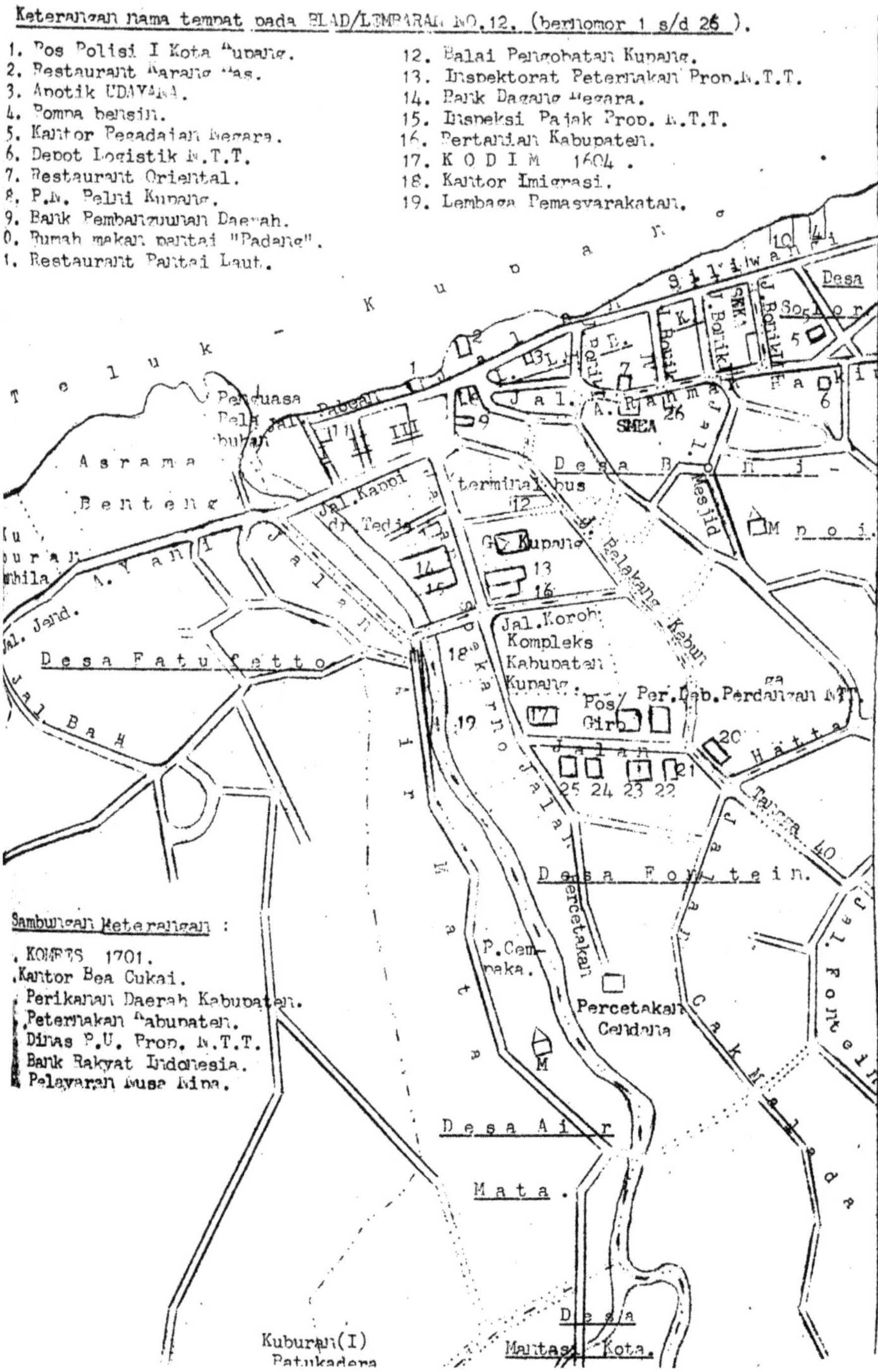

Figure 23. Kupang, 1973 (Sidik 1973).

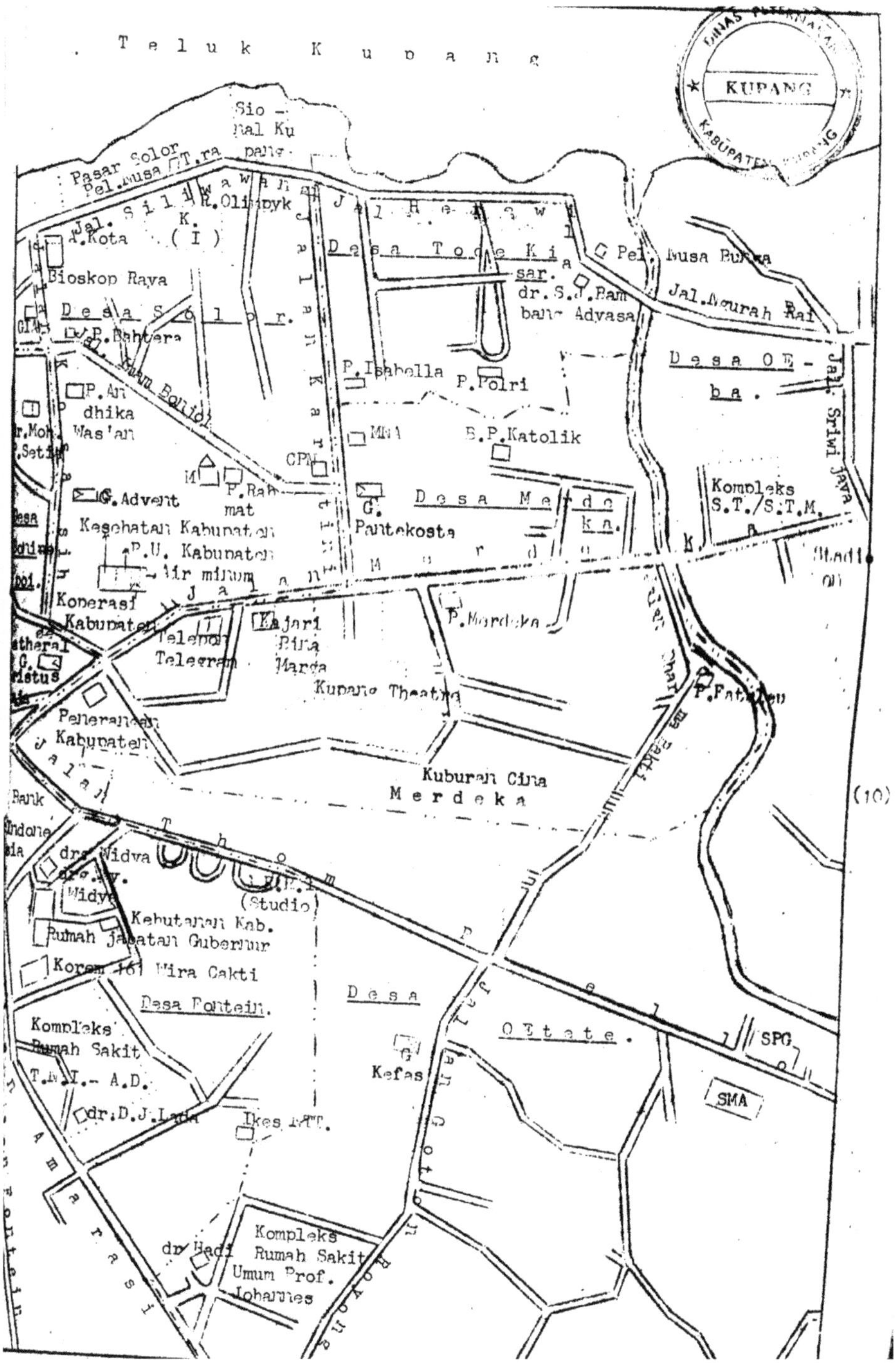
T e l u k   K u p a n g
KUPANG
Pasar Solor
Bioskop Raya
D e s a S o l o r.
P. Isabella
P. Polri
B.P. Katolik
Jal. Ngurah Rai
D e s a O E - b a .
Kompleks S.T./S.T.M.
D e s a M e r d e k a.
G. Advent
Kesehatan Kabupaten
G. Pantekosta
Koperasi Kabupaten
Kajari
Bina Marga
Kuburan Cina
M e r d e k a
Rumah Jabatan Gubernur
Korem 161 Wira Cakti
Desa Fontein.
D e s a O E t e t e .
Kompleks Rumah Sakit T.N.I. - A.D.
G. Kefas
SPG
SMA
Kompleks Rumah Sakit Umum Prof. Johannes

(10)

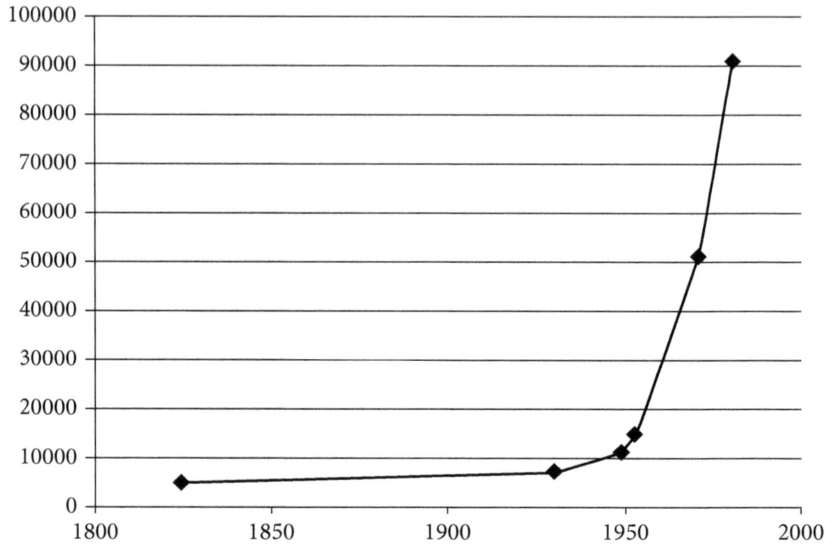

Figure 24. Kupang town population (data from Leirissa et al 1984).

that, contrary to the image of friendly torpitude that clings to them, all experienced severe disruption.[3] The number of trained civil servants was too low to do all that needed doing; the communications, transport and housing infrastructure to support them was broken. Local tax revenues and national subsidies were just enough to reconstruct the worst of the war damage, but not to house the influx of new civil servants, to repair the leaking school roofs, or to lay on piped water for the slum dwellers who were now also citizens with rights. Rampant smuggling exacerbated the budgetary problems by robbing the state of import tariffs and export duties. Young men in the heartlands who fought as irregular guerrillas in the revolutionary war against the Dutch threatened to join criminal bands unless they were given a job. Under the guise of 'national integration' many were sent to the outer islands as state-sponsored transmigrants or teachers, despite poor qualifications. For years after the Pacific War and the revolution had ended, violence remained close to the surface in these provincial towns. Criminality exploded repeatedly into local revolts, which invited military intervention in many towns. As in the days of the

[3] The following notes are drawn from a survey by my research assistant Basilius Triharyanto of news items concerning eight provincial towns in the national daily *Merdeka* throughout the 1950s. The towns were Ambon, Banjarmasin, Bengkulu, Kupang, Makassar, Malang, Palembang, and Pontianak.

Dutch pacification decades earlier, the town once more became a military base for forays into a countryside that the soldiers regarded as inhospitable, ignorant and impoverished. But this time the military were themselves wracked with factionalism and intrigue, making their interventions less effective than they might have been.

That national and local governments achieved anything at all in these chaotic circumstances was not due to the successful rolling out of machine-like centralized institutions, but to the local social forces that emerged in and through these new institutions. It is the socially embedded nature of these institutions that gave them their power, as the following sections will demonstrate.

Bureaucracy

How large was the bureaucracy that was to bring forth Kupang's new indigenous middle class? Figures for the size of the civil service in Kupang in this period are imprecise but when placed in a province-wide context they reveal an astonishing growth. Few could have predicted in 1950 that government employment would come to sustain a substantial proportion of Kupang's population. Timor was at first part of the province of Lesser Sunda Islands, which stretched from Bali to Timor. Modern government at this end of the archipelago was thin on the ground. The total number of Lesser Sunda Islands provincial government officials in the late colonial period was a mere 300, and this declined to 50 under the State of East Indonesia NIT immediately after the Pacific War. A good many of these were posted in the provincial capital in Singaraja, Bali. After the transfer of sovereignty in late 1949 Dutch officials were at first replaced by older Indonesians with experience but who were really ready to retire. By the end of 1953 the total provincial corps had gone up to 329, many of them young and without experience. Three years later it had crept up to 438. The governor had only asked for 400, and he was of the opinion that few had any real work to do (Reksodihardjo 1960 [1957]:I, 59–61). But in late 1958 Kupang became the capital of its own province called East Nusa Tenggara, much smaller than Nusa Tenggara. The provincial corps rose to about 1500, the biggest concentration of them based in Kupang. The governor alone had a staff of 260, each of the 12 districts had 65, and every government service had another 20–45 (Sumarto 1962:168–175, Tari 1972:I, 96).

The state indirectly sustained many more people than this, though clear figures are hard to find. The rajas each received money to pay their own staff (up to a couple of dozen – though these were about to be transferred to the local government payroll). Catholic and Protestant missions who ran virtually the entire education system in the Christian part of Lesser Sundas received state money to pay some of their teachers, particularly in the towns. Teachers became more visible in the civil service statistics as time went on, but statistics remained speculative. Until well into the New Order even the government did not know exactly how many people were on its payroll. One 1967 estimate had 33,112 civil servants in NTT, of whom just under half (15,819) were paid by the central state ('pegawai negeri,' including teachers), and the rest by provincial and district governments (17,293, 'pegawai otonoom'). NTT had 8,513 primary school teachers in 1967 – 1,172 in Kupang.[4] In addition there were 2,746 retired civil servants and military officers, some of whom had gone into business (Sidik et al 1968:51, 55).[5]

Even these higher numbers are by no means complete. Not listed were the hundreds of parliamentarians on good salaries at the provincial and district levels, and their staff; the thousands of village and subdistrict officials who received payments not amounting to salaries; the hundreds or thousands of private sector workers, such as construction workers, dependent on government building contracts. Thousands more worked for state-owned commercial entities, such as the post office, banks, the shipping line, two airlines, the pawn shop, the electricity company, the state oil company, construction companies, etc. (a list without numbers is in Chalik 1971:187–8). The biggest uncounted government labour pool was the military. The army, air force, navy and police all had headquarters and other bases in Kupang. Any reasonable estimate will run into thousands here as well. The army also maintained thousands of poorly paid auxiliaries, such as civil guards (*hansip*) posted in small towns all over the province.

---

[4] Ende, NTT's other major town, had 1,253; rural districts had 400–800 teachers each; almost all taught at religious schools.

[5] There are other estimates. Governor El Tari in 1969 reported a smaller number of civil servants in NTT: 24,082. Of these 12,132 were paid centrally through the province – most of them primary school teachers (9,010), and another large group (2,119) seconded to the districts. The districts employed another 7,062 (including 549 in Kupang) – this is much lower than the Sidik estimate and accounts for the difference. Then there were 4,193 casual workers, and about a thousand more in state-owned corporations and central government offices (direktorat) (Tari 1969:8).

Another estimate the next year put the number of centrally funded civil servants at 'about' 13,000. Five thousand of these had been recently employed, many in the education, justice, and religion departments, where they replaced sacked Sukarno loyalists. The great bulk of these civil servants were poorly educated people on a low salary scale. The better educated ones, particularly teachers, tended to be young. This report did not mention district-level civil servants (BPS 1970:9–15).

From these vague estimates, often lacking geographical specifics, it is difficult to hazard a guess at the proportion of Kupang's working population partly or wholly employed by the state. If half the town's population of 51,000 in 1971 was of working age, then it would be surprising to me if the number of those dependent mainly on the state for their income (many would have needed second jobs as well) was less than 5,000 or 20% of these.

By some counts, the number of bureaucrats had outstripped the number of private traders. In 1967 the provincial government knew of just 5,082 traders in all of NTT. Eighty percent of them were petty traders. Forty percent, even at the petty end, were Chinese (Sidik et al 1968:52). These numbers should probably be taken as an indication of the number of fairly established traders; the number of fishers and farmers who sold their own produce at market more casually must have been far larger than this. Kupang lay not only in the most feudal part of the province (see Chapter 4) but the most backward, in every economic sense, as well. Of the 36 registered companies (CV and NV) in the province of Lesser Sunda Islands in 1956, 30 were based in Bali, six in Lombok, while none was to be found further east. Of the 43 indigenous (non-Chinese) businesses that had received credit from a state bank only two were located in Timor. One was Raja Nisnoni's ICAFF meat canning factory (see Chapter 8). A list of industries that had received help with mechanization included not one in Timor. Bali had 38 small hotels in 1956 (the tourist boom was yet to come!), but that was luxury compared with Timor, which had just five, all in Kupang and all apparently Chinese-owned. A government survey of small industries, such as shoemaking, weaving or ice lollies, found 233 establishments in Bali, 147 in Lombok, 32 in Sumbawa, and only 25 in Timor. Only Flores and Sumba had fewer (Reksodihardjo 1957:II, 120–184). The region was simply left behind by the modern world. Agriculture and fisheries remained entirely unmechanized, and hesitant attempts to introduce motorized machinery failed repeatedly.[6] The road into Timor's interior remained an unsurfaced single lane until it was sealed after the military invaded neighbouring Portuguese Timor in late 1975. Its bridges, repaired since the Pacific War, were continually washed away again in the

[6] There was no motorized fishing in Lesser Sunda. A single venture with a motorboat called Majang I in 1952 failed (Reksodihardjo 1960 [1957]:I, 115). An attempt to reduce food shortages by introducing mechanical tillage on 2,500 hectares near Kefamenanu in West Timor – the Sekon project – failed as well (Ormeling 1956:218–20). There were just three tractors in all of Sumba in the mid-1950s (*Bentara*, 1 July 1954) (Sidik et al 1968: appendix).

monsoons; people mainly used the network of bridle tracks that covered the island.

Economic statistics reinforce the picture of government as easily the fastest growing sector in these years. In 1971 NTT was still overwhelmingly agrarian, making up 71% of provincial Regional Gross Domestic Product (RGDP). But in the four preceding years the government share of RGDP had doubled from 3.7% to 6.3% (Pemda NTT 1973: x-xii).[7] Although this still looked smaller than trade at 17.7%, much of the latter also came from the state through state-owned corporations. In any case, in the decade 1975–86 the government's share of RGDP nearly doubled from 10.1% to 19.5%, exceeding trade. The state sector was growing at the expense of agriculture, which had declined to 53.9% by 1986 (Barlow et al 1991:243). The bureaucratic town was rapidly displacing the agrarian countryside. As far as the indigenous population was concerned, Kupang had become the heart of an alternative economy, funded by the central state and run by an educated middle class.[8]

Feeding this growing number of town dwellers from a dry landscape was a major problem. The subsistence agriculture in the hinterland hardly produced enough to feed its peasant population, let alone cities full of civil servants. All of Nusa Tenggara in the 1960s was regarded as a malnutrition area, since the population relied to a large extent on the poorly nutritious cassava root; it was the only region so categorized outside Java (which also suffered malnutrition) (Napitupulu 1968). Peasants ate rice only on ceremonial occasions, but townsfolk ate it routinely. NTT produced small surpluses in maize and tubers, but for rice the shortfall had long been chronic, and this shortfall grew larger as the towns grew bigger. Almost all the rice, petrol and kerosine imported into NTT was for the use of civil servants and soldiers. Chinese traders have been keeping Kupang alive with their rice-importing skills since 1731 (Ormeling 1956:130). In 1953 Kupang was importing 150 tons of rice a month from Java (Kementerian Penerangan Sunda Ketjil 1953:226), but it was not enough. Kupang was essentially a rice-eating parasite weighing heavily on the delicate tissue of the rocky eastern archipelago's subsistence economy. On two occasions, in 1953 and 1955, Kupang's streets saw demonstrations demanding cheaper rice. Since there was no free market in rice, all rice distribution being

[7] This report uses constant prices. Another uses prevailing prices to reach slightly different figures for the same period: agriculture declines from 72% to 67%, government more than doubles from 2.5% to 5.8% (Tim Penyusun Repelita ke II NTT 1972:11–4).

[8] NTT exports did shoot up after 1966 – from approximately US$ 200,000 in the early 1960s to around US$ 2.3 million ten years later (Pemda NTT 1973:62).

organized by the government, these became politically laden events (see Chapter 7). In 1966, NTT's rice production was 57,000 tons, but the shortfall amounted to 123,000 tons. This led the author of the report that noted this disturbing statistic to suggest that NTT should look seriously at limiting the number of its civil servants (Sidik et al 1968:54).

These somewhat confusing figures broadly confirm a picture we have discussed earlier in the book (see Chapter 2), which is that of an urban employment market dominated by rising government investment and by trade, in sharp contrast with a surrounding subsistence agrarian economy in decline. By itself this occupational breakdown does not tell us much about social relations within the town, since both government service and trade cover a wide range of incomes. But when combined with political action it does become meaningful. The educated personalities who people this book make up a political class that, after independence, is almost entirely drawn from the upper levels of the bureaucracy. As late as 1973, education remained the privilege of a tiny few in NTT. Just 1.5% of both men and women had completed secondary school, and 0.2% had a tertiary qualification (Pemda NTT 1973:83). Comparable national figures about this time were 13.1% and 0.8% respectively – multiples of the NTT figures. By contrast, 61% of men and 80% of women in NTT aged ten or over had either never gone to school or not completed primary school, compared with 16% of men and 31.8% of women nationally (Kawuryan 1998:33, quoting 1976 Sakernas data). This tiny middle class with secondary schooling or higher, amounting to just 1.7% of the population, was concentrated mainly in the towns dotted around the agrarian landscape where it made up a larger proportion of the population. But it did not become a political force by acting alone. Its members were tied together with all civil servants through the manifold bureaucratic and political organizations that they led. All civil servants and their families, no matter how poorly paid, were rapidly turning themselves into a class apart from both the subsistence peasants and the traders by their regular salaries, and by their access to perks, such as cheap loans and employment for their relatives. They all shared an emerging common culture of religion and bodily discipline symbolized by the uniform. The top levels of the trade occupations, meanwhile, were almost entirely Chinese (with some ethnic Arabs), and they had no or only tenuous patrimonial links with indigenous petty traders. Thus we have the following ethnicized class division: a predominantly bureaucratic indigenous lower-middle and middle class with political clout, a commercial Chinese middle class with little (and diminishing) direct political clout, and an indigenous lower class predominantly involved in the agrarian sector and petty trade and for most of our period almost entirely without access to the state (Evers and Gerke 1994).

How did the bureaucratic lower-middle and middle classes act together to exert their influence in this provincial town? Subsequent chapters will examine the material advantages they had over others, which gave them resources of patronage and the power of sabotage. In this chapter we focus on the cultural influences that radiated from the prestigious buildings they occupied – government buildings, but also churches and military headquarters.

The Military

The military's task at this time was less to defend the country against foreign aggressors than to put down the armed Darul Islam rebellion mainly in West Java, and to extend central government authority to regions that had lived quietly under Dutch rule after World War II instead of participating in revolution. Their first challenge in those formerly Dutch-ruled regions was simply to get boots on the ground. We saw in Chapter 5 that they moved into the colonial military barracks on the eastern outskirts of the old town in 1950. Each major island in the Lesser Sundas now had a 'territorial' Military Area Officer (Perwira Daerah Militer, PDM) occupying former colonial barracks in the biggest town. Each had some garrison troops under his command. They lacked the resources to spread beyond the towns. Not till after General Suharto's New Order came to power in 1966 were troops stationed permanently in small towns and villages everywhere.

From the moment those boots stepped on land their wearers had to start communicating. Talking was their main resource. That is why the army appointed locals to territorial positions as much as possible. The 24-year old Lieutenant El Tari, who grew up in Kupang, got his first posting as PDM in Ende in 1950.[9] The main objective in 1950 was defensive and inward-looking. It was to stop the revolt of former Netherlands Indies troops in Ambon (the Republik Maluku Selatan, RMS) from spreading to the equally Christian islands towards the southwest. The outskirts of town were not a good place from which to launch a 'charm offensive,' but they did offer some protection against the anti-Javanese sentiments that

[9] *Bentara*, 28 June 1950.

caused considerable unrest in Kupang in the first year (Doko 1981a:61). The senior territorial officer in Kupang was Lt. Col. R.A. Kosasih, a Muslim from West Java who had first brought republican troops to Timor. When he did address Kupang's elite in May 1951 it was not at his barracks, but in what was still called Kampong Belanda. Rather than inspiring new legitimacy, his speech was one of puzzled incomprehension. He admonished his audience of local government leaders for allowing their people to live in houses 'like chicken coops,' to eat salted maize (instead of rice), and to sleep under trees (instead of in a bed). They were weakening their bodies with home-brewed liquor known as *sopi*. 'Don't you feel ashamed when outsiders see you?,' he thundered ineffectually. 'Rajas, please bury this outdated drinking habit, which only holds up progress!' He also berated the elite for being 'drunk with luxury' and warned them not merely to 'represent the wealthy few.'[10]

When other Javanese officers tried to take their urge to discipline the population beyond a speech they found themselves humiliated. Major Sukrendo, officer in charge of the Kupang garrison, ordered everyone in town and its surrounding kampongs, including schoolboys and -girls, to take part in a five-day war exercise, beginning at 5 a.m. on 15 November 1950. 'The enemy' had landed and occupied all the city's strategic points. The next day Sukrendo expressed disappointment that people had switched their lights and radios on before the end of curfew and were going about their business, not taking the exercise seriously. He sagely declared general success and abandoned the rest of the exercise.[11] We hear little more of the military after this until the eruption of the Permesta and PRRI revolts in Sumatra and Sulawesi in 1957 and 1958. As in Maluku in 1950, troops in the eastern archipelago, most of them locals in accordance with national policy, threatened to go along with the rebels. These rebels had more success than any before them by actually mobilizing the anti-Javanese sentiment their elders had feared (see Chapter 8). But it lasted only a moment. Martial law was declared all over the archipelago, rebellious officers were gradually side-lined, and officers loyal to Jakarta took over many of the functions of civilian administrators (Harvey 1977).

10 Speech by Komando Pasukan 'C' Territoriaal Timor, 21 May 1951: 'tidakkah saudara merasa malu djika dipandang dari luar daerah... mabuk kemewahan.... Djangan sampai terdjadi bahwa Wakil Rakjat hanja mewakili segolongan hartawan-hartawan.... Hapuskanlah minuman sopi jang berbahaja itu! Adat kuno jang usang jang menghambat kemadjuan rakjat kuburkanlah!' (Kana 1969:App. 15, 225).

11 *Bentara*, 1 December 1950.

Talking was still not their strong point, however. In the province of Nusa Tenggara (the name for the Lesser Sunda Islands since June 1954), culturally alien military officers once again tried to build power by inflicting humiliating disciplinary measures on their hapless populations. As soon as Captain Boediman, the Javanese PDM and martial law administrator in Ende in 1958–59, arrived he began to push through an energetic list of measures to bring order to the town. He removed hordes of goats running wild on the streets, organized neighbourhood work parties to clear drains while he drove around town in his jeep, forced youth into village security details known as OKD (organisasi keamanan desa), made everyone turn up to flag-raising ceremonies on the 17th of every month, restricted the sale of cigarettes, forced the Chinese to attach name plates to their front doors, closed down a nascent arts faculty for unclear reasons after its opening just two weeks earlier, and shut down two local Catholic newspapers. All this without consulting anyone else, civilian administrator Manteiro said with mock admiration in his farewell speech for the officer a few months later.[12]

The Church

More effective at developing face-to-face power was the church. Its membership expanded dramatically in this period, just as the Indonesian state was expanding into many new areas of life (Figure 26). If we take seriously an insight from Talal Asad (1993), these two phenomena are connected. According to Asad, the Islamic religious experience is authentic not when it reaches heights of private spirituality, as in a secular democracy, but only when it is communitarian and sanctioned in state ritual. In the same way the booming church membership in Timor should be seen as the cultural correlate of the simultaneous blooming of government. The church was populated by civil servants, and the civil service by church members. The white shirts and shoes that they wore to church were only affordable to those on a salary – this simple fact overshadows all intricacies of text, cognition, or meaning. Church membership was voluntary, yet when people joined the church, political power was being generated. This will become obvious in subsequent chapters when we come to consider the 1955 election, the 1959 formation of the province of East Nusa Tenggara, and particularly the dreadful anti-communist denouement of 1965/66. Church growth is a good example of the 'soft' modalities of seduction and

12 'Masa Kerdja Kapten Boediman,' *Bentara*, 15 July 1959.

inducement. To examine the link between church and state power in Timor we first look briefly at the institutional history of the church, then at the elaboration of a new hierarchy of prestige elaborated in its buildings, and finally at the lifestyles and norms the church promoted.

The church in Kupang has always been a 'civil servants church,' wrote the Australian missionary Gordon Dicker, who worked there from 1955 to 1962 (1959:52). The ecclesiastical rapprochement with bureaucracy went back a century and a half (Fox 1980). The autocratic King William I ordered all Protestants in the Indies to gather in one church, the Indies Church (Indische Kerk), which fell under the Department of Trade and Colonies. Later it seemed more practical to place it under the Department of Education, Worship and Industry. All ministers were paid out of the state treasury. Their sense of mission in Kupang was largely confined to the small number of (Indo-)Europeans who worshipped in the stately building that still stands in the heart of town. But this did not prevent some native elites from realizing very early that religion was important to good relations with the foreigners. Rotenese rajas converted to Christianity early in the eighteenth century with practically no outside help. Batavia was impressed, and the Rotenese shrewdly turned this warmth of feeling to their advantage by requesting free schooling. This prescient long-term strategy led to the Rotenese being the most educated indigenes in this part of the archipelago, and they continue to dominate the local bureaucracy to the present day.

From the early nineteenth century onwards, quite outside the Indische Kerk, zealous Protestant missionaries began to evangelize indigenous societies in this part of the archipelago. But even in 1900 only a sixth of the most intensely evangelized island of Rote was Christian. Religion was an elite affair. Language was one obstacle: ordinary Rotenese did not speak Malay, which was the language of the state *and* of the church (Fox 1977). In Timor proper, serious work outside Kupang only began with the arrival of the Dutch missionary Piet Middelkoop and his wife Jet in 1922 (Jong 2006). They settled at Kapan, the military base in the newly pacified Amanuban kingdom in South Central Timor. He pioneered the study of the local Dawan language, and spent years translating the Christian gospels into it. They later moved a short distance to Soë, which subsequently became the symbolic heart of the church in Timor. The Middelkoops's motivations were purely spiritual, but the conservative Resident in Kupang at the time, A.J.L Couvreur, attached strategic importance to the mission, which would create wedges of loyalty to the Dutch in regions otherwise threatened by Islam (Kwantes 1975–82:II, 115). State funding for ministers and teachers at mission schools was the practical side of this strategy. When Indonesia became independent, the church in Timor was caught unprepared. Whereas other ethnic Protestant churches around the archipelago had been arranging their independence from the colonial Netherlands Indies Church since the 1930s, in Timor this did not happen until 1947. It renamed itself the Timor Evangelical Church (Gereja Masehi Injil Timor, GMIT).

Neither missionary exertions nor official strategizing produced mass conversions before the Second World War. Not even in Rote, where an elite had long been Christianized, did ordinary people begin to enter the church until the 1950s (Figure 26). When they did, it was as part of a transformational movement that was much larger than the church. Unexpectedly, urban young people began flooding into GMIT during the 1950s. They saw it as their way of becoming Indonesian, of expressing the optimism that shone in the eyes of everyone associated with the new state. The state that promised emancipation and prosperity was embodied for them in their own brightly coloured skirts and new shirts. Australian ex-missionary Colville Crowe showed me two photos taken outside the still-bombed out church in Soë in about 1961. One was taken after the Dawan-language service, still run the way the Reverend Middelkoop had written it. A few illiterate peasants dressed in sarongs stood around, the shame of backwardness evident in their body postures. The other was taken just after the Indonesian-language service. A crowd of confident, educated young people in floral dresses or white shirts and trousers were happily streaming onto the street. Gordon Dicker (1959:52) made a special note of the fascination for politics among these young worshippers.

Key to their postures was the glad adoption of new bodily rituals. The clothes they wore to church were in fact the same ones they wore to the office (Figure 25). Indeed the church required all male worshippers to wear a uniform of white shirt and dark trousers to church festivals, such as Easter and Ascension Day (Dicker 1959:52). There was little singing: attending to the sermon was the central ritual element. Like the speeches at political rallies, these were long, formulaic, and delivered in Indonesian. An indispensable skill was to be able to recite long passages out of the large Indonesian Bible one carried to the new concrete building on Sunday mornings. Rote memorization was required for the baptism and confirmation rituals that opened the door to church membership, even for barely literate people. It was the only book most of them read (Lay 2014:167). During the apocalyptic days of famine and military purges at the end of 1965, the recitation of long bible passages from memory was a marked feature of the frenzied evangelistic meetings (Brookes 1977:29) (see also Chapter 9). But even in normal times, the Christian practice of praying before meals became a class marker noticed by the poor (see Box 'How the big people eat' below). These cultural markers of belonging had little ethical content. Dicker observed despairingly that the well-thumbed Bibles and full Sunday services failed to make everyday Christian behaviour any different from heathen (Dicker 1959:64).

GMIT became the normative institution *par excellence* in Timor. Its rapid growth in the 1950s produced an equally rapid shift in the Timorese status system. Values that had once been exclusively urban spread to the countryside. Where once the rajas clothed in traditional *ikat* sarong had defined status simply by who they were, now ministers and evangelists, the town-educated children of *fetor* or even of peasants, told people status could be achieved through learning. They created new values by exhorting their flocks from pulpits each week in modern Indonesian while wearing conservative western black trousers. Displacing the rajas was an important part of the church's seductive appeal in Timor. Some reverends provoked spectacular clashes with the local ruler. Camplong was one of the strongholds of the mission not far from Soë in South Central Timor. In the run-up to the national election campaign of 1955 W.H.M. (Hans) Nisnoni, the raja of Fatuleo and younger brother to Kupang's Alfons Nisnoni, supported a secular party. But the reverend urged his flock to vote for the Protestant party Parkindo. Realizing the church was fast becoming an alternative arena of power, Nisnoni even went as far as forming his own breakaway church. But the reverend got the numbers for Parkindo, and the breakaway church collapsed.[13] In Central Rote the reverends continually criticized the aristocracy for 'wasteful' funeral ceremonies and polygamy (Cooley 1976:349). Whenever indigenous church ministers served in an area not their own, they tended to be harsh on local customs, whereas ministers who served in their own cultural area were regarded as paternal figures (Brookes 1977:79).

Hans Nisnoni's ageing father Nicolaas had worked out even before the 1950s that the status of aristocrats was declining in favour of that of church ministers. He became a patron of the church during World War II. His considerable wealth was later said to have been 'central' to church financing during the Japanese occupation. He became an interlocutor for many local affairs of state to the Japanese masters and, with the missionaries in detention, these also came to include the church (Noach 1972:15). Three of

13 Dicker 1959:49. District-level election results are available in Alfian (1971).

the four top church leaders, known as moderators, in the period 1951–1975 were from feudal families. Other aristocrats saw the light only later. Koesa Nope, the Raja of Amanuban who became district chief of South Central Timor in 1961 and who was famous for his polygamy, affluence and autocracy, decided only after the turning point of 1 October 1965 to throw in his lot with the church. He is said to have joined the evangelistic teams whose miraculous healings were putting Satan on the defensive out in the villages. He bade farewell to the secular PNI-affiliated political party that he had supported hitherto, and embraced Parkindo together with about 150,000 of his subjects. Later he would become an equally fervent Golkar supporter.[14]

How the Big People Eat

Born into a poor family in Sabu, Cornelis Lay's father came to Kupang as a young man and eventually became an itinerant petty trader known as a papalele. *His mother saved enough from her stall at the market to send one son to senior high school. It was there, in the mid-1970s, that he first went into the homes of children whose parents worked for the state. One of these was Ge, from an Indo-European family whose father had been a Dutch military officer.* (GvK).

Both Ge's parents knew me well, and my parents knew very well that Ge belonged to the "big people" (*anak orang besar*) who were prepared to be friends with "little people" (*orang kecil*). These terms were very common social classifiers. "Big people" was a general category for all bureaucrats (*pejabat*). I suspect it reflects the Sabunese custom of addressing officials as "Mone Ae" –"big person." The term "boss" was also used, or even repeated for emphasis as "boss boss." We often said "he's a boss boss kid" (*itu bos bos pung ana*), sometimes adding the word "big" so it became "big boss." It was used for officials and for anyone with money, including big Chinese traders. In the market, traders with strong capital were called "big papalele" (*papalele besar*). The term "businessman" (*pengusaha*) was hardly ever used. "Rich person" (*orang kaya*) was only used when gossiping about a friend or neighbour who "didn't want to mix." Occasionally the phrase was "now he's really become someone" (*su jadi orang na*), indicating social mobility for the whole family of someone who had become a civil servant. Lower class people were generally called "people with woes" (*orang susah*) or "little people" (*orang kecil*). This was the general term for the lower classes, among families like our own and those of officials or businesspeople alike. Ge was called a "big people's kid" because his

[14] Koch 1971 (available online http://www.webrevival.net/en/books/rev_indonesia2.html, accessed 12 July 2012).

father, a full-blood Dutchman, was a police lieutenant colonel, a former Dutch policeman who had decided to become an Indonesian citizen. As I recall he was one of the most senior policemen in Kupang, besides the Ully family.

Going in and out of the houses of friends whose parents were mainly officials like this gave me an opportunity to see how the "big people" lived. There was little noticeable difference, except that my friends did not have to do any chores. They had a servant to do everything for them – cook, clean, wash dishes and clothes, and even make drinks. This was so different to the world I lived in every day, where we had to do everything ourselves. I also saw that their daily needs were never something to be discussed, unlike the houses of most lower class people that were kept busy every day with the problem of "eating." Children and parents always talked about the rice or the salt being finished. Parents in wealthy families routinely discussed "appetite" instead: "what do you feel like eating?" (*bosong mau makan apa?*). Whereas in most of our homes the commonest expression was "Hey go and borrow some rice from neighbour so-and-so" (*we lu pi pinjam beras do di ...*).

I also noticed their lives were much neater and more hygienic. The water they drank had to be boiled first. They washed their hands before eating, and some even started the meal with prayer. That was something we never did at home, except at Christmas and New Year (*kunci taon*). Their lives were so organized that they had a fixed time for their meals; and the same for drinks. Whereas in our world eating time was set by how hungry the stomach was, and you might say drinking time had no place in our agenda at all. Whenever they ate they sat down at the table, at a plate with a spoon and fork neatly laid on either side. Every type of food had its own dish and even spoon. We never had such order in our home. We usually just took our food straight out of the rice pot or out of the frying pan (*tacu*) whenever we felt hungry. We sat anywhere as we ate. There was no dining table, no dining room. In short, the main difference between our world and that of the"big people" was that for them eating was a cultural event, whereas for us it was simply a matter of survival, of filling the stomach.

(*Lay 2014:167–8*).

The seductive attraction of participating in rituals of modernity was one of the church's modalities of power. Inducement was another, as the church served increasingly as an informal patronage channel for the benefits of the state. The conversions of the 1950s made the church large enough to be an independent force, but it by no means took its distance from the local state. The ecclesiastical structure mirrored that of the modern state. Each time the state redefined the boundaries of its districts (*kabupaten* in 1956, and *kecamatan* in 1961), the church adapted the boundaries of its own districts known as *classis* (Cooley 1976:343–9).

Finances were one obvious reason for this postcolonial proximity to the state. Even those among the 90% of Timorese subsisting in small villages who felt inclined to donate to the church were unable to produce a surplus. In 1947 the Dutch mission gave the young GMIT a sizeable 'liquidation fund,' and said goodbye. When this money ran out in 1955, the problem of maintaining educated ministers in the style to which their class entitled them became pressing – there were 94 by 1971. Freedom from state control was fine in theory, but a vow of poverty was not really an option and the state was the only source of cash. The first Indonesian governor of Lesser Sunda set aside his secularizing instincts and agreed to continue financing the Protestant and Catholic schools in the province. GMIT set up an Economic Foundation (Yayasan Perekonomian) to try to channel more state money its way. It signed a joint development project with the Agriculture Department in 1957, for example, as part of the new five year plan adopted by the government. However, the arrangement apparently helped prominent individuals more than the church as an institution. The foundation joined a long list of project failures caused by mismanagement and corruption (Noach 1972:21, 26). Corrupt practices were as common within the church as they were within government. For example, the Americans had donated a truck in the mid-1950s to help the Kupang church cope with reduced foreign funding, but instead of being used to help transport church members it was rented out commercially (Dicker 1959:80–2).

A more fundamental reason for the rapprochement was that bureaucrats and ministers came from the same urban social milieu. Working together seemed only logical (Brookes 1977:78–9). In Alor, a rugged island off Timor's north coast, one old reverend had by the mid-1970s been 20 years a member of the local assembly and seven years on the district governing council (Badan Pekerja Harian, to assist the district chief). Conversely NTT's governor after 1965, the non-aristocratic Maj.-Gen. El Tari, let it be widely known that he was a faithful member of the church. 'Thus was forged the bond between religion, politics and government in NTT,' wrote the church historian Frank Cooley (1976:348). Together they shaped the new provincial establishment of which Maryanov (1959:63) had written: 'The definition of problems takes place within this group, and it sets the climate of opinion in which problems are discussed and solved.' This also meant that the church remained culturally confined to the new middle class. It did not attempt to deal even caritatively with social problems that afflicted the poor, which Dicker listed as drunkenness, gambling, sexual promiscuity, the neglect of widows and orphans, and, among the rural majority, seasonal 'normal hunger' (*lapar biasa*) (Dicker 1959:71).

Disconnected

The resources the new middle class of bureaucrats deployed to expand its authority could only be effective if they had local purchase. Geography was the most basic resource. The major institutions had their key offices in town. The new buildings may have looked like ramshackle blocks of concrete to cosmopolitan visitors, but Timor had never seen such edifices before. Of course buildings alone were not enough. The seductive new rituals associated with them – particularly those of the church – created social capital among the equally new bureaucratic middle class, and among those aspiring to become like them. Networks of church affiliation energized local policy networks, helping them overcome parochial defensiveness and building links between town and countryside. They underpinned a self-conscious cultural establishment that was more open and thus less elitist than the little pre-war clique of educated indigenous clerks and teachers had been. Central state power could expand in this period only because state power became geographically *and* socially embedded within Middle Indonesia. Social networks, both existing and new, were the key resource, since information could only pass from one person to another if they were already connected.

All this also helps to explain why the military, despite their far superior national resources, were so much less successful at rising to this local hegemonic challenge than the church. Their uninviting barracks on the outskirts of town, their culturally alien repertoire of public action – heavy on humiliation and light on respect – and simply their absence beyond the town boundaries, made it an uphill task for them.

The main problem with the outreach efforts by both the military and the church, however, was that it did not connect with the problems the poor majority in and around Kupang were experiencing. Building alliances across the class divides that increasingly separated the secure from the insecure and the town from the countryside required more than middle class rituals of belonging. In the next chapter we see that the same spaces could also function in more seductive ways to generate liberating forms of political power.

Figure 25. Oeba church, Kupang, mid-1950s (source: Dra. Ruth Heny A. Nitbani-Markus).

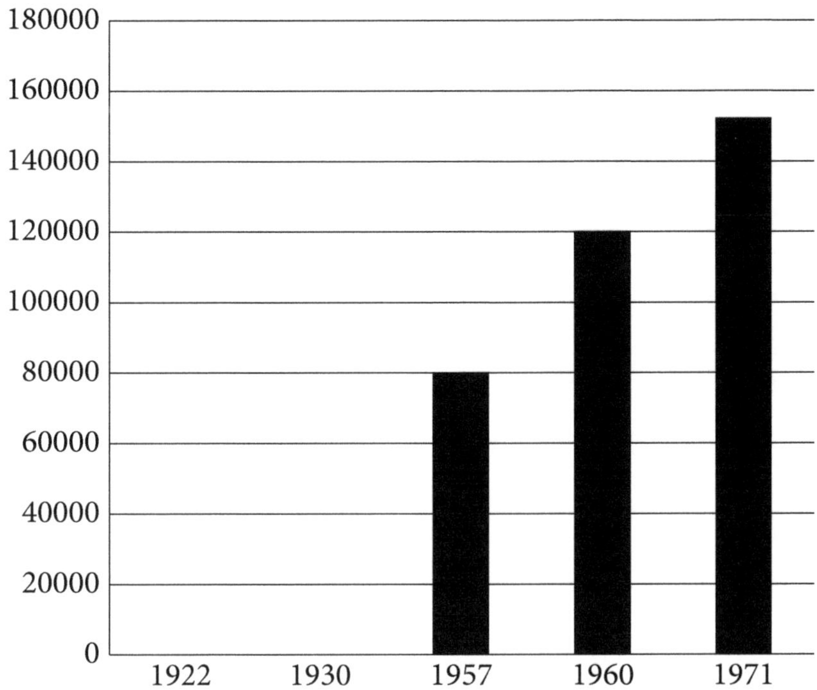

Figure 26. GMIT membership (source: Brookes 1990:265).[15]

[15] GMIT itself claimed much higher membership figures than this in the early 1950s. Where Brookes records only 80,000 in 1957, GMIT claimed 310,000 in 1953 (Anonymous 1956:19). The latter adds a regional breakdown, showing the biggest concentration in Alor (91,000), followed by Soë (69,000); out of a population of 120,000 in the wider district of Kupang, 41% were said to be 'without religion.' Presumably the difference arises from loose versus strict notions of membership – ranging from inflated claims of evangelistic success, through nominal adherence, to being listed on the communion roll (with attendant financial obligations). The caution shown by Brookes (who was an Australian missionary in Kupang in the 1970s) seems advisable here.

CHAPTER SEVEN

THE SEDUCTRESS (1955–1965)

> This new anti-feudal law offers a special leap, a leap up for one group, a leap down for another.
>
> (Timor assembly chairperson E.R. Herewila, speaking at the opening of the new session, held on the front veranda of the Kupang government offices, 5 August 1950 - Kana 1969:218)

The mere symbolic act of raising a flag in an elite Jakarta suburb on 17 August 1945 had meant nothing to most people in Kupang, let alone in its hinterland. Yet today the event is ritually re-enacted in Kupang's schools and offices with the same militaristic precision as it is everywhere in Indonesia. The ritual is bureaucratically enforced from the centre, yet at some point the republican ideals that inspired the flag also came to have meaning in Kupang. How did this happen? Meaning arises in interpersonal relations; it requires proximity. Visualizing national power as an essence or a flow does not explain how a set of meanings in one socio-spatial setting can be actualized thousands of kilometres away. The present chapter investigates the process by which emancipatory republican meanings in revolutionary Java – where they in turn formed part of a much older global history of communication – travelled across time and distance. Years after 17 August 1945, Timorese subsistence farmers put them to work, transformed yet recognisably republican, as resources in their own mini French revolution in the hills behind Kupang. In Java republicanism implied many things, from cultural 'anti-feudalism' to anti-colonial agitation and (for many) some kind of state socialism. But in Timor it mainly came to signify an end to real feudal privileges in the countryside.

A highly mobilizational Japanese military regime in Java had created intense social dislocation there. In the power vacuum that followed the surrender, a chaos of local revolutionary movements sprang up. By contrast, Timor had been spared the worst excesses of war despite the bombing of the towns, and afterwards it was brought quickly back under colonial control. Where Java was being united under a new revolutionary regime, Timor after the Pacific War integrated with the rest of this part of the archipelago on the basis of a developed form of the pre-war neo-traditionalism.

The Dutch under Lieutenant Governor General van Mook were working towards a federal construction in the area that they controlled, which covered most of the former Netherlands Indies including Timor. The construct was by 1948 being negotiated through the Federal Consultative Assembly (Bijeenkomst voor Federaal Overleg, BFO). BFO territories were constituted by layer upon layer of semi-autonomous entities, each practising a conservative politics of the soil. At the most local level were the little kingdoms led by 'traditional' rulers that, to most people living in them, represented the natural units of political community.

When the Dutch colonial project finally collapsed and Republican troops landed in Timor in 1950, they were hardly received enthusiastically (Chapter 5). Yet in the years that followed, republican mobilization was seen all over Indonesia, even in places that had experienced no national revolution in the late 1940s. Associational power of the kind that Hannah Arendt recognized as true power began to taken on new forms also in Timor. Among the newly literate young bureaucrats and teachers in town, the invitation from the church to participate in its Sunday spectacles of word, hymn and sacrament excited tremendous energy (Chapter 6). Among the poor, however, much more explicitly political ideas now proved their seductive power, even in rural areas far from the main arenas of nationalist agitation. This chapter considers the role Kupang played in mediating that seductive power. At first, anarchic peasant revolts took place in the surprisingly polarized and weakly policed rural islands of the Lesser Sunda Islands. In this respect the periphery did share some of the political instability of the heartlands, except that in the periphery it did not escalate into a revolution (Kahin 1985). Later, some political parties led by educated townspeople mobilized similar sentiments in a more orderly, and more effective, fashion, starting with the 1955 national elections.

Insurrection

During the two decades that followed 17 August 1945, the myths of the revolution, of freedom, prosperity, education and progress, penetrated places far from Java at a rate out of proportion to any organized propaganda. Sometimes it took just a single individual who had seen the new republican state with their own eyes to trigger a 'me too' uprising. In February 1955 a demobilized soldier named Arsad (or Arsyad) returned to the sleepy little town of Kalabahi, district capital of Alor Island, next to Timor. He had been away a long time as sergeant in the Indonesian armed forces TNI. What he saw incensed him: 'Alor is still the same Alor I left

30 years before.' The youths he gathered around him tied red cloth around their waists for magical invulnerability, and then attacked the local police barracks, radio station, government buildings and shops with knives and arrows. Two days later security assistance arrived by slow boat from Kupang, and Arsad, who had promoted himself to captain, surrendered unconditionally with 125 of his followers. While the rebels' exact motivation remains a puzzle, the quoted explanation at least suggests the myth of progress had struck root even among these young people in Kalabahi.[1] And it suggests that when myths of modernity detonate in a poor, unequal rural and small-town society whose institutions are moreover in flux, they can produce severe governability problems.

We have already seen (Chapter 4) that rural dissatisfaction with some of the more regressive rajas grew in step with the awareness that higher authorities were no longer prepared to back the rajas to the hilt. But rural protests were unlikely to be effective without urban partners. The peri-urban tax revolts inspired by the intellectual Chris Pandie in the mid-1920s collapsed once Pandie was arrested, and no one took his place. After the war another such outbreak of protest, this time more rural, occurred in Adonara, an island off the eastern tip of Flores marked for its poverty-driven out-migration.[2] Some of Pandie's followers had started a group in Lamahala, on the south coast of Adonara, in 1927. Although it too was quickly suppressed, its memory survived the war (Farram 2004:131). Like Chris Pandie, Buang Duran, once a Catholic school teacher, had been politicized by meetings with a PKI activist in Java. He had travelled to Java to trade during the Japanese occupation and met him in Semarang. Upon his return to his home village on the east coast of Adonara, soon after the Japanese capitulation, he started a revolt against the Dutch colonial administration over taxes (Barnes 2003). The Dutch arrested him twice, the second time sentencing him to four years labour. But the association he had named Indonesian Farmers Union (Persatuan Kaum Tani Indonesia, PKTI) grew even while he was in jail, spreading also to the PKI villages on the south coast. Upon the transfer of sovereignty to Indonesia in 1949 he was released and subsequently had good relations with the local military commander. His ideology was an eclectic mix of Marxism, nationalism, and messianism, like many other 'home-grown' communist movements around Indonesia in the late 1940s (e.g. Lucas 1991). Everyone should be equal – rajas were no exception, everyone should work for the

---

1 *Bentara*, 15 March 1955, 15 April 1955; Farram 2004:75, 296.

2 Reports on Adonara poverty and inequality, and out-migration, are in *Bentara*, 1 July 1957, 1 October 1948.

government and would become wealthy, and a ship would bring the first instalments soon. But they also propagated hygiene and practised deliberate cleanliness. They built bridges and roads (Reksodihardjo 1957:II, 205–7, 1960 [1957]:35).

However, things soon turned nasty. Allied movements led by Buang Duran's relatives began to question his anti-clericalism, and then turned into rivals. In January 1951 clashes between these groups drew the attention of the police and military. This had the effect of uniting the factions against the government in October that year. Several people died in the ensuing fracas, and thousands were detained by the nervous and poorly equipped new government. More died during an attempted jail break in nearby Larantuka, on the eastern extremity of Flores Island. It was led by Buang Duran's lieutenant. In March 1954 Duran was convicted of sedition and sentenced to 18 years jail in Madura (off Java). He continued to correspond by letter with his followers, some of whom were drawn to the PKI (Reksodihardjo 1960 [1957]:35). In late 1965 he was released from prison and returned to Adonara a broken man, only to be caught up in the military anti-communist pogrom that followed the events of 1 October in Jakarta. Although he himself had never been a PKI member, the military had him murdered in Larantuka in March 1966. In Buang Duran's home village in Adonara, surviving followers still proudly called themselves 'communist' in 2000, and showed a visitor the CCP-like uniform of blue trousers and shirt and red scarf that they wore (Barnes 2003:1). Buang Duran's movement has entirely disappeared from today's local historical textbooks.

Clearly, these sporadic insurrectionary movements lacking allies were easily suppressed, even by the poorly resourced state apparatus in the eastern archipelago. But the rapid and complex processes of state formation that swirled through the archipelago and through Kupang in the years after independence created many new opportunities to build more resilient movements through alliances between the rural poor and the emerging urban middle class.

Political Parties

Parties were central to the new democracy, but it took years for them to penetrate from their elite bases in town to the broader rural society. The Dutch did not try hard to introduce democracy over the heads of the rajas during the few years they were back in charge after World War II (Netti and Itta 1997). They did persuade the rajas to accept governing councils (Dewan Pemerintahan Daerah, DPD) to rule alongside them, but in practice the rajas themselves appointed their own DPD, so little changed. At the island level, that is the residency, one level above the rajas, executive power was held by an island head (kepala daerah), also assisted by a DPD, and legislative power was held by a regional parliament (Dewan Perwakilan Rakyat Daerah, DPRD). These two institutions survived the transition to independence and were constantly sniping at each other in the early years, even though their personnel swapped frequently and the separation of powers was fuzzy, to say the least. When the DPRD Timor was first constituted in October 1946, the rajas considered it a mere formality, and they simply appointed its members themselves. But the new DPRD Timor in October-November 1949 was elected. Candidates did not represent a political party but a district or (for the Dutch and Chinese not bound to the soil) an ethnicity. Michael Marcus, for example (see Chapter 3), was chosen to represent Amanuban, and Herewila Sabu island.

Political parties only became interesting to local elites once the talk of national elections began to firm up in 1954. After those elections they continued to grow in importance for a decade. The elections failed to create a stable national government. Indonesia drifted into increasingly authoritarian politics in which, strangely enough, party mobilization grew more and more urgent (Lev 1966). Mobilization for the 1955 election campaign in Timor was far less intense than that which swept Java (Feith 1957), but it did pass along the most vital social connections then linking town and countryside. Occupying the central points in these networks were two rivalling elites, the declining rajas and the rising bureaucrats. The rajas had been central to the Dutch practice of 'betting on the strong.' In 1955 they simply commanded their subjects to vote their way. Church leaders continued the colonial policy of co-opting rajas. Flores turned out a near-unanimous Catholic Party vote in this way in 1955. The Protestant church in Timor was a little less wedded to the rajas. Some rajas went with the Protestant party Parkindo, while others struck out on their own with various home-grown secular parties loosely affiliated with the highly factionalized national PNI, tied to the bureaucracy. The modern administrators and teachers in town, meanwhile, mainly joined Parkindo, which was fast becoming the new establishment. The fascination with religion was nearly universal outside Java.[3]

---

[3] Religious and localist or ethnic parties dominated outside Java. They achieved over 50% of the vote everywhere there except in some plantation areas such as Deli Serdang.

Parties in Timor lacked even the basics of institutionalization in 1955 – branch organizations were not established until the early 1960s. They were an arena for local prominents to test their popularity. They offered educated young people a chance to show the rajas it was time to move over. Young civil servants, church ministers and teachers – idealistic and ambitious for a bigger role – formed left wings within both Parkindo and PNI. Membership of national parties like PNI gave them access to networks stretching to Jakarta that largely bypassed the Protestant and aristocratic local establishments in town and countryside. Sukarnoist ideals inspired people in the lower levels of the church and its associated network of schools, and in parts of the state including the military, the public prosecutor's office, and the state schools. The PNI and later the PKI gave them organizing resources to reach out to the masses. Of course, their reaching out to the countryside had paternalistic elements. In turn, peasants saw in these initiatives an opportunity to steal a march on their petty local oppressors, to organize in their own way, and to discover new patrons in town. The first cross-class alliances were born out of the republican anti-feudal campaign of the early 1950s. The communist campaign for peasant and land rights built on these a decade later. We look at each in turn.

Anti-Feudal Movements

The central ideologue for modernity in Kupang in the 1950s was the charismatic nationalist E.R. Herewila (1906–1969) (Figure 27). He was another of the new politicians who found his true calling upon independence after rising from peasant origins into the lower levels of the colonial bureaucracy. Herewila was part of the republican surge in towns all over the archipelago in the 1950s (Amal 1992, Asnan 2007, Magenda 1991, Zed 1991). As an official with the republican Information Department it was his job to promote national institutions at the expense of local ones. The department gave him certain central resources to do that in Kupang – propaganda films, national legislation, some influence over

---

Religious and ethnic voting was stronger outside the towns than within them. Such voting probably reflects clientelistic relations in rural and small-town economies little penetrated by capital. Class-based politics, on the contrary, were seen in plantation/ mining areas, and in a Java disturbed by the revolution – as seen in higher votes for the PKI in those areas.

The electoral results also demonstrate that eastern Indonesia was poorly integrated with the rest of Indonesia at this time. The Big Four parties (PNI, PKI, Masyumi, and Nahdatul Ulama) that dominated the national result in fact drew most of their votes from Java and parts of Sumatra. Particularly in eastern Indonesia they had little impact. Thanks to Dwight King for letting me have a digitized version of the 1955 election results in Alfian (1971). Similar conclusions were drawn by Feith (1957, 2007 [1962]).

appointments – but most of his resources were local. The fire in his speeches derived from an experience of dispossession by the rajas that he knew was common all over this region. Educated commoners everywhere were challenging feudalists to get their hands on the new levers of power and on the rents these could yield. Their struggles were local, negotiated affairs. National legislation could be ignored for years where it did not suit local power-holders. The transition from colonial indirect rule to the modern government promised by the republican revolution of 1945 therefore took longer in Timor than anywhere else in Indonesia.

In his twenties before the war, Herewila had combined a clerical job in forestry in Makassar with organizing for the Timorsch Verbond.[4] This was a self-improvement association for teachers, policemen and other low-ranking officials from Sabu, Rote and Kupang who lived scattered throughout the Netherlands Indies. Herewila belonged to a small radical nationalist wing that had felt inspired by Sukarno just before his incarceration in the early 1930s. Their activism began to turn from the 'spiritual' objectives of their moderate founders to exposing abuses by colonial officials in Timor through their own newspapers. Some of these efforts were successful (Ardhana 2005, Farram 2004). Herewila only finished primary school, but he became a cosmopolitan from travelling the world. In the early 1920s a French geologist working in the Kupang area invited him to be his assistant in Morocco. Back in Makassar he amazed an old aunt with his stories of having seen Jerusalem. 'I thought the Holy City was in heaven,' she said. Like so many gifted young men he imitated the oratory of Sukarno, dropping French-accented loanwords into his speeches. During the Japanese occupation he rose to head of the traffic department, and was then invited to sit on a board advising the local Imperial Japanese Navy government. After the war his oratorical talent led him to the NIT Ministry of Information in Makassar, where he worked under fellow-Sabunese I.H. Doko, younger but better educated than him and also a Timor activist since before the war. In 1950 his office was incorporated into the republican Ministry of Information. Promoting Jakarta's views on the antiquated raja system in Eastern Indonesia was the most exciting part of his job. He had written in the 1930s of his contempt for the rajas after one of them had robbed him of his hereditary land in Sabu.[5] Besides

[4] 'Riwayat hidup singkat almarhum R.E. Here Wila', anonymous, unpublished document dated 1969, in the private archive of Herewila's son Dami Herewila (Kupang, 15 July 2011).

[5] 'Keterangan E.R. Here memang benar?,' *Tjinta Kebenaran*, 20 March 1936, quoting *Soeara Timoer*, January 1936; 'Toean E.R. Here contra beberapa bangsawan Savoe,' *Tjinta Kebenaran*, 20 May 1936.

Figure 27. E.R. Herewila in the mid-1950s (courtesy private collection of Ruth Heny A. Nitbani-Markus).

the Ministry of Information he had a speaking platform in the island-wide parliament (DPR), which he chaired until 1956. Doubling up positions in the executive and legislative branches was not considered improper at that time. All the new rulers in Kupang led busy lives. In this slow-moving town, his constant travel by air and sea gave him an aura of prestige.[6]

[6] Herewila revealed a month's schedule in a note to a Dutch missionary in 1954 to explain why he could not help check the latter's bible translation (Onvlee 1953–55): 6 September: leave for Jakarta; 21 September: arrive back in Kupang from Jakarta; 23 September: to Singaraja (provincial capital in Bali); 26 September: return to Kupang to

Eastern Indonesia formally joined the independent Republic of Indonesia to form the Republic of the United States of Indonesia (Republik Indonesia Serikat, RIS) on 27 December 1949. Its system of local government based on autocratic rajas was not immediately replaced with a republican one. Indeed, the power of the rajas initially grew. In September 1949 the Dutch Resident officially transferred his authority to the Rajas Council in Timor (Dewan Radja-Radja). The revolutionary Republic of Indonesia, which was to dominate the RIS, was against this construction because it stood in the way of central control. Republicans within the former BFO (federal) territories did support the system's continuation, but only out of the pragmatic consideration that it worked and would take time to democratize. But they also realized the rajas' legitimacy was in decline. Herewila told the council in his speech on behalf of the ministry (Kana 1969:App 5, 160f) that from now on the struggle lay within Timor, between 'the people' and the rajas. Some of the latter continued to think they had come down from heaven like 'gods.' The root of Timor's problem was that the Dutch had betted on the strong instead of on the people, and even Indonesian independence might not be up to the task of displacing them:

> Of course this transfer merely hands power from the Dutch bureaucrats to the Rajas Council; it does not return the people's human rights, yet surely *this* has been the purpose of all this struggle and sacrifice.... Those rights were stolen by greed and avarice long ago; some of them are in Dutch hands, some in the hands of our own brothers who turned themselves into aristocrats, and some are with the Tribal Heads, and all of this is permitted by the rubbery colonial laws.'[7]

Main spokesperson for the rajas in the Timor assembly was the school teacher Benjamin Sahetapy Engel (1916–2008), curiously enough of Ambonese origin. When the outgoing NIT Interior Minister Lanto Daeng Pasewang visited the government offices in Kupang in mid-1950 to gauge

---

prepare visit of Vice President; 9 October: to Sabu (missing out on Protestant church synod 10–17 October); 24 October: arrive back in Kupang to prepare Timor parliamentary session which will start on 15 November and run for about 20 days.

7 'Memang segala penjerahan itu hanja penjerahan kuasa dari Pamongpradja Belanda sadja kepada Dewan Radja-Radja, tetapi belum pengembalian hak azasi manusianja rakjat dan sesungguhnja inilah ada tudjuan segala perdjuangan dan pengorbanan.... Hak asasi itu telah dirampok oleh loba dan tamak sepandjang perkembangan masa sebahagian ada dalam tangan Belanda, sebahagian dalam tangan orang-orang saudara sendiri jang telah mendjadikan dirinja bangsawan, dan sebahagian ada pada Kepala-Kepala Suku, dan semuanja itu dibenarkan oleh Undang-Undang karet dari Kolonial.'

reactions to a mildly reformist law on the structure of government (Law No.44 of June 1950), he ran into a storm of conservative reaction. Sahetapy Engel spoke for the rajas when he said he was all in favour of democracy but 'it should not be implemented in a way that – I am sorry to say it a bit harshly – is revolutionary.' It might 'muddy the waters' in those places where customary law (*adatrecht*) remained strong. Political parties would bring demagoguery. What was the point of caving in to the 'political atmosphere' if the wind might change again at any time? The minister responded that nothing would ever improve if 'people just want to leave things as they are.' Herewila, on the contrary, had already before this meeting condemned Law 44 as too little too late. In a speech to the NIT parliament in Makassar he said that the people still saw the same unaccountable officials and the same 'rajas who are once again fully sovereign in their domains.'[8] Why was the government unable to democratize these domains but insisted instead on protecting their 'historical rights'? 'Our state is democratic at its head, dualistic in its chest, and its hands and feet are feudal-monarchistic.' He hammered at his theme again in August 1950 in an address to the first Timor parliamentary meeting after the adoption of the unitary state. It was held on the veranda of the government office in Kupang (later parliament moved into a nearby temporary building in the ruined town). He thanked the progressives among the rajas for thinking ahead in step with the times and not upping the ante with parliament. Law 44, he said not without humour (Kana 1969:App 12, 220), 'offers a special leap, a leap up for one group, a leap down for another.'[9] He moved the Timor parliament to make its first motion a symbolic one – a law banning the raja's corvee tax.

At the same time Herewila was quick to see new dangers lurking in Kupang's democracy. People had been conditioned with authoritarianism: 'They are not only 75% illiterate, but their souls are immobilized, from birth they live and breathe and are educated in aristocracy and fascism; for them it is not easy to make this special leap' (Kana 1969:218). The new elites, too, were thus far failing to live up to their high calling, he told the NIT parliament on 22 March 1950:

> The lower layers of our people are illiterate and politically blind, their souls have been anaesthetized under an aristocratic and fascist education and they are incapable of practising their democratic rights, the human rights

---

[8] Speech to NIT parliament, 29 March 1950 (Kana 1969: App 7, 169).

[9] 'Undang-undang ini jang memberikan lontjatan istimewa, lontjatan naik bagi satu golongan dan lontjat turun bagi lain golongan.'

> that they have obtained. The upper layers and the intellectuals received those rights in the first place as a material benefit, and very few of them are able to marry that feeling for material things with a sense of responsibility or a feeling of obligation to the people and the nation.[10]

Inexperienced politicians, he said, were like passengers suddenly thrust into the driver's seat of a car hurtling along a rocky road with bad bridges. Herewila loved his red government Chevrolet (its wreck still stands in the family yard today). More to the point, he went on, many politicians were as corrupt and nepotistic as the rajas had been. Ethnic and family cliques were seizing government money for themselves, and civil society was too weak to stop them. The intellectuals were out of touch with the broader society from the town to the village, he said, and hijacking government programmes for their own interests. Having been thrown into politics from an apolitical background, they were now good at 'sabotage' but not at 'captivating the soul of their people.' He warned in another speech of 'neo-colonialism of us against ourselves... provincialism and the family system... neo-colonialism of the intellectuals.'[11] The danger of ethnic factionalism – 'calling the Rotenese and Sabunese little rajas in Timor, and the Javanese the new colonizers of Indonesia' – was real. Its results could be even worse than the feudalism of the rajas. The Indonesian ideal was to rise above all this:

> I am convinced that in five or ten years' time our people will be so advanced, intermarrying and overcoming every kind of provincialism, that the question of federalism or unitarism will no longer be one of provincialism but simply one of profit or loss for the state (Kana 1969:220).

Herewila kept up the preaching throughout his remaining career, which ended with aggravated diabetes in the early 1960s. Eager young men loved to frequent his house by the beach in Kampong Tode, just east of Kupang's China town, for irreverent political talk. But such was his reputation for iconoclasm outside Kupang that Herewila was rarely welcomed in the little raja-run towns of the interior. Over 50 years later a man who had been the young administrator in Atambua in the 1950s could still recall to me how shocked he had been when, during a visit to Kupang, he heard Herewila make razor-sharp jokes about the rajas.

---

[10] 'Kaum kita didaerah ini jang bukan sadja buta huruf 75%, tapi jang djiwanja sudah lumpuh, sedjak dilahirkan hidup dan menghirup serta pendidikan aristokrat dan fascis, baginja tidak mudah melaksanakan lontjatan istimewa itu.'

[11] Speech to mark the dissolution of the Ruler's Council (Dewan Radja-Radja), 2 November 1950, at the government office in Kupang, attended by 50 civilian and military elites (*Bentara*, 1 December 1950).

Democracy in this settler town with a mission on the edge of Timor may have been corrupt, nepotistic and ideologically naïve, but it did involve more people in public affairs than ever before. Herewila's anti-feudal talk struck a chord among educated young people in town. It only took a shout of 'feudalism' uttered in the midst of the ever-shifting factional politics of the Kampong Belanda offices to rouse a crowd of student protestors. Two episodes will illustrate – the unseating of J.S. Amalo, the head of the Timor island government, in 1954, and the resignation of Alfons Nisnoni as raja of Kupang in 1956. J.S. (Jaap) Amalo was an aristocratic Rotenese, trained in the colonial bureaucracy, who sat in the Timor assembly. When the incumbent Timor head, Raja H.A. Koroh, fell ill and died in March 1951, the Indonesian minister of the interior chose Amalo out of three candidates (one of them Doko) to replace him. Amalo was a poor administrator. He much preferred fishing all night off the Kupang pier. Complaints started immediately. He tried resigning in November, but the provincial governor would not let him. In March 1952 the Timor parliament under Herewila passed a censure motion condemning his chaotic budgeting and (the Herewila touch) his pandering to the most regressive of the rajas, namely those of Amanuban, Amanatun, and Mollo. In November of that year Herewila forced Amalo to sit through a parliamentary interrogation that lasted all night. Herewila's view that Amalo was 'feudal' got plenty of exposure in the local paper *Timor Sedar* (which has not survived), while Amalo's angry retorts that Herewila was an uneducated demagogue only made things worse.

In November and December 1953 big demonstrations turned out in the streets of Kupang. Young people banged metal dinner plates and shouted 'We want rice! We want rice!' It was the time of year when subsistence food stocks run low, and some now recall there was real hunger in the town, but others say the 'hunger' was exaggerated for political effect. In the midst of these demos Amalo lost his last friend when the moderate Sahetapy Engel announced he was no longer able to support a man who was 'lazy and neglectful of his duties.' Amalo resigned in May 1954. Unable to decide who among the quarrelling local elite should replace him – Herewila wanted the job but Sahetapy Engel blocked him - Amalo was replaced by an acting head, a Javanese bureaucrat. This man thought Kupang was such a hole that he never turned up in the office either and soon absented himself to Java on 'sick leave.'[12] Democracy had come to Kupang.

---

[12] *Bentara,* 15 October 1954, 15 November 1954.

Townsfolk were discomfited by these rowdy protests against distinguished men in high office. But Herewila said demonstrations were now normal in Jakarta; they belonged to the creation of 'a new society.' Just like China had united against the Japanese colonizer only to fall into an internal struggle between the elite led by Chiang Kai-shek and the 'impoverished masses' led by Mao Zedong, so Timor was engaged in a conflict against those 'whose soul still bears the signs of colonialism,' he said, somewhat tendentiously.[13] Rowdy demonstrations by school students, hungry or not, soon became commonplace in the mid-sized towns of Nusa Tenggara province. In February 1955 high school and even primary school students joined a 1500-strong mass meeting in Kupang's Royal movie theatre (the new name for Tjiong Koen Siong's Sunlie, later called Raya). Afterwards they walked to the Timor government office in Kupang because, once more, they were hungry. Not a grain of rice, corn or beans could be bought anywhere in town. Civil servants with insufficient time to work their own gardens were the worst affected. But the demonstrators blamed corrupt officials rather than the weather for their hunger. The rally was organized by labour unions in town demanding more say in the government-run food distribution system. The Catholic newspaper *Bentara* that reported it worried that demonstrations were 'impolite' and could plant rebellion in the hearts of young students.[14] But the church organized demonstrations as well. 'Ten thousand' Catholic high school students protested in Ende in November 1954, because a Jakarta newspaper had insulted 'Christ the Messiah' in a story about President Sukarno's polygamous marriage to Hartini the previous year.[15]

Herewila's mobilizational tactics also eventually pushed Alfons Nisnoni to resign as Raja of Kupang district. For a while it looked as if the Nisnoni family fortunes had improved rather than declined. Alfons had taken over from his ageing father Nicolaas late in the Imperial Japanese Navy administration, and the Indonesian interior minister had accepted his arguments for the historical primacy of his family in the Kupang district in 1951 (there were, of course, other claimants with impressive lineages…) (Anon 1956). He lived with his family in the small but comfortable stone 'palace' the Dutch had built for his father in Bakunase, in the hills behind Kupang

[13] *Bentara,* 1 July 1954.

[14] *Bentara,* 15 November 1954.

[15] Both 'impolite' and 'ten thousand' in *Bentara,* 15 November 1954. See also Kana 1969: App.20, 237–8, Netti and Itta 1997:88–9, 101–2; *Bentara,* 1 July 1954; interviews with Hendrik Ataupah, Kupang, 20 July 2010, and Blasius Manek, Atambua, 2 August 2010; B. Sahetapy Engel, 'Surat terbuka,' Djakarta, 1 December 1953, in private archive of Leopold Nisnoni.

town. The town's elite used to gather at his home for dances. Under the Dutch, the directly ruled town had been closed to him politically, but this changed during the Second World War. To keep things simple, the conservative Japanese Navy regime gave the raja control over the town as well. The NIT had kept the arrangement, and when the bombed-out town became a municipality in September 1949 it was up to Raja Nisnoni to select the mayor.[16] When that man succumbed to ethnicized fights over how the ravaged town should be rebuilt, Alfons briefly took over as mayor himself.[17]

He was not a bad planner, but the town had never been enamoured of rajas and after 1950 its republicanism grew more vociferous. Herewila in particular was the bane of his life. Alfons Nisnoni never recognized him as the legitimate speaker of the Timor assembly. 'Herewila has no following,' he used to say. The 1955 election result was to prove that Herewila did indeed have little following in most of rural Timor, but Kupang was different.[18] The Timor assembly under Herewila gradually legislated away Nisnoni's powers. It began by outlawing tribute as its first act in late 1949 (compensating the rajas with a bigger salary - Ormeling 1956:81–2). It then took away his judicial powers in September 1954 (taking over three years to implement national Emergency Law no.1 of 1951 on this issue). In any case, Alfons Nisnoni was a poor magistrate. He was deciding only one in three or four cases, and had already built up an enormous backlog by 1952 (Anon 1956). Finance was the most sensitive pressure point. The paternalistic Dutch had managed all the Timor rajas' funds from Kupang, but after the war the impoverished government let rajas manage their own money, while giving them no central state funds. Raja Nisnoni's budget in the mid-1950s stood at a substantial half a million rupiah,[19] collected from local taxes such as the slaughter tax. He spent it on around 600 staff (many of them still Dutch), and on his meat-canning business ICAFF. But the Timor assembly gradually throttled his income by, for example, outlawing a schools tax and a road tax. Above all it refused to condemn tax

---

16 *Bentara*, 1 January 1950.

17 There were complaints about too many Florinese migrants getting labouring work, of privileged officials seizing undamaged houses for themselves, of elite suburbs like Fatufeto and Fontein being prioritized over the impoverished suburbs of Kampung Solor and Merdeka, not to mention over Airmata with its brothel and its mosque. Chinese shop owners, meanwhile, who had been worst hit by the bombs, were left to rebuild the commercial district with their own means. Interview Hendrik Ataupah, Kupang, 20 July 2010.

18 Interview, Blasius Manek, Atambua, 1 August 2010; 'Alfons Nisnoni Radja Kupang 1945–1955', undated, anonymous document, in the private archive of Leopold Nisnoni (June 2009).

19 US$ 44,000 at the official exchange rate of Rp 11.4/ US$, or US$ 16,000 at the black market rate of Rp 31/ US$ reported for 1956 (http://en.wikipedia.org/wiki/Indonesian_rupiah).

avoidance, which rose alarmingly from an estimated 27% in 1954 to a massive 62% in 1955 (Anon 1956). The raja had lost his subjects. The erosion of respect dispirited this large, slow-moving gentleman with thick glasses, and in early 1956 he asked the Indonesian interior minister to relieve him of his post. To save face, he claimed his allowance of 1300 rupiah a month was 'not commensurate with his position' (actually it was a large income for those days) (Anon 1956). The government let him take leave, and in February he handed over to an elected official, H. Oematan (of mixed Timorese aristocratic and Chinese descent). Alfons Nisnoni received a government pension to the end of his life (Liliweri et al 1984:106).[20]

The Herewila message of 'human rights now spreading unstoppably from town to village' (as he put it in a 1951 speech to parliament - Kana 1969:230) also triggered republican movements in the interior.[21] They sought links with urban organizations that would help them in their search for more independence. If peasants in the interior of Timor had ever believed their raja was the centre of the universe, they now became aware that powerful people above the rajas were openly disparaging the rajas. They knew about Herewila, speaker of Timor's parliament. He himself was rarely invited to speak in the interior, but his messages were repeated by disaffected *fetor* and idealistic school teachers who learned them during visits to Kupang. All politics in the interior in the period 1949 to 1965 challenged the rajas. Their language of tradition and kinship was questioned in the hills, far from their palaces, by dissidents who did their best to attract allies in Kupang by deploying a language of popular sovereignty. The modern and the traditional interwove ambiguously in the framing of this contention. By the early 1960s, political party organizers were building district and village committees that were held together by

---

20 Elsewhere in Timor the kingdoms finally came to an end only in 1962. The rajas usually became subdistrict heads (*camat*). The 'pre-existing rights' of the rajas have become the subject of discussion again in decentralized Indonesia after 1998 (Banunaek 2007).

21 The events described in the next few paragraphs were reconstructed from interviews with old participants conducted in Amanuban and Amanatun, South Central Timor district, in July 2011. My most valuable informants were Daniel Teneo, Johan Christian Sapai, Melianus Babis, Salmon Neonloni, and Yunus Tafuli; thanks to Yanni Tahun for facilitating most of these interviews in July 2011. Memories five or six decades old are never flawless, and when cross-checked these memories too often proved most inaccurate, even those most confidently stated. They also came from village elites, who preferred to highlight their roles in intra-elite fights rather than to discuss broader social change. Several ordinary farmers told me apologetically they were still too afraid to speak about the anti-feudal politics of the period, which ended in such horrible blood-letting in this area. Nevertheless in their main lines the various versions concurred in the story presented here. Other informants' names are given in this book's acknowledgements.

kinship alliances and fuelled by memories of betrayals generations old. Peasants participated in political rallies and cooperatives while dreaming of utopias couched in Timorese messianic terms. This ambiguity has subsequently been poorly understood. Elite New Order writers have preferred to see only the tradition, while ignoring the modern institutions that awakened the dreams.[22]

The district of South Central Timor was created in 1958 out of the three kingdoms of Amanuban, Amanatun, and Mollo (Figure 12). Amanuban was easily the largest of the three. By 1949 it was in the hands of Koesa Nope (1924–1980), second son of the ageing lord Pa'e Nope whom the Dutch had appointed in 1923. Koesa Nope had been educated as a modern bureaucrat in Makassar just after World War II. He was not first in line to the throne, but Herewila and the new political elite in Kupang thought his good education would make him a modernizer. Herewila agreed to help him up, provided he drop his ambition to be chair of the Timor Rajas Council (Dewan Radja-Radja Timor), which should go to the older raja of Amarasi, H.A. Koroh, also a modernizer. But once appointed raja he began to behave like his father had done in order to maintain his power. That included appointing his relatives to positions of *fetor* and *temukung*. He did not have to wait long for the first challenge on precisely this point. Pa'e Nope had had about 70 children by his dozens of wives. The struggle between them over his succession inevitably spilled out of the family to the new institutions in Kupang, and to the villages ruled by lesser nobles. Nepotism was not merely an affront to Timorese norms, in which the nobles carry the raja, it was also a sin against the new republicanism.

In 1950 the Fa'ot family based in Noemeto, just west of the 'palace' in Niki Niki, mobilized demonstrations by thousands of villagers demanding that the *fetor*, a Nope, be replaced by a Fa'ot family member. The raja was continuing to levy the traditional tributes known as *abeat* and *etu* despite the ban on them by the Timor parliament the previous year. Four truckloads of peasants – a huge convoy in those days – travelled to Kupang to voice their complaints to parliamentary speaker Herewila. It had all been

---

[22] Several western scholars have echoed post-1965 public opinion in Kupang that those who took part in PKI activities had no understanding of communist doctrine and were easily duped by offers of untold wealth. The opinion recalls the paternalism of the Dutch Resident who wrote in 1927 that many of the people 'associated with [Pandie's] Sarekat Ra'jat called themselves communist without there being any appearance of communism and they having no understanding of the term' (Farram 2004:132). More perspicacious was Barnes' conclusion about Buang Duran's PKTI, whose ideology of modernity with social harmony, he wrote, was 'very much within the mainstream of Indonesian political thought until October 1965' (Barnes 2003:25).

organized by an ex-soldier named Yakobus Hitarihun, who had married into the Fa'ot family but had seen something of the world. The dispute had escalated by means of non-traditional techniques, but at core it was a traditional problem, and Koesa Nope solved it in the traditional way. He took one of the Fa'ot women as a wife, thus tying the Fa'ot clan to him with kinship ties. A Hitarihun son grew up in the Nope *sonaf* or palace (actually a modest house, which still stands[23]). The *fetor*'s domain (*kefetoran*) remained in Nope hands. The modern state was as yet absent in the interior of Timor.

The first institution to make an impact there was the political party. The next challenge to Koesa Nope came towards the mid-1950s from a group of junior high school teachers from prominent local families who made good use of this new instrument. Lui Babis and Gabriel Isu had been at senior high school in Makassar together with Koesa Nope in the late 1940s. But now they turned against him, and they used the political party as their weapon. Talked about for years, national elections were finally held in September 1955. The family of Lui Babis had roots in the rugged hills of Noemuke, south of Niki Niki, where several of them were known as *meo*, warriors (Figure 28). The Isu family was based in Noebunu, also near Timor's rather fertile south coast, where an older brother of Gabriel was *fetor*. Democratic competition was the perfect outlet for factional rivalry.

Many places in Timor saw no campaigning. Rajas in rural Catholic areas told farmers to vote Catholic Party. Catholic Party votes in Catholic areas averaged around 90%. 'We just voted as we were told,' one old farmer recalled to me with a smile, and the uniform results in many rural areas bear him out (Alfian 1971, Pemda NTT 1966). Protestant ministers expected the same result when they told parishioners from their pulpits to vote Parkindo. But the Protestant church was still growing in rural Timor at this time, and it only captured a third to two-thirds of the votes in its home areas, mostly in the towns. Many rural rajas in Protestant areas looked to various secular parties to feed them. Some followed the advice of Sahetapy Engel, Kupang-based advisor and spokesperson for many of them, to choose the Partai Rakyat Nasional, National People's Party PRN, a party that cultivated outer island votes. But others went their own way. Alfons Nisnoni had his own local party with the equally grand name National Front (Front Nasional, not to be confused with other parties of the same name in the early 1960s).

---

[23] A photograph is at 'Menyapa yang datang (1),' *Pos Kupang*, 24 September 2012 (http://kupang.tribunnews.com/2012/09/24/menyapa-yang-datang-1) (accessed 17 August 2013).

Figure 28. Recent funeral monument for a meo (warrior) member of the Babis clan, just north of Kuanfatu, Amanuban, South Central Timor (photo: Gerry van Klinken).

Sahetapy's nemesis Herewila was the first Kupang politician not to look to the politics of the soil in which the church and the rajas were rooted. His Indonesian National Party (Partai Nasional Indonesia, PNI) was the one that civil servants were expected to join. But the party was wracked with factionalism in Jakarta, and he had few civil servants in Timor to work with. In 1955 he found himself leading a local breakaway grandiosely called the People's Front (Front Rakjat), with a rooster as its symbol. Of the four biggest parties active in Timor, only Herewila's PNI-affiliated Front Rakjat lacked authoritative patrons in the interior. This led it to mobilize on popular discontent with the rajas, which was already rumbling in South Central Timor. The Indonesian republic, mediated to the countryside by the town, provided locally marginal groups with an attractive emancipatory agenda. Here it won nearly a third of the votes by portraying itself as a party of 'popular sovereignty' (*kedaulatan rakyat*). All its leading lights in TTS were either *temukung* or *fetor* themselves, or related to them. They included the well-connected teachers Lui Babis and Gabriel Isu, already mentioned; others were Neno Boimau, Sofian Un and Key Nabuasa. Vague memories survive of a youth organization called Indonesian Youth Generation (Angkatan Pemuda Indonesia, API), suggestive of the 1945 revolution. Lui Babis was a persuasive orator. He called the raja a leech (*a'susu* in Dawan, *lintah darat* in Indonesian) for constantly demanding cattle, goats, and women. He invited one of the best educated Timorese teachers in Kupang, Alexander Z. Nomleni, to make speeches in villages off the main road. Nomleni had connections in Soë, which he visited often to see his mother. He later went into politics full-time.

At around this time Raja Koesa Nope struck back at Lui Babis with a court case. Rumours that Babis had beaten someone to death are denied by others who say the case was purely political, and I do not know the truth of it. Babis spent about two years in jail shortly after the election, first in Soë then in Kupang. However, his older brother Leno continued to agitate against the raja. It seems that eventually the ruling *fetor*, A.F.H. Nope, retreated to Soë, leaving the field to Leno Babis as de facto *fetor*. The latter cemented his position at a public meeting in 1959, after which Koesa Nope was forced to formalize the appointment. In less dramatic ways several other locally powerful families in southern Amanuban also increased their autonomy. Despite his conviction, Lui Babis's career took off upon his release. He became a member of parliament in Jakarta, married a Muslim, and converted to Islam (an easy-going version that did not prevent him eating pork). The mosque he built still stands at Kuanfatu.

PKI

By the early 1960s the genie of popular participation in politics was out of the bottle. Peasants no longer moved automatically on the command of their patrons. Raja Koesa Nope survived the final dissolution of his kingdom in 1961 when he was appointed district head of South Central Timor (Tari 1972:I, 98–9). He reportedly declared 'the kingdom never ends!' Opposition never ended either. Powerful families side-lined by the raja continued to protect farmers who wanted rights. The PNI had declined, but an energetically expanding communist party had taken its place. Teachers in the towns facilitated new networks that produced organizational innovations such as cooperatives. In this section we examine the role of urban brokers in the expansion of social capital that took place in South Central Timor, which by 1963 had NTT's largest concentration of BTI farmers union membership. Facilitated by educated teachers in the towns, they enthusiastically built cooperatives and learned new skills – the villages of Kusi and Tuapakas in southern Amanuban had strong cooperatives (Sekda TTS [1978]:68f).

The occasion for this mobilizational activity in Kupang in the early 1960s was created by crisis in Jakarta. The abolition of parliamentary democracy in the late 1950s did not so much weaken the political parties as tie them more closely to the interests of the two great executive powers in Jakarta, President Sukarno and the armed forces. Indonesia's authoritarian turn is usually dated from the abandonment of the democratic 1950 constitution in July 1959, though this followed upon the declaration of martial law a little earlier (March 1957), and was in turn followed by the suspension of parliament a little later (March 1960). But Guided Democracy had even more populist politics than the liberal period that preceded it. Unable to negotiate compromise solutions to their differences in parliament, rivals took their followers onto the streets. The effect was highly polarizing, as the political middle disappeared. All parties began to form new mass organizations in 1960, except Masyumi and the Indonesian Socialist Party PSI, which were banned that year.

PNI had lost the 1955 election in Timor to parties with links to rajas and churches. It had lost its direction nationally after this as well, and soon became a classic patronage party, weakened by factionalism and rent-seeking, in which the membership system lapsed (Rocamora 1974:252, 315–6). Its conservative bureaucratic and business leadership confusingly tried to stay close to the increasingly leftist-sounding President Sukarno. At the same time it adopted an anti-communist ideology echoing that of the religious parties Masyumi and NU, in order to resist encroachment from the more radical PKI. But out in the districts this anti-communism made little sense and PNI and PKI sympathizers often worked together. When BTI began mobilizing nationally from 1961 onwards, it found the ground prepared in southern Amanuban and Amanatun. The local families in the southern coastal regions, who had used PNI to keep the Raja of Amanuban at a distance in the 1950s, saw little reason to stop now. Herewila was not part of this – the PNI fraction he supported was anti-communist – though some of his protégés were. Again, power was generated in Timor as ideas and organizational forms from Jakarta became resources for embryonic alliances that linked urban workers and rural peasants with rising middle class elites. Teachers excited by the promise of a new world played the central role in these cross-class alliances.

The Communist Party PKI had by far the best mobilizational skills, and Sukarno was keen to make use of them. The armed forces began cultivating links with more conservative groups, mainly religious ones. Under Sukarno's protective umbrella, the PKI organized faster and better than any of the others. With its affiliated organizations for farmers (BTI), youth (Pemuda Rakjat, PR), women (Gerwani), labour (Sobsi), artists, journalists, government workers and intellectuals, it rapidly built up a hierarchy of committees and conferences from provincial to village level – also outside Java where PKI had till then been weak. By 1964 PKI general secretary D.N. Aidit could claim there were PKI committees in 100% of Indonesia's provinces or major islands, in 93% of districts and large towns, in 83% of subdistricts and small towns, and in 62% of villages or institutions at an equivalent level (Pauker 1964:37).[24] The PKI had won few votes in this part of Indonesia in the 1955 election – just 4,500 in the whole region that was soon to become East Nusa Tenggara – most of them in East Flores (Alfian 1971). But from 1960 the party and its affiliates began mobilizing aggressively all over Indonesia, engaged in a high-stakes national gamble for territory.

For its middle class members, the PKI offered access to jobs just like any other party. Educated people moved easily from one party to another, and sometimes combined membership in several. Agustinus Roboth, a teacher in Soë, was active in both the PKI and Parkindo (Sekda TTS [1978]). Michael Marcus, ex-teacher and now finance manager in the Soë government offices, moved to the PKI in mid-1960 after years of service in Timor-level political offices in the PNI under Herewila's wing (Tari 1972:I, 253). Urban communist activism focused on the demand for communist representation in the local government and parliament. As part of his agenda

24 The highest regional level was the Comite Daerah Besar CDB, Comite Pulau Besar CPB, and Comite Djakarta Raya CRD, totalling 27 units. Comite Seksi, or CS, operated at the level of district of city (kabupaten, kota); Comite Sub-Seksi, CSS, operated at the sub-district level (kecamatan); Resort Comite, RC, at village (desa) and factory level.

of balancing the politically hostile military, President Sukarno had been pressing the doctrine of Nasakom since 1960. This envisaged all state institutions having representatives from each of the three ideological persuasions – nationalist, religious and communist. Sukarno's rivals hated this idea, but all parties were pushing for 'proportional' appointments to the increasingly politicized bureaucracy. 'Democracy' meant that official appointments should be made through a party and not on the basis of bureaucratic merit. When in 1965 Nasakom eventually became policy, local governments in NTT reluctantly agreed to allocate a nominal one extra seat to the PKI in the provincial parliament (it went to H.H. Motu), one in the provincial advisory body BPH,[25] and one in to the district-level representative assemblies in Kupang (Abraham Neno) and in West Sumba (Pura Tanja Pandjang) (Tari 1972:I, 277).

Outreach to non-elites was a unique PKI skill. If other parties existed mainly for their executives, the PKI had members who paid dues and ran neighbourhood branches, almost like a liberal democratic party. Government officials, who also wished to reach out to the wider public, at first regarded the PKI as an ally. Lesser Sunda Islands Governor Sarimin Reksodihardjo, a man hardly enamoured of local political parties that in his view contributed little beyond 'continual opposition,' thought highly of civil society organizations mobilizing people for development work. He wrote in 1957: 'The efforts of the farmer's organizations (BTI, Petani, Gerakan Tani Indonesia), the women's organizations, the youth organizations, and others, are truly constructive' (Reksodihardjo 1960 [1957]:I, 36–7). BTI referred to the Barisan Tani Indonesia, the Indonesian Farmers Union, easily the most successful of the communist organizations in Indonesia. The party knew the importance of cross-class alliances to build associational power. The 1959 PKI National Peasants Conference urged organizers to 'go down' (*turun ke bawah, turba*) among the peasants. They had to combine the promotion of structural solutions with 'small but successful' actions alongside the peasants, such as the provision of cheap seeds and tools, and building bridges together. The idea was to wean peasants off their dependence on patrons within the aristocracy, the bureaucracy or the major religions (Huizer 1974:100–1). For farmers in Timor it was a stunning new experience to belong to an organization that set them on a footing of equality with the government. It was led by white-shirted office-bearers who distributed aid to them in times of hunger and who spoke to officials whenever the raja grabbed their land.

[25] Badan Pemerintah Harian.

The PKI agrarian programme did not diverge greatly from the modernization paradigm of the 1950s, as western technocrats envisaged it. Mechanization would produce economies of scale, and land reform was widely thought to be essential. The problem in Timor was (and remains today) how to produce enough food for a growing population on dry, marginal land without washing the soil away through over-production. The absence of individual land rights left peasants with a 'loose' connection with the land that, it was thought, gave them little motivation to deal seriously with Timor's serious soil erosion problem. The 'evolution' therefore, according to Ormeling (1956:84), was towards individual land tenure for peasants. The United States through the World Bank was actively promoting this solution in the 1950s, partly for ecological reasons and partly to deflect communist influence in developing countries (White 2005).

Under the energetic BTI organizer Asmu in Jakarta, land reform became the union's key programme in 1960. This was the year the national land reform legislation was passed (UU 56/ Prp/1960 about land reform and the Basic Agrarian Law UUPA of 1960). An implementing bureaucracy (agraria) was established all over the country and also in Kupang. A land reform seminar held under government auspices in Kupang on 27–30 April 1961, at which experts and activists shared their knowledge of the issues involved, underlined the mainstream nature of the campaign (Sidik et al 1968:49).[26] Land reform faced a serious shortage of statistics on land-owning practices throughout the vast archipelago, which was only partially relieved by the agricultural census of 1963. Nevertheless, the government went ahead with a hierarchy of Land Reform Committees at every level of government. The district (*kabupaten*) was the key level. The committees were drawn from various elements of government and civil society, including the local BTI secretary. Timor was not first in line for land reform. Phase I was implemented in the second half of 1964 and covered Java, Bali, and West Nusa Tenggara. Kalimantan was scheduled for Phase II (Utrecht 1969). This means little was achieved in Timor until the rise of the New Order put an end to the BTI and eventually to the idea of land reform itself.

It was never very clear what precisely land reform would mean for Timor's communally held rural land, but it *was* clear that it involved confronting the rajas, hitherto the main partners for government development programmes. Land ownership problems were becoming urgent for another reason too – Kupang town was expanding rapidly into rural land

26 They were A.A. Bere Tallo (Belu); OE.A. Kapita (Sumba) and Jan Djong (Flores).

claimed by the rajas. Real or imagined land title grievances became hot issues, even before the formal process had started in NTT. In Seba, the largest little town on the island of Sabu, teachers affiliated with the PKI mobilized demonstrations urging the raja named Ludji to socialize his land. They reminded listeners that Sabu had known no rajas until the colonial Dutch had imposed them less than a lifetime earlier. The subdistrict chief, a PNI man, tried to protect Ludji from harm but urged him privately to return land he had acquired under the cover of aristocratic privilege. The extended drought of 1964–1965 caused tempers to fray. The PKI handed out assistance, provoking PNI rage. When some houses were burned down in Seba in July 1965 – probably accidentally as farmers routinely burned grass – it became politicized into a PKI vs. PNI issue. The opportunity for PNI revenge came only with the new regime (see next chapter). Similar mobilization over land also produced tensions in Babao, east of Kupang (Kolimon and Wetangterah 2012:125–38, 227–8).

Heading up NTT's first BTI branch in Soë, the capital of South Central Timor district – two months *before* the provincial branch was established in September 1960 – was Michael Marcus (Tari 1972:I, 253). He became known in Kupang as an expert on land reform.[27] Marcus was from Rote and belonged to the new political class that emerged after independence (see Chapter 3). By 1960 this former school teacher, politician and now government administrator was nearing retirement. He worked in the local government finance office, having left his family for their schooling in the Fontein house in Kupang. Politics was a spare-time activity. Survivors of the anti-communist purges of 1965/66 recall that they thought his move to the PKI was unusual for an established bureaucrat. Had he been pushed against his will? Patronage available to progressives from Herewila had declined after the PNI's thrashing in the 1955 elections in Timor and the leadership splits that followed. Perhaps Simon Bubu, the wealthy PKI labour union boss in Kupang on whose land Marcus owned a house, had press-ganged him into service for a rapidly expanding communist party in search of cadre? More likely, however, he was less driven by necessity than that. Michael Marcus was a gregarious man who had been all over the interior of Timor as a teacher for a decade. Teachers were at the coalface

[27] One report quotes a paper by him on 'the role of adat' in Timor and Sumba presented at a symposium on the economic and financial development of East Nusa Tenggara on 17–25 November 1966 (Sidik et al 1968:49). His paper was presented together with one by the former editor of *Bentara* magazine, the priest A.A. Conterius SVD representing Flores. However, Marcus had already been executed by then. Was the paper presented posthumously, perhaps implying a veiled protest against his execution?

of every social renewal project in rural NTT. They taught about the world at church schools, taught the gospel in church, and served on local committees for all the political parties (Kolimon and Wetangterah 2012:131–2). Marcus's network with equally eager middle class modernizers was wide; they all believed in the salvific potential of politics. When PKI leader Njoto said in 1965, 'we are the men who are modernizing life in the villages; we are the men introducing the twentieth century' (Mortimer 1974:409), he might have been overstating his case, but for people like Marcus it was the literal truth. In Soë he was introduced to the PKI by the radical PKI activist B. Paulus Kanuru, with whom he shared an office (Netti and Itta 1997:110–1, Sekda TTS [1978]:63–7). Kanuru had been a primary school teacher in Kefamenanu in the early 1950s. When he moved to Soë in 1955 just after the elections he set up a PKI secretariat there. Kanuru's wife was uneducated but had family connections in the region, and she started a Gerwani group (Kolimon and Wetangterah 2012:256). Four of Marcus' oldest sons and daughters also joined leftist organizations in those innocent days. Although his wife had a withdrawn personality, she came from a relatively influential clan in the Soë area. For Marcus, the very act of marrying her – most educated Rotenese regarded the Timorese as backwards – was a bit of cross-class alliance. The Nenobais came from western Amanuban, and some of its members had joined in the widespread dissatisfaction with the ruling Nope clan. The merging of historical inter-clan grievances with modern party activism was a characteristic feature of the highly-embedded politics of rural Timor at this time (McWilliam 1999).

Under Marcus' leadership, the southern part of South Central Timor became one of the strongest BTI areas in NTT. The first provincial governor after the military takeover in 1966, El Tari, published a table showing BTI membership by district in NTT in 1963 (Tari 1972:I, 263) (Table 1). South Central Timor ranked first with over 25,000 members, with high concentrations also in Belu (in Timor) and Manggarai (in Flores). 'Membership' may have meant no more than just registration for free agricultural tools, yet the numbers suggest a significant level of mobilization. Local elites had their own troubles with Koesa Nope's transformation from raja to district head, but their clients had a bigger agenda. The farmers who ran the village branches, and the teachers in Soë who gave mid-level leadership,[28] thought less about opposing the Nope family than

[28] Three Soë teachers active in the BTI were Yohanes Mauboy, Daniel Sonlae, and Simon Petrus Kase.

Table 1. BTI 'membership' in East Nusa Tenggara province by district in 1963 (Tari 1972:I, 263). Shaded: the three largest BTI districts. (NB: original document incorrectly reports bottom right cell as 77,026.)

Nr.	District branch (DPT BTI)	Sub-branches	Neighbourhood groups	Members
1	Kupang	5	82	4,000
2	South Central Timur	14	302	25,073
3	North Central Timur	3	9	189
4	Belu	8	0	16,166
5	East Flores	13	14	1,470
6	Ngada	0	8	800
7	Ende	0	11	6,106
8	Sikka	8	26	1,987
9	East Sumba	2	22	1,755
10	Manggarai	13	80	12,000
11	West Sumba	3	10	2,261
12	Alor/ Pantar	4	17	5,000
13	Rote/ Kupang district	3	8	444
14	Sabu/ Kupang district	0	11	775
	Totals	76	600	78,026

about gaining access to the state. It was a marvel that subsistence farmers wearing sarongs without shirts could talk as equals with their own city people in white shirts. They had been the object of election campaigns and government development plans, but now BTI officials talked back to arrogant officials on their behalf. When drought struck in 1964, BTI was the only organization handing out food aid to distressed farmers. The farmers who headed up the BTI branch in Kusi village would walk to Kupang for a political meeting, 150 km away along foot trails. They brought along their members' contributions in kind for the BTI Cooperative – cloths, and even cattle – hoping to get it back in the future with interest. The BTI and PKI were unique among Indonesian political organizations in being largely financed by ordinary members (Feith 1957:27). Upon their return, sometimes bearing gifts of agricultural tools, the delegates called the village together for a report; this was also an occasion for shouting party slogans. In villages as widely spaced as Oinlasi in southern Timor and Lamboya in central Sumba I heard how the BTI was known for its cooperative farming. Peasants had a long tradition of working together on preparing subsistence gardens, but these reports suggest the BTI helped solve some of the collective action problems that normally bedevil these collaborative efforts in rural Timor.

This did not mean that peasant BTI organizers suddenly became twentieth century apparatchiks. The deference its leaders enjoyed did not always derive from modern performativity. The Kupang agricultural economist Hendrik Ataupah saw the popularity of BTI in southern Amanuban as little more than traditional messianism. He advised the provincial government to combat it by building a road through the rugged hills into Tuapakas and thus reduce its isolation. The BTI leader in Tuapakas was Susanamanu, a ladies man who also chaired the communist women's movement Gerwani. Many women were camped with their children in temporary huts around his house; apparently they believed having sex with him would bring them great benefits.[29] Balthasar Klau, the BTI leader in Belu, was a marginalized but ambitious aristocrat who mobilized peasant support through the BTI by producing piles of cloths apparently out of nowhere. He promised to deliver more if they supported him. Belu was another strong BTI basis (Farram 2002).

Peasant suspicion frequently overrode good judgment. At the height of the Irian Jaya confrontation in 1962, an aeroplane passed over the little town of Kefamenanu just as an explosion was heard. A policeman rang the district chief, Piet Salasa, to say a bomb had been dropped. Salasa went to the place of the incident and found a drunken policeman who had fallen into the fire with his shotgun, which set off the ammunition. However, the local BTI leader insisted it had been a bomb attack called in by a foreign priest. A month later military commander Paikun came from Kupang and asked about 'the bomb.' He had heard about it from the BTI. In March 1965 a German priest called Hans Smit was counting the collection in front of his congregation in Belu district. He held up each note before dropping it on the table; the total came to the price of half an egg. Somehow a rural Catholic teacher had the idea this was an insult to the President of the Republic of Indonesia, and the story spread that the pastor had burnt the notes with his image. He was charged with subversion by a local judge who was afraid of the PKI and the story went national. Finally the Supreme Court allowed him to leave the country for 'medical treatment.'[30]

---

[29] Interview, Hendrikus Ataupah, Kupang, 31 July 2011.

[30] Interview Piet Salasa, Kupang, 19 July 2010; 'Kegiatan subversi di Nustengtim,' *Harian Rakjat*, 24 April 1965; interview Centis da Costa, Jakarta, 11 June 2010.

Such tales of peasant dreams and suspicions awakened by the BTI are legion in Timor's history as told today. Modern emancipatory repertoires produced unexpected effects in closed, hierarchical peasant societies where the modern state had hardly penetrated. But just how illegitimate or destructive they were is no easy question to answer. They do not differ in principle from the invigorating impact that the modern political language had on the equally primordial status conflicts between rival elite families in Timor. If the BTI goal was to wean peasants off dependence on their traditional patrons, its work in Timor appears not to have been so far wide of this mark. The seductive modality of power highlighted in this chapter generated new forms of associational power among the poor majority. Urban middle class intellectuals – particularly teachers – facilitated the process by bending the resources of political parties and other state institutions to the greater public good. More importantly, the (semi) educated town dwellers had 'set a climate of opinion' (as Gerald Maryanov put it - 1959:63) in which the poor were no longer passive subjects but active citizens. The new republican sentiment in town made politics a matter for a whole class of people previously excluded from it. Kupang was here playing the generative role of agrarian modernizer that towns ought to play, in the vision of John Mellor (1976) and others.

However, associational modalities of generating power tend to run into trouble when social inequalities are structurally entrenched. Hannah Arendt paid insufficient attention to this reality in her work. In Timor such inequalities were sharp. Mobilization among the poor soon began to provoke reactions among privileged members of the community. Particularly in the countryside, the very act of encouraging peasants to think they had friends in high places challenged the existing hierarchy. Hendrikus Ataupah explained to me the risks that this entailed:

> Every aristocratic family has a 'pillar.' For example in Sumba they are known as *Umbu*. He holds up a place where others can sit. He never speaks out, but he can order his shadow bodyguard to speak. This is probably a former slave, even if he wears nice clothes. He has lots of rights. If he kills, he will be a hero in the family. Now the BTI wanted to displace the pillar! But this is very difficult to do.[31]

In Soë that 'pillar' was Koesa Nope, the Raja of Amanuban and district chief of South Central Timor. He lived in his palace (*sonaf*) in Niki-Niki just outside Soë and was the province's largest cattle owner. Photographs show him literally towering over the peasant-born men of the same age

[31] Interview with Hendrikus Ataupah, Kupang, 30 June 2009.

(see Chapter 8) (Alfons Nisnoni was tall too - perhaps suggestive of the better nutrition raja's children had enjoyed). The state's struggles had become, at this provincial level, a class struggle. How this confrontation reached its denouement here and in other parts of Timor that had its own pillars, is the subject of the next chapter.

Emancipatory Connections

In the face of widespread perceptions that democracy in developing countries inevitably equates to a feast of elite patronage interspersed with communitarian xenophobia and ethnic violence, doing little for the ordinary citizen, the stories in this chapter paint a more complex picture. Previous chapters have demonstrated that top-down, instrumental forms of power are not very effective at achieving their goals. This one goes on to illustrate that new cross-class, bottom-up associational forms of power can develop even in situations with low institutional maturity. Emancipatory political agendas have their own appeal wherever people feel oppressed. Superior centralized organization was certainly a condition for facilitating this kind of mobilization, but ultimately the energy came from local people who found each other around ideals of improvement through political action. Middle class townsfolk, particularly teachers, were the vital mediatory link in this generation of new social capital.

CHAPTER EIGHT

THE GATEKEEPER (1950S–1970S)

> Cooperatives not based on people's participation flourished but lacked a strong basis. Combined with cheating in some cooperatives both by management and outsiders, these weaknesses were only exposed once the excessive facilities given to the cooperatives were no longer available.
>
> (NTT Governor El Tari official report 1972:II, 455)

Idealistic teachers making common cause with rebellious peasants was one aspect of life in Kupang in the 1950s and '60s, but most people just wanted to make a living in these insecure times. This chapter describes a more limited form of power generation, among a rising group of senior bureaucrats and their dependents. They formed the core of a new provincial establishment. The exercise of power can only be sustained by mobilizing certain resources, and this chapter focuses on material ones. The key resource was not money as such but the capacity to control its flow across space. Once again, it was their highly political intermediate functions that gave provincial elites access to resources out of proportion to their position in pure market or state institutions. 'Cheating,' as the NTT governor put it so frankly in the 1972 report quoted at the head of this chapter, was the key to both the possibilities and the limitations of these resources.

Two earlier chapters have already traced in a synthetic way the outlines of the argument developed here. A rather unconventional notion of class necessary to make sense of the story in this book was introduced in Chapter 1 with a discussion of two important papers. Aage Sørensen (2000) argued that exploitation can be explained by asking who controls *any* kind of asset. Bureaucratic resources such as targeted subsidies and the policing of regulations form powerful assets. Michal Kalecki (1972) reasoned that the varieties of state socialism common in several newly independent countries in the 1950s and '60s had been more favourable to a politically savvy lower-middle class than to 'pure' capitalists in the upper- and upper-middle classes. Chapter 2 applies these ideas synthetically to a broad history of Middle Indonesia. The beating heart of post-independence provincial urbanization was a new and largely bureaucratic indigenous middle class. Their economic muscle was exercised in the rent-seeking politics associated with state intervention in the economy in the 1950s and '60s. The present chapter aims to put flesh on these assertions by reconstructing bureaucratic economic behaviour in a particular town.

Indonesia wrote socialism into its constitution (articles 33 and 34), but it never adopted the creed in an integral way, restrained, as it was, by being within the US sphere of influence from 1945 and throughout the Cold War. But the US was subsequently more concerned to control foreign policy, and Indonesia did adopt socialist-sounding ideological motifs for domestic matters. Socialist language was *de rigeur* across the political spectrum. There were historical reasons for this. The nationalists had found their voice during the Depression of the 1930s. The colonial state itself had intervened to protect vulnerable populations from out-of-control market forces at that time. The Japanese occupation had seen a war economy run entirely along command lines. The promise of welfare for all, which gave the national revolution its popular energy, was premised on extensive redistribution of resources. A government floundering to assert its authority in the 1950s sought to buy political stability by appeasing the noisiest provincial groups. Unable to give them real money, it gave them the gift of the means of primitive accumulation.

Four economic and political processes that help explain the rise of this provincial middle class are discussed below. The first was *Indonesianisasi*, a deliberate policy to create a new class of indigenous urban entrepreneurs who could both compete and work together with more established Chinese operators. A steady trickle of government funding preferentially targeted this group in stricken provincial economies. Next, these entrepreneurial urban officials resorted to political action to increase their leverage over this funding. They pushed Jakarta for more government and greater autonomy in their home territory, at the price of sabotage if they didn't get it. This section on localism adds a crucial territorial dimension to Kalecki's intermediate class analysis. Third, 'cheating' increased as they discovered that scarcity could be a source of wealth for those in gatekeeping positions. And fourth, exploitative practices produced social tensions with disadvantaged groups. An undercurrent of violence led to militarization. By the late 1960s the indigenous ruling class in town had established a strong gatekeeping position for itself in Middle Indonesia, even in the midst of economic crisis, lower class disaffection, and authoritarian policies emanating from the centre. The next chapter examines the tragic consequences of pursuing this increasingly exploitative new local constellation of power.

Indonesianisasi

A major part of the constitutional goal of popular welfare through expanded democratic control over the economy was to 'Indonesianize' it (Sutter 1959). *Indonesianisasi* developed a late colonial policy ideal of excluding the Chinese from those levels of the economy below big capital, which the Dutch thought indigenes should be able to handle. All the Indonesian political parties participating in the colonial proto-parliament called the Volksraad had supported significant state intervention in the economy. State banks out-competed Chinese moneylenders with their small credit schemes for indigenous small and medium entrepreneurs. State-sponsored cooperatives expanded rapidly after 1927, and state intervention generally grew in scope during the Depression. The Japanese occupation further stimulated the indigenization of the economy in order to make up the shortfall caused by the loss of imports. State-sponsored trade organizations attempted to displace Chinese private enterprise. Chinese traders were driven from the villages and were excluded by means of a licensing system from many economic sectors, except where it concerned their own community needs (Wertheim 1955). In post-war revolutionary Indonesia, nationalizing everything from sugar and textile production to rice distribution and land title was the main policy promoted under Vice-President Mohd. Hatta, a Dutch-trained economist.

The historian's wasteland that is Kupang in the 1950s and '60s has left us only snippets of information about the economy, and practically nothing from the earlier parts of that period. Most of the termite-ravaged remnants of 'grey' government literature, still held in private collections, dates from the mid- to late 1960s, and so do most of the stories I heard from old people in Kupang about the economy. Precision and completeness is therefore no longer possible, and we shall have to range across the period to get an impression of the way *Indonesianisasi* created an indigenous provincial establishment.

The private economy in town was tiny (Chapter 6). Above the itinerant Sabunese small traders, most of its practitioners were ethnic Chinese while a few were Arab. Chinese before the war had made up 13% of the urban population, though this decreased as the town grew. All but one of the 'factories' in town were Chinese-owned: three made ice, three lemonade, and one, owned by Ang Hauw Lang, produced clove cigarettes. The Arab entrepreneur Umar Baktir had a little weaving plant. None was very reliable – breakdowns were common (Anonymous 1956).

Live cattle were the island's major export, but the value of imports greatly exceeded exports such as these. Rice, cement, textile (mainly sarongs), and Indonesian-made cigarettes were big import items at the harbour. Biggest import of them all was paper money, whose value exceeded the island's entire exports (Anon 1956:14)! The provincial government in the 1950s regulated basic supplies on a quota system. State-owned corporations worked with both international capital and local Chinese entrepreneurs. However, the scarcities created by unattractive markets and poor infrastructure still offered possibilities for good profits. Private suppliers of modern consumables insisted on a monopoly or at least a duopoly. All gasoline and kerosine was distributed in the province by BPM, a subsidiary of Royal Dutch Shell. Sugar was monopolized by the semi-government company Nivas – Timor got allocated 50 tons a year. All soap came from the Dutch multinational Unilever, cement from Portland Padang, cigarettes from British BAT (based in Surabaya) and the Belgian company Faroka (Malang). Tires came from Goodyear in Bogor and Dunlop. Government services came to Timor via Bali, which also had by far the most developed economy in the province, but goods came directly from Java on the Pelni ships. Kupang had only one fuel agent, the famous Tjiong Koen Siong; he was also the sole Goodyear agent (Reksodihardjo 1960 [1957]:II, 7–8).

An ideological commitment to privileging indigenous ('national') business over ethnic Chinese ('foreign') was one thing, finding the resources to carry it through another. The result was often a so-called Ali-Baba construction. For example, one regulation stated that only national entrepreneurs could operate land transport, but this simply resulted in Chinese bus and truck operators taking a sleeping indigenous partner while continuing business as usual (Reksodihardjo 1960 [1957]:II, 3). Chinese entrepreneurs continued to dominate the trade in agricultural products, such as coffee, soy, onions, garlic, and copra.[1] Kupang's only experiment in *Indonesianisasi* also produced an Ali-Baba construction. The town had manufactured hardly anything until the opening of a small meat-canning factory in Kupang in 1952, grandly called the Indonesian Canning and Freezing Factory (ICAFF). It was run by an indigenous director – Raja Alfons Nisnoni – and underwritten by the state, but its managers were all Chinese. There was only one similar plant in the Lesser Sunda Islands, in Bali (Anon 1956). A photograph of white-gowned workers supervising

[1] Reksodihardjo 1960 [1957]:9. An example of indigenous protests against this Chinese 'abuse' is the article 'Ada bisikan begini,' *Bentara,* 31 December 1959.

gleaming machinery at ICAFF proudly decorated government reports (Kementerian Penerangan Sunda Ketjil 1953:232–4). In reality the venture was never economic.

In the early 1950s Alfons Nisnoni still had plenty of political opportunities, but even then he realized times were changing. Like the Balinese aristocrats in C. Geertz's *Peddlers and Princes* (1963c), he began to ponder how he could convert his political capital into economic. Lesser Sunda Islands Governor Susanto Tirtoprodjo persuaded him that meat processing would add value to Timor's (raja-dominated) cattle industry. Nisnoni would provide local political cover, joined by Sahetapy Engel the educated former parliamentarian and protector of the Timorese rajas. They first had to try raising local money. No one in Kupang wished to invest their own, but several Chinese agreed to lend their names. One was the venerable Tjiong Koen Siong, whose star, however, was in decline because his children lacked his skills to carry on the business. No doubt helped by the governor, the group then obtained a loan for indigenous entrepreneurs from the State Industry Bank (Bank Industri Negara) (Ormeling 1956:198). Raja Nisnoni supplied the land, across the road from his little palace at Bakunase. Salaried ethnic Chinese managers came from Java. This was a typical provincial Ali-Baba construction. An indigenous face attracted government investment and political protection, while Chinese did the work with no risk.

The local government licensed ICAFF to employ 50 workers and to slaughter 30 head of cattle a day (Anonymous 1956, Ormeling 1956). Production of corned beef, sausage and liver paté reached an impressive 148 tons the first year 1953, and nearly doubled to 264 tons the next (Figure 29). Canned meat was suddenly Kupang's major export, accounting for over a third of the value of goods transiting the harbour (Anonymous 1956) (live cattle were next). But the year after that it was down to 177 tons, and production did not recover again. The cattle quota was never filled because the factory could not pay the price they fetched at export (Lalamentik 1961:6, Ormeling 1956). Even so, canned beef from Bali cost less in Kupang than ICAFF's local product. The ethnic Chinese managers gambled away the factory's remaining cash. The huge inflation of the late 1950s and early 1960s, including a massive currency devaluation (*sanering*) in August 1959, left the factory unable to order tinplate (Pemda NTT 1966:32). An expensive fire that same year added to its woes.[2] The doors

2 *Bentara*, 22 October 1959.

Figure 29. ICAFF label (courtesy of Mr. Leopold Nisnoni).

closed in 1963, and today only a concrete slab reminds passers-by of Kupang's first industrial experiment (Doko 1982:44–5). By the mid-1960s most of the other little ventures in town had shut as well. Umar Baktir's weaving factory had run out of money to buy cotton thread, and several little soap factories had died after caustic soda became unavailable. Big plans to produce silk or to turn Timor into 'Indonesia's cotton belt' came to nothing (Sidik et al 1968:100–2). Clearly, merely waiting on Jakarta to scale up the *Indonesianisasi* policy was not going to significantly improve incomes for the new indigenous elite in Kupang. The answer instead was to expand state services, expand local control over them, and see where this might produce positive spinoffs for those working in Kupang's government buildings (still the temporary ones in the former Kampong Belanda).

Localism

Expanding state services was essential if general welfare in the region was to improve. The war had destroyed most of the little that the Dutch had achieved in Timor in agriculture, health, education and communications. Only some of the infrastructure had been rebuilt after the war, and soon after that the economy deteriorated so badly that many of these gains were once more reversed. Agricultural development faced failure after failure. In the years 1946–49 the NIT under Dutch patronage had started an ambitious programme to mechanize tillage. The Sekon pilot scheme on 2,500 hectares of subsistence land near Kefamenanu aimed to demonstrate that tractors could improve the island's food supply (Ormeling 1956). But by 1950 it had been declared a failure and the tractors moved to Southeast Sulawesi (Kana 1969:App. 11, 191f). In 1954 Raja Alfons Nisnoni of Kupang district acquired a Ferguson tractor for his agriculture department. People were invited to come and watch it at work in the gardens near his house. After that it seems to have been used exclusively on his own lands at Bakunase (Anonymous 1956).

Education and health services were in an appalling state. By 1953 the number of primary and junior secondary schools in Kupang was two or three times higher than before the war, reflecting the town's growth and upward social mobility. Even these were forced to turn children away due to insufficient space. But many teachers were unqualified. Ninety percent of the buildings were substandard, and half were considered 'pig sties' as rainwater poured in through the roof and goats walked through broken walls to sleep in them at night. The town's only senior high school (SMA) was still being used for residential housing. Housing remained in short supply, due to wartime bombing and the demand from civil servants pouring into Kupang with the opening of new government offices (Kementerian Penerangan Sunda Ketjil 1953:227–8). In that same year there were just four doctors in all of Timor, among a population of 440,000 afflicted by endemic malaria and respiratory diseases.[3] One was stationed in Atambua, one in Soë, and two in the new government-funded hospital in Kupang. All were Dutch. There was also an Indonesian dentist, an ethnic Chinese.[4]

Transport infrastructure was equally poor. One ship from Java visited the eastern islands each month, but so unpredictably that people joked that the company's initials KPM stood for '*Kom Pas Morgen*' (Coming Tomorrow).[5] Another came fortnightly from Makassar, and some small government 'white ships' took passengers incidentally among the Lesser Sunda islands (Dick 1986:131, Kementerian Penerangan Sunda Ketjil 1953:229). Students from the interior wishing to study in Java first spent days traveling to Kupang on horseback, then several more days to obtain a ticket. If, as often happened, the ship was full they could try again next month.[6] A Garuda DC-3 Dakota flew members of the elite to and from Java once a week (in the late 1950s replaced by a Convair CV-240), with a smaller De Havilland Heron flying twice a week via Makassar. Telephone connections into the interior, wrecked during the war, had been restored only to the head offices of the rajas (Kementerian Penerangan Sunda Ketjil 1953:220).

---

[3] Disease statistics for the early 1970s are in Pemda NTT (1973).

[4] Kementerian Penerangan Sunda Ketjil 1953. Four years later there were still only 17 in the entire province from Bali to Timor (Dicker 2007:56, Reksodihardjo 1960 [1957]:II, 78).

[5] Koninklijke Paketvaart Maatschappij, Royal Packet Company. In fact the service deteriorated markedly after the 1957 Pelni takeover.

[6] *Bentara*, 1 August 1954.

The political class in the region felt strongly that this sad state of affairs was the result of leadership failure. The bureaucrat-politicians in Java were not doing enough to help because they lacked local knowledge. One editorial from Flores in 1954 said the Javanese shouted a lot of slogans about national unity but 'did not know how to ride a horse without stirrups up and down the mountains of Sumba or Timor.' The answer was to let locals take over on their own turf. Java had outlawed federalism in 1950, but if they did not want federalism to return by popular acclamation they should not wait for an 'anti-colonial' reaction to arise outside Java and Sumatra. Java should immediately extend maximum autonomy, appointing locals at least to all the middle and lower level positions.[7] Like the Kupang intellectuals who had argued in the 1930s that indigeneity was the main qualification for public office (Chapter 5), the urban opinion-makers of the 1950s wished to be gatekeepers to their own domains. Their preoccupation with localist politics soon began to undermine the wider goal of improving popular welfare.

The main problem in their view was how to take Jakarta's money and still run their own show – how to have their cake and eat it too. This dilemma had only one solution – the threat of sabotage. Considering how shaky Indonesia's independent state still was, such a threat was likely to be quite effective. The first localist agitation concerned religion. When the Ministry of Religious Affairs began sending out officials to establish provincial and district offices in May 1951, all were Muslims, while Kupang was predominantly Protestant. The town erupted in protest. It took eighteen months until Jakarta agreed to appoint a Protestant to head the local office, with a Muslim deputy. Bali – predominantly Hindu – saw similar protests (Reksodihardjo 1960 [1957]:I, 28).

The ultimate sabotage was the deliberate instigation of political instability. Only an alliance between disaffected elements in the regions *and* at the centre had any chance of instilling real fear of disintegration in Jakarta. This was a technique used to devastating effect in 1965/66. As then, so in 1957 the threat came from an alliance between military officers opposed to Sukarno and civilian notables all over the archipelago with localist agendas. When troops in Sulawesi declared the Permesta revolt in March 1957, they mobilized localist sentiments among the wider population in Sulawesi, and the feeling spread also to Kupang (Harvey 1977). The town was part of the military region led from Makassar and its population of

[7] *Bentara* (poorly legible – vol.14, probably 15 December 1954).

around 23,000 made it worth courting. Nusa Tenggara provincial governor Susanto Tirtoprodjo had just been replaced by Sarimin Reksodihardjo, leaving a vacuum of civilian authority. Anyway he was far away in the provincial capital in Bali. The regional commander, Lt. Col. Ventje Sumual, flew to Kupang to address a large crowd on the football field on 13 April. The local military commander, Major Kodiowa, an energetic and also popular mobilizer, required all men aged 21 or over to attend. The enthusiastic cry 'evict all the Javanese!' rang out. Stirring up the locals was the tall and popular 26-year old Victor ('Vicky') Koroh, the only son of the late Raja H.A. Koroh. He had studied in Makassar. Violence came readily to hand. When a policeman roughed up Koroh during an incident on the street, emotions exploded among the youth and made the town ungovernable for a month. The rebellious military officers boosted their populist following by skilfully exploiting anti-police feelings among the population (Banunaek 2007:94–5). After the rally a convoy of open military jeeps carrying gun-toting soldiers led marchers around a town in which demonstrations were still astonishing occasions. Some shooting was heard.[8] The local head of police, a Javanese man named Soemantri, was put under house arrest for several days.

The feeling ran strongest among students, teachers and minor civil servants. Albert Loni (a pseudonym), then 18 and still at high school, told me how the events stimulated a sense of injustice among these young men and women dreaming of a career. New media were bringing national events into their simple Kupang homes. There was no local newspaper in the 1950s, but he and his mates listened to the radio and read his father's old subscription copies of *Indonesia Raja*, a Jakarta newspaper that often reported regional dissatisfaction around Indonesia. Timor was sending its sandalwood, its beeswax and its dried meat to Java, but what was it getting in return? they wanted to know. They behaved insolently to Javanese teachers and policemen that year. They could understand that a shortage of educated Timorese meant Javanese held the senior bureaucratic positions. But when Jakarta also sent poorly qualified ex-revolutionary fighters to Timor to fill more accessible jobs, such as those of teachers and policemen, simply to get rid of them in Java, resentment in Timor rose. 'These were the jobs *we* had in mind,' he told me. A locally born teacher with the (Batak) name Turman Silalahi led the movement against Javanese teachers under the slogan 'When one hurts we all hurt.' Many outside

[8] A description comes from Mrs. Ruth Dicker, who was in Kupang at the time and who showed me her diary entry for that day during my visit with her in 2009.

teachers felt intimidated enough to leave, temporarily causing a serious shortage in Timor. The localist protesters in April and May 1957 gave the name Destar Merah (Red Cap) to their anti-Java and anti-communist movement to remove Muslim and/ or Javanese teachers, police, and government officials.[9]

Jakarta's response to the Permesta revolt combined a little stick of repression with a big carrot of a new province. Timor had little need of the stick, since the revolt was reigned in before it had spread to Timor's military ranks, and those few officers most implicated soon slipped away across the border to Portuguese Timor. The carrot was in any case more effective. What Jakarta could offer Kupang's youthful and increasingly educated public was essentially the gift of the means of primitive accumulation. In the face of subtle threats of sabotage by these aspiring members of the new intermediate class, appeasement became the centre's most trusted technique for maintaining stability. Increasing government services in remote areas was an important development aim, and, if this could be achieved only through unfair distribution of the state's resources, that was the price to be paid. As the Dutch had betted on rajas wearing sarongs, so the republic now began betting on western-educated men and women in the towns. At the end of 1958 the new province was carved out of the Lesser Sunda Islands (by then called Nusa Tenggara). It was called East Nusa Tenggara and its capital was Kupang.

Subdivision of large administrative units has been a popular tactic among Indonesian provincial officials ever since independence. It pulls control over state resources closer to home. The campaign for a new province had been running since 1953. It was conducted entirely by bureaucrats, who deployed a populist rhetoric. Administrative boundary changes had held little interest for politically involved Indonesians in late colonial times, unless they concerned the little kingdoms.[10] But the democratic

---

9 Farram (2004:298), quoting Francillon (1967:35); also Dicker (2007:7).

10 The Dutch maintained multiple levels of government. A province called the Great East (Groote Oost) was created for the entire east in 1938. Underneath that lay the residency – Kupang was the seat of the Residency Timor and Dependencies, which included Timor, Sumba, Flores, and Sumbawa. Below that came first the district (*afdeeling*, one for every major island in the residency) and then the sub-district (*onderafdeeling*), which covered several self-ruled kingdoms. The Japanese created the Lesser Sunda province out of the Great East, and the Republic of Indonesia maintained that division after the Pacific War. But the Republic did not control the area, and the Dutch returned it to a larger unit, renamed the State of East Indonesia (Negara Indonesia Timur, NIT). The Lesser Sunda Islands re-emerged late in 1949 after the Dutch recognized Indonesian independence. It was an administrative province, meaning its governor was centrally appointed and not monitored by a provincial legislative assembly. The residency had been abolished,

and corrupt 1950s thoroughly politicized such boundaries. For a while the key unit of local government was the island government – one for each major island, corresponding to the colonial *afdeeling.* However, Jakarta soon determined to dissolve the island governments and to make the much larger province the basic unit of regional autonomy. From that point on, getting one of their own became the most interesting issue on the local elite agenda. Each island government – run by 'autodidacts in government' – as former NTT governor Ben Mboi called them (2009: 8–22) – fought their own campaign for a piece of the action. Timor's drive was publicly funded through the long-serving head of Timor who followed Jaap Amalo, Stephen nDoen.

The first regional conference devoted to the issue took place in Ende in June 1954, and the second in Singaraja in December.[11] Island governments suppressed their rivalry to pressure Jakarta together. The Indonesian interior minister, with an eye on the upcoming elections, made encouraging noises in a meeting in March 1955 (Figure 30). When the election year confirmed the overwhelming strength of religion outside Java, subsequent lobbying took on a strongly religious tone. Party congresses in 1956 and 1957 – again dominated by bureaucrats – debated provincial boundary proposals – promoting especially those that would give their party hegemony in any new province based on the religious demography. But Kupang argued along historical lines that any new province should take as its basis the former residency of Timor and Dependencies, covering Timor, Sumba, Flores, and Sumbawa, and which had its base in Kupang (Cribb 2000). This postcolonial argument moved PNI-dominated Jakarta more than the religious one. Jakarta's arm had been twisted by the regional revolts of 1957. Despite protests from Flores that it did not want a reinvented colonialism, and that it and not Timor was producing most of the region's surplus, Kupang became the capital. But religion had the last word on the boundaries. Majority Muslim Lombok and Sumbawa became West Nusa Tenggara, the Protestants and Catholics were allowed to fight it out among themselves in East Nusa Tenggara, while Hindu Bali (which had hardly been interested in the new-province scheme) got its own tiny province.

---

but island governments corresponding to the former afdeeling had been maintained and democratized since independence – Timor, Sumba, Flores, Sumbawa, Lombok and Bali each had one of their own, with a corresponding legislative assembly.

[11] *Bentara,* 1 August 1954; 1 January 1955; 1 March 1955; 15 May 1955. All correspondence summarized in Hermanus (1985:Vol.3).

Figure 30. Timor government delegation in Jakarta to lobby for a new province, March 1955. From left to right (as supplied): Sa'iah, da Costa (North Central Timor), Koesa Nope (South Central Timor), E.R. Herewila, Michael Marcus, Benufinit, Burhanudin Lelang (Alor) (photo courtesy Dra. Ruth Heny A. Nitbani-Markus).

Ethnic, religious and territorial politics brought many benefits to its practitioners, even under martial law conditions after 1957. In vain did the military commander for Nusa Tenggara, Lt. Col. Minggu, warn at the ceremony inaugurating the new province that it was intended to strengthen national unity and was not to be about politics or autonomy.[12] Religious and ethnic parties gained over 50% of the vote in the 1955 national elections everywhere outside Java, except in some plantation areas.[13] Their highest returns typically came from rural hinterlands of towns, such as Pontianak and Bengkulu, rather than from the towns themselves. These areas had been little penetrated by capitalism and lacked a history of revolutionary mobilization. Their small indigenous middle classes relied to a great extent on state intervention in the local economy. Party leaders drew their votes from communal patron-client networks. This was

[12] The speech is included in a booklet apparently produced in Kupang in relation to the ceremony marking the creation of NTT province in late 1958. The title page is missing. The booklet is in the archive of Mr. Leopold Nisnoni, Kupang.

[13] See Footnote 3 of Chapter 7.

precisely the type of economy that Kalecki had sketched as the home of the intermediate classes. Explicitly class-based mobilization, by contrast, had supplanted these rural and small-town patron-client politics in revolutionary Java and in those areas outside Java most affected by plantation and mining capitalism.

Within Timor, all factionalism had to do with ethnic identities. In Africa, state formation actually stimulated communalism. To maintain order within pre-capitalist economies 'the [colonial African] state had to convert its superior coercive force over Africans into a legitimate authority accepted by Africans and therefore mediated through their own pre-existing or emergent relations of power' (Lonsdale and Berman 1979). Something similar was happening in Timor. Spatial ethnic segregation had been built into Kupang's urban fabric since colonial times. Sabunese lived in Fontein and Fatufeto, Rotenese in Kuanino and Oebobo, Chinese in the commercial old town, while few Timorese were found anywhere (Leirissa et al 1984:56).[14] But rather than fading under modernization, ethnic clientelism became more entrenched as the rents from government administration grew. Modern politics homogenized numerous little local identities into just three, each with its widely accepted stereotypical attributes, and with its political turf known as *kapling* – from the Dutch *kaveling* or land parcel. Most Rotenese adhered to Parkindo, most Sabunese to the secular PNI, while ethnic Timorese tended to follow the bossist preferences of their rajas (which the two other ethnic groups despised as 'feudal'). Most Timorese rajas who did not go with Parkindo supported the secular party PRN, because their Sabunese rival Herewila was already with the main secular party PNI. Herewila had often preached against this type of ethnic chauvinism. As early as November 1950 he had warned, in a speech in Kupang, of 'neo-colonialism between ourselves ... a neo-colonialism of the intellectuals [who will introduce] provincialism and the family system.'[15] But even he was unable to escape from it. By the mid-New Order several observers noted that the majority of Kupang's adult population, even if they lived in ethnically mixed kampongs, belonged to an ethnic association, for protection and solidarity.[16]

---

14 Since then, class has become more important than ethnicity as the basis for spatial segregation (Tidey 2012, ditto Colombijn 2010).

15 *Bentara* 2 November 1950. Similar sentiments were expressed in a speech to the opening of the Timor parliament on 22 February 1951 (Kana 1969: App18, 230) – afterwards much quoted, for example by Doko (1981a:72).

16 The Indonesian term for these organizations is 'ikatan kekeluargaan,' meaning 'family bond' (Leirissa et al 1984:58). Widiyatmika (1983:64) (similarly Vel 2007) observed that

Even the militarization that followed the end of liberal democracy in 1959 did not sweep away the ethnic *kapling*. When I asked a former Kupang bureaucrat if they found military rule oppressive, he answered: 'No, they were all our people.' John Smail, in his study on the military politics of the 1956 regional revolt in North Sumatra, described the local units as less like a division of the Indonesian army and more like 'the military element in and of North Sumatra.' In a memorable image he wrote that the military were 'laid over this society like a thin wet sheet over a body, picking up a perfect imprint of the complexities of its shape' (Smail 1968:132). He could have been writing about Kupang. Regardless of the violence the military could deploy, no ethnic outsider ever made it big through the military in Kupang. The first military resort commander (*danrem*) under Guided Democracy, Lt. Col. Paikun from Pasundan in West Java, felt in 1964 he had a chance of making it to the provincial governor's office. He had the rank to please Jakarta, and as a publicity stunt for his local constituency had built Kupang's gigantic football stadium at Merdeka. But the provincial parliament refused to endorse him. Instead the job went to local boy El Tari, then just a captain. When the early New Order military forced all political parties to replace their top people with soldiers, Parkindo appointed Captain Manafe, a Rotenese who (so I was told) 'happened to be military,' to sit in parliament for them.

All Ministry of the Interior offices in the early 1960s were PNI. Since most schools in NTT were run by churches, Parkindo had a powerful influence in the Education Department, beginning with its provincial head I.H. Doko. But PNI had a foot in the door in education too, since the central government provided substantial subsidies to church schools. So a teacher in PNI-loyal Sabu, for example, was well advised to join PNI if he wanted a transfer or a promotion, while one in Parkindo-loyal Rote should do the opposite. Fist fights between teachers affiliated with PNI and Parkindo were not uncommon. The polarization was caused by structural change in Jakarta: in 1961 President Sukarno split the Ministry of Education, Knowledge and Culture into a communist-controlled Department of Basic Education and Culture and an army-controlled Department of Higher Education and Knowledge. The split was undone after a year but the polarization lasted longer.[17]

---

such associations in Kupang were particularly strong among non-locals – from Sumba, Flores, Solor, Sunda, and South Sulawesi. The study on ethnic clientelism by Dagang (2004) is discussed in Chapter 11.

[17] 'Ketika itu, Presiden Soekarno membagi Kementerian Pendidikan, Pengetahuan, dan Kebudayaan (PPK) menjadi Departemen Pendidikan Dasar dan Kebudayaan (PDK) serta

Each *kapling* produced its rents. The legacy of the revolution had been 'economic dishonesty in its many forms (such as corruption, black-marketeering, smuggling) and its passive tolerance… distrust of foreign investment [and the] belief that private enterprise is dishonorable' (Sutter 1959:I, 692–3). The nationally dominant political party PNI was a major proponent of the statist ideas that produced this corruption. Although in practice the policy left big capital alone, provincial capital was closely tied to state regulation. Since top PNI politicians were mainly bureaucrats and well-connected businessmen, and since the party earned most of its money from rents on business straddling the public-private divide (Rocamora 1974), politicians and bureaucrats alike often became involved in business relying on state subsidies. *Mutatis mutandis,* the same applied to all the other parties except the PKI. The habit among provincial politicians to skip between the legislative and executive branches of government throughout their careers made politicized predation on the state a matter of the urban bureaucratic elite as a whole rather than of any institution in particular.

The new province was a moment for Kupang's bureaucratic elite to savour. The rajas were finally about to disappear. Kupang would see a massive state-funded building programme, though budgets remained far from adequate. Former bureaucrats recalled to me that corruption began to head for the skies, from this time onwards and into the New Order. When so much of the cash in NTT circulated through the hands of a small group of people who also set the rules of conduct, primitive accumulation was the natural outcome. Amidst NTT's oceans of poverty, the state increasingly became the means, for those who had exclusive access to it, to live in comfort.

White Collar Crime

One example of the spoils available comes from a service company owned by the Kupang district government. PD Tjendana ran a couple of trucks – also used as the town's only buses – a hostel and a printery. We only have annual reports for 1970 and 1971 (PD Tjendana 1970, 1971), but there is no reason to think the picture was radically different throughout the 1960s. Its most lucrative business was 'trade.' By this was meant not free trade in an open market but government procurement in a regulated one. The

Departemen Pendidikan Tinggi dan Pengetahuan (PTP)' (Agus Suwignyo, 'Tiga Menteri Pendidikan?', *Kompas*, 20 October 2011).

central government sent out rice, as part of the civil servants' salaries, and building materials under its five-year development plans. In the past this flow of goods had been entrusted to the hard-working ethnic Chinese entrepreneur Ong Teo Piet, or Pieter Nerius (who had begun building his connections with government after arriving in Kupang in 1952 – Adam et al 1997:108). But the district government now insisted that local distribution be handled by PD Tjendana, from whence the goods were passed, duly marked up, to other government agencies. In 1970 trade had a turnover of Rp 8.3 million, which could buy a lot more in those days than the formal equivalent of US$23,000 would suggest. Rp 1.9 million or 23% of this was profit.

Its two trucks, meanwhile, were running at a loss of Rp 230,000. Yet shady deals on fuel purchases ensured that PD Tjendana was still making good money for the staff. The Air Force at the Penfui aerodrome had engineered a monopoly on fuel sales. The official price of a drum of fuel was Rp 8,000, but air force officers would sell it to a PD Tjendana staff member for Rp 16,000. The latter would then sell it to PD Tjendana for Rp 20,000. This was done with the approval of the boss, former Timor head and NTT assistant governor W.C.H. Oematan, who shared in the profit. The extra costs, of course, were borne by the bus passengers. The printery – the only one in town – only had to fill a demand for about a ream of printed paper a day (41,000 sheets in a year), yet it made a profit of Rp 670,000. Its main customers were other government departments, who were forced to pay exorbitant prices to stencil their reports.

The company tried issuing shares to the public but no one would buy. Yet when it offered them to its staff, the terms were suddenly very attractive. Each member obtained 100 shares at a nominal value of Rp 250 a share. PD Tjendana paid a dividend in 1970 of Rp 73.50 a share, equivalent to a healthy 29% return on investment. Salaries at PD Tjendana were generous. The company's part-time commissioners included Sahetapy Engel and Alfons Nisnoni. For the privilege of signing off on annual reports they received Rp 750 a month, almost double the regular monthly salary of Rp 400 for a civil servant in those days. The full-time director of the printery earned Rp 3,000 a month.

PD Tjendana was just one of a rich field of rent-seeking ventures consisting of cooperatives, state-owned corporations, and 'foundations' (*yayasan*) that sought to provide alternative, state-run distribution networks to undercut the Chinese. Many sold cheap daily consumption goods, such as soap, kerosene, sugar, and coffee; others exported sandalwood or cattle. The cooperatives got a big boost as the economy nosedived from 1960 onwards. By 1967 their number in every district was nearly half the number of Chinese shops (Sidik et al 1968:64–8, App. III/8). They were heavily politicized, serving as stepping stones to higher office and as slush funds and barrels of political pork; and they proved to be corrupt and inefficient. The army was well represented among them; cooperatives provided one of the links that bound it to local society. Among NTT's foremost New Order civilian politicians who came up through the cooperatives were Canisius Parera, who went from Livestock Cooperative manager in Kupang to anti-communist youth leader in late 1965, and Jan Kiapoli, who had spent years running various cooperatives in Flores and Timor before becoming speaker of the provincial parliament in 1965.

Kupang had no newspaper in this period (which perhaps says something about the narrowing social base of its civil society), but we gain glimpses of the regular corruption scandals from the region's only news journal, *Bentara*, based in Flores. The stories begin in the year 1959, when NTT became a province and the state apparatus began to expand rapidly. The militarization of government silenced checks and balances and introduced a new cynicism among those in power. Scarcity became a resource for those who controlled flows. In June 1959 a shipment of 96,000 yards of textile arrived at the harbour in Ende. It was the first instalment of 800,000 yards of textile intended for civil servants in all of East Nusa Tenggara, a small part of the war reparations Japan was paying Indonesia. The civil servants cooperative had to sell the textile cheaply to its members, who would make clothes out of it and store the proceeds with the government. Soon it emerged that some local officials were pocketing the proceeds themselves. St. nDoen, the district chief of East Flores, was put under house arrest.[18] The Copra Foundation meanwhile, big in Flores and intended to maintain prices and ensure state revenue by centralizing all copra trade, had long been a well-known money spinner for its administrators. But this diversion of public resources into private pockets produced only censorious finger-wagging by the military commander.[19]

---

18 'Barang pampasan untuk pegawai pemerintah dan pegawai2 dari seluruh Flores,' *Bentara,* 15 July 1959; 'Persoalan pembagian/ pendjualan kain pampasan perang di Flotim,' *Bentara,* 17 March 1960; 'Ada orang jang mentjatut kain2 pampasan,' *Bentara,* 24 March 1960. The name resembles that of Stephen nDoen, the later provincial secretary, but some chronological inconsistencies raise the possibility that it was someone else.

19 'Kapten Suratman/ Pupekuper Flores: Kita harus bekerdja keras tjepat,' *Bentara,* 1 August 1959. It played a major role as slush fund in the 1950s factional politics of Maumere, capital of Sikka district – see Anonymous 1974.

Shipping services had become erratic since Jakarta nationalized the Dutch-owned shipping line KPM in 1957. East Nusa Tenggara had been totally dependent on it for its export and import. The state-owned line Pelni that took over the service found it more remunerative to deploy its ships elsewhere than in eastern Indonesia. Everyone with authority to regulate transport – whether of copra from Flores, of lontar sap from Rote, or of cattle from Sumba or Timor – squeezed the desperate owners whose products were languishing at the harbour. When the boat did arrive, Pelni crews asked for 'you-know-I-know' bribes to load the goods (*uang Tahu Sama Tahu*, or *uang TST* – the expression is still used today).[20] Fifteen years later an Australian report on the cattle industry made it clear that the problem continued to weaken the province's main export (Collier and Tjakrawerdaja 1974). It began with village officials demanding a 'village administration fee' equivalent to a US dollar a head to let the beast pass out of its borders, continued with payments to the Jakarta shipping office to ensure a ship actually arrived, and did not end until further charges had been paid once it did arrive, including a US$200 'expedition fee' (*uang lancar*) for each shipment; all this on top of the official rates.

The state subsidies passed to the cooperatives helped to buy political loyalties, and could thus be considered 'transfer rents' to ensure political stability. Amidst the political crisis of 1965 the central government under cabinet minister Leimena disbursed a US$3.8 million 'crash program' designed to stimulate the moribund economy in the regions and, more importantly, to retain loyalties there. The point man to pick projects in NTT was the military deputy governor, (by now) Major El Tari. He allocated some money to the army-led cooperative Gerkopin (Sidik et al 1968:65), but most went to a state-owned company called Fajar Ternak whose aim it was to seize and reinvigorate the cattle export sector.[21] Soon afterwards the leadership of this company passed to El Tari's military colleague Is Tibuludji, who expanded its activities into sandalwood, cattle skins, coffee and copra. Soldiers rarely make good businesspeople. While Fajar Ternak did successfully use its leverage with Jakarta to bring fuel and vehicles into Timor, its cattle exporting skills were abysmal. After valiantly announcing it was going to export 20,000 head of cattle, the company managed to export a grand total of just 537. In short, it did not take long

---

20 'Suara-suara dari Nusa Tenggara Timur,' *Bentara*, 3 December 1959.

21 It was led for a while by the entrepreneurial bureaucrat J.L. Indradewa, who had made his name in the early 1950s as an intellectual spokesman for the rajas in Flores, and who went on to become wealthy in Jakarta.

for the whole crash programme to … crash. The economic crisis had ensured undercapitalization. Politics were to blame too. El Tari, by now NTT governor, tried shifting some of the blame to the defeated communists, who had also politicized cooperatives. But he had to confess that the real causes of the failures were 'mis-management,' 'poor accountability' and plain 'cheating' (Tari 1972:II, 416–39, 453–5). The ethnic Chinese businesspeople, who were supposed to have been displaced by all this government investment, meanwhile, proved that it was not at all impossible to make money even in a poor society and amidst a hostile political environment (Sidik et al 1968:66).

Governor El Tari frequently stressed the 'heroic' nature of his work. He certainly had heroic discretion in the disbursement of funds. Sixty percent of expenditures in his budgets in the period 1968–70 were marked simply 'other.' (The biggest single marked item, by the way, was education, at 22%). He also did not have to give an accounting to local taxpayers, because 85% of his budget came directly from Jakarta (Tari 1969:5–7). All the office holders in the Livestock Cooperative, the governor among them, for example, awarded themselves allowances of Rp 4–5,000 a month – over 10 times the official salary of a regular civil servant. Building projects were awarded to friends and allies with little thought for their usefulness. In the early 1970s Governor El Tari ordered the construction of not one but two sandalwood oil factories on the outskirts of Kupang, even though there was almost no sandalwood left in Timor (Doko 1982:45–6).

Albert Loni gave me a glimpse into the ease with which money flowed to people within the system, even while the governor complained about lack of resources and arbitrary cuts made by officials above him. By the early 1960s Loni was a university student in Bandung on a NTT government scholarship (won through family connections). His allowance was about ten times the salary of a working civil servant. For the return transport to Kupang in 1964 he was given half a million rupiah in cash – about US$2,000,[22] enough for many luxurious air tickets, even after half of it had been spent on unofficial payments to various officials. 'It was white collar crime,' he acknowledged to me, 'but it was all legally approved with stamps and letters.' Back in Kupang as a high school sports teacher, he, like most civil servants in those crisis-ridden years spent much of his time on business ventures. A friend from the air force base brought drums of fuel, which Albert then sold on a profit-sharing basis. He took cheap transistor

[22] Using historical exchange rates at http://fx.sauder.ubc.ca (accessed 17 August 2013).

radios and rice consignments intended for civil servants and sold them at high prices on the open market in the interior. When he felt in 1971 that his promotion chances were inadequate, he decided to migrate to Australia. In order to support his wife in Kupang for a year while she was waiting for a visa, he asked Governor El Tari for an interest-free loan of Rp 150,000. He invested it and fed his family for a year on the interest.

These stories do not describe personal mendacity so much as a system that Fred Riggs called the 'sala' bureaucracy (Riggs 1964:267–71). In Thailand, a 'sala' is a pavilion adjacent to the temple that serves as a community meeting place for entertainment, business, worship and other public purposes. Riggs turned it into a metaphor for the mixture of motives and practices found in public offices. Civil servants deal with people both officially as clients, and commercially as customers. The entire arsenal of tricks, described in studies on the bureaucracy elsewhere at this time, from brokerage on resale of merchandise to mark-ups on acquisitions were routine in Kupang also. Roelof van Zeeveld Oostingh (1970:189–90) concluded his dissertation on this topic at the time with the words: '[A] new structural category has evolved in incipient form – that of the *pegawai negeri* [civil servant] as an entrepreneur.... [T]he individuals who fill the ranks of *pegawai negeri* are civil servants who are rooted in the broader base of Indonesian society ....'

Militarization

Popular dissatisfaction with these exploitative practices began to brew around Indonesia in the early 1960s. In 1963 the journalist Mochtar Lubis wrote a novel about them that soon acquired the status of a classic. He was under house arrest in Jakarta for previous exposés in *Indonesia Raja*. This delayed the novel's distribution in Indonesia for a time, but an English translation appeared the same year – *Twilight in Jakarta* (1963) – and a Malaysian one the next year. It described the extravagant lifestyles of apparatchiks who raised money for their political parties and for themselves by manipulating import licences, while the poor went hungry. *Twilight in Jakarta* captured the essence of hundreds of similar stories in the press.

Towards the end of 1964 the PKI began to mobilize on the discontent. The party's cultural institute Lekra produced a song that became popular about the 'bureaucratic capitalist' (*kapitalis birokrat,* abbreviated *kabir*) and another about the 'three town devils.' Party conventions began to rail against 'village devils' and 'town devils.' The first were usually listed at seven: landlords who refused to implement the land reform law, officials who defended them, the middlemen who oppressed farmers, the religious who demanded offerings, 'bandits' who worked for the landlords, moneylenders, and usurers. The short list of urban devils condemned bureaucratic capitalists (*kabir*), manipulators and corruptors. A longer list had five: the petty bourgeoisie who extract riches without a thought for negative social consequences, speculators, manipulators, vested interests and bureaucratic capitalists.[23] It was a caricature of the establishment in Middle Indonesia, but not one it could afford to ignore.

The potential for violence hastened a rapprochement between provincial civilian and national military elites. Civilian elites in the provinces clearly felt a growing need for protection from non-elite anger at their anti-social behaviour. But central military leaders, who were moving to seize control of what they felt was a deteriorating situation (Crouch 1988, Sundhaussen 1982), also had a stake in provincial partnerships. They realized that the road to increased political influence in Jakarta lay via the provinces. No one did more to build the army into a political force than General A.H. Nasution, army chief of staff for most of the 1950s and early 1960s. Success in Jakarta, where the military top brass increasingly saw the well-organized communist party PKI as its greatest rival, came only through appeasing several regional revolts. He had already begun in late 1951 to design a permanent territorial system modelled on the revolutionary guerrilla strategy in Java. The plan was to politicize and regionalize the military by concentrating military, administrative and political powers in regional military commands. Eastern Indonesia was covered by military region VII (Tentara dan Territorium VII, or T&T VII). In each T&T, several Military District Commands (Perwira Distrik Militer, PDM) had to liaise with the civilian population.

Each major island in the Lesser Sunda Islands had a PDM led by a lieutenant drawn from a local ethnic group. Indigenizing military leadership was supposed to prevent a recurrence of the popular resentment that, for example, had faced the Siliwangi troops upon landing in Kupang in 1950 (Chapter 5). The PDM in Kupang in 1955 was Is Tibuludji. Born in Kupang in 1922 and trained as a teacher in Bandung along with Doko, he was swept into the republican military in Java by the revolution. He was among the first PDM posted to the eastern archipelago when he went to Waingapu

---

23 *Harian Rakjat*, 12 January 1965.

in Sumba in July 1953. Ende in Flores was next, followed by Kupang in 1955 (Passar 2005:277–9). The PDM had an infantry regiment at his disposal, which as time went on was increasingly made up of locally recruited soldiers. Under him a number of non-commissioned officers were distributed in the districts, known as BODM (Bintara Onder-Distrik Militer, Military Sub-district Non-Commissioned Officers).

Territorializing military politics in this way carried with it the risk that warlordism would fragment the country. Nasution's chief skill lay in negotiating with prima donna local commanders. Whenever another internal military revolt broke out, he would, as far as possible, put it down using troops from the same region who remained loyal to the centre. Thus El Tari, who was to become NTT governor, was deployed to fight the RMS revolt in Ambon in 1950. His unit of mainly ex-KNIL troops did little or no fighting. They were told to persuade rebellious Timorese KNIL troops to switch sides. A mission to the Sulawesi region in the late 1950s to confront troops loyal to Permesta also involved mainly negotiation (Setwilda 1978). To soldiers like El Tari, political conflicts and military factionalism looked like two sides of the same coin.

Military embeddedness in provincial society – Smail's 'thin wet sheet over a body' – arose as much from Jakarta's inability to pay its troops properly as from ethnic rivalries and charismatic personalities. In 1951, the military spent only 55% on commodities compared with the amount spent by the colonial army KNIL in 1949; soldiers earned only 40%, and their housing allowance was only 20% of what KNIL soldiers had received two years earlier (Sundhaussen 1982:69). This forced soldiers to 'live off the land.' They formed alliances with local business interests, such as the state-run Copra Foundation (Yayasan Copra) which was big in Flores, and these in turn required connections with local political parties. Military warlords would never have launched the Permesta revolt in 1957 if their interests had not been bundled with those of local business. Permesta leaders demanded extensive financial autonomy for their copra-rich region, more local personnel in government positions, greater military autonomy from civilian politicians in Jakarta, and the return of Vice-President Hatta (an outer island intellectual who had resigned after conflict with President Sukarno).

Nasution cajoled and threatened, sent in troops when bluff needed to be called, but only rarely ordered them to shoot. Appeasement was his central tactic. Considering Jakarta had little to offer by way of extra resources, granting permission to build new military and civilian government structures in restive regions beyond Java amounted (once more) to handing gifts of primitive accumulation to the embryonic middle classes that inhabited provincial towns all over Indonesia. As the military expanded its territorial footprint, they became increasingly valuable local rent-seeking allies, and these armed alliances grew increasingly militant in the late 1950s. Martial law was declared in March 1957. In 1958 Nasution divided the eastern Indonesian T&T VII into four military regions and renamed them Kodam (Komando Daerah Militer, Regional Military Command). Each corresponded with a civilian province. Kodam XVI/ Udayana, based in Denpasar, Bali, covered the province of Nusa Tenggara. Officers now enjoyed increased promotion opportunities (Sundhaussen 1982:125). In March 1960 the army announced a new territorial warfare doctrine that distributed troops over more places on the map.[24] The main purpose of these territorial units was not so much to retail violence as to mobilize and raise funds, that is, to build links with local middle class allies. In order to contain the political advances of the PKI, military officers engaged in civic action, indoctrination, and cultural activity through a proliferation of allied organizations for youth, veterans, trade unions, the religious, peasants, and political activists (Sundhaussen 1982:138–143, 175).

Gatekeepers

The local predatory regime described in this chapter in many ways resembled the 'bureaucratic capitalists' long recognized by Southeast Asia scholars such as Fred Riggs (1966) and notably Richard Robison (1978). Military officers controlled access to certain markets and thus reaped profits from foreign and Chinese capital. The line between private and public interests was blurred, authority was patrimonial, and the purpose of this rent-seeking behaviour was not to accumulate productive capital but to raise funds for politics. In certain respects it also reflected the much older patterns that Marx famously characterized as the Asiatic mode of

[24] The PDM was now called a Korem (Komando Resort Militer, Resort Military Command), led by a colonel; the BODM at district level, previously led by a NCO, became a Kodim (Komando Distrik Militer, Military District Command) led by a captain or a major with 100 officers and men. A new military unit was introduced in 1962 at subdistrict (kecamatan) level known as Koramil (Komando Rayon Militer, Subdistrict Military Command) under a lieutenant with a small staff. And in 1963 a NCO known as Babinsa (Bintara Pembina Desa, non-commissioned officer for village guidance) was placed in many villages.

production. The economy was kept in a state of stagnation by the strict division between self-sufficient peasant communities cut off from world markets on the one hand, and an authoritarian mercantilist state on the other (Evers 1987).

These familiar images, however, obscure several features of the story that has come to light in Kupang. Three such features stand out, and recognizing how essential they are will sensitize us to the socially and spatially embedded nature of similar local regimes everywhere. The first feature is that this story is historical rather than timeless. The Asiatic mode of production in particular is too ahistorical to be a useful instrument for understanding the details of Middle Indonesia in this period. Too much had changed even in Timor since the Dutch had insisted, anachronistically, on rajas, with virtual monopoly powers over the distribution of land and credit, for the Asiatic mode of production to be a realistic picture of both the colonial and post-colonial period. The resources that underlay the constellation of power as it developed historically in Kupang in the 1950s and '60s did not go back aeons; they were specific to the immediate post-war period. The military, who came to play such central predatory roles in the economy of Kupang, could hardly have risen to those roles under any other circumstances. In late colonial times the military were politically unimportant, and by the late 1990s they had virtually disappeared from the formal political stage again. Their role in our period was boosted by the rapidly increased levels of political contention that followed the transition to a democratic independence in 1950. Democracy brought development programmes designed to appeal to key constituencies, but it also created social tensions that directly fed into an increased political role for the armed forces.

The second feature of the story presented here is that it is rooted in 'society' rather than in certain institutions. The notion of bureaucratic capitalism is sensitive to contemporary politics, but its institutional emphasis threatens to isolate it from its surrounding society. Recognizing the social embeddedness of institutions (particularly at their lower levels) helps reinsert the predation of bureaucratic capitalism back into the social process. If this research strategy does not exactly make the predation look more acceptable, it at least helps explain its tenacity in Indonesia. Smail's image of the 'thin wet sheet' undermines any over-confidence in institutional dynamics as the sole explanation for political outcomes. Social forces must become part of the picture. If the state had been merely 'soft' (Myrdal 1968), it would have been unable to accomplish what it did in this period. When seen from below, the state is not weak but strong, because it reaches into all areas of social life. William Reno (1995) memorably coined the phrase 'shadow state' to describe a state whose strength is derived not from institutional discipline but from the social capital of local ruling state elites. It is by their personal authority that the state reaches across institutional boundaries into society (hence the communal networks in Kupang) and into the market (hence the cooperatives and the Ali-Baba constructions).

A single institution such as the military harboured conflicting interests at different levels of the polity. At the local level these conformed rather closely with societal divisions, such as ethnicity, religion, political preference, and urbanity. Negotiation rather than lines of command determined outcomes both within institutions and across their boundaries. Local elites remained boss on their own turf in this period. They saw the military as just another channel for accessing the resources of the state – as a service to them. An individual belonged first to the local ruling class (mainly by virtue of their education), and only then to this or that state institution. Such embeddedness of the state in society leads the researcher's interest from institutional towards societal forces. The (admittedly somewhat unconventional) class character of the forces described in this chapter has a greater concreteness than the military or bureaucratic institutions that they inhabit.

The third interesting feature of the present story is that it matters *where* it plays out – it has a spatial aspect missing from more conventional images of Asiatic predation. Researchers who study the bureaucracy purely in abstract terms of the quality of governance overlook the map. Indonesian policymakers, by contrast, are acutely aware of this spatiality. They often worry more about the bureaucracy's spatial reach than about its more abstract qualities. When urging the need for national unity, they use the term 'Archipelagic Perspective' (*Wawasan Nusantara*). In the period under discussion, maintaining cohesion over distance could only be achieved by 'soft' tactics. Even the military adopted them. Appeasement by the gift of the means of primitive accumulation to urban elites was the main instrument to bridge the distance. Mushtaq Khan and Jomo called this price tag on stability a 'political transfer rent' (Khan and Jomo K.S. 2000). Kupang's middle classes largely owe their existence, and their relative autonomy, to the town's spatial distance from Jakarta. Indonesia owes its existence to the success of their appeasement. Members of the middle class in Kupang were gatekeepers for Timor on behalf of the nation.

CHAPTER NINE

THE MAKING OF MIDDLE INDONESIA (1962–1965)

Three town devils, getting rich,
Use their power as they please!
But here come the People wanting justice!
Hayo, bayo, smash those three wild devils![1]

The contrary tendencies in the previous two chapters inevitably led to conflict. In important respects, Middle Indonesia was born out of the violent resolution of that polarizing process. This chapter begins with the seductive mobilization left incomplete at the end of Chapter 7. By the early 1960s this broad movement for modernization and even for peasant rights was transforming increasingly into a protest against the urban gatekeepers of the new state, described in Chapter 8. The second half of the present chapter turns to the growing reaction among privileged parts of the community – rural landlords and ex-rajas in the countryside, and in the town religious conservatives who voiced bureaucratic concerns. As the optimistic cross-class coalitions that had underlain the political work of earlier years began to break down, embryonic rival coalitions formed along class lines. The best resourced of these broad coalitions ultimately came out on top. This became the new establishment in town, the core of what we have called Middle Indonesia. Just what the nature of those resources was, what role geography played in them, and how they were deployed in this brief, violent and constitutive episode of provincial class conflict, is the burden of this chapter.

Rapid state formation had by the early 1960s created a new urban middle class. It was busy building a still-tenuous hegemony in town, and it had little grip in the countryside. Its core was conservative – bureaucratic, localist, and religious. It worried increasingly that further expanding citizenship rights to rural folk might become costly to themselves. As in colonial times, it preferred to limit modernization to technocratic reform. In

[1] Second stanza of PKI song *Ganjang Tiga Setan Kota* (Smash the Three Town Devils), by Subronto K. Atmodjo, 1965 (*Harian Rakjat Minggu*, 3 October 1965). The original runs: 'Tiga setan kota, makin kaja,/ Gunakan pangkatnja sekehendaknja! / Tapi [illegible] datang Rakjat tuntut balas! / Hajo, bajo, ganjang tiga setan ganas!'

the swirl of competing notions of the kind of national freedom (*merdeka*) that Indonesia ought to pursue, it adhered to what Indonesian intellectuals in the 1950s called 'green' concepts (Alers 1956). These were rigid ideas of moral rights, prejudged values held by established elites including Muslims, Christians, feudalists and Stalinists. At the same time the very expansion of the middle class also created many energetic individuals whose ambitions could not be fulfilled through existing local patronage. These people were likely to be attracted to the open-ended 'red' notions of freedom, which arose spontaneously out of the people under slogans like popular sovereignty (*kedaulatan rakyat*).

From the mid-1950s onwards, politically active townsfolk increasingly built links with (or were sought out by) national institutions. Whether focused on education or rural development, policing or transport infrastructure, all institutions within Indonesia's 'soft state' at this time (Myrdal 1968) were highly politicized. Educated townsfolk played crucial mediating roles in these fluid influence-peddling coalitions, all trying to build authority throughout Indonesia's vast territory, as previous chapters have explored. Conservatives in town increasingly built links with the military, while progressives built them with the communists favoured by the President. Both these organizations were centrally controlled, but both were forced to take considerable risks by mobilizing provincial elites whose loyalty was by no means guaranteed. A remark made about the communist party by the (astute but politically unsavoury) American intelligence analyst Guy Pauker[2] could as well be applied to the military at this time:

> [O]nce issues are broadcast into society, they are likely to gain a life of their own and continue a self-propelled course, beyond the control of the elite at the top. The initiative comes almost exclusively from the small group of leaders at the top, but they cannot count on popular response unless they have the support of the intermediate strata, that increasingly large segment of the population with a mind of its own, the reference groups and opinion leaders for the broad popular masses below (Pauker 1958:137).

Mobilizing the Poor

The PKI only began to organize vigorously in the regions far from Java in the late 1950s. Most organizations in this period were brittle and lacked

---

[2] He later became a hard-line senior CIA advisor, who urged the Indonesian military to remove President Sukarno and to assume 'full responsibility' for the nation's leadership (Scott 1985).

commitment. But by 1958 this party had made itself into the most important intermediate organization in the country by adopting organizational techniques from abroad. Like the Italian communists, the PKI under Aidit operated within the bounds of democracy, trying gradually to move politics to the left rather than aiming for revolution. Where the PKI differed from other political parties was in its approach to membership (see Chapter 7). All the other parties were essentially instruments for intra-elite manipulation, avoiding contact with ordinary people between elections, and living off rents extracted from the state and big business. The PKI, however, made a direct appeal to a class of people who had never been mobilized before. Its populism proved attractive to individuals not tied to the local establishment. These unhampered souls are still recalled in Kupang as *orang bebas*, free people. Unlike the educated, who were mostly 'bound' (*terikat*) to bureaucratic organizations in local government and the church, they could afford to indulge their dreams in the prestigious but somewhat dangerous PKI. Like the young anti-feudal activists of a decade earlier, they looked to Jakarta rather than to Kupang for support. The PKI was particularly good at finding people like this. It is they who also populated the communist women's movement Gerwani, the party's urban trade union Sobsi, and its cultural organization Lekra (the only place in town to offer music and theatre outside the church).

Mr. Costa was a bicycle repairman in the heart of old Kupang aged about 45 or 50. His wife was from Madiun in East Java. She rode around town on her bicycle selling clothes. Costa led an urban village-level PKI unit and had a PKI sign in front of his house. He was witty and insolent. When the government car drove by with a loudspeaker to make an announcement he would shout at it: 'You can talk, an ounce for two cents!' To a customer waiting while he fixed their bicycle he would sometimes whisper mischievously: 'If some time I were to tell you to kill the Catholic priest would you do it?'[3]

In charge of the leftist trade union Sobsi was Simon Bubu, Kupang's most colourful communist in the early 1960s. He became rich in Kupang's shadow economy, helped by the town's thuggish politics. At the same time he was a generous patron of his workers, and he tried hard to make himself acceptable to the town's religious establishment. An ethnic Sabunese,

---

[3] Interview with Eleanor Toma, Buraen, 21 June 2009. This could refer to the then 65-year old SVD priest Johann Nelissen (http://www.svdcuria.org/public/infonews/misc/obit/rip1875-.pdf, accessed 19 July 2011).

he had a large number of tough men at his disposal, as boss of Kupang's harbour workers from the 1940s.[4]

He was also in a powerful position to extract rents from the town's import-dependent economy. According to some accounts these advantages had first begun to bear fruit during the Japanese occupation when, amidst general scarcity, he was able to buy a large tract of land in Bakunase, then the centre of government. His blessings multiplied in the chaotic 1950s, when he bought more land all over town. One leafy parcel lay at the end of the valley in Fontein, a predominantly Sabunese suburb just west of the town centre. He allowed his most loyal labourers and political associates to build their houses on his land. In the 1950s his political base was the PNI, home to the bureaucrats who ran the harbour and the ships. When the national PNI split into left and right wings in the early 1960s and Kupang's PNI went right, Simon Bubu joined the disaffected leftist exodus to the PKI. Michael Marcus, who owned a house on Bubu's land at Fontein, joined him. They both needed protection from allegations of corruption – that standard weapon in Kupang's factional fights – and Herewila (who had stayed with the rightist PNI) was no longer willing or able to supply it. But the PKI now offered connections to Jakarta, as good as any the PNI had ever had.

Tough as he was, Simon Bubu and his clients were as zealous about their Christian faith as any white-shirted pen-pusher in town. But they wanted religion on their own terms. They felt patronized by the bureaucrats' congregation of GMIT in the suburb of Airnona where Bubu lived. Bubu encouraged a breakaway called the Gospel Tent (Gereja Kemah Ibadat) in 1956. Sectarian breaches for political reasons were not unusual in GMIT, as we saw in the case of Hans Nisnoni. Their biggest problem was to persuade an ordained minister to lead the sacrament of Holy Communion. In 1961, with food once more scarce, Bubu had some of his men carry bags of American relief rice to the house of the young female minister in charge at Airnona, Rev. Margreta Gertruida Noelik. But she angrily refused to break regulations to service the breakaways on the sly.

[4] Kupang's harbour may have been a conduit for communist ideas for decades. Between the 1920s and the 1950s, thousands of Rotenese and Sabunese passed through it on their way to or from the pearling industry in Broome, Australia. Australian journalist Michael Grant has compiled a database of 20,000 names from shipping lists (personal communication, Kupang, 17 June 2009). Besides ideas, they smuggled back cigarettes (*Pewarta Timoer*, 3 February 1940).

By this time Simon Bubu was the provincial secretary of the PKI in NTT. He lived next door to Sutarman, the energetic provincial secretary of the farmers union BTI. Bubu died suddenly in 1962. Some say he was poisoned after chairing a PKI meeting in Soë, Timor's PKI heartland. At his funeral it appeared that church leaders hated the PKI more than PKI leaders hated the church. The preacher criticized the dead man for his communism. When the deputy party secretary, Sam Piry, who had himself been banned from Holy Communion for communism, spoke out on Bubu's behalf, youths from the Airnona GMIT stormed the house of mourning. Police had to be called to save the women.

The PKI and its affiliates dominated Kupang's mobilizational agenda from 1962 onwards. Participants revelled in the feeling that they were on the right side of national politics, a government report recalled some years later, while at the same time being able to express themselves through 'mass rallies focused on dissatisfaction' (Tari 1972:I, 260). The first moves had begun the previous year. PKI youth organization Pemuda Rakjat held a congress in Kupang on 20–22 July 1961 at which they condemned the murder of Patrice Lumumba and killings in Angola and welcomed the Cuban revolution. For Indonesia they demanded elections, lower prices, higher civil service salaries, better schooling, communist representation in the provincial parliament, land reform, and an end to the rule of the rajas. They were preparing to join the Jakarta congress that September. A week earlier the PKI labour union Sobsi had held a public meeting in Kupang's famous cinema, now renamed the Bioskop Raya, for a lecture about the anti-colonial struggle of the Sonbai kingdom of old, and to support demands for higher civil service salaries. The following October, Sobsi held its provincial conference in Kupang and elected Octavianus Marcus, the son of Michael Marcus, as its secretary (Tari 1972:I, 258–60).

Protest against established elite privileges increasingly began to replace these moderate modernizing demands in the early 1960s. Much existing literature on the communist mobilization of this period overlooks the depth of resentment that the exploitative and cynical practices described in previous chapters created. Instead it echoes New Order propaganda in portraying provincial communist sympathizers as passive clients misled by devious patrons. Certainly clientelism played a role in most political practices of that period. And propaganda of the crudest kind was as effective among a poorly educated public in Timor as it was in Europe and North America at about the same time. But none of this is enough to discount the reality of class resentments, which burned for a while with considerable intensity even in Kupang.

In 1962 the provincial party started a weekly 12-page bulletin called *Pelopor.* Some say it was stencilled in red, but no copies survive to check. Old people today recall a strident tone that went far beyond Herewila's witty irreverence. It routinely lambasted respected local figures. Raja Alfons Nisnoni was 'feudal,' the Australian foreign missionary Gordon Dicker was 'imperialist,' as was an intellectual like Hendrikus Ataupah, who was about leave for the USA on a postgraduate scholarship. Its editor was Paulus Kanuru, originally a primary school teacher in Kefamenanu in the early 1950s. He was a fat man, already a radical activist when he moved to Soë in mid-1955 (Netti and Itta 1997:110–1).

Raucous PKI mobilization in town sometimes provoked violence there (far more than in the country, where BTI activities were more often seen as benign). Fist fights and beatings were a regular part of politics in Timor since the mid-1950s,[5] and they became more frequent as the temperature rose in the early 1960s. Similar mobilization took place all over the archipelago in the late 1950s and early 1960s. It has been extensively described for Bali, for example, by Geoffrey Robinson (1995). The Catholic anti-communist activist Kanis Pari (Canisius Parera, then aged 35) later recalled how aggressive the 'three town devils' agitprop sounded in his ears: 'Three years before 1965, the NTT governor was practically lame, his communist advisor Th. Rissi decided everything. Then in 1964/65 military commander Sutarmadji was PKI, ditto the military police, the economy ran through their Copra Foundation, they controlled food, etc., etc., etc... "Crush the town devils and the village devils" pointed the way. I was their prime target. Because my group stood up with the *Pos Kupang* stencil, I got aggressive anonymous letters, mysterious phone calls' (Wawa 2004:180f). He was exaggerating the degree of PKI influence, but the aggression was real.

Theatricality was a key mobilizational tool for all parties, and also for the government. As an official report put it wryly a few years later, the government promoted gigantic rallies to 'Smash Malaysia!' as a way of reducing social tensions arising from the ideological contest between the religions and the communists. The Dwikora Command was formed in

---

[5] For example, a Chinese Catholic member of the Timor parliament visiting Kefamenanu ahead of elections was beaten up in October 1954 by 'a people's gang' (*gerombolan rakyat*) while the local head of government stood by (*Bentara* ,15 October 1954, 15 April 1955). BTI executives complained to the military authorities in Kupang in March 1965 ('on behalf of 155,000 members'!) about a local government official who had threatened violence against BTI peasants who refused to pay their taxes in the words: 'In Russia things are good because it is a nation of law, but Indonesia is just a nation of beatings' (*negara pukul*) (*Harian Rakjat*, 22 March 1965).

May 1964 to channel these unifying energies. All the local parties participated fanatically in these rallies. As a result, everyone 'competed with each other to prove themselves the dominant force in implementing the Dwikora Command.' On 13 April 1964 the National Front, the government mobilizational organization, held a 'Big Roll-Call' (*Apel Besar*) in Kupang at which 10,000 participants pledged to destroy the Puppet State Malaysia. Similar meetings were held at district level throughout NTT (Tari 1972:I, 266).

The PKI had an especially innovative theatrical repertoire. Its mobilizational activities remained within the bounds of democratic practice, but in town they were sometimes shockingly shrill. From 1962 onwards it set new standards of agitprop that other parties could only emulate (and did). Kupang saw show-of-force mass rallies, prominent signs in front of its numerous local branch 'offices,' and a local newspaper named *Pelopor*, full of personal attacks on non-communist elites (including the military after 1963), which complemented the imported national communist daily *Harian Rakjat*.

Harian Rakjat reported a constant round of public rallies all over the country at which the rank-and-file echoed central party demands, vented outrage at imperialist atrocities overseas, but also gave voice to local concerns, such as the desire to create a new province. Massed choirs sang rousing melodies to provincial audiences, hoping to make it into extravagant national competitions. The exhilaration of organized collectivity was new to the small towns of the eastern archipelago. The tiny town of Namlea, on Buru Island in Maluku, became the proud owner of a 'Marxist library,' consisting of 35 new books.[6] The women's organization Gerwani in tiny Kapuas, inland from Banjarmasin, condemned 'US imperialism and foreign military bases.' The provincial PKI secretary of West Kalimantan told a Gerwani meeting in the Chen Chiang building in Pontianak they should tell their husbands to give them more freedom to take part in social activities.[7] Kupang had seen rallies on the Bakunase sports field during the Japanese occupation, and occasional street processions around election time in the 1950s, but the rallies of the early 1960s took the technique to another level of spectacle. An entertainment-starved town found them fascinating. The town's new Merdeka football stadium provided a venue for gatherings of such a size that they left the

6 *Harian Rakjat*, 27 February 1965.
7 *Harian Rakjat*, 10 April 1965, 9 July 1965.

venerable Kupang cinema down the hill looking puny. It had been built in 1962/63 on the military shooting range by the military area commander (*danrem*), Lt. Col. Paikun. Although it lacks a roof and is now in a serious state of decay, it remains in use today. Paikun was a builder – his tour of duty 1959–1964 also left behind a lot of new housing. The provincial PKI may have been the first to make use of this space for politics, but all the other parties – PNI, Parkindo, Partai Katolik – held rallies there too as a 'show of force.' To celebrate Labour Day in 1963, the PKI brought together all its affiliate organizations from a wide area for a huge rally in the Merdeka stadium. PKI gatherings in the early 1960s were not unique in their militancy, but they did out-perform the other political parties. They added an oppositional undertone to the rally that unsettled the town's political class. Although all the town's military and civilian worthies were in attendance – PKI was after all an official party enjoying the president's favours – some posters were seen criticizing Governor W.J. Lalamentik. Lalamentik was an experienced bureaucrat, originally from Menado, whose retiring personality kept him signing papers in his office for fear of unpleasant confrontations outside (Liliweri et al 1984:112, Tari 1972:I, 263).

To mark the 45th anniversary of the party's founding on 23 May 1965, branches were encouraged to go all out for a massive display of strength. Eager to please with exact numbers, the Kupang correspondent for the national *Harian Rakjat* reported that '5,793' people took part in a procession of members and supporters. The day, 29 May, had begun with a rally in the Merdeka football stadium organized by the youth branch Pemuda Rakjat. Provincial deputy secretary Sam Piry had addressed the crowd. Towards evening, by the light of flaming torches, a kilometre-long procession then left the stadium. BTI farmers, who at home rarely acted demonstratively, marched behind banners naming their village, carrying their new hoes on their shoulders and singing 'Nasakom Bersatu' (Nasakom Unite). Snaking around the normally quiet town, the procession eventually arrived at the provincial PKI headquarters in Naikoten, where they were welcomed and fed by Piry, along with the entire town's other political party leaders and senior government officials, including the governor. Also present was Sardjono from the PKI Central Committee in Jakarta. Piry spoke once more, first on the encouraging leftward move at the national level and the progress towards Nasakom (government policy to place PKI representatives in every government agency). Then his speech adopted a darker tone, moving on to the need for 'iron discipline' among communists as they faced local obstacles, conventionally referred to as 'pure Manipol forces.'[8]

The Kupang rally of 29 May 1965 had been preceded a week earlier by celebrations at village level in the vicinity of Kupang. In rural villages they had gone well, such as the gathering of about 1,000 'PKI members and candidate members' in Buraen south of Kupang, which enjoyed the popular dances and the declamation of revolutionary poems by farmers' children. But in the semi-urban kampongs on the outskirts of Kupang some village chiefs belonging to rival parties took exception to what they saw as displays of insubordination. In Oepura, Nunhila, Kuanino, and Oebobo, PKI branches had planted signboards announcing their presence, and hung out banners with slogans like 'Let us race to become communists who are Red and Expert!' According to a later government report, Kupang was 'flooded with posters reflecting the political temperature.' Some condemned non-revolutionary leaders in general ('Hypocritical Manipolists ... step aside!,' 'Smash Manikebu!'),[9] others urged the new land reform judges to side with the 'pillars of the revolution,' others again insisted on the destruction of the 'New Colonial and Imperialist Project called Malaysia' (Tari 1972:I, 279). Such signs were flashpoints all over the archipelago. The Oebobo village chief was a Parkindo man. He ordered the removal of the signs as soon as they went up. Knife-wielding men surrounded the house of the PKI village secretary.[10]

Sam Piry

Samuel Nicodemus Piry (1922–1966) (Figure 31) was a middle class vanguard intellectual. His father was an ethnic Sabunese colonial government official in Waingapu, Sumba. Older brother Yakob discovered the PKI when he was in Java during the 1945 Revolution, then became a convinced communist during

(*Continued*)

[8] *Harian Rakjat*, 5 June 1965, 23 August 1965. This Sardjono is not the same as the man imprisoned in Digul by the Dutch, who was executed by the Republic in 1948.

[9] Manikebu refers to the Cultural Manifesto (Manifesto Kebudayaan), a 1963 statement urging artistic freedom that was regarded as anti-communist; Manipol to the Political Manifesto Sukarno had issued in 1959, which some had tried to turn against Sukarno; Nekolim, routinely applied to Malaysia with which Indonesia was on a war footing, was an acronym meaning New Colonial and Imperial Forces.

[10] He was secretary of the Resort Committee (RC). These committees were based in villages and in institutions like factories; each had less than a hundred members (Pauker 1964:37).

(*Cont.*)

university studies in Leiden, the Netherlands. In the 1950s Sam worked as clerk in the Christian hospital in Waingapu, and was active in Parkindo. But when the PKI began its recruitment drive later in the decade, Yakob persuaded Sam to join up. Sam began by handling subscriptions to the national PKI paper *Harian Rakjat,* the only newspaper to reach Waingapu. His son Ratu collected them from the post office on his bicycle and took them to educated subscribers around town – Chinese shopowners and a few senior government officials. Sam was severe with his own children if they did not study, and read legal and political texts even at the dinner table. The PKI had good government connections; policemen would come to his home asking for help with promotion.

His connection with Yakob led to an appointment as deputy provincial secretary, and in 1960 as member of the prestigious Temporary People's Consultative Assembly (MPRS) in Jakarta. This required a move to Kupang with a large young family, at first sleeping at Simon Bubu's home in Airnona before a new house became available on the outskirts of town at Oebobo. He had the right to a car, but it never arrived. The house was often full of PKI activists, especially primary school teachers. If they had come from out of town – Sabu, Soë, Kefamenanu – they slept overnight in the garage. On public occasions it was Sam Piry rather than As Rissi who addressed the crowd.

After the events in Jakarta on 1 October 1965, none of this prestige helped him. A couple of days later, on a moonlit night, GMIT youths surrounded Simon Bubu's house where he was staying. They began throwing stones. Some were armed with grenades given by sympathetic soldiers. BTI youths quickly gathered from all over Kupang to defend him, but they realized the military were in touch with the church youths and avoided a fight. When Piry rang military commander Soetarmadji asking for protection as a MPRS member, troops came and deposited him in the athlete's quarters at the football stadium. He was never released again. Soldiers tortured him with electricity for information, and later detained him at the old jail. Some time in 1966 soldiers took him out to Tanah Merah, on the eastern outskirts of town, and told him to run. He was shot as he ran and left to die. His body was never identified.

Reaction

These mobilizational tactics were intended to polarize, and they did. In rural areas a reaction came from village and subdistrict chiefs who had been harried about land reform. The 'pillars' had only recently been stripped of their last claims as sole rulers of the soil under what remained of the Dutch indirect rule system. Rajas, *fetor*, and another layer

Figure 31. Deputy Secretary of provincial PKI, Samuel Piry (right with dark glasses), at an undated (approx. 1964) meeting in Waingapu with the district chief of East Sumba (Lesu Djaga Dapangole, standing), military officers and government officials. The photo gives a glimpse of provincial status relations before 1965. While the district chief nervously reads his prepared text and his officials appear to listen intently, the military officers and PKI secretary from out of town can afford to display their nonchalance (photo courtesy Mr. Ratu Piry, Waingapu).

of dependents known as *temukung*, no longer had a place in the modern administrative system. Many had been re-appointed under the new system, but they now had to put up with central orders and political party interference. What bothered them most was the central government's land reform policy, loudly supported by their own peasants through the PKI.

The first symbolic land redistributions were already taking place. At a ceremony in Kupang on 24 September 1964 to mark National Farmers Day, some hundreds of hectares of state land were redistributed in the districts of Kupang, South Central Timor, East Flores, Sikka and Manggarai (both the latter also in Flores). On 29 October 1964 district level rulers from around the province met in Kupang and declared they were ready to redistribute thousands of hectares of land considered state-owned to the farmers who were working it. More land reform conferences were held in Kupang late in 1964 to set targets and build the special land reform court, on which farmers' representatives from various organizations would also sit (23–27 November, 5 December, 10 December). The provincial BTI had been mobilizing popular participation in the reforms since 1962, while at the same time consolidating its own organization and appointing new leaders (all named in official reports – Tari 1972:I, 269–270). Michael Marcus and his South Central Timor BTI never took over land by force, as in the unilateral actions in Java, but they did urge farmers to withhold local taxes until the government had implemented the land reform act (Tari 1972:I, 26). Individual land ownership title for peasants, with credit to finance the transfer, remained an official policy objective in Nusa Tenggara Timor until about 1968 (Sidik et al 1968:72), but after that it faded.

The PKI anniversary committee told the assembled mass on 29 May that the number of participants in the procession would have far exceeded five thousand 'if evil village-level power-holders in various subdistricts had not prevented farmers from taking part in this big procession.' Some subdistrict chiefs had imposed a ban on villagers leaving for town. Beatings had occurred, leading to at least one injured schoolteacher.

Overshadowing reaction by rural landlords and ex-rajas in vehemence, however, was the religious reaction in town. Disputes over the boundaries of bureaucratic fiefdoms were primarily urban and religious. Religion had put the brakes on the secular Jakarta party PNI in the 1950s, and it was now turned against the PKI. Central Committee member Sardjono used his speech at the 29 May rally to defend the PKI against charges that it was 'against Pancasila,' the national ideology that places God first.

One of those who embodied the mobilizational potential of religious reaction in town was Kanis Pari. He discovered a gift for oratory when still a teacher in the 1950s. Borrowing the proletarian title 'Bung Kanis' during a visit from 'Bung (Su)Karno,' he began to write for the Catholic news magazine *Bentara*. The style was vividly Sukarnoist but the substance far from it. During the 1955 election he did sterling work turning Florinese voters away from the secular PNI towards the conservative Catholic Party. By 1960 he was in Kupang, working for the Livestock Cooperative and soon producing an anti-communist news bulletin called *Pos Kupang*. His lifestyle was Spartan, he lived for politics and never married, and he had a magnetic personality for young men who loved the thrill of action. He organized Catholic students into a branch of the national organization PMKRI in 1963, and other youth into the Catholic youth organization AMKRI the following year. The students he trained 'totally,' so they could become part of an anti-communist action when the time came.

Kanis Pari felt himself to be the target of the PKI's noisy campaign to 'crush the town devils and crush the village devils,' as we saw above. By this time the list of town devils had ballooned from three to five, and the fifth – the 'bureaucratic capitalist' (*kapitalis birokrat, kabir*) – was not wholly inapplicable to him. The Livestock Cooperative was one of the more lucrative government ventures in town (Chapter 8). Recalling the hostile environment in Kupang afterwards, he told an audience (somewhat mixing his metaphors): 'Kupang was no baby on the PKI map.' Politics in Kupang were highly personal. PKI activists from the *Pelopor* paper intimidated Pari with anonymous pamphlets and mysterious phone calls. Party sympathizers in the tiny telephone exchange listened in on his conversations. The real power, Pari felt, lay with Thobias ('As') Rissi, the PKI provincial secretary. Rissi was a rather humourless man, the son of a Protestant preacher from Rote, who always walked everywhere in town wearing a white shirt and white trousers. He was the provincial PKI secretary and a member of the prestigious People's Consultative Assembly in Jakarta, but he was a poor public speaker. In private, though, he had a sharp tongue and persuaded much new talent to join the party.

Polarization split the Protestant churches, GMIT which was dominant in Timor and GKS (Gereja Kristen Sumba) in Sumba. Many church school teachers felt attracted to the PKI programme for the mix of reasons that has already been reviewed – the exhilaration of being at the forefront of change they believed in, solidarity with the poor whom they knew well, and, most importantly for a teacher whose salary was partly subsidized by the state, the satisfaction of being on the right side of national politics. Teachers in the towns of Kupang, Lelogama and Soë heeded the call most clearly (Peters 1973:54). Even some ministers felt attracted by the integrative possibilities of the cross-class coalition that PKI power generation implied.

Protestant church leaders, on the contrary, saw the PKI as their rival, both for the affections of the poor, among whom they were just beginning to make inroads, and for those of the government.[11] Church relations with government were mainly about money. After independence most state subsidies for the church dried up but not for the schools (see Chapter 6). The quid pro quo for this arrangement became clear in 1964. As the state

[11] Theological objections to communism seemed not to be a major concern to Protestants. Whereas most Catholics had been made well aware of these objections, only a few of the most highly educated Protestants ever voiced them in this region. The GKS synod in Sumba had issued a condemnation of communism at its synod in 1957, but the impulse seemed to come mainly from Dutch missionaries.

grew more assertive, the suggestion arose that Nasakom might also apply to those institutions the state was subsidizing. Church leaders feared schools might have to appoint some teachers approved by the PKI. An increasingly communist government might force them to teach 'atheistic' doctrines at the many church-run primary schools in Timor. Some panicky church officeholders even worried the PKI might insist on placing its representatives on local congregational councils. Synod chairperson Rev. Radja Haba started a committee in 1964 to protect the 'Christian character' of the schools. Later that year he attracted much attention with a public lecture on this theme. The Kupang district chief, the former *fetor* Oematan, was persuaded to intervene on behalf of the church against the wishes of the provincial parliament. Political pressure on the church eased with the suppression of the PKI, and the church thought back on this escape with relief. The church historian M.A. Noach wrote: '[I]n a situation that is humanly impossible, the Lord will act, and cleanse the schools and the church from communist elements' (1972:24–5). Ironically, the flow of state subsidies still began to decline from 1967.

Protestant church leaders were just as suspicious of efforts to mobilize the poor as were senior Catholics and, for that matter, most senior bureaucrats. But there were many poor within the church, and not all believers were prepared to defend a Protestant establishment that had filled elite rice bowls but had done little for others. Leaders began to speak of 'PKI infiltration.' In 1958 the then-synod secretary Radja Haba had written an influential article in a church bulletin warning of this (Brookes 1977:85), and early in 1960 the GMIT synod felt compelled to remove one minister for being a member of the PKI. At the end of that year it issued an ultimatum to members of local church councils to 'choose' between the PKI and the church. In March 1961 the synod became so concerned about the spread of communism among its members that it contemplated a 'frontal attack' in the form of public rallies to expose the dangers of communism. But, fearing this might backfire, it fell back simply on trying to blow some life into what even they acknowledged were 'lifeless' sermons. This half-hearted response, according to the missionary Dicker, did little to prevent people from joining the communist party (Dicker 2007:121). On the contrary, the 1960 ultimatum later led several ministers in Amarasi to leave the GMIT in June 1964 and join a breakaway church, calling on other communist Christians to join them (Brookes 1977:98). The loss of discipline within the church continued, leading an American investigator to say afterwards that '[c]ommunists had invaded the churches and in many places practically controlled them' (Peters 1973:54).

The flashpoint for confrontation was the town of Soë in South Central Timor. This was where Michael Marcus, himself an active church member, was successfully mobilizing farmers for the Indonesian Farmers Union BTI. But this was also where the pioneering missionary Piet Middelkoop had lived from 1922 until 1957, and where the theological college stood. The first mass conversions had taken place near here in the 1920s, at the mission base in the garrison settlement of Kapan 20 km from Soë. The outreach from town to countryside had become highly competitive. The BTI was better than the church at bridging the class gap that yawned there. By 1965, according to the church historian Graham Brookes (1977:84), the BTI was 'practically in control of many villages and districts.' BTI village activists told a Soë doctor they would only allow him to make his visits to a village polyclinic if he agreed to do so under PKI 'auspices.' What precise form of acknowledgement they wanted from him is not clear from these words – one of my informants thought the issue was part of the village-level resistance to raja-cum-district chief Koesa Nope – but the doctor stubbornly refused to give it (Dicker 2007:110–1). Medicine as a field for ideological contestation had a history in Timor. In March 1961 the American hospital ship SS Hope, a military-civilian partnership, anchored in Kupang harbour for two and a half weeks to provide medical help to a poor and isolated area of Indonesia. Locals flocked to this white marvel of technology to get their cavities filled and to eat apples. But it was also a show of force in a nation on the frontline of the cold war. Dicker wrote afterwards that 'except for the Communists, everyone felt unusually fortunate that Kupang was on the vessel's itinerary' (Dicker 2007:118–9).[12]

In August 1965 a remarkable 'spiritual revival' burst out in Timor. The build-up to this moment lasted almost a year, and about another year later it was all over. Ecclesiastical scholars have written mainly about its spontaneous visions and miracles, but it seems clear the events also reflected the extraordinary class tensions between town and countryside then reaching a peak of intensity. Like the earlier sermonizing against drinking and in favour of bible recitation and correct clothing for worship, these

---

[12] Project HOPE (Health Opportunities for People Everywhere) was started in 1958 by an ex-US Navy officer and had the free use of a navy ship. It operated under the Geneva Convention like a military hospital ship. Its first mission was to Indonesia (http://en.wikipedia.org/wiki/Project_HOPE; (http://www.globalsecurity.org/military/systems/ship/ah-ngo.htm, accessed 19 July 2012; 'White fleet ship starts her mission,' *Life* magazine, 19 December 1960, p74–9). Governor Lalamentik, who had studied in the United States, translated a little booklet with statistics about NTT into English especially for the occasion of this visit (Lalamentik 1961).

events too began as a contestation over the body. This time the disease was political. In October 1964 the GMIT congregation in the small town of Niki-Niki, the seat of the Nope clan 35 km east of Soë, wrote a letter to church leaders. They implored them to send a 'healing team.' There were literally sick people in Niki-Niki, but the more serious problem was that 'parties.... have spread like an epidemic.' The crisis-ridden church was delighted when a young Rotenese teacher called Johanes Ratuwalu, son of a minister, declared he had heard God's voice calling him to volunteer for the healing ministry. His faith mission soon brought wellness to many people, particularly in Amarasi south of Kupang. However, just as the church was about to ordain him and give him a car, the man abandoned his mission and went to Alor. He was last reported to have become 'crazy about money, crazy about women, and crazy about status' (Brookes 1977:97–100, 1980:111).

A year later another young teacher arose, this time in Soë itself. Miss Priscilla 'Hennie' Tunliu had grown up in the home of the missionary Pieter Middelkoop for seventeen years; her mother had been a protégé. She then married a minister and was given a scholarship to study at Satya Wacana University, a new Christian university in Central Java where students were constantly reminded of the incompatibility of communism with their faith. Here she developed a strong sense of nationalism. Once back in Soë she was soon very senior as director of the two Christian high schools. Her first vision occurred on the evening of 16 August 1965, at a church thanksgiving service for Independence Day (17 August). The next morning Jesus spoke to her again with a message urging action. This led her to travel to Batu Malang, in East Java, to ask the foreign-funded evangelistic mission based there to send a mission to the youth of Timor.

Well-organized teams were soon fanning out from Soë to retake possession of the countryside. Its spectacularly successful healings and conversions owed much to Timorese messianism. The enthusiastic but poorly educated young preachers 'vied with each other in telling stories of the greatest miracles' – birds sang gospel songs, stones preached and sang, people walked on water, water changed into wine, the dead were raised. Nothing was impossible (Peters 1973:28–32). The atmosphere was apocalyptic. Rising tensions caused by the escalating conflict between the PKI and the establishment were exacerbated by economic and even natural calamaties. Terrible inflation had caused cattle exports to collapse. Anthrax was raging among the cattle. Drought had by December 1965 struck 170,000 people in the Amanuban kingdom with famine, out of a total population of 200,000–250,000. To top it all a strange comet appeared in the sky (Brookes 1990:274, Pemda NTT 1966).

The massed 'conversions' (many were already nominal Christians) began on 26 September 1965, just days before events in far-away Jakarta were to bring a radical regime change also to Timor (Brookes 1980). Within weeks the mission teams were operating in the midst of a bloody crack-down on the PKI throughout Timor. We have little information about how the young missionaries were able to do their work amidst the purges. An occasional hint suggests they were politically aware. The leader of Team 17, an illiterate woman named Mrs. Boimau, announced triumphantly at one point that she had had a vision predicting that 'before long Indonesia would govern the world and that President Suharto would become president of the world.' The declaration apparently created some resistance on the part of her hearers, perhaps because they knew President Suharto as none other than General Suharto who had sent the troops down on them (Brookes 1977:114).

The mission to bring communist heathens into the fold was at first marvellously fruitful. Thousands of rural people flocked into the church in the months after the military crackdown (described in the next chapter). In the old Amanuban kingdom in South Central Timor, 60% of the church's membership had joined immediately after the regime change (Brookes 1980:86). Heathens were known as *khalaik*, from *khalayak*, meaning creature, a reference to the animist reverence for what Muslims call creatures of God. To the church, the term translated to ignorance, but to the military after 1 October 1965 it translated to wilful atheism and communism. In South Central Timor, terrified *khalaik* peasants entered the church in such droves that a sub-district chief was reported able soon afterwards to tell the military: 'There are no *khalaik* here' (Cooley 1976:347).

However, the mission eventually proved to be a mixed blessing for the church. The military were swarming all over the countryside. Under this intense surveillance many ministers were reluctant to associate with the unpredictable charismatic phenomena the evangelistic teams were unleashing. Conservative churchmen also worried about the dominant women who often led these teams, and they suspected men and women were sleeping together on tour. By the end of 1967, just as the military began allowing foreigners to travel into the interior of Timor again, most healing teams had ceased to exist. Their job was done. The church had reined them in and was giving them 'further training' in a new institute in Soë, under the Rev. Y.M.E. Daniels. He said with satisfaction: 'The Lord used the coup to make the people seek the Lord, and revived the church to gather in the people.' Not long afterwards, American missionary Frank Cooley observed that indigenous church life in Soë seemed, on the whole, little changed (though the conversion of the Chinese does date to this period) (Brookes 1977:129, 145, 151–2, Peters 1973:56, 100, 155).

In the purges that followed, thousands of civil servants plunged back to the lower class when they lost their jobs. Mrs. Yulianti Meno of Soë was one of them. She had delayed marrying her teacher husband Kristofel Meno in the early 1970s because the military had detained him for three months due to his PKI affiliation. By 1975 things seemed to have blown over, he went back to teaching, and they married. But five years later a new purge broke out and he was fired. He lost his state pension, their children became 'PKI kids' with no chance of a civil service career, and not even the pastor would defend their rights. To pay for the children's education Yulianti did people's laundry, babysat, and sold dried fish (Kolimon and Wetangterah 2012:263–6).

Meanwhile careers for those on the right side of politics blossomed. Protestant student leader Melkianus Adoe, for example, thanks to his activism in 'crushing the PKI' enjoyed a varied career in Kupang in government broadcasting, state banking, and the state political party Golkar culminating in the provincial parliament (Adam et al 1997:198). Kanis Pari talked Governor El Tari into employing 'thousands' of his young anti-communist protégés (Wawa 2004: xxiv, 313).

Betting on the Strong

The interactions between national and local interests in this key moment of Indonesia's history were complex and dynamic. This chapter has adopted a contentious politics approach that attempts to do justice to both. At the national level, polarization had produced two big power blocs, a 'red,' mobilizational, broadly progressive one around the president and the PKI, and a 'green,' reactionary one around the military and religious parties (Alers 1956). Each deployed mobilizational strategies based on the resources and opportunities available to them. Provincial constituencies were an indispensable resource. The Jakarta actors had to deal skilfully with a huge network of intermediate organizations based in the provincial towns.

This chapter has traced a parallel process of polarization and mobilization in one such town. Until 1961, polarization had not been marked in Kupang. But as its urban middle class members invented new ways of excluding the poor from state rents, the cross-class coalition aiming to seduce the rural and urban poor into participating in the modern state began to falter. With the coalition sabotaged from within, vague hopes among the poor for a 'red' new social order crystalized into protest against the new rulers. 'Red' PKI propaganda from Jakarta provided the idiom for this protest. From 'green' Jakarta's point of view, the choice familiar from colonial times became urgent once more – to bet on the people or on the strong. The people were more numerous, and the PKI mobilizational network in the towns was impressive. But the party had not counted on the strength of provincial conservatism. It was forced to rely on townsfolk who were rather marginal to an urban establishment that was growing increasingly assertive. Teachers, lower level clergy and trade unionists hoped to bypass the conservative establishment by mobilizing urban 'free people' and rural 'mountain people.' They found themselves increasingly at odds with white-collar townsfolk led by senior bureaucrats and their local business allies, senior clergy, former aristocrats, and upwardly mobile students.

A vertical coalition between this provincial establishment – the new strong – and the military in Jakarta was by no means a natural one. The locals were religious and anxious to protect their turf; the military were generally secular and nationalist. But they were broadly united in the 'green' values of order and hierarchy. Indonesia was not a democracy from 1959 onwards. Long subversive of democracy, the military allied pragmatically with those provincial actors least committed to national, secular democracy in the period 1964–66. This was blatant cynicism, but also reflected a growing degree of military embeddedness in provincial middle classes, a decade after Kupang's integration into Indonesia. If the choice for betting on the strong was easily made, the cost was to be high. Abandoning the most broadly associational forms of power generation was sure to leave behind social dysfunctionalities.

From 1960 onwards and particularly from 1963, local conflict escalated as each side undertook innovative actions in response to opportunities and to threats from the other side. The initiative lay with the PKI. Its supporters made the most of the opportunity of presidential protection to recruit unreached people of the lower classes on justice issues that had been framed for them by the revolutionary discourse of *merdeka:* freedom and independence, land rights for peasants, workers' rights for harbour labourers and – for urban young people – civil rights, the right to freedom of expression and to engage in the arts. Their repertoire ranged from routine lobbying through official channels to episodic theatrical events designed to recruit new members, increase support from the centre and intimidate enemies. The anti-feudal, anti-clerical language grew increasingly shrill.

The local official and religious establishment at first reacted hesitantly to this threatening language. On the one hand it had enough control over the machinery of office that yielded it rents not to have to fear the worst. But on the other, *should* it become necessary to counter-mobilize, its elitism had left it with minimal organizational resources among the 'free people.' Non-communist political parties had no branches outside Kupang, and they were in any case oriented more towards elite rent-seeking and communal competition than seeking contact with the masses. The churches were divided between conservatives at the top and young progressives at the grass roots. Their leaders feared the church might lose if the confrontation escalated, though they gave their blessing to an evangelistic campaign that tried to shift the escalation to the spiritual domain. The military initially had even fewer organizational resources to mobilize. But since the early 1960s it had considerably expanded its territorial presence, and established a variety of mobilizational organizations that sought contact with the population. As the next chapter will explain in detail, it used these to approach religious conservatives who shared concerns about communism. It was precisely the lack of associational resources both in the centre and in the provinces that led the reactionary alliance to engage in a bloody crackdown.

Escalating confrontation between the two broad coalitions in 1965 led to a violent and one-sided denouement that ended further experiments in democratic reform for the rest of the century. There were many problems in the period after 1961, and many of them were outside the town's control. But of those within the grasp of the political class in Kupang, the biggest problem had been its own decision to sabotage the cross-class alliances that had been building up until then. Thus Middle Indonesia was born. It at once holds the country together because it controls the towns with central state rents, yet also destabilized it with its undercurrent of disenfranchisement and class violence.

CHAPTER TEN

A KILLING TOWN (1965–1967)

> Not even the gecko would make a sound and not even the cock would crow.
>
> (Pak Kobus, East Kupang – Kolimon and Wetangterah 2012:226).

> After my husband did not come home, I felt terribly sad. I wept out loud, but some people warned me: 'Don't weep out loud, or they will come and get you too. So I wept, but only after pushing my mouth into the pillow.'
>
> (Mama Ribka, Alor – Kolimon and Wetangterah 2012:305).[1]

> The victor's cause pleased the gods, but that of the vanquished pleased Cato.
>
> (Lucan, *The Civil War*, I.128)

This chapter reaches into the dark heart of Kupang's history. This is what my friends told me not to write, indeed, what the government today continues to declare was 'not a gross violation of human rights.'[2] The fear the New Order worked hard to instil continues to hamper research into what precisely happened during the anti-communist pogroms. Years after it ended, standard New Order narratives still dominate the accounts researchers take over from local informants, as Steve Farram's otherwise remarkably detailed work illustrates (2002). That the historical authenticity of these accounts is dubious at best became obvious in a more recent report (Kolimon and Wetangterah 2012). Young female church activists in Kupang here bring to light the experiences of women caught in the pogroms, in seven case studies. Once one becomes aware that the mainstream narratives represent internalized regime propaganda, they can still serve a wry analytical purpose. They indicate how shallow democratic

---

[1] 'Ya, ada pulang datang, tidak nasehat anak-anak atau pesan-pesan … habis keluar malam, tidak tau kemana. Setelah bapak … tidak pulang, saya pung perasaan sedih sekali. Saya menangis keras-keras, tapi ada yang tegur bilang, "Jangan menangis keras-keras; nanti mama juga dijemput." Jadi kita menangis, tapi tutup mulut di bantal baru menangis' (Mama Ribka, interviewed by the report authors, 12 September 2010, Kadelang hamlet, East Kalabahi Timur village, Alor – Kolimon and Wetangterah 2012:305).

[2] 'PKI purge not a gross violation of human rights, says AGO,' *Jakarta Post*, 11 November 2012.

reform has been and how high a degree of moral legitimacy an only superficially reformed provincial state continues to enjoy. Katharine McGregor raised a similar question when, in a recent edited volume on the 1965 killings, she observed that every single attempt to memorialize mass graves in the newly democratic Indonesia has been thwarted by thugs with conservative religious and military backing (Kammen and McGregor 2012:234–62). Such ironic legitimacy reflects extensive middle class complicity in the pogroms. This chapter chooses to explore the class-biased embeddedness of the state in provincial society by examining how the pogroms were organized in and around Kupang.

A nascent cross-class coalition led mainly by teachers had brought renewal to the surrounding countryside in the 1950s, but by the early 1960s it was beginning to break down. For provincial conservatives higher up in the rapidly expanding bureaucracy, the prospect grew increasingly unpleasant of having to share the resources of the state for a greater good, just as they had learned to manipulate them for their own good. This bottom-up conflict was the subject of previous chapters. We now turn to the role played in Kupang by the nation's supreme top-down institution, the military. The events in Jakarta on 1 October 1965 had made its senior officers determined to carry out an anti-communist purge, but they could not do it without local allies. Chapter 6 showed that they had done a poor job of finding these in the 1950s, but they had worked hard on it since then and intensified their efforts that October 1965. Since the early 1960s those members of the urban middle class who felt most threatened by the communists were increasingly ready to be wooed, though certainly without realizing the depths of antisocial behaviour to which the alliance would expose them. They ranged from students who were active in religious clubs and were planning civil service careers, through businesspeople dependent on government work, to bureaucrats and village heads guarding economic gates.

Military

Chapter 8 explained how the army under chief of staff General Nasution evolved into an increasingly effective political organization. It began to expand into the provinces. Its only rival was the PKI, and it often found itself scrambling to imitate organizational techniques whose effectiveness had been proven by them. From the late 1950s it began to greatly elaborate the 'territorial' system whose origins lay in the revolutionary struggle. The rather conservative social structure outside Java made the military feel more confident there than they did in Java that they could find allies there.

President Sukarno also had to mobilize to survive, and the military were increasingly his rivals. In an ever more byzantine game, Sukarno vied with them to continually stimulate new mobilizational and control organizations at the regional level. Each side set up joint civilian-military organizations whose ostensible purposes diverged wildly from their real ones. Some were created to curry local favour by dispensing patronage, others to sabotage rival organizations or to coup them from within. They mobilized on issues of real concern to provincials – ideological ones such as religion, but also material ones such as land reform and bureaucratic employment. Their strategy of continually upping the ante threatened to escalate provincial confrontations to dangerous levels. When the denouement did come, it quickly became a remarkably one-sided obliteration of the communists. But this could not have been achieved without the partnerships that had been formed in the two to three years leading up to 1 October 1965 and that were tempered in the fire of the action-charged months that followed.

In March 1962 army headquarters created a new section that aimed to insert officers into every field of civilian government activity. It intended to counter the Sukarno government's increasingly insistent Nasakom line, which essentially required a PKI representative in every government organization. It was called the Sixth Special Army Section for Work Affairs (Seksi Khusus Urusan Karya Angkatan Darat, SUAD VI) (Sundhaussen 1982:143). It led to a further militarization of the already authoritarian government structure in NTT. Governor Lalamentik got a military deputy to look over his shoulder in May 1965 – his name was Major El Tari. The speaker of the provincial parliament had had one since 1960, named Major R. Margono.

The military had begun to penetrate the villages during the regional revolts of the mid-to-late 1950s. It formed village militias to 'protect' the population against rebels, then extended them all over the archipelago even where there had been no rebellion. In Kupang they were known as the Peoples Defence Organization (Organisasi Pertahanan Rakyat, OPR).[3] In 1962 they were nationally standardized as Civil Guards or Hansip (Pertahanan Sipil). During the purges in NTT they were under the

[3] Elsewhere they were variously known as Village Security Front (Barisan Keamanan Kampung, BKK), Village Security Front (Barisan Keamanan Desa, BKD), or Village Security Organization (Organisasi Keamanan Desa, OKD).

command of deputy governor Captain El Tari, and he remained in charge after becoming governor. Though poorly trained and ideologically unreliable (with lots of PKI sympathies), they were his main conduit for coercion directly against the village population.

In order to cultivate civilian allies in the political parties the military subverted a political programme kicked off by President Sukarno. Ostensibly to support his campaign to Crush Malaysia, it built security organizations all over the country in September 1964 known as Pepelrada (Penguasa Pelaksanaan Dwikora Daerah) (Sundhaussen 1982:186). This was the military answer to an earlier organization with emergency powers known as Peperda, which Sukarno had set up in 1959 in the hope that it would displace the military from local political control. Pepelrada was a national military organization with tentacles reaching down to the local level, similar to the Kopkamtib that was later so crucial to the New Order's regime of state terror.[4] Civilians were co-opted into the organization, as were the police (who were part of the military by this time). Pepelrada had less to do with Malaysia than with Indonesia's own 'hearts and minds' campaign in the regions. When the PKI started openly challenging the army from 1963 (which Feith (1964) at the time saw as a turning point in favour of the PKI), Pepelrada became the main military means for confronting the PKI at the local level.

The regional revolts had led to martial law around the country, and even after this was lifted in May 1963 the military worked hard to hold onto its grip. Martial law had given the army a strong role in a provincial and district-level consultative mechanism called Tjatur Tunggal, in which army and police commanders worked with governors, district heads and local prosecutors (Sundhaussen 1982:175). In March 1964 the mechanism was expanded and renamed Pantja Tunggal. When Pepelrada was formed later that year, part of its task was to chair the Pantja Tunggal. In Kupang, the provincial Pepelrada was headed up by the provincial police chief, R. Gurbada, replaced in May 1965 by Hardono. Its other members were the politician M.A. da Gomez (Front Nasional), the prosecutor Amir Hamzah, a representative from the governor's office, and a junior soldier named Lt. Rompas to look after 'operations' (Tari 1972:I, 267). Since the police had been progressively integrated into the military from 1960, this meant Pepelrada was effectively controlled by the provincial military commander (*danrem*).

[4] Kopkamtib stands for Komando Operasi Pemulihan Keamanan dan Ketertiban, or Operational Command for the Restoration of Order and Security (Tanter 1990).

'Wild' Killings

The military have never acknowledged organizing the killings. Even those internal reports that have come to light write instead of 'excesses' carried out by 'the people.' This is actually not completely false, except that 'the people' were social organizations working in close tandem with military intelligence. It is possible to distinguish a phase of 'wild' killings that lasted for a few weeks, from the 'systematic' and much more bloody phase that started late in October 1965, may have peaked in February 1966, and ran to at least February 1967. In the first phase, social groups allied with the army took most of the initiative. The military at this time was busy with its own internal purges, and then took some time to lay its plans for an organized extermination. In the second phase, those same social groups increasingly became tools in the hands of intelligence officers. Organized into various mobilizational fronts for propaganda purposes, they became willing accessories in an increasingly institutionalized purge. Though civilian actors no longer had the initiative, they remained involved because it was obvious to them that the alternative was to forfeit any kind of future in provincial Indonesia.

The wild phase started as soon as radio news bulletins made it clear that the communist putsch in Jakarta had failed. Protestant youth groups, some among them armed but 'off-duty' policemen, swung into action. They surrounded the Kupang jail and pressured the jail governor into releasing a Protestant village head who had earlier been arrested for 'insulting' the PKI by pulling out one of its signs. Pepelrada received orders from Gen. Suharto in Jakarta on 19 October 1965 to ban all parties associated with the 'G30S' event of 1 October (Sundhaussen 1982:214). Two days later, as the military governor wrote in his report of 1972, 'the emotions of the people of Kupang city, and their zeal to crush the G30S/ PKI, spontaneously reached a peak.' GMIT youths threw rocks on the roof of the home of the PKI's provincial secretary Thobias ('As') Rissi. They also targeted the homes of other PKI leaders – everyone knew where all the town's elite lived. They pulled out all the remaining PKI signs, which they had seen as such a provocation. The next day, 22 October, youths belonging to civil organizations close to the military began seizing PKI members who, they said, 'had secretly contravened the Pepelrada order against holding meetings.' This too, said the report (not believably), was not an organized 'demonstration' but 'spontaneity.' Several BTI members who happened to be visiting Kupang, and who were known derisively in town as 'mountain people' (*orang gunung*) were dragged out onto the streets and lynched by thugs around this time. Then on 20 November 1965 representatives from all the non-communist parties, led by the Catholics, held a rally at the Friars Field (today's Catholic University), 'with the permission of Pepelrada.' As if still not quite sure who to trust, they expressed support for Sukarno *and* for the military, and demanded, like all the rallies that year had done, that 'New Colonialism and Imperialism be crushed.' But then they added a new demand to disband the PKI and 'eliminate it down to its roots.' Its leaders should be 'crushed in accord with revolutionary justice' (Tari 1972:I, 284–7). The sudden reversal of fortunes sparked exhilaration and a savage bloodlust among many lower-middle class male youths in religious groups – matched by terror everywhere else it should be added. Arbitrary arrests and killings continued even during the holy season of Christmas.

That communism and religion were incompatible had been a theme of (particularly) Catholic preaching for many years, but even so, it only began to ring bells, even among educated young people, in late 1965 as national politics reached alarming levels of intensity. One young man heard in 1965 on a broadcast from Radio Malaysia (which was forbidden, since Indonesia and Malaysia were on a war footing) that Indonesia's own former Vice-President Mohammad Hatta had once written about the incompatibility between communism and religion. This astonished him and he spoke with his friends about it excitedly. The idea offered a powerful incentive to oppose the Sukarno government. When things got hot in late 1965, the Catholic activist Kanis Pari drew on his corps of trained cadres in the Catholic student and youth organizations to form an anti-communist militia called the Catholic Readiness Column (Barisan Katolik Siaga, Barkas). He later immodestly claimed to have single-handedly crushed the PKI in NTT. The moment of truth, he recalled, was initiating the big anti-PKI rally in Kupang on 20 November 1965, together with some younger officials from the governor's office, and with Daniel Adoe, the civilian chief of staff at Pepelrada. Altogether he claimed to have given 'guidance' to 'thousands' of young people through tireless activities before and after 1965. Afterwards he talked Governor El Tari into employing most of them as civil servants on the basis of their anti-communist credentials. In 1966 he travelled to Jakarta to take part in the anti-communist youth and student fronts KAPI and KAMI (Wawa 2004).[5]

---

[5] KAMI (Kesatuan Aksi Mahasiswa Indonesia, or Indonesian Student Action Front), came first, followed by KAPI (Kesatuan Aksi Pelajar Indonesia, or Indonesian Scholars Action Front). Two similar organizations were KAPPI (Kesatuan Aksi Pemuda Pelajar

Exactly as in Jakarta, but with a slight delay, anti-communist youth fronts were formalized under military patronage in May 1966. Its activists continued to be involved in executions until early 1967. The Protestant, Catholic and Muslim youth and student organizations that later joined in KAPI and KAMI began picking up PKI leaders from their homes in November 1965. They did this in coordination with the chief of staff of the district military command (Kodim), Major M. Noor. The youths handed them over to the military in such numbers that the old colonial jail ran out of space and many were held in the Merdeka football stadium. From there, beginning in January and peaking between February and April 1966, the military began taking them out at night to their executions. Bravado such as Pari's is common in the memoirs of Kupang public figures who won their spurs in 1965/66. The senior Florinese bureaucrat Yan Kiapoli even said Kanis was a Johnny-come-lately in the anti-communist struggle (Liliweri et al 1984:86–99).

Institutionalized Killing

The reasons for the low profile initially taken by the military in this first wave of killing were internal. In October 1965, the *danrem* in Kupang was Lt. Col. Soetarmadji. His immediate superior in the Udayana Military Area Command was Brig.-Gen. Sjafiuddin, based in Denpasar, Bali. Jakarta politicking had factionalized the armed forces, and Sjafiuddin was known as a Sukarnoist. He had openly expressed his loyalties to the PKI at the 1965 May Day rally in Denpasar. When the situation changed dramatically in Jakarta, the new military strong man, Gen. Suharto, initially doubted Sjafiuddin's readiness to obey. Bali experienced 'a near total breakdown in the normal line of command' (Robinson 1995:231–3). It took a month for Sjafiuddin to fall into line with the new reality, and only then did he also begin persecuting PKI members, aided by fresh anti-communist troops arriving in December. Kupang's Soetarmadji had been a protégé of Sjafiuddin. When Suharto, in mid-October 1965 (well ahead of the formal banning on 12 March 1966), ordered Pepelrada nationwide to crack down on the PKI and its affiliates, Soetarmadji may have been slow to act. He was removed from his post, accused of being 'involved' in G30S (Tari 1972:I, 30), and detained in Bali, but never charged (Kopkamtibda

Indonesia, Indonesian Youth and Scholars Action Front), and KASI (Kesatuan Aksi Sarjana Indonesia, Indonesian Graduates Action Front).

Nusra 1975b). His replacement Lt. Col. Abdul Djalal lost no time following Suharto's order. Djalal had been the first *danrem* in Kupang in 1958, and he had commanded the local battalion 743 (formerly known as 712) in combat operations in Ambon. The senior military men at this time all came from outside Kupang – Djalal was Madurese. He was assisted by his chief of staff (Kasrem), Lt. Col, M.H. Moesa S.B. After the New Year, with the completion of internal army purges, the ready participation of middle class civilians permitted the military to take their anti-communist actions to a more systematic level.

As the military shifted gears the process of mass murder began to look more institutionalized. Increasingly after the end of October, arrests were made by men in uniform sent by Pepelrada. Initially its office was located among the complex of government offices at Kampong Belanda, but in the course of 1966 the need for the pretence that this was a joint civilian-military operation grew weaker and the military commander (*danrem*) moved it conveniently close to his official residence in Kartini Street. It was located in a shop-front on the eastern side of the Ani Apothecary, just in front of the later Kupang Theatre. Many mobile police (*brimob*) were there, but people knew the soldier Lt. Col. Djalal was in charge. He was a short man, slightly bald. As he drove past in his jeep 'monitoring' events people said to each other: 'There goes the man who has been given the job of wiping out the PKI.' 'Everyone said, if you end up at Pepelrada, that is the end,' a woman who was a schoolgirl in Kupang at the time told me.

The house of Mr. Costa, the PKI bicycle repairman, lay next to the first Pepelrada office in town. Officers picked him up as one of the first, and took him straight to his execution. Many others of his class followed. When the killings were over, it was reportedly difficult for years to have basic repairs, such as plumbing done, as so many tradesmen had disappeared (Farram 2002:44). After initially holding detainees at the football field during the first few days in October, they were kept mainly at the old jail. But this small building filled up quickly, and after a short stay they would be taken out secretly and murdered on the outskirts of town.

Djalal played the central role of organizing executions, while the military governor Tari coordinated behind the scenes. Both men had access to an array of forces to execute orders, but most of these lay outside their immediate institution and thus required them to communicate. Pepelrada connected Djalal with elite civilian players in the anti-communist political parties. For logistics he had Battalion 743 and his own territorial troops, which both possessed trucks to transport prisoners. When the need grew greater he requisitioned civilian trucks, among them the famous ex-US

Army Chevrolet called 'Raksasa,' owned by the Indo-European Barbier family. The military did not yet have posts out in the subdistricts and villages at this time, but the police had a much stronger presence, and they had been under military command since 1960. Also under military command, through El Tari's nominally civilian office of governor, were thousands of Hansip civil guards distributed around the villages. It was generally they who, on the direct orders of the village head, arrested fellow-villager BTI members. The village heads received their orders from higher up and eventually from the military. Sometimes Hansip men were also ordered to do the actual killing. Once the New Order was established, the governor used Hansip to give military training to all civil servants and to bring in Golkar votes during the 1971 election. Governor El Tari wrote in 1972 that Hansip had been a way to 'plant the New Order' (Tari 1972:I, 46).

Despite their overwhelming coercive capacities, the military continued to pay a great deal of attention to involving their civilian allies within the bureaucracy, the political parties, and the religious organizations. Key people from all these middle class sectors sat on joint committees that ensured that a complex programme of extermination was implemented smoothly, that is, without provoking a mass backlash. These civilian allies helped create moral panics about PKI conspiracies, vetted lists of victims, and participated in their public humiliation and even execution. They then used their opinion-making powers to create a climate of impunity for perpetrators while reinforcing ostracism of surviving PKI sympathizers. A few illustrations of each of these steps will have to suffice in this short chapter.

A recurring element in the early phases was the deliberate instigation of mass hysteria about PKI intentions. Almost everywhere older people still swear to researchers that the pogroms were justified because their own names had been on PKI death lists, though no one has ever produced one as evidence.[6] In Kupang the PKI 'death list' story that could have fathered all the others was the military claim that the PKI had intended to murder General Ahmad Yani during an official visit a few days before 1 October (Tari 1972:I, 32–33). Yani was actually killed during the botched kidnapping operation by pro-communist military conspirators in Jakarta on 1 October. Perhaps the inventors of this unlikely provincial story hoped

---

[6] Farram gives them some credit (Farram 2002:40–1). Siegel, on the contrary, argued years ago (à la Derrida and with equal disdain for everyday meanings) that the death list hysteria reflected, not political circumstances but, 'the dread of the failure of reading' (Siegel 1979).

to borrow the aura of the ultimate showdown for their own town. Even a little town like Waikabubak, in the interior of the subsistence agrarian island of Sumba, produced a PKI conspiracy. Its Chinese and Arab traders, and Sabunese, Rotenese and Ambonese civil servants, had every reason to feel vulnerable amid growing communist mobilization among the peasants. Execrable roads kept the town isolated from the port of Waingapu. In January 1966 a rumour flew around town that the PKI was planning to detonate a bomb that would kill government officials and volunteers planting trees in a re-vegetation project five kilometres beyond the town boundary. The PKI was already no longer a force by that time, yet in the ensuing hysteria, bands of church youths and government officials rounded up many communist party activists. The state prosecutor held them in the town's jail, where the men and women were tortured by being hung upside down and beaten (End 1987:612–7, Halsema 1995:73–4, Kolimon and Wetangterah 2012:36).

No matter how implausible the scenarios that did the rounds, they always unleashed mobs eager to take part in rituals of public humiliation, torture and even public executions against well-known PKI members. Breakdown of law and order appears to have been part of the plan. As in Kupang, people in the harbour town of Waingapu in Sumba raided Chinese shops in January 1966 once it was clear the military was on their side. Christian teachers coordinated attacks on the Chinese school in town (Kolimon and Wetangterah 2012:83). On 11 January 1966 those PKI leaders still alive in Kupang were paraded before all the political party leaders and senior officials who sat on the provincial Pantja Tunggal. All knew each other well. Now the tables were turned on the loud-mouths of the 'town devils' and the 'village devils.' They were forced to acknowledge the 'superiority of Pancasila as the only life view' and to declare their party disbanded. The following week, 17 January 1966, the military-controlled National Front held a 'gigantic roll-call' in the Merdeka football stadium.[7] Ten thousand participants from all non-PKI parties yelled their demands to smash (*membubarkan*) the PKI. The military accommodated these demands by establishing a NTT Research and Evaluation Agency (Badan Penelitian and Pertimbangan). Its ostensible purpose was both to expedite the effort to suppress the PKI and all its members as well as to

[7] The National Front was set up in Jakarta in 1960 as yet another 'coordinating' body to be fought over between Sukarno and the armed forces. In most regions it was run by military commanders (Sundhaussen 1982:152).

'prevent excesses that may occur as a result of this suppression.' In order to ensure its 'objectivity' it contained representatives of all the non-communist political parties and was chaired by a military police lawyer, Mr. W.A. Mokalu. Under this veil of legality, most of the provincial PKI leaders, whose names once stood clearly on published lists of state appointments, and who were last seen being humiliated on 11 January, disappeared without a trace. One of the few to survive was provincial PKI secretary As Rissi, who was reprieved for revealing much information to his interrogators and instead given a long sentence in a Lombok prison – more on this below.

Most of those killed were never tried. No military court was convened in Kupang, but a few cases apparently went to civilian judges. Convictions were overwhelmingly determined within the executive agencies. Death lists were compiled by military intelligence (Kasi Intel), headed in Kupang by a Javanese officer. Presumably the senior PKI/ BTI names were drawn from the party committee lists that had routinely appeared in government reports alongside all the others. Junior names were based on lists of those who had received assistance during the previous year's drought, or perhaps simply on what the wave of arrests at village level had thrown up. These lists were then vetted by the political party representatives. It seems likely that the euphemistically named NTT Research and Evaluation Agency was the place where this happened in Kupang. No official membership list of this agency has so far turned up, but some evidence suggests all anti-communist parties had senior representatives there. I.H. Doko, for example, is thought to have been one of several representing Parkindo.[8]

How difficult was it to break the civilian reluctance to be drawn into approving the death sentences? A remarkable account from Maumere suggests that when Mephistopheles did knock on the door, the bargain was made within a few hours (see box). In this case the joint military-civilian organization that vetted the lists was simply named Operations Command (Komando Operasi, Komop).

---

[8] Two other senior Parkindo figures mentioned in interviews as 'having the power over life and death' by their involvement with Pepelrada include Parkindo chairperson, Rev. Andreas ('Ande') Tule, and the former GMKI activist and civil servant Sol Therik. Most stories about these civilian collaborators highlight actions that saved lives, while leaving their consent to the deaths unspoken. I have no information about other parties, such as Partai Katolik and PNI, but there is no reason to think they would not have been similarly involved.

The Meeting to Decide Who Should be "Secured"

This unique description of the process by which the military sought middle-class participation in the atrocities of 1965/66 comes from an anonymous account (Anonymous 1974:75–6) written in Maumere, capital of Sikka district in (largely Catholic) Flores. It did not have a Pepelrada office, but the military there had a similar institution named Komop (Komando Operasi). The translation is my own (GvK).

In the afternoon of 27 February 1966 a meeting was held in the Sikka district parliamentary chambers between the Komop chief of staff, the head of the G30S Investigations Team and leaders of political parties, social organizations and Golkar. The meeting was led by Karel Elkel, the head of the Investigations Team and (someone delegated by) the Komop chief of staff, Sergeant Major Jos. U. Tokoh. The political leaders were asked their opinion, or more precisely were asked to decide who should be "secured" out of this second wave of arrests. The Catholic leaders among them through their spokespersons, E.P. da Gomez and Herman Joseph, then said that the Catholic organizations did not feel competent to decide which individuals should be "secured". This was a matter for the appropriate authorities, according to instruction no.22 of the Crush Malaysia Command (Komando Ganyang Malaysia, Kogam). The Catholic organizations were only able to offer assistance where necessary. Those chairing the meeting had a problem with this opinion, and so they ended it and reconvened in the official residence of the Komop chief of staff, Major Soemarno, which was also the Komop headquarters. There was extreme pressure on all parties and organizations to attend. With the argument of "taking joint responsibility" the parties and organizations were forced to take a stand on "securing" those individuals who had been arrested on suspicion of involvement in G30S. The meeting proceeded. One by one the names of the detainees were read out, the reason why they had been detained and the nature of their supposed offence. The atmosphere was edgy; it made the hairs on their necks stand up, because each of the military personnel in the room had his weapon in his hand. In this situation the parties and organizations one by one had to state clearly their attitude to the detainees whose names had been read out. The PNI party represented by Th. M. Sogo said among other things: "We have to wipe out G30S/ PKI to its very roots, so no one can be absolved."

That night 24 people affiliated with PKI and PNI in Maumere were classified as Category A ("secured"). This horrible and cruel decision was immediately implemented by "securing" respectively eight people in Lela/ Kuarwang, eight in Nita, and another eight in Koting. Among the victims of this malignancy were Sukasno, Suprapto, M. Said, Ignasius Ila, B. Tasi, Tua Buar, Karang Betel and Viator Nurak. Those present at this flawed meeting were Soemarno, I. Pati, J.M. Masar, J.U. Tokoh, J. Pulor, A. Muslimin, C. Jantje, S.R. Abdullah and Niko Kopong, all from the armed forces Abri; from the G30 Investigations

Team there was Prosecutor Karel and Fronas J.P. Meak, and Niko Bela from Hansip. The Catholic parties and organizations were represented by A.I. Sadipun and E.P. da Gomez, the Islamic party Nahdatul Ulama by Umar Salia, Parkindo by W.S. Pandy and PNI by Th.M. Sogo.

This night of 27 February 1966 was the moment that Catholic leaders started losing their grip, or to put it more strongly they had already abandoned Catholic principles. The leaders did not have the courage to raise their voices to fight for justice and truth because they were afraid of the guns in their faces, afraid of the threat of death for defending truth and justice. And from this one wrong turn arose the long and complex series of problems in the political chessgame that have afflicted Sikka district ever since.

Similar committees appear to have existed everywhere. Their ad hoc naming suggests a degree of improvisation and confirms the importance the military attached to local participation. In the small market town of Oesao, about 30 km east of Kupang along the road into the interior, the same committee was called PKI Extermination Team (Tim Pembasmi PKI) (Kolimon and Wetangterah 2012:222–3). It was formed in December 1965 and consisted of a representative from both the Protestant political party Parkindo and the secular bureaucratic party PNI, and a policeman, all locals. They sat in the village office and were presented with lists of farmers who had accepted government assistance during the drought of 1964–65 under the Mekatani programme. The PKI had apparently presented this as a party programme to win new members. Capturing government programmes for political purposes was then a common tactic – so, for example, PNI controlled Interior Affairs, while Parkindo had influence in Education. Other non-PKI party leaders and local officials were called in as witnesses. Under strict military intelligence supervision, the Extermination Team had to separate core organizers of PKI/ BTI/ Gerwani local branches from the small fry. If caught trying to exempt a neighbour or relative, they were forced to add five more victims to the list. There were no penalties for excessive zeal, for example against unpopular individuals. Soldiers then took the unlucky to the subdistrict capital of Babao at night using a truck seized from a Chinese businessman. After several days they were then taken out at night in groups of about 20, and shot by soldiers, policemen, or trusted civilians. Any survivors had their throats cut to make sure. A new mass grave was dug for each group. Seven such graves in the vicinity of Tanah Putih village near Babao, the home village of the *fetor* and subdistrict head, were filled between late December 1965 and early February 1966. Together they are thought to hold over a hundred bodies. Other mass grave sites are at Pulu Thie village, Oesao itself, and Tanah Merah village (the latter is also a repository from Kupang city that is mentioned in other reports). The terror was such that 'not even the gecko would make a sound and not even the cock would crow.'[9]

Anti-communism was an urban middle class passion, directed mainly at Jakarta's Nasakom policy and at the growing assertiveness of the rural poor. The urban poor, by contrast, had been mobilized by the PKI, albeit unevenly. An account written much later by an academic who remembered his life as a kampong boy depicts how stunned the normally convivial kampong community had been when the military teams drove in looking for certain individuals (see box).[10] One brave woman spoke out on behalf of a neighbour, but she then fatalistically betrayed another neighbour instead. This account of a Kupang kampong in the 1960s is no doubt coloured by the author's youthful innocence, and by the forgetfulness enforced by the middle class establishment since then. But it also suggests that the anti-communist heroism that lower-middle class activists recall until the present time did not have its home in the poorer kampongs.

A Very Quiet Area

As engrossed as the religious middle class was in the pogroms, so disengaged were the urban poor. They experienced them almost as a natural phenomenon, a tragedy akin to a drowning or a rock rolling off the hill onto a house. [Extract from a manuscript by Cornelis Lay, then the 6-year old son of a Sabunese harbour worker who lived in a Sabunese kampung in Fontein, Kupang, named Dendeng, a couple of kilometres along a dead-end road running west from the old town centre. Other extracts from this manuscript are translated in Lay 2014.]

As everywhere in Kupang, neighbours in Dendeng communicated in a big voice. In fact it was more like a shout, called "maruak". But as I remember there was never any serious fighting in the neighborhood. I feel Dendeng was a very quiet area. Nothing out of the ordinary ever happened there, except in 1965 – 1966.

Towards the end of 1965 we were told not to be outside the house after dark. We children had little idea what was going on, but people said "there is a war".

[9] 'Cicak saja tidak berbunyi dan ayam saja tidak berkokok,' (Pak Kobus, in East Kupang – Kolimon and Wetangterah 2012:226).

[10] Similar stories of severed heads to the one related in the box have been heard all over Indonesia throughout the twentieth century. Gregory Forth (2009) finds they 'articulate relations between local communities and various categories of outsiders in the context of nation-building.'

We often heard shooting at night, and sometimes flashes of fire between the two hills that lay on either side of the Dendeng creek. But war between who and who, we had no idea. A short time later there was another disturbance. Parents strictly forbade their kids from going out at night. We heard there were people running around wearing "spring shoes" – allowing them to jump vast distances – and they were kidnapping children. The rumour said these children would have their heads cut off and put into the foundation of a new building or a bridge to strengthen the construction. We never knew where this story came from, but practically everyone in town believed it.

There were a few other events that disturbed the quiet at Dendeng. The first one I didn't see but everyone was talking about it when I got home from school. This was late 1965 or early 1966. Early one morning before dawn a group of soldiers came to collect Uncle Wielawa. He was our neighbour and his door was always open for food or gossip. They accused him of being "a PKI person" and said he had to be "secured" (diamankan). When the vehicle with him in it started to move away, Nene Mia Duru Kana, the oldest person in the kampung, stopped it and told the agents they had the wrong person. Words flew back and forth. But in the end they let him go after Nene Mia had explained that the one they were after was Uncle Lawa, an activist said to be connected with the PKI who lived just below the Mondolang family home. Uncle Lawa was eventually arrested, I don't know what happened to him after that. His two sons, Mien and Adi Papa, were our playmates but they never told us anything about their father.

The second big thing that happened in Dendeng was when a huge rock became dislodged from the eastern slope above the kampung and rolled down onto the front of the Wielawa family home. Two daughters, Kakak Yane and Mince, died instantly. This was in the late 1960s. The third thing was when a part of the dam burst in the early 1970s killing our neighbour, A'a Minggus Djo. And oh yes in between those two occasions the only other event to disturb the peace was the drowning of a Timorese boy who worked at the shop "Sudirman". Other than that, Dendeng was a very quiet area.

The most basic purpose of the executions themselves was to physically eliminate the PKI. But they also had to inspire terror among the lower classes and to tie the middle-class elite to a new regime. The first of these extra effects were achieved through spectacular public executions, the second by issuing 'invitations' to anti-communist party activists to observe and even take part in executions. The public burning of John Timu, secretary of the Ende PKI branch and a militant man, in late 1965 or early 1966 was one example (see Chapter 3). He had fled to Surabaya, but was persuaded to return by assurances from Ben Mboi, a Florinese army officer who later became NTT governor. The military arrested him and put up a poster at the central monument advertising the place and time of his execution. This was carried out in daylight by Muslim activists belonging to Ansor. Along the way to Tanjung, a few kilometres east of Ende, he was slashed with razors and dragged along the ground. Barely alive, he faced the flames in silence, watched by a large crowd. Several such burnings took place in Ende. Human heads were placed at the Ende monument as a public warning.

In Sabu, soldiers invited everyone in the little main town of Seba to troop along behind the execution party for 31 communists, on the evening of 29 March 1966 (Kolimon and Wetangterah 2012:141–7). The joint committee that had condemned them was here known as the Judgment Forum (Forum Pengadilan). Two people from the crowd were assigned to hold each bound prisoner, whom they often knew well, to ensure they would not run. The crowd took an hour to walk from the general hospital to the end of the Terdamu airstrip, where more people were already waiting by a large hole two metres deep. By the light of portable gas lamps, the appointed guards lowered each prisoner into the hole, where soldiers shot them.

Civilian participation in rural killings seems to have been driven more by coercion and curiosity than by hatred. The BTI had been no enemy in rural Timor except to some landlords. A rural primary school teacher at Buraen took me to a site in Amarasi district where, according to locals, 33 people had been murdered, in two groups. The graves lay in a swampy patch within an area of dark rainforest between Buraen and Oekabiti.[11] He told me that for years villagers passing the site on foot would hang small gifts of food or betel nut on the bushes to appease the spirits. After fastidiously clearing the undergrowth with his machete, looking for 'snakes' (which I suspected were spiritual), he asked me to bow my head and then prayed simply: 'Lord, we are here to learn about the unjust acts of people against people. Help us to know the truth of this event.' The killing took place early in 1966. The prisoners were all from Amarasi district, but from other villages, so locals did not know them personally. They had first been detained at the 'round house' in Baun – the raja's ballroom, where he had danced so often with his *fetor* and their women. Raja Victor Koroh had passed the order to make the arrests to his *fetor*, who passed it to their

[11] Approximately at 10 degrees 15 minutes 39 seconds south, 123 degrees 50 minutes 39 seconds east.

village heads (*temukung*). About three hundred had been detained at the round house. Most the raja then ordered released, the rest he sent to their deaths. The basis for these instant and undocumented decisions will forever remain cloudy. Stories abound about acts of social revenge against peasant upstarts. Hendrikus Ataupah traced the murder in 1966 of the deputy chairperson of the provincial BTI, a man named Th. ('Tontje') Timu, to the insult that the Raja of Amarasi had experienced at the hands of Timu's and some other rebellious families in Baun in the 1920s. The rebels had accused the raja of having raped one of their women. This had led the Dutch to discipline him.[12] Forty years later he had his revenge.

Every subdistrict in Amarasi appears to have had its own execution sites, and perhaps that was the case in most of the province's subdistricts. Where in other villages soldiers or perhaps mobile police did the killing, near Baun villagers (presumably members of Hansip) were forced to do it themselves, much to their own horror. There was as yet no military post there; soldiers were a rare sight. The village head (*temukung*) told his villagers to dig two large holes on the edge of the swamp, five metres square and about a metre deep. Police (some say soldiers from outside the area) then brought the condemned persons to the edge one by one. Two villagers would hold him or her down while others hacked into them crudely with machetes. Some victims were still groaning in pain as others fell on top of them. Then the soil was heaped over them. It was raining. Traumatized men returned home covered in mud and blood, unable to sleep or eat meat for months. Too many such stories came my way to record here; they resemble those recorded by Farram. Sometimes victims dug their own graves. However, most executions were carried out by soldiers, apparently largely from the territorial Battalion 743, but also by other military units and even by the police and civilian auxiliaries. They usually happened at night, in groups of ten or twenty, often by bullet, sometimes by bayonet or machete. Sometimes local villagers or anti-communist political party activists participated.

Elite civilians were occasionally encouraged to participate in these mass executions on the outskirts of Kupang. So productive was such participation thought to be in military minds that even a western visitor to Kupang at this time was invited to witness a massacre: 'I was told I could

12 Interview, Kupang, 30 June 2009. Timu appears in this capacity in an official report (Tari 1972:I, 270).

come along, but I was warned that I'd have to help with the project. They make sure that anybody who sees these things becomes involved in the killing in some way' (King 1966:89). A detailed description of one particular mass execution witnessed only by invited loyalists came to me from two sources.[13] The time was February 1967. An anti-communist party activist at the time told me he accompanied the condemned prisoners from the moment they were collected from the old colonial jail to the fatal shots. The evening began with him standing in the dark next to the head jailer's residence, just outside the door of the jail. He heard prisoners weep in distress when their names were called. More than a year had passed since the worst of the troubles. They had been lulled into thinking the time for executions was past. A kick in the backside kept the slow ones moving towards the truck. Other party representatives in KAPI/ KAMI were observing too. The greatest sadism came from members of right-wing student associations, who nursed a bitter hatred towards the once privileged leftist student association CGMI.[14]

Earlier that day soldiers had turned up in a truck at Oebelo village, some distance east of Tanah Merah, off the main road at 22 km from Kupang.[15] A Timorese farmer who then lived in a hut on his fields told me they dug a large hole, about four metres deep, a couple of hundred metres off the road. They were not Timorese, and did not ask permission from or even speak with any of the farmers working their fields in this flat area with lontar palms and scrub. It was raining, but the water had not yet

---

13 One was a farmer who still lives near there, the other a civilian anti-communist activist in Kupang at the time. Strangely enough the farmer does not remember seeing any civilians there. Although both seemed sure they were speaking of the same events, there were many executions at different locations in that general area in 1966/1967, so perhaps they were mistaken and had described different events. The activist remembered being present at at least three similar occasions.

14 Concentrasi Gerakan Mahasiswa Indonesia, or Indonesian Student Movement Concentration. The head of CGMI at Kupang's Universitas Cendana, Inyo Kanadjara, son of the former acting district head of South Central Timor, got away with his life because he had a friend in Pepelrada. But his father was murdered, as were all his senior CGMI colleagues. The CGMI rivals mentioned in this interview as particularly cruel belonged to the Islamic Students Association (Himpunan Mahasiswa Islam, HMI) and the Indonesian National Students Movement (Gerakan Mahasiswa Nasional Indonesia, GMNI). Other anti-communist student associations active in Kupang at this time were the (Protestant) Christian Student Movement of Indonesia (Gerakan Mahasiswa Kristen Indonesia, GMKI), and the (Catholic) Persatuan Mahasiswa Katolik Republik Indonesia, PMKRI.

15 The coordinates of the three neighbouring mass graves, according to eyewitnesses who wish to remain anonymous, are these: 10 degrees 6 minutes 41.36 seconds south, and 123 degrees 45 minutes 33.39 seconds east; 45.32 seconds south, 32.19 seconds east; 45.31 seconds south, 31.06 seconds east.

soaked in, so the hole was dry on the bottom. In the evening several truckloads of fully-armed soldiers arrived at the entrance to the track. Some took up positions up and down the road to stop any passing traffic. One truck had about 20 prisoners in it, their eyes blindfolded and their hands tied behind their backs. The farmer did not recognize any of them. Some seemed to be from Rote. Actually his own village of Oebelo had PKI officials who also disappeared, but these were taken to their deaths elsewhere. When rain prevented the truck from driving off the bitumen road, prisoners were thrown onto the ground 'like sacks of rice, some landing on their heads, some on their buttocks.' Curious bystanders were ordered to grab each one – four to a prisoner. 'Don't let them get away, these are evil people,' the soldiers told them. As soldiers called out numbers, one by one the prisoners were stood up on the edge of the hole, and shot in the back of the head, upon which they toppled into the hole. A few days later the same thing – the hole, the trucks, the prisoners, the shots. And a few days after that it happened for a third time. One man somehow managed to save himself by feigning death and then crawling out of the grave after everyone had left. Another delayed his death by a few days by claiming vigorously he could show them a secret PKI weapons cache, which was never found. At the hole later that night some civilians took bayonets and joined in the wild stabbing amid yells of 'this is how we deal with village devils.' The vicious intra-elite rivalry is a reminder that by no means all the tensions in Kupang were class-based. Much later that night my informant came home with blood-soaked trousers. Soon afterwards his little daughter was afflicted with convulsions, which kept returning for two years. His wife blamed the spirits of the dead.

Where it was felt the aim of middle-class complicity had been achieved, the killings became routine affairs carried out at night and without public dramas. An example of a secret execution was that of seven people in Waingapu, East Sumba, on 1 March 1966. They were shot at night in the mangroves 3 km outside town, while residents were under curfew. Another 13 were taken out to sea on a barge from the Waingapu jetty in August 1966. They were secretly disposed of at sea (Kolimon and Wetangterah 2012:91–3). Among the thousands secretly executed were several who figure prominently in this book: top provincial organizers like the inflammatory PKI journalist Paulus Kanuru (see Chapter 7) and the provincial deputy secretary of the PKI Sam Piry; district organizers like BTI organizer in South Central Timor Michael Marcus (see Chapter 3) and Soë parliamentarian Agustinus Roboth (Chapter 7); and rank-and-file activists like the Soë teachers (Chapter 7).

Mass graves lie along all three roads out of Kupang city, to the east, south and west. None have been exhumed. Most often used for execution was the barren stretch of land on either side of the road east towards Soë. Tanah Merah, a hamlet in Tarus village on the eastern side of Kupang, is widely known though unmarked by any monument. Years later bus passengers with a hazy idea of what had happened there would abuse villagers as they passed the area for having themselves been communists. There appear to be graves in a number of places on either side of this road for several kilometres. One of them is at Oebelo, at kilometre 22 along the same road (see above). A second significant site lies in a former guava grove at kilometre 10 out of Kupang, on the road south to Baun. Some accounts say this place was used to bury people already executed elsewhere, perhaps because it was closer to town. Here the gruesome memory is of human feet sticking out of shallow rocky graves, and of heads dug up by dogs. A third is described as lying in West Kupang at Pohon Nitas, in the suburb of Manulai. Beyond Kupang many subdistricts had their own execution and burial sites (see above). The stories are particularly abundant in Amarasi south of Kupang, around Soë the capital of South Central Timor district, and in Belu the Catholic area near Portuguese Timor. All these areas had significant BTI adherence.

Women affiliated with the women's movement Gerwani were murdered as well. More were imprisoned, and some escaped with their lives by offering their bodies to officers. Abdul Djalal himself took a Gerwani woman as a concubine. In December 1965 soldiers arrested the district-level PKI coordinator in Waingapu, an Information Department official named Mbulu-Dima. He was secretly executed in the mangroves 3 km out of town one night in March 1966. Police also arrested his wife, and the arresting police officer later 'married' her, perhaps as a kind of trophy (Kolimon and Wetangterah 2012:91–2). Women were at most risk of sexual abuse during the obligatory periodic reporting to the military, especially if they had been widowed by the pogrom. The wives of PKI officials often had a function in the women's movement Gerwani. These were the circumstances under which a widow, whose name is given as Mama Koba, was raped by the most senior military officer in Kalabahi, Alor, Buterpra Ahmad (Kolimon and Wetangterah 2012:325).

Afterwards, middle class opinion-makers in religious institutions affirmed regime propaganda, perpetuating a climate of impunity for the crimes committed and exacerbating the social ostracism of survivors. Even where some within the church protested the killings on humanitarian grounds at the time, the final word was one of complicity. In Alor, for example, several ministers circumambulated the main town of Kalabahi for six days in their robes to protest the killing of church members who, according to them, had been unstained by the PKI. They confronted Buterpra Ahmad on the seventh. But other church officials complied with Ahmad's demand to fetch Alor PKI chairman Sem Talmaka from hiding in his mountainous home village and surrendered him for execution. On 5 May 1966 all religious leaders in Alor issued a joint statement thanking God for delivering the nation from the PKI, 'which not only rejected God but also proved a hindrance to inner rest and worship of Him.'[16]

The synod of the Sumba Christian Church, GKS, on 4 December 1965 ordered an anti-communist declaration it had drawn up in 1957 to be read out again from all pulpits. GKS members 'involved' in the PKI were banned from Holy Communion until they had publicly confessed their sins, and stripped of any ecclesiastical functions they may have had. Such discipline had thus far only been imposed for sexual transgressions. In the communal societies of East Nusa Tenggara, such condemnation from on high led whole families to be socially ostracized for generations. Widows were seen as sinners and criminals, as atheists, bearers of a disease. 'I was accused of being a temptress, a bad woman,' one of them in Waingapu told the authors of *Memori-memori terlarang* (Kolimon and Wetangterah 2012:78). 'I was just a girl, it was too heavy. They saw me as filth.'[17]

Numbers

How many people became the victims of this sudden and bloody regime change? If officials in Jakarta did keep accounts they have remained a closely guarded secret, and the same is true in this remote part of Indonesia. A Protestant church source a decade after the events described here put the estimate for all of NTT at 'about 2,000 killed' (Cooley 1976), and Farram (2002:43) years later regarded this as still the only reasonable estimate we have.

Since then two kinds of evidence has emerged that, while sketchy, both suggest a figure perhaps three times as high. The first comes from newly

---

16 'Bangsa-Negara dan Pemerintah dihindarkan Tuhan dari malapetaka 'GESTOK' yang menyangkal tetapi juga menghambat ketentraman batin serta ibadah kepada Tuhan yang Maha Esa' (Kolimon and Wetangterah 2012:323).

17 'Saya dituduh macam-macam, saya dibilang perempuan penggoda, perempuan yang tidak baik [menangis]. Padahal itu semua tidak benar [terdiam beberapa saat]... Ya ampun, godaan sangat berat waktu saya masih gadis. Saya dianggap perempuan kotor.'

discovered district-level demographic data for the period 1961 to 1969 (Kantor Sensus NTT 1971). Tables show that the provincial population in 1966 was about 30,000 less than would be expected, with male adults and children in Kupang district the most affected. However, plotting the underlying district data reveals that the figures are of poor quality, while most districts with apparently good data show no unusual shifts.[18] Major population declines are evident only in Kupang and Alor, each based on a few points only. If real, they could reflect killing of men, which might have been greatest around Kupang, but more likely are due to increased out-migration led by men. More convincing is the subtly undulating population graph for South Central Timor, of central concern in the present study. It suggests slowed population growth over the period 1965–1966. The loss here looks to be equivalent to at most a couple of thousand. Again, if real this could have been due to the killings, but it could also have been caused by (drought-related?) emigration to town.

A different but no less fraught technique is to compare current estimates of numbers killed in some districts with the officially recorded number of BTI branches in those districts in the 1960s. If the number killed per branch is consistent, it could be used to generalize across all districts in NTT. Unfortunately the numbers are not very consistent. Yet another technique is to assume that the nationally estimated ratio of those killed to those detained also applied in NTT, and thence to calculate the dead from an estimate (see below) of those detained in NTT. Both approaches suggest a number of dead considerably higher than 2,000, and range from a low of 5–6,000 and a high of 13,600.[19]

Information about prisoners is only slightly less difficult to obtain. According to figures kept by the extrajudicial military intelligence agency

[18] In Belu and Ende unusually straight graphs suggest that annual points were not measured but interpolated between endpoints, and this may be the case for parts of the Manggarai and Alor data too. For East Sumba most data is missing. A sudden jump in the proportion of adults to children in Manggarai, Alor, Kupang and North Central Timor suggests a changed definition of the child in the mid-1960s. The graphs for North Central Timor, Sikka, Ngada and West Sumba look normal. Poor data quality is probably due to poor education and weak motivation among local officials in NTT at this time (I am grateful to Colin Barlow for this observation).

[19] For some districts we have both an estimate of the number of BTI branches in 1963 ('Branches' in the table below, from Tari 1972) and an estimate of the number killed ('Killed' in the table below, drawn from Kolimon et al 2012, and for Sikka from Prior 2011). Using the Tari data for this purpose is problematic for at least two reasons: the 1963 BTI branch tally would have increased by 1965 (Chapter 7), and Tari did not count other PKI-affiliated organizations, some of which were numerous (Gerwani). Meanwhile, the figures in Kolimon et al are highly uncertain.

Kopkamtib, set up in November 1965 to secure the transition, the number of long-term detainees from this part of the country was in the low hundreds. The Udayana Military Area Command that included Bali, West Nusa Tenggara and East Nusa Tenggara, was holding 274 prisoners in 1969, most of them from the western parts (Kopkamtib 1969).[20] The big detainer was the Central Java command, totalling nearly 50,000. By 1975 the number of Udayana detainees had grown slightly to 389, as more were arrested in subsequent years (Kopkamtibda Nusra 1975b). Among them was the provincial PKI secretary As Rissi. However, the number of short-term detainees, labelled 'Category C' and not recorded here, had been much larger. Most of these were released by 1968, but they remained subject to surveillance and reinvestigation for years. Released suspects were under orders to report and could not be rehired for the bureaucracy. An internal military report indicates soldiers had their hands full with the large number of these short-term detainees in the aftermath of the purge. How could they possibly, it complained, give 'ideological guidance to these ex-G30S/ PKI Category C people... in view of their huge numbers down to the village level'? How were they, to mention another problem discussed

---

District	Killed	Branches	Multiplier
East Sumba	20	22	0.9
West Sumba	22	10	2.2
Sabu	37	11	3.4
Alor/ Pantar	384	17	22.6
Sikka	800–2,000	26	31–77

The ratio of Branches to Killed ('Multiplier' in the table) varies from a low 0.9 in East Sumba to a high 31–77 in Sikka. Low values could be due to local military restraint (often mentioned in Sumba), or shipping victims out to be killed in Kupang (e.g. from Sabu). The high Sikka value may be due to most killings being ethnic rather than BTI-based. The real value is therefore likely to lie in between these extremes. Perhaps the Alor/ Pantar value of 22.6 is close to the provincial average – the number killed here is actually an underestimate since it counts only those near Kalabahi. This would lead (for 600 BTI branches province-wide) to 13,600 deaths. A more modest estimate for the multiplier of 10 would lead to 6,000 deaths.

Yet another estimate is deduced from the national ratio of those killed to those ever detained. That ratio is thought to be approximately 1:3 (500,000 killed, to 1.5 million detained – Vickers 2005:159–60). In NTT the number ever detained may have been around 20,000 – see below. If the ratio in NTT is the same as the national average, the number killed would be 7,000.

20 This report appears to indicate the origin of detainees, not their place of detention. The Maluku military command is listed as having only 170 detainees, even though Buru Island, in Maluku, was the destination for a very large cohort of prisoners, especially from Java.

in the report, to issue a letter of dismissal for someone who had been secretly shot dead? How were they to answer members of the public whose family home had been seized because one family member was suspect (Kopkamtibda Nusra 1975a)?[21]

An intriguing set of figures indicates that the number of people kept under surveillance in NTT may indeed have run to the tens of thousands. The possibility of rural revolt seems to have been the main worry. In order to learn how realistic this fear was, the military conducted a 'registration' of political affiliations in rural villages in December 1966. A total of just over 2 million people lived in the area in which the registration was conducted, which corresponds roughly to the rural population in NTT at this time. The total of all political party members and sympathizers came to about 780,000, which would correspond roughly to the rural adult voting population. The resulting table, broken down by district, reported 'members' and 'sympathizers' for all the seven then-legal political parties (differing significantly from the 1955 list of legal parties). Curiously it also reported adherents of two leftist parties that had recently been banned, namely PKI and Partindo, formerly an urban party. The report does not explain how this registration was conducted.[22] Clearly it could not have been a voluntary exercise. All electoral activity had been banned. Moreover it is inconceivable that, after the terror a few months earlier, anyone would voluntarily list themselves as a member of a banned political party. It therefore seems likely the figures were gathered by local officials, such as sub-district and village chiefs, who had earlier cooperated with the murders. Perhaps the list of PKI and Partindo 'members' was simply the list of those ever detained for alleged communist sympathies.

A total of 17,105 were reported to be 'ex-PKI members,' plus another 800 'ex-PKI sympathizers.' Another 4,164 were said to be BTI, without breakdown by district. In addition, 667 were reportedly members of or sympathizers with Partindo (Pemda NTT 1966: appendix). These people were

[21] The reports makes clear that Kopkamtib in this region of Indonesia was stretched to the limit by its many other tasks as well. They included monitoring smuggling, narcotics, prostitution, 'hippies' (who should be prevented from entering Indonesia), foreign fishermen, and visiting ships' crews who distributed hammer and sickle symbols. They had to suppress dissent among intellectuals, among the religious, and even within the armed forces. The way to do this was to appoint military people to every designated professional organization, for supervision. All this required budgets as well as manpower.

[22] The same table (slightly simplified by leaving out non-party sympathizers and others totalling about 60,000) occurs in Tari (1969), where it is attributed to a 'census.' There was no national civilian census in this year; it was probably a military exercise. It was repeated in 1968.

kept under permanent surveillance by the extrajudicial military security organization Kopkamtib, which reported a few years later that '21,483' people had no voting rights in the upcoming 1971 election (Gubernur NTT 1970:14). The biggest concentrations of leftist adherents were in the district of Kupang, in Belu (Timor) and in Manggarai (Flores). These were also areas of high BTI sympathies in 1963, according to the 1972 report quoted above. But South Central Timor, reportedly a BTI heartland in 1963, reported almost no PKI members here. Instead, it reported a high level of 'non-party' adherence. Perhaps this indicates that local officials in this area were permitted to hide their region's PKI past under the label 'non-party.' 'Non-party' affiliations totalled 57,035, spread out over Belu, Ende, South Central Timor and North Central Timor. In all but the last, BTI mobilization had been high in 1963, and mobilization may have spread into North Central Timor by 1965. If we add the reported PKI figures to the 'non-party' figures, the total of 79,771 is not far off the reported 77,026 BTI 'members' in 1963. The areas of densest leftist affiliation reported in 1969 and 1963 also show some correspondence. The figures suggest the military were concerned that up to 10% of the rural adult population continued to have a doubtful ideological orientation. It is from these people that the 'huge number' of rural short-term detainees had come. Whether these areas also suffered the greatest number of deaths in 1965/66 is more difficult to say.

Provincial Society

This chapter has shown how thoroughly the military carried out their gruesome task in NTT. But it has also brought provincial society back into the picture. In this respect it underscores the conclusions of other recent work, which has similarly stressed the collaboration of middle class individuals affiliated with religious and political organizations in the killings (Kammen and McGregor 2012, Kolimon and Wetangterah 2012, Sulistyo 2000). Considering the ramshackle affair that was the state in 1965 – in terms of territorial coverage, infrastructure, and personnel – such a quick and complete extermination of an influential rival political party was a remarkable achievement. But precisely this discrepancy between state coercive capacity and effectiveness should provoke our curiosity. How was it possible for a few hundred soldiers, many of them not native to the region, to kill so many individuals and detain so many more, mainly lower class but also elite, without provoking a massive backlash? Kupang was left short of bicycle repairmen, the whole province was short of teachers and bureaucrats, the crimes committed in every town and village had been beyond numbering, yet today the whole affair has been all but forgotten. With hardly any exceptions, mass graves remain unmarked, prayers over the bones within them remain unsaid, compensation for the loss of livelihoods and homes remains unpaid, yet killers have lived out their old age amid universal respect. Why?

Certainly one answer must be the one explored in this chapter. Behind its welcoming façade, society in East Nusa Tenggara remains deeply divided along the lines of class. The town has been the major source of this divide. As the town grew from small beginnings, many of its new middle class reached out across the divide as teachers and intellectual vanguard party organizers. But as the contradictions sharpened in the early 1960s, anxieties grew and the new middle class overwhelmingly chose to close a Faustian bargain with the military. Local civilian middle class religious, political and bureaucratic organizations provided everything the military lacked to make a success of the extermination of rival fellow citizens. Their most respected political party heavyweights sat on joint civilian-military committees that condemned thousands to summary execution at every level. Their opinion-makers thanked God from the pulpit for saving the nation from their political enemies and wrote the textbooks that taught the same in schools.

It is no surprise that those young people who dream today, as did the young in the 1950s, of once more building a civil society from below see it as their first challenge to confront the events recounted in this chapter.

CHAPTER ELEVEN

CONSOLIDATING MIDDLE INDONESIA (1966–1986)

> In the process of political emancipation – especially if this is not accompanied by armed struggle – representatives of the lower-middle-class rise in a way naturally to power.
>
> (Kalecki 1972:162)

By the mid-1970s the New Order was well established in Jakarta. The commander of the armed forces was simultaneously the president. The first toll road was being built out of Jakarta. The chunky locally designed Toyota Kijang motorcar appeared in 1977 and quickly came to symbolize middle class prosperity, also in provincial towns like Kupang. This chapter describes first the consolidation phase in the provinces, still using the broad class-brush of previous chapters. It then reviews once more the main lines of the argument this book has been making about the process by which Middle Indonesia was made. Put baldly, the argument is that Middle Indonesia was a political project for townsfolk who were not necessarily rich and powerful on a national level, but whose disproportionate power to assert their will arose from their indispensable mediating role for the central state in the provinces, and hence from their exclusionary access to rents from the local state.

Consolidation in the first place entailed neutering collective antagonists. Most to be feared for their numbers and their unpredictability were the rural and urban poor. The previous chapter described how terror tactics reversed lower-class political mobilization. Terror had to remain an option, but permanent neutering also required longer term techniques of monitoring and social engineering. Instrumental modalities of power were at the forefront here. The 'security approach' introduced a new fragility into Middle Indonesia, as New Order cynicism replaced the naïve trust and optimism of the 1950s. The central government attempted to assuage the anguish by investing in rural development schemes (Henley 2012).

Dealing with those who threatened the provincial middle classes from a higher position on the social scale presented a much more delicate problem. They ranged from local aristocrats and wealthy Chinese entrepreneurs to the generals in Jakarta and to global capital. The means here were primarily political. Provincial middle classes were mobilized on the basis of the petit bourgeois values of nationalism, indigeneity, a horror of atheism, and an aversion to what in Indonesia was called 'free-fight capitalism.' One of these superior antagonists had already been dealt with by 1965. The native aristocracy who had once stood above them had lost their autonomy by 1962 (although they remained socially influential) (see Chapter 7). Far far above them, there was Jakarta, the hand that fed them but that also threatened to overrule them. The administrative province of Nusa Tenggara Timur, Jakarta's gift of the means of primitive accumulation, had been won following the anti-Javanese protests at the time of Permesta in 1957 (see Chapter 6). The one remaining locally dominant group in Kupang not yet domesticated were the rich Chinese. Their capacity for independent economic networking represented a threat to Kupang's political class. Finally, consolidation also required strengthening internal ranks by rewarding loyalists. All these political programmes, fought intermittently but more or less consciously, were energized by limited forms of associational power – limited because they lacked the cross-class character of the vision of the 1950s; associational because they appealed to the 'green' conservative values that had become common among provincial middle classes by the 1960s (Alers 1956). This chapter therefore deals with external action against the poor and against the Chinese, and internal action in favour of loyalists.

The Poor

These always remained the most numerous of antagonists. Months after the killings had stopped, but with the horror still fresh in people's minds, a new fear arose in military minds. They now worried that the horror might turn into cross-class sympathy for the victims and then into an anti-government reaction. The special security command Kopkamtib established propaganda teams to travel around Kupang and out into the districts. Their mission was to 'coach' people on the correct way to view the killings. In Timor the teams were led by Captain J.W. Manafe, intelligence chief for the regional military command (Kasi I Rem 161), and also a Parkindo activist. South Central Timor district had seen the strongest BTI presence and now became a special focus for propaganda (Tari 1972:1, 305). The teams were known as Team Kempen Pembantu Pelaksana Kopkamtibda. Military reports reveal they were still at work in late 1968 and early 1969, nearly two years later. Team members had learned by heart a gruesome if prolix catechism of state-sanctioned murder. One item in the manual they read (which was not a secret document) confronted likely criticism head-on:

> Question: The Indonesian people are known abroad as a civilized nation because they have Pancasila. Yet in reality the Indonesian nation has committed mass murder against the Communists. Is that not a betrayal of Pancasila itself?
>
> Answer: We must look at this problem through the law of cause and effect. The Indonesian people only began to move spontaneously after the treachery and the cruelty committed by PKI members at Lubang Buaya [the place in Jakarta where army generals were murdered on 1 October 1965] and in other areas in Indonesia. Acts to destroy PKI agents were precisely aimed at saving Pancasila from an Atheist movement, and this cannot be classified as a barbaric act because on the contrary it is based on humanitarian considerations, especially after seeing the reality that according to seized PKI documents there was a plan for G30S/ PKI to carry out mass killings should they succeed (Kopkamtib 1968:II, 18).[1]

Figure 32. Governor Brig.-Gen. El Tari, at a banquet for National Sports Week, approximately 1971 (photo courtesy Mr. Leopold Nisnoni).

[1] Pancasila was the main pillar in military anti-communist ideology. The original ran: 'Pertanjaan: Bangsa Indonesia diluar negeri terkenal sebagai Bangsa jang berkeadaban tinggi karena memiliki PANTJASILA. Tetapi dalam kenjataan Bangsa Indonesia telah melakukan pembunuhan masal terhadap orang[2] Komunis. Apakah itu bukanlah suatu

A more daunting task for Governor Maj.-Gen. El Tari than keeping up the threat of state terror was to extend state control into the interior. This was in fact a matter of introducing modern government there for the first time. Till then, the state in the districts had amounted to little more than the crumbling remnants of the Dutch indirect-rule system. A few provincial officials had tried to cajole the traditional rulers to look up from their nepotistic micro-politics, but they had been even less resourced than the Dutch *controleurs* had been, and achieved little success. Most education and health services were provided by the church. El Tari's task was doubly difficult because it had to start with dismantling the little that already existed. He was under instructions to prioritize 'cleansing' the apparatus of those with doubtful loyalties to the new military order. His predecessor had already replaced the rajas with modern district administrators in 1962, but had still appointed people with local roots – something the military now wished to review. El Tari's American-educated advisor Hendrik Ataupah travelled into the interior on inspection tours. Dispensing with the idea that local administrators should have local roots, he saw only incompetency and illiteracy. Lui Babis, calling himself Aba Soleh after his conversion to Islam, had kept up a rivalry with the Nope clan from his home base in southern central Timor, in the process permitting the communist BTI to flourish. He had been made subdistrict head of Noemuke. But Ataupah now found a horse tethered inside his office. Cow manure on the typewriter indicated that the precious equipment had rarely been used. Instead of typing reports, Aba Soleh was fond of singing traditional Timorese poems (*pantun*) of an evening, alternating in friendly competition with the local BTI leader.[2] Under the guise of rejuvenating an ageing corps, El Tari replaced Babis and six other district chiefs – more than half the total of 12 (Nahak et al 2009:39, Tari 1972:I, 98–9, 138f). Military screeners sacked many other bureaucrats further down the ladder for ideological contamination. The many vacancies were filled by pro-military loyalists from town.

---

pengingkaran terhadap PANTJASILA itu sendiri? Djawab: Kita harus melihat persoalannja dari hukum sebab dan akibat. Rakjat Indonesia baru bergerak setjara spontan setelah penghianatan dan kekedjaman jang dilakukan oleh anggauta PKI di Lubang Buaja dan lain[2] daerah di Indonesia. Tindakan penghantjuran oknum[2] PKI djustru dilakukan untuk menjelamatkan PANTJASILA dari suatu gerakan A-Theisme dan ini tidak dapat diklasifikasikan sebagai tindakan biadab karena djustru berlandaskan pertimbangan kemanusiaan, terutama setelah melihat kenjataan bahwa menurut dokument[2] PKI jang dapat disita menundjukan [sic] adanja rentjana pembunuhan masal oleh G.30.S./PKI apabila gerakan berhasil.'

[2] Interview, Hendrikus Ataupah, Kupang, 31 July 2011.

Most invasive was the modernization of village administration. NTT had known over four and a half thousand village units. These had by no means been primordial entities – they were the result of the Dutch pacification campaign, which involved concentrating agrarian populations in settlements and appointing leaders to coordinate with the authorities. But the late colonial village administration had retained some connection with local custom, being structured into a genealogical rather than a territorial hierarchy and carrying a variety of local customary names for its institutions (Cunningham 1962, Warren 1993). Now these villages were reorganized into less than 1,700 units known as 'New Style Villages' (Desa Gaya Baru), all on a standard model laid down in Jakarta (and still building on colonial practices).[3] Village officials remained without a salary but they now received grants and bonuses for good performance that increasingly tied them to the bureaucracy (Tari 1972:I, 84–5). Many physically new villages were built as well, also on a uniform pattern. A bureaucratic manual issued in Kupang in 1973 explaining how officials should design these villages is reminiscent of the sterile Soviet village plans James Scott so memorably described in *Seeing like a State* (1998:215). The layout was to be functional, with designated areas for government offices, market and commercial buildings, school, church and mosque, and neat residences all distributed along a grid of straight roads for the motor vehicle (Figure 33, Figure 34). Walter Christaller's central place theory was quoted, not as an explanation for existing village distribution but as a prescriptive ideal for efficient 'service delivery' (Direktorat Pemerintahan 1973). The manual was as silent on consultation as it was on respecting existing arrangements such as land rights, sacred places or natural flows. Most of the New Style Villages were constructed in the former kingdom of Amarasi, where Raja Koroh had become the subdistrict head. Villagers in Buraen told me they were built without any consideration of existing rights. Vicky Koroh told villagers communal land rights no longer existed. He himself claimed vast lands on the basis of his traditional rights while paying no land tax on it.

It seems Governor El Tari did commit to some land reform in the early years of the New Order (Tari 1972:I, 435–7). He claimed to have redistributed 35,995 hectares of aristocratic hunting lands to 33,404 families in various parts of Flores.[4] He also bought small 'excess' parcels from some

---

[3] Colonial resettlement schemes had never been off the agenda. A detailed village reorganization plan ready for Nusa Tenggara in 1955 failed only because there was no money to implement it (*Bentara*, 1 April 1955).

[4] I have corrected an apparent misprint in the original that, if true, would have meant 35 *million* hectares were redistributed. Kupang historian Munandjar Widiyatmika told me

Figure 33. Traditional spread-out village (Direktorat Pemerintahan 1973).

aristocrats near Kupang – Alfons Nisnoni lost 22 hectares of wet-rice land to the farmers working the fields,[5] Koesa Nope lost a remarkably extensive 591 hectares of dry gardens to 724 farming families. Other noble

he had seen farmers living on these redistributed lands with his own eyes; they were located in Mbai (Ngada), Lembor and Paka (both in Manggarai) and Mautenda (Ende) (interview, Kupang, 18 June 2009). Curiously, El Tari's Florinese successor, Ben Mboi, denied that any land was redistributed under Governor El Tari (interview, Kupang, 19 June 2009).

5 Alfons Nisnoni was the only significant aristocrat in Timor to have lost all his official connections. He apparently also lost a couple of hundred hectares above Bakunase in a

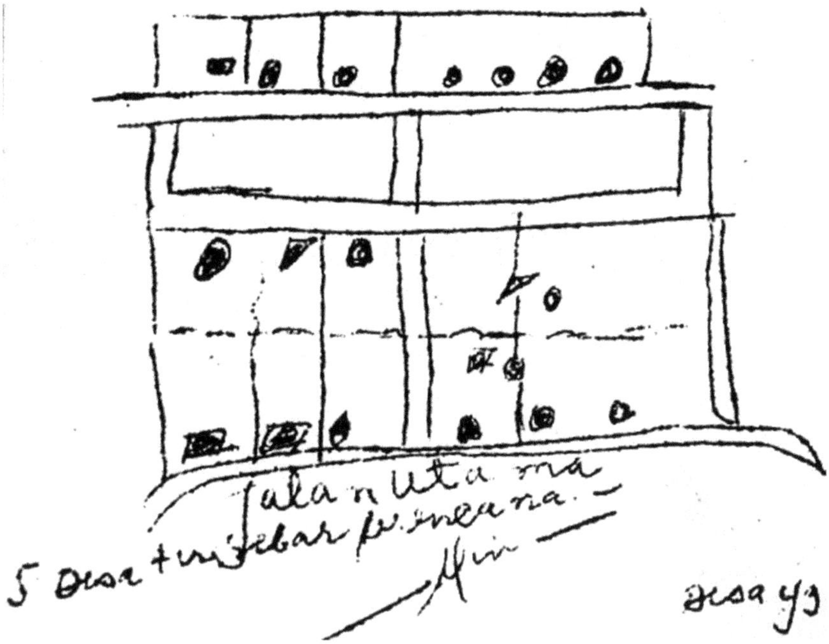

Figure 34. Planned spread-out village (Direktorat Pemerintahan 1973).

families had their land holdings investigated too – the Amtiran, Oematan, and Funay were mentioned. Whatever the truth of these claims, the programme was clearly not sustained and not consultative. Where a government-sponsored seminar on land reform in 1961 had been attended mainly by rural land owners (Sidik et al 1968), the next land-title seminar in Kupang demanded rights for the city. The 1972 symposium was attended by 'city people,' and the message was that traditional rights no longer existed, since all customary land belonged to the state (Direktorat Agraria NTT 1973:43, Panitya 1972). The urban fringe was expanding and the city administrators wanted to reduce trouble from aristocrats demanding extortionate payments for peri-urban land.

Kalecki had already described the fascination with religion in the 'intermediate regime.' Religion played a central role in the efforts by the quintessentially petty bourgeois provincial New Order to subjugate the rural poor in NTT as well. Chapter 9 described how government officials had shocked villagers in late 1965 by suddenly demanding they

court case around 1960. However, the family retains large lands even now (interview Munandjar Widiyatmika, Kupang, 18 June 2009).

change their religion. This involved abandoning local names and adopting new ones. Now they went on to insist on a complete civilizational makeover for the rural poor – how to dress, eat, talk, and build their houses. The ubiquitous knot of hair (*konde*) traditionally worn by rural men (Figure 35) was now seen as a heathen symbol of the *khalaik*. The only village in which the *konde* survives today is Boti, in the southern hills of South Central Timor district. In October 1967 the gospel was brought to Boti by a Rotenese military officer named Pello (Kolimon and Wetangterah 2012:283–5). His unit gathered all the men and the raja at the village office. When their demands for conversions met reluctance they brought out a brass-tipped cane. Men were beaten and told to stand shirtless in the sun for hours. Fearing the raja would be killed, enough men then pledged conversion to satisfy the soldiers. Those who converted moved away from the ritual sites of the village, but a small core of traditionalists remained behind. Their elders later argued successfully that they should be exempt from the policy to abandon their way of life, since there had in fact been no communist organization in their village. Moreover, they added defiantly, they had seen enough suffering caused elsewhere by people named Matthew, Mark, Luke, and John not to wish to adopt these names themselves. Today the village is an exotic tourist attraction. Brochures describe its proud long-haired pagan inhabitants as 'Indonesian Amish,' but do not mention the reason that they are alone in Timor.[6]

Officials began requiring rural people to wear shoes, shirts, and (for the women) bras. The church readily cooperated. Wife and husband reverends Len and Robert Tahun had been local missionaries to Oinlasi in southern South Central Timor since 1964, and they still lived there when I visited them in 2010 and 2011. Healthy bodies and modesty were good things, they told me. Women accustomed to preparing tubers had to learn to cook rice for visiting dignitaries, whose numbers increased as the state established a presence even in small subdistricts. Subdistrict capital Oinlasi had till then possessed only a police station, but soon government buildings appeared up and down the main street and there was even a government high school.

Governor Brig. Gen. El Tari tried at first to stimulate the rural economy mainly by slogans. Lacking both a land reform programme and serious money, he addressed the island's notorious soil erosion by simply calling on peasants to 'plant, plant, plant, and plant again!' Several statues in Dili and Soë still show him holding up a coconut shoot to symbolize this

[6] 'Berliburlah ke Boti,' *Pos Kupang*, 1 November 2009.

exhortatory mode of government. It was reminiscent of the forced coconut plantation programme carried out by the Raja of Amarasi in the 1930s. But (as was noted in Chapter 3) he did not match it with financial incentives to busy subsistence farmers, and it all came to nothing. Once real New Order oil money began to flow, rural development programmes became more sophisticated. Technical specialists built roads and telephone lines, introduced new fertilizers, and enhanced the skills of local officials. Although the Green Revolution worked better on Java's irrigated rice fields than Timor's maize, agricultural productivity did appear to rise and absolute poverty certainly declined. As it did everywhere in Indonesia, the New Order brought technical inclusiveness without empowerment.

Nevertheless success was modest. Health indicators for NTT have stayed among the worst in Southeast Asia. Infant mortality, child malnutrition, malaria, and sexually transmitted diseases remain major problems. In the most recent World Food Programme nutritional map for Indonesia, the number of underweight infants in the province NTT rates as by far the nation's worst. All of Timor is shown in the worst category, 'very bad to critical,' with more than 30% of infants aged less than five underweight (WFP 2009). The latest WFP map of food insecurity for Indonesia maps all of Indonesian Timor to the two worst levels of food insecurity, along with all of Sumba and large parts of Papua. The WFP links these poor health indicators to the large proportion of the population in these districts living below the national poverty line, the large number of households without access to electricity, the large number of children under five years who are underweight, the number of villages not accessible to four-wheeled vehicles, and the fact that many households have no access to clean water.[7] Part of the reason was certainly that the local government regarded expenditure on health, education and other welfare as 'a residual item of public consumption' (Barlow et al 1991:46). When a group of scholars in the 1980s returned to 'the Timor problem,' they discovered that soil erosion had grown ever worse. 'The contemporary surface of Timor can only be described as a degraded landscape,' one of them concluded (Barlow et al 1991:35). Ormeling had estimated that the Indonesian part of Timor had 280,000 hectares available for subsistence food crops; the rest was only suitable for cattle grazing or enclosing for forestry. Subsistence requires most of the land to lie fallow most of the time. Ormeling thought a 12-year cycle was sustainable. But even in the

[7] See a stream of similar reports online at http://www.ntt-academia.org/index.html, accessed 19 July 2012.

1950s there was not enough land in Timor for such a long cycle. Since then it has only been shortened. By 1986 the population of rural Timor had more than doubled, and the area planted with non-wet rice food crops at any one time was estimated at 133,000 hectares, or almost half Ormeling's total available area. Government investment in the Green Revolution, according to some figures, did nearly double yields for wet and dry rice, maize, cassava, and sweet potatoes since the late 1970s (though this is disputed by Pellolika et al in Barlow). But the researchers concluded that degradation of land due to overexploitation was widespread, in Timor and all over NTT (Barlow et al 1991:246, 249, 121–44, 15).

The reason why the New Order failed to solve the Timor problem was as political as it had been under the Dutch. A marginal landscape like this can feed everyone only if access to scarce resources is shared equally. But precisely the assumption of equal rights was unpalatable to Kupang's policymakers. Control over farming land has remained unequal. In the mid-1980s, 41% of farm land in NTT was controlled by 15% of households. Where the average holding was 1.23 hectares, this upper group held an average of 4.42 hectares (Barlow et al 1991:255–7). After El Tari's initial gesture the land reform programme was abandoned. Unequal cattle ownership was an even bigger contributor to the Timor problem, but this too remained unaddressed for the same reason. Ormeling had identified cattle as both an ecological scourge and a source of inequality, but 30 years later their population had increased nearly five-fold to 520,000 (though Ormeling did acknowledge under-reporting had been a problem in his day) (Barlow et al 1991:246–8).[8] The tracks they left on hillsides, and the tendency for cattle owners to burn grass in order to produce 'green pick,' were exacerbating soil erosion and causing landslides. Cattle, agreed the editors of the volume, had produced 'widespread environmental destruction, while there has further been a marked shift to a more uneven

[8] In between the studies by Barlow and Ormeling comes the useful study of the cattle industry by Soedarma (1968). At this time the Timor cattle population was 333,278, with the biggest concentration in South Central Timor, where they were regarded as the greatest obstacle to re-vegetation. One visible expression of the clashing interests between cattle owners and peasants was their different attitudes to the lantana invasion. Peasants liked lantana because it stopped the cattle and meant they had fewer fences to build, but owners hated it and persuaded the government to launch an expensive and ultimately successful eradication campaign. Yet cattle were bringing in little by way of taxation, since they were rarely consumed. Despite all these disadvantages, nothing was done about them because they were owned by 'rajas, *fetor* and *temukung*... leaders and power holders who are respected by the people and whose cooperation is essential to the government for local administration' (Soedarma et al 1968:28).

Figure 35. Rural Timorese male and female hairstyles and clothing, respectively in Belu and Kolbano, circa 1909 (KITLV image nrs. resp. 26829, 26823).

distribution of income' (Barlow et al 1991:232). Two others warned that growing livestock numbers were putting such pressure on land that food supply problems were occurring during the already normally lean period from June to November (Barlow et al 1991:87–8, 140). It proved politically impossible to regulate the maximum number of cattle per unit area. Cattle ownership had become even more concentrated in wealthy hands than it had been in Ormeling's day. The 4.5% of farmers with herds of more than 25 owned 48.4% of all cattle and buffalo, whereas 55% of farmer households had just one or two beasts (Barlow et al 1991:92, 20, 257).

Hendrikus Ataupah, another of the researchers in this collection, wrote that '[t]he effect of the conflict between land cultivators and animal breeders has been the disappearance of grasslands in the NTT.' He called it the 'tragedy of common access to property.' The 'traditional leaders,' who exercised authority in the villages, also tended to be owners of large animal farms. They resisted any attempt to regulate cattle numbers. Formal regional government bureaucrats, as well as merchants and other influential figures, often owned large animals as well. 'Therefore,' Ataupah concluded sombrely, 'the rivalry and conflict of interests between the land cultivators and owners of animals has further intensified as the numbers in each group grow' (Barlow et al 1991:226). No doubt this was also the reason that cattle were not part of the planning that, according to the researchers, was so sorely necessary (Barlow et al 1991:85–104). Ataupah had put his finger on the reason for the inaction – it was what Wertheim had called 'betting on the strong.' The problem had not been a lack of technical capacity or funding, but a middle class that had hijacked the development agenda. Communist-led Kerala has the highest Human Development Index in India. If Indonesia's embryonic politics of rural empowerment of the 1950s had been sustained, instead of being abruptly reversed in the mid-1960s, Timor might have had better social statistics too.[9]

The Chinese

Back in town the new political class and its middle class dependents also had to deal with a threat from above. Most of the private money in town

[9] Another government report concluded that soil erosion in NTT was the worst in South Central Timor and in Kupang district (Pemda NTT 1972:33) – these had been the areas of greatest BTI mobilization over land.

was held by the small but vibrant Chinese commercial middle class. Anti-Chinese measures had been intermittent and largely driven by national politics in the 1950s (Coppel 1983), but they gradually assumed a local dimension as well, and the combination produced a highly public campaign to humiliate the Chinese during the events around 1965.

It started with growing irritation over Chinese middle-class cosmopolitanism. Young musicians jammed every Saturday evening at the clubhouse of the association Chung Hua Chung Hui in downtown Kupang. Hawaiian guitarist Sjors Lie told me his father, agent for the state shipping line KPM, started the Chung Hua Hawaiian Band in 1940. It played at all the town's most important weddings, including the week-long celebration for that of Raja Alfons Nisnoni. He also played the clarinet and had an enormous gramophone collection ranging from Beethoven to Batak songs. The old (1920s) Chinese school offered the best sports in town – including ping pong and basketball – and put on open air theatre performances in the playground. In the 1930s little indigenous Kupang newspapers like *Tjermin Timoer* and *Tjinta Kebenaran* had openly expressed their admiration for successful Chinese entrepreneurs in town. But after independence the ascendant indigenous lower-middle class more and more gave voice to xenophobic sentiments. It became increasingly fashionable to regard Chinese cosmopolitanism with wary eyes and give vent to feelings that native Indonesians had been kept down economically by the Chinese 'foreigner,' just as they had been kept down politically by the Dutch and their aristocratic allies. Whatever Cold War geostrategic calculations may have lain behind Jakarta's anti-Chinese measures, to Kupang's emerging lower-middle class they were meaningful primarily in terms of protecting their own new-found political dominance. As early as 1950, the news that some remarkably aware Chinese youths in the small Florinese mountain-town of Ruteng had sent a telegram to congratulate Mao Zedong on his new government triggered an anxious reaction in the Florinese Catholic magazine *Bentara*. Such a dangerous sign of communism among a people who were growing rich on Flores, a reader warned, should stimulate fresh efforts to build indigenous cooperatives that might slow them down. Illogically suggesting the Chinese were both communist *and* capitalist, he wrote: 'We will fight this capitalism whose materialism is so damaging to us.'[10]

---

10 'Waspada,' *Bentara*, 15 March 1950.

The military's social base lay among these small-town parochials. Populist anti-Chinese measures had been part of its policy of 'uniting with the people' (*manunggal dengan rakyat*) for years before 1965 (Mackie et al 1976), and it was to remain so for many years after it (Purdey 2006). Whenever the military took potentially unpopular measures against political rivals, it knew race was a sure-fire button to push with the small-town petit bourgeoisie to short-circuit a backlash. Just when it had successfully struck down a series of regional rebellions, instituted local martial law regimes, and won the dissolution of parliament in the period 1957–1959, the military had energetically implemented a regulation to remove Chinese from the rural and small-town economy. Presidential Instruction No.10/ 1959 ordered the Chinese out of the interior and into district and provincial capitals, and 'repatriated' those Chinese who refused to adopt Indonesian nationality. In NTT the government ordered all small trade to cease for a time, in order to force reluctant Chinese traders to leave the villages for the towns (Sekda TTS [1978]:82f). Villagers could not be blamed for interpreting this measure as a withdrawal of protection from the Chinese. I heard, for example, that a Chinese shopkeeper in the small village of Oihana (between Soë and Oinlasi) had his shop raided and burned by opportunistic villagers before he fled. El Tari, then still a captain, headed the screening committee tasked by his military commander with drawing up lists of Chinese in NTT. According to the local government report quoted above there were, for example, 743 ethnic Chinese in South Central Timor, of whom 199 'returned' to China (they would all have gone – they had already sold their property – were it not for the chronic shortage of shipping).

After the military takeover at the end of 1965 the government was anxious to regain popularity among an indigenous lower-middle class that had seen many of its sons and daughters arbitrarily fired from the bureaucracy. It once more withdrew its protection from the Chinese. The emerging Suharto regime held China responsible for the communist putsch in Jakarta of 1 October 1965 and regarded all ethnic Chinese Indonesians as a disloyal potential fifth column. On 12 January 1966 the military mobilized a large anti-communist student rally in Jakarta that demanded a ban on the PKI, a new cabinet, and lower prices.[11] The latter was a dig at the Chinese shopkeepers, who were popularly thought to be both communists and economic hoarders. Similar rallies were later organized all over the archipelago, also in Kupang in May (Tari 1972:I, 287–90). The

[11] These were the Three People's Demands, Tri Tuntutan Rakyat, abbreviated Tritura.

distinctive characteristic of the 'intermediate regime' identified by Kalecki (see Chapter 1) is that it earns its income through political manipulation rather than on the free market. Protecting its interests often involves putting political considerations above those of economic efficiency. Many of Governor El Tari's early New Order policies should be seen in this light. He sacked many well-trained teachers and other civil servants, but most directly damaging were his anti-Chinese measures. El Tari's personal involvement in anti-Chinese attacks went back to his membership in the revolutionary Laskar Sunda Kecil, which participated in the so-called Bandung Sea of Fire incident of May 1946 mainly by burning Chinese businesses.[12] The gravest attacks on Kupang's Chinese middle class occurred after October 1965. Chinese became targets for humiliation, intimidation and fleecing.

Lt. Col. Abdul Djalal, the Pepelrada commander in Kupang, for a time ordered the shopkeepers to attend daily roll calls in front of the district chief's office, where he harangued them about Pancasila and told them to lower their prices by 50%. One Timorese man told me that as a newly married young civil servant these enforced discounts permitted him to furnish his government house comfortably despite the economic crisis. Personal friendships with several Chinese shopkeepers' sons did not prevent him from taking advantage of the opportunity. Later that year the new Suharto cabinet suggested that all Chinese Indonesians should adopt Indonesian-sounding names. The following year the president banned the public display of Chinese characters, and his cabinet officially replaced the polite designation 'Tionghoa' for Chinese with the (in Indonesian derogatory-sounding) term 'Chinese' (*Cina*). The last insult was again the occasion for looting of Chinese shops in Kupang. No one came to their defence. The shops were already nearly empty due to the economic crisis, and in the past the provincial government had begged the Chinese to do what they could to keep up supplies, but not this time. The Dutch priest Boumans wrote in his autobiography that anti-Chinese intimidation had caused economic crisis in Flores, and Kupang would have been the same (Boumans 2005:78–83).

---

[12] El Tari's membership of Laskar Sunda Kecil is deduced from his list of medals in the unpublished obituary entitled 'Hasil penelusuran kisah pejuang: Penelusuran perjuangan pahlawan El Tari, E.R. Herewilla, Tom Pello dan H.A. Koroh,' in the archive of Mr. Leopold Nisnoni, Kupang. It is confirmed in 'Dalam kenangan, Bapak L. Say' (anonymous blog, quoting from the book by E.P. da Gomez, 'Menantang badai di bumi gempa tsunami,' no date), 28 November 2008, http://www.inimaumere.com/2008_11_28_archive.html, accessed 20 October 2011. On the role of Laskar Sunda Kecil in Bandung see Smail (1964:153).

Sjors Lie's Hawaiian band had accepted an invitation from a leftist organization to perform at an Independence Day celebration in the sports stadium on 17 August 1965. They had played the saccharine 'Lovely Hula Hands' and got the audience dancing. Soon after 1 October 1965 this performance led to trouble. Sjors was told to report to the Timor military headquarters (Kodim), just above the old town, at 10 p.m. A lot of other Chinese were there too. Representatives from the anti-communist religious parties Parkindo and Partai Katolik sat on the other side of the table. The Chinese were given a meal, then ordered onto a truck under military guard. They drove all night along the winding road into the interior. Everyone was sure they would be executed, and no doubt they were meant to feel this way. By midday the next day they pulled in to Soë, where they saw Muslim youths trampling on the Chinese flags that the military had years ago required all Chinese to put up in front of their shop-houses. The Chinese were told to get down from the truck and clean up. After that they were driven back to Kupang and released. Seah Liang Sie, the young ethnic Chinese man who had organized the patriotic 17 August Independence Day event, was executed on the same day as PKI organizer Paulus Kanuru.

In April 1966 the new military regime in Kupang seized the two Chinese schools and the clubhouse. This happened all over Indonesia, in retaliation for mainland Chinese condemnation of the killings committed by the military (Tari 1972:I, 289). The clubhouse eventually became the Golkar headquarters, the schools went to the state education department. A number of Chinese were murdered. One of them was Fu Tjien, a keen young basketballer who had operated the stencil machine for the communist broadsheet *Pelopor* and had sold the broadsheet on the streets. Chinese religion had to disappear as well. Abdul Djalal might also have been the 'military officer' who according to James Fox told the Chinese in Kupang they had two weeks to choose a new religion (Fox 1980:243). Until then there had been only one Chinese Protestant in town, a shopkeeper named Tjioe Tek Giok, who converted in 1955.[13] Now they flocked to comply. Of the four clan houses in Kupang, only one survives today, empty of worshippers (Figure 36).

---

[13] Tjioe Tek Giok (1893–1963) owned Toko Semarang. The Japanese appointed him leader of the Chinese community in Kupang, a position the Dutch confirmed. He was the only Chinese permitted to attend the Dutch *societeit* (interview with Gordon Dicker, Sydney, 16 December 2009).

Figure 36. The Lay clan house in Kupang in 1910, the only one in the city to survive today (KITLV image nr. 503525).

Once the social hierarchy had been firmly established, the same 'Ali Baba' arrangements simply continued to enrich both Chinese entrepreneurs and indigenous operators alike at the expense of the state budget. Niti Susanto came to Kupang from Soë with his father Pieter Nerius (Ong Teo Piet) as a small child in 1952 (Adam et al 1997:108) (see Chapter 8). Their Toko Piet soon became as essential to the local economy as Tjiong Koen Siong's had been before the war. It sold bicycles to the general public, and imported fuel, rice, and building materials for the government through inflated Ali Baba arrangements. In January 1966 the military encouraged looters to clean out the shop completely. Niti Susanto had just taken it over, merely 15 years old. The threat of violence was so serious that the Florinese Catholic Party activist Anton Langoday offered the family protective shelter. But the business survived. It supplied Governor El Tari and then Governor Ben Mboi with fuel and other essentials. Today it retails motorcycles and marine equipment, runs a small airline, has built an airport, and still sells petrol. Niti Susanto still sits in his poorly lit back office with a calculator and no computer, but takes his annual holidays in Europe.

Kupang became a more indigenous, less ethnically Chinese town. In 1930 ethnic Chinese made up 13% of the town's 7,000 inhabitants (see Chapter 4). Immediately after the war Chinese shops had expanded up the hill along the new shopping street of Kuanino. An aerial photograph taken in the mid-1950s shows that the vast Chinese cemetery on the southern side of town was actually inhibiting the growth of the town.[14] But once Kupang became the provincial capital in 1959 the huge influx of indigenous people from elsewhere in NTT overwhelmed any increase in the ethnic Chinese population. By 1971 they made up only 3% of Kupang city's population of 44,800 (Kantor Sensus NTT 1971:55). Chinese symbols began to retreat from Kupang's town centre in the early 1960s. The first great post-war builder in Kupang, Lt. Col. Paikun, moved the Chinese cemetery in 1963. A few years later the town's tallest building arose in the same space, a four-storey state bank. Across the road stood the official residence of Governor El Tari. It had beautiful views over the ocean, and El Tari loved it there, but disturbed Chinese ghosts made the place for the average Kupang inhabitant 'a sacred place with powerful forces. Most people did not dare to go there.' Doko (1982:30–1), who described this evocative scene as part of an imagined drive around the town with a foreign visitor, saw more new than old along the way. The bombed-out Dutch government buildings near the harbour had been replaced in the 1950s and '60s. In the old part of town the Chinese-owned Bioskop Raya movie theatre still screened Kung Fu movies for its traditional clientele. But a brand-new Kupang Theatre further up the hill, owned by Umar Baktir of Arab descent, now catered for much larger Indonesian audiences. They sat in air-conditioned comfort and preferred Indonesian movies, especially on religion.

Internal Consolidation

Action against outsiders – the poor, the Chinese – had helped unify the indigenous middle class, but more was necessary to create the long-lasting support the new regime in Jakarta saw as essential. Even under the New Order, associational modalities of power were always more important than instrumental ones in holding Indonesia together. An ideological newspeak to control dissidence within the middle class was one requirement. It could only be established by deploying locally legitimate

[14] It is shown on Parera's sketch map for 1946 (see Figure 22), and Ormeling (1956:130–41) has an aerial photograph.

authority. More tangible inducements for people to act like loyalists, even if they felt like rebels, were money and jobs.

Enforcing a newspeak was not difficult, given the complicity of most of its spiritual and political leaders in the pogroms. If Captain Manafe's Team Kempen Pembantu Pelaksana Kopkamtibda had adopted a defensive tone among the poor, his message enjoyed a warm reception among their fellows in Kupang's middle class. Its stock phrases soon became commonplaces in all out-loud discourse from urban opinion makers – the PKI death lists, the PKI's negativity towards God and government, indeed towards all humanity. It soon became possible to proclaim in one breath both that the PKI had been historically insignificant in NTT thanks to the population's religiosity, and that those who had resisted this apparently insignificant force were heroes (Liliweri et al 1984:86f). The murders became a taboo, even at the closed history seminar within Kupang's state university, as we saw in Chapter 3.

We know of only one place in NTT where guilty finger-pointing of the kind Kopkamtib had feared actually did take place within the urban establishment, albeit muted. The killings in the Sikka district of Flores had been largely rural and ethnic rather than anti-communist. One priest in this intensely Catholic society spoke out against them at the time, and some active laymen had timorously lobbied Jakarta to stop them. That seemed to be the end of it, but in 1974 one of the local elites who had approved the killing lists committed an account to paper of the lead-up to the murders that did not fit the propaganda clichés (Anonymous 1974). After circulating in photocopied form for decades, it is now about to be published.[15] This remarkable document, written in the third person, exculpates no one and culminates in the confession that at the crucial moment the participants had 'abandoned Catholic principles' (p75–6). It uses archival sources to build a detailed history of elite factionalism in the little town of Maumere from the early 1950s to the early 1970s.[16] Were it not for rare gems such as this, even the worst events in human history can be forgotten within the span of a lifetime.

---

15 Personal communication, John Prior, Maumere, June 2010.

16 Too complicated to unravel here (but see Van Klinken 2013b), it starts with families from old local kingdoms battling over the rents extracted from various branches of the local state, and ends with two broad coalitional factions aligned with opposing power centres in Jakarta. The local establishment (including the church) lines up with the military, while the ethnic challengers line up with the secular political parties PNI and PKI. At least 800 rural clients on the latter side are thought to have died in 1965/66. Careers opened up for the former, who hid their twinges of guilt.

Money and jobs as the price put upon the loyalty of those who had been on the right side of the Suharto coup were the final indispensable element. The dominance of Kupang's new indigenous middle class had been due to state intervention in the market (see Chapter 8). Post-colonial anti-capitalist ideology had bought Jakarta chunks of influence in the provinces. Economists call the deliberate creation of rents to ensure political stability 'political transfer rents' (Khan and Jomo K.S. 2000). When taken to the extremes as in the early 1960s, they paralyzed the economy and fuelled discord. In December 1965 the value of the hugely inflated rupiah was adjusted by making a Rp 1,000 note worth just one rupiah. The creeping military coup of those same months quickly ended mass politics, but not the need to continue lubricating the machinery. On the contrary, the only way the men known mainly for their ruthlessness could ensure middle class support in far-flung regions was to offer more attractive incentives than their predecessors had done. Their own soldiers were part of that middle class – they all belonged to local families. The price tag on their loyalty had risen quickly. Soldiers now rapidly took over existing channels of state finance. The story of Major Is Tibuludji and his state-funded Fajar Ternak cattle-cum-fuel-cum-sandalwood business was told in Chapter 8. Nearly every subdistrict in NTT had a branch of the Livestock Cooperative, where it was accompanied with the usual muffled complaints about cheating and factional politicization. (The Rote administration, for example, refused to deal with them because of their secretive book-keeping practices – Heo 1972:71). Numerous other cooperatives graced local economies, supplying subsidized goods to various collectivities of civil servants and regulating markets for important export products. Thanks to government subsidies, Kupang was only about 25% more expensive to live in than the average city in Indonesia (Perdagangan 1971).

Jakarta initially had to scrape the bottom of its coffers for funds, but after 1973 the oil boom made it much easier (Booth 1992). The so-called Presidential Instruction disbursement (Instruksi Presiden, Inpres) was the major instrument to relieve poverty by stimulating development. Eastern Indonesia received proportionately more central government subsidies than provinces in core areas (Ravallion 1988). But the biggest grants did not go to the poorest provinces, and it seems political loyalty was at least as important a consideration. The biggest grants were going to places whose urban middle classes were dominated by civil servants, including NTT.[17]

[17] By my calculation there exists a high correlation (0.64) between the per capita Inpres grant by province for 1985 and the proportion of the urban (rather, non-agricultural) working population that were civil servants in 1990 (derived from BPS 1990).

These were frontier provinces with little industry, and where the state had put down a strong footprint only in the previous 50 years or so. Local state elites were able to pressure Jakarta into giving them preferential treatment even if that made little economic sense.[18]

State resources from Jakarta were spent disproportionately on the small urban middle class. Of the NTT provincial government's income of Rp 20.5 billion in 1979/80, 89% came as transfers from Jakarta (Barlow et al 1991:262–3). By 1986 government accounted for 19.5% of the gross regional domestic product (GRDP), nearly double what it had been a decade earlier and now second only to agriculture. The trend of rapid growth in government had been noted since early in the New Order (Tim Penyusun Repelita ke II NTT 1972:14). The government share in GRDP had doubled from 2.5% to 5.8% in the four years between 1967 and 1971, while agriculture declined from 72% to 67%. (Trade stayed the same at 17–18%.) This would be good if the money benefitted the whole population equally, but at least 68% and more likely 86% of the government budget was spent on salaries and pensions for civil servants. Estimated at 4.5% of the provincial working population in 1990 and less before that (BPS 1990), civil servants therefore received more than three times their fair share of government expenditure (Barlow et al 1991:243–4). The share of agriculture in the provincial GRDP, meanwhile, had declined further from 69.1% in 1975 to 53.9% by 1986, even though 81.5% of the population still said in 1990 that their main income came from that sector (BPS 1990). The lion's share of the agricultural GRDP came not from food crops but from livestock and smallholder tree crops for export, such as coffee and cocoa, both controlled by better-off farmers and townsfolk.

A skewed distribution of household income was the result. In town the biggest group – 53.8% – earned over Rp 200,000 a month, whereas in the country the biggest group – 41.6% – earned just Rp 50–100,000 (Barlow et al 1991:258). Compared with urban-rural inequalities around the more industrialized cities of Java this was not dramatic, but the gap was widening and it was enough to underscore the class differences that underlay the town's growth.

---

[18] Provinces with a very high 'preference weight' were Bengkulu, Central Kalimantan, East Kalimantan (not particularly poor), Maluku and Irian Jaya. In the second rank were Aceh, Riau, Jambi, West and East Nusa Tenggara, West Kalimantan, North Sulawesi, and Central Sulawesi. Southeast Sulawesi, West Sumatra and South Kalimantan were almost in the same category. Regionalist activism – including more or less veiled threats of secession – was strong in these state-dependent provinces in the 1950s and also around 1998. At the bottom were the Javanese provinces and Jakarta, and Lampung (Ravallion 1988: Table I).

Relations with the less fortunate were idealized in philanthropic images. Benedictus Mboi, NTT governor in 1978–1988, visualized society as a series of concentric circles, like a medieval cosmos kept in motion by higher powers. In the inner circle were 'the people,' shaded and passive. Surrounding this, another circle was marked 'government and elite who empathize with the suffering people.' Beyond that were higher circles marked 'resources such as law, technology, natural and human resources,' and finally the deity – 'resource management' (Mboi and edited by Basri K. 2009:82). The next governor built the gigantic bronze Social Responsibility Statue (*Patung Kepedulian*) that still stands at a major intersection in Kupang. A 'rich man,' tie and business suit fluttering energetically, is lifting up a 'poor man' whose limbs flail like a paralytic (Soh and Indrayana 2008:146). Locals joke the bronze Good Samaritan is actually the governor moving the peasant out of his way (Campbell-Nelson 1993). Elitism has deep roots in Kupang's postcolonial middle class psyche. But in the late colonial years they at least thought of themselves as vanguard intellectuals when one of them wrote: 'The intellectuals give leadership to the impoverished people or the masses. Meanwhile the masses with the strength of their bodies, with their work, give sustenance to the intellectuals' (see Chapter 5). Now the masses had lost all their agency and understood only force. A 1973 provincial government forward planning document breezily dismissed the bulk of its citizens as 'feudalistic, followers, apathetic, and irrational.' The hope of the future lay with 'leadership cadres who are honest, capable, rational, programme-oriented and who understand the region.' Their task was to bring about 'a change of mental attitude by means of persuasion, stimulation, and if necessary by force' (Pemda NTT 1973:81, 108, 110).

Middle Indonesia Today

The introduction to this book promised to investigate what holds Indonesia together. This led it to develop a fresh curiosity about the spatial dimension to the study of power in Indonesia, which opened new perspectives on the apparently constitutive role that middle classes in provincial towns play in the nation as a whole. The book then set out to investigate this claim by examining the history of state formation within and around one particular town over the five decades in which Indonesia was most vigorously under construction. Associational modalities of power (to use John Allen's phrase) played a more significant role in this history than did the more conventional instrumental ones. The book then went on to reconstruct a process of what might be called mutual constitution, of Kupang's urban community and in particular its middle classes on the one hand, and the Indonesian state in this region on the other, roughly between 1930 and 1986. Now is the time to take stock of the project. What difference does this history make to the way we think about Indonesia today? What have we learned about the way power operates in this social zone Middle Indonesia?

At first glance the history makes little difference today. The story of poverty and unrest in the immediate post-war years at the heart of this book appears to be of historical interest only. Kupang's population has continued to grow, reaching around 340,000 in 2010 (BPS Kota Kupang 2011:47). Healthy, well-dressed young men and women zigzag their new motorcycles-on-credit through clogged streets lined with well-stocked stores (which are however still owned by Chinese entrepreneurs). More people come and go by air from Penfui airport than by passenger ship from the 1960s-era harbour at Tenau. Teenagers who live in villages three hours' drive into the hills of Timor check Facebook accounts on their smartphones (even if the road remains bad). Once Suharto resigned in 1998, soldiers disappeared from Kupang's formal politics as well. Numerous elections since then have allowed the people to choose who will be their local and national representatives, their successive presidents and governors.

Kupang's prosperity is part of a worldwide trend, in which local politics do not appear to be particularly constitutive. Whether a nation's politics are centralist or federalist, socialist or capitalist, democratic or authoritarian, the twentieth century has seen poverty decline all over the world. Only the most rabidly isolationist regimes and those struck by HIV/ AIDS have not shared in it.[19] For Indonesia too, it would have been possible to tell this story of growing welfare by describing, not the unevenness of space but its uniform shrinkage as one new technology after another washed across the globe. The increased mobility as mass transport costs plummeted, the long-distance coordination facilitated by the adoption of clocks and watches, the rush of new communication and information technologies, the promiscuous power of new techniques of planning and organization greedily appropriated by armies, political parties and the

[19] See the striking animated historical statistics presented by Hans Rosling (http://www.ted.com/talks/hans_rosling_shows_the_best_stats_you_ve_ever_seen.html, accessed 19 July 2012).

religious alike. Apparently without the need for local politics, they brought increased welfare levels to all parts of Indonesia, especially after the end of the period that this book describes.

Yet unevenness persists in the social landscape of Kupang and environs. Only a few years ago the national *Tempo* magazine began its report on malnutrition in the country with this story:

> The girl was lying frail with an empty gaze. Her abdomen was bloated and her ribs protruded. Despite her pre-adolescent age, she weighed only 10 kilograms. The physician in charge diagnosed Kristin Lubalu, the girl, with *busung lapar*. The affliction was worsened by tuberculosis, which also consumed her. 'I'm the second of three siblings,' she said as *Tempo* saw her at the Bhayangkara Hospital, Kupang, East Nusa Tenggara (NTT). Kristin's dwelling is always inundated in the wet season and scorched in the dry season. 'Our house has an earth floor and an iron-sheet roof,' she added. Suddenly Kristin gagged. She wept and endured pain before vomiting. A yellow liquid poured from her mouth. She tried to stand from time to time but failed. Her skinny legs were unable to support her distended stomach.[20]

NTT accounted for more than a third of the nation's deaths due to malnutrition in that year. All of NTT's districts except the city of Kupang are officially classified as regions of extreme poverty (*daerah tertinggal*), the highest proportion among all the provinces of Indonesia.[21] Intra-rural, intra-urban, and between urban-rural inequalities remained relatively high in NTT considering it has no industry (Akita and Lukman 1999). Inequality has a strong spatial component – as urbanization increases, so does inequality. It will continue to increase at least for a time, if the Kuznets Curve is correct, which predicts inequality will rise while the economy develops and will only decline once a certain average income has been reached. While the curve remains a controversial expectation (Cameron 2002), Akita and Lukman used it to estimate that Indonesia as a whole will not reach that peak until 53.2% of its households are urban. If now, as feared by some economists who think the New Order at least got its economic policy right, the revival of democracy results in more 1960s style rent-seeking behaviour and less growth (Timmer 2004), the revenge of the nation's spatiality will be complete.

Inequality drives the social motor of a society. Subnational politics are still being produced by the same spatialized social divisions that first

20 'We only eat porridge and salt,' *Tempo*, 21–27 June 2005.

21 http://www.kemenegpdt.go.id/hal/300027/183-kab-daerah-tertinggal (accessed 10 August 2013). Figures for Papua are also very high.

produced those politics in the 1950s and '60s. Examples abound in Sylvia Tidey's (2012) recent ethnographic dissertation on the bureaucracy in Kupang. Corruption scandals are almost as loud today as they were when Subronto K. Atmodjo composed his mocking 'Three Town Devils' song in 1965, while the amounts involved are far larger. Bureaucratic jobbery still dominates the promises on local electoral hustings, but the socially embedded ethnic favouritism that appears to everyone to rule the actual distribution of jobs (Dagang 2004) inevitably fuels discontent after the elections, as it has done since the formation of the Timorsch Verbond in the 1930s. Both the promises and the discontent arise from a middle class that still works largely for the state, and still by the same loose rules that favour the strong. The localism that led Christian youths to trash Muslim fishers' houses in the clashes of November 1998 resembled the riotous behaviour towards Javanese at the time of the 1957 Permesta movement, and it still arises from a feeling that turf needs to be defended against outsiders. The talk of new districts and provinces remains as interesting to the urban political class in NTT today as it was when NTT was carved out of Nusa Tenggara in 1958. The middle class, which today sets tastes, rules of prestige, and agendas for social change, was born in that period. The one difference is that the battle for dominance that it fought so bloodily in the mid-1960s has never had to be fought again. In short, social, economic and political graininess, always with a spatial dimension, continues to defy the homogenizing effects of technical innovations. Nor should we assume that graininess is slowly disappearing. Much globalization talk today suggests that it is, but then so did much modernization talk in the 1950s and '60s. The complex reality can only be understood by means of spatially-sensitive historical and ethnographic fieldwork.

Ultimately the question of the persistence or otherwise of social unevenness is one of power, and not of naturalized processes of differentiation or homogenization arising from topography or technical innovation. What is the nature of that power? Much has been made in this book of notions of associational power. It brings large numbers of people spread over wide areas into the picture in a way that more elitist ideas of instrumental power focusing on central players cannot. At first, brokerage was a key mechanism for bringing different groups of people together around a common national project even where their historical experiences had very little in common. The total amount of social capital in a society is increased by cosmopolitan individuals like I.H. Doko, E.R. Herewila and Sam Piry who travelled between one place and another. The town and its small educated middle class functioned as a node in the spread of innovative new ideas. Particularly the progressive political parties of the late 1950s and early 1960s bridged divides – between town and country, rich and poor and notably between peasants and the middle class. Their emancipatory agendas spoke to oppressive hierarchies created in the late colonial process of state formation, and thus generated substantial new forms of power. Even the inherently authoritarian armed forces, churches and bureaucrats deployed 'soft' modalities of power to win influence. This part of the story shows that the image of the 'generative' town that inspired John Mellor (1976) and Michael Lipton (1977) to propose alternatives to urban bias was not some unattainable Gandhian idealism. Even today it still has the power to inspire young citizens in and around Indonesia's provincial towns to recover that role for their town. They can be encouraged by the suggestion that, as towns grow in size, their civil societies similarly grow in maturity. Perhaps the savagery that marked Kupang's conflicts, particularly in the mid-1960s, *partly* reflected the destructive explosions of violence that typically take place in societies with rather closed social structures (Coser 1956).

Any more than the poverty of the 1950s and '60s, however, the episode of immense violence that stands at the heart of this book cannot be dismissed as a relic of a now-irrelevant past. It was in part produced by the social divisions that had grown sharper before it, and helped make them even sharper afterwards. In the second half of the book, the storyline of associational power that was developed in the first half experiences considerable erosion. Instead of crossing social divides, the urban social movements of the second half of the book widened them. Key actors in Jakarta abandoned soft modalities of power and adopted instrumental ones that increased conflict and reduced social capital. The colonial policy of 'betting on the strong' was back, this time focused on the bureaucratic middle class in town rather than on the feudal rajas in their rural domains. The story of nationally constitutive power became less integrative than it had initially appeared to be. Mechanisms that increased social 'graininess' rather than reduce it through political means gained strength. Sharpened local divisions were caused by factionalism in Jakarta, and by the rapidity with which new state institutions were introduced into an almost feudal rurality. But at the local level – and this is the level that for local people is the most real – the most divisive mechanism was class exploitation. The sharpest division was between the urban indigenous bureaucratic middle class and the rest. The other salient social divisions – especially the ethnic and religious ones so characteristic of provincial society – rarely challenged the overarching class divide.

At the top stood the political class that defined the agenda for action. It was they who were to gain the most from the 'white collar crime' in which they were engaged. But this elite had a large constituency, a political public (as Herbert Feith called them, 2007 [1962]:109–13) of ordinary civil servants of many kinds. Seen from a national level they belonged to a lower-middle class, but their access to the resources of the state differed in degree rather than in kind from that of their superiors. They were 'bound' (*terikat*) to the state in ways the 'free people' (*orang bebas*) or the 'mountain people' (*orang gunung*) were not. By deliberately informalizing state rules they created a Gramscian civil society in which state and middle class society were embedded in each other (Hedman 2006).

They 'held Indonesia together' on their own terms. Towards the poor, these have been partly the terms of terror – which is a kind of abject integration of the kind produced by domestic violence, slavery, or racism. Like other state resources, terror too is more effective when it is socially embedded. But largely they are the terms of clientelism, which respects authority and terror. The patronage democracy that characterizes provincial politics (Van Klinken 2009b, Simandjuntak 2010) is their invention. Patronage helps temper inequalities, but does not empower. Towards the powerful in Jakarta, they are the terms of rent-seeking and economic stagnation. From that side, Middle Indonesia experiences neoliberal reform and globalization as a threat.

That so many features of the social landscape in a provincial town today can be traced to the process of state formation over half a century ago suggests Middle Indonesia has some underlying reality. Yet the historical inelasticity of Middle Indonesia should not be exaggerated either. Economic and cultural globalization, or at least a regional variant on it centred in East Asia, is gradually undermining the conservative bastions of Middle Indonesia. Nor need we exaggerate the oppressive aspects of Middle Indonesia. Despite the unexhumed mass graves that surround the towns, Middle Indonesia offers a homeliness of familiar places and faces, and even some kind of emancipatory potential rooted in narratives of 'local wisdom' that resists bossy outsiders. Its residents are proud to belong. The challenge for them now is to rediscover the larger emancipatory potential that lies hidden in the history of Middle Indonesia's younger years, when Hannah Arendt's 'power to' get things done together had a tangible reality. The current phase of democracy and economic growth is their best opportunity in decades. Reformasi has made possible a different coalition of interests from that of the New Order. The extent to which that can improve life for all and reduce the legacy of social polarization left by the New Order in Kupang and its hinterland remains as yet an open question. The possibilities certainly do extend to reaching once again across class boundaries to those who, as Herewila put it, 'from birth [...] live and breathe and are educated in aristocracy and fascism,' so together they can make 'a special leap up.'

REFERENCES

Abeyasekere, Susan. 1989. *Jakarta: A History*. rev. ed. Singapore: Oxford University Press.

Adam, Jacobus Andreas Soekarno Hatta, et al. 1997. *Baktiku Untuk Nusa Tenggara Timur: Apa Yang Telah Mereka Lalukan Adalah Teladan Buat Kita!* Kupang: Yayasan Citra Insan Pembaru.

ADB. 2010. Key Indicators for Asia and the Pacific 2010: The Rise of Asia's Middle Class (Special Chapter). Manila: Asian Development Bank.

Akita, Takahiro, and Rizal Affandi Lukman. 1999. "Spatial Patterns of Expenditure Inequalities in Indonesia: 1987, 1990 and 1993." *Bulletin of Indonesian Economic Studies* 35 (2):67–90.

Alers, Henri J.H. 1956. *Om Een Rode of Groene Merdeka: 10 Jaren Binnenlandse Politiek: Indonesië, 1945–1953*. Eindhoven: Vulkaan.

Alfian. 1971. *Hasil Pemilihan Umum 1955 Untuk Dewan Perwalikan Rakjat (Dpr)*. Djakarta: Lembaga Ekonomi dan Kemasjarakatan Nasional.

Allen, John. 2003. *Lost Geographies of Power*. Malden, MA: Blackwell Publications.

Amal, Ichlasul. 1992. *Regional and Central Government in Indonesian Politics: West Sumatra and South Sulawesi, 1949–1979*. Yogyakarta: Gadjah Mada University Press.

Anderson, Benedict R. O'G. 1972. *Java in a Time of Revolution: Occupation and Resistance 1944–1946*. Ithaca, NY: Cornell University Press.

——. 1991. *Imagined Communities: Reflections on the Origin and Spread of Nationalism*. 2 ed. London/ New York: Verso.

Angelini, John, and Kenichi Hirose. 2004. Extension of Social Security Coverage for the Informal Economy in Indonesia: Surveys in the Urban and Rural Informal Economy. *Working Paper 11*. Manila, Philippines: International Labour Organization, Subregional Office for South-East Asia and the Pacific.

Anonymous. 1956. Tentang Pemerintahan Swapradja. Kupang: [Djawatan Penerangan Daerah Timor].

Anonymous. 1974. *Menjaring Angin: Kronik Percaturan Politik Di Maumere, Ntt, Jelang, Selama Dan Pasca Pembantaian 20 Pebruari – 29 April 1966*. Ende: [unpublished mss].

Antlöv, Hans. 2003. Civic Engagement in Local Government Renewal in Indonesia. *Logolink SEA: Citizen participation in local governance: experiences from Thailand, Indonesia and the Philippines*. Manila: Institute for Popular Democracy.

Ardhana, I Ketut. 2000. *Nusa Tenggara Nach Einrichtung Der Kolonialherrschaft 1915 Bis 1950*. PhD, Lehrstuhl für Südostasienkunde, Universität Passau, Passau.

——. 2005. *Penataan Nusa Tenggara Pada Masa Kolonial 1915–1950*. Jakarta: Grafika.

Arendt, Hannah. 1958. *The Human Condition*. Chicago/ London: University of Chicago Press.

Armstrong, Warwick R., and Terry G. McGee. 1968. "Revolutionary Change and the Third World City: A Theory of Urban Involution." *Civilisations* 18 (3):353–76.

Asad, Talal. 1993. *Genealogies of Religion: Discipline and Reasons of Power in Christianity and Islam*. Baltimore, MD: John Hopkins University Press.

Asnan, Gusti. 2007. *Memikir Ulang Regionalisme: Sumatera Barat Tahun 1950-An*. Jakarta: Obor.

Ataupah, H. 1995. Land Tenure Di Daerah Aliran Sungai Mina: Laporan Akhir. Kupang: NTT Watershed Management Planning Project.

Banunaek, Don Yesriel Yohan Kus. 2007. *Raja Raja Amanatun Yang Berkuasa*. Yogyakarta: Pustaka Pelajar.

Barker, Joshua. 2005. "Engineers and Political Dreams: Indonesia in the Satellite Age." *Current Anthropology* 46 (5):703–27.

Barlow, Colin, Alex Bellis, and Kate Andrews. 1991. Nusa Tenggara Timur: The Challenges of Development. *Political and social change monograph no.12*. Canberra: Australian National University, Research School of Pacific and Asian Studies, Department of Political and Social Change.

Barnes, R.H. 2003. "Fransiskus/Usman Buang Duran: Catholic, Muslim, Communist." *Bijdragen tot de Taal-, Land- en Volkenkunde* 159 (1):1–29.

Barron, Patrick, and David Madden. 2003. Violence and Conflict Resolution in "Non-Conflict" Regions: The Case of Lampung, Indonesia. Jakarta: World Bank.

Basile, Elisabetta, and Barbara Harriss-White. 2003. "The Politics of Accumulation in Small Town India." In *Corporate Capitalism in Contemporary South Asia: Conventional Wisdoms and South Asian Realities*, edited by Ananya Mukherjee Reed, 92–105. Palgrave Macmillan.

Bates, Robert H. 2008. "Domestic Interests and Control Regimes." In *The Political Economy of Economic Growth in Africa, 1960–2000*, edited by Benno J. Ndulu, Stephen A. O'Connell, Robert H. Bates, Paul Collier and Chukwuma C. Soludo, 176–201. Cambridge [UK]: Cambridge University Press.

Benda, Harry J. 1966. "The Pattern of Administrative Reforms in the Closing Years of Dutch Rule in Indonesia." *Journal of Asian Studies* 25 (4):589–605.

Boenga, H., et al. 1996. *I. H. Doko: Perjuangan Dan Pengabdiannya: Suatu Biografi Singkat*. Kupang: Kanwil P&K.

Boer, M.G. de, and J.C. Westermann. 1941. *Een Halve Eeuw Paketvaart, 1891–1941*. 2 vols. Amsterdam: DeBussy, Koninklijk Paketvaart-Maatschappij.

Bongenaar, Karel E.M. 2005. *De Ontwikkeling Van Het Zelfbesturend Landschap in Nederlandsch-Indie: 1855–1942*. Zutphen, Netherlands: Walburg Pers.

Boone, Catherine. 1998. "State Building in the African Countryside: Structure and Politics at the Grassroots." *Journal of Development Studies* 34 (4):1–31.

——. 2003. *Political Topographies of the African State: Territorial Authority and Institutional Choice*. Cambridge: Cambridge University Press.

Booth, Anne, ed. 1992. *The Oil Boom and After: Indonesian Economic Policy and Performance in the Soeharto Era, South-East Asian Social Science Monographs*. Singapore: Oxford University Press.

Boumans, Nicolaas Jozef. 2005. *Pekerja Kebun-Nya: Otobiografi Nicolaas Jozef Boumans, Svd*. Ende: Nusa Indah.

BPS. 1970. *Statistik Pegawai Pemerintah Bali Dan Nusa Tenggara, 1 Djuni 1969*. Djakarta: Biro Pusat Statistik.

——. 1990. *Statistical Yearbook of Indonesia 1990*. Jakarta: Biro Pusat Statistik.

BPS Kota Kupang. 2011. Kota Kupang Dalam Angka 2011. Kupang: Badan Pusat Statistik Kota Kupang.

Breuilly, John. 1982. *Nationalism and the State*. New York: St. Martin's Press.

Brookes, Graham F. 1977. *Spirit Movements in Timor: A Survey*. MTh qual., Melbourne College of Divinity, Melbourne.

——. 1980. *The Influences of Some Primal Religious Experiences on the Beliefs and Practices of Atoni Christians and Their Challenge to the Protestant Evangelical Church of Timor*. MTh, Melbourne College of Divinity, Melbourne.

——. 1990. "Spirit Movements on Timor." In *Cargo Cults and Millenarian Movements: Transoceanic Comparisons of New Religious Movements*, edited by G.W. Trompf, 263–91. Berlin: Mouton de Gruyter.

Bruner, Edward M. 1961. "Urbanization and Ethnic Identity in North Sumatra." *American Anthropologist* 63 (3):508–21.

Buli, J., et al. 1977–78. *Sejarah Daerah Nusa Tenggara Timur*. Kupang: Departemen Pendidikan dan Kebudayaan, Pusat Penelitian Sejarah dan Budaya, Proyek Penelitian dan Pencatatan Kebudayaan Daerah.

Cameron, Lisa. 2002. "Growth with or without Equity? The Distributional Impact of Indonesian Development." *Asian-Pacific Economic Literature* 16 (2):1–17.

Campbell-Nelson, Karen. 1993. "Menduga Makna Sebuah Patung." *Berita GMIT* 6:24–5.
Chalik, A., ed. 1971. *Laporan Penelitian Tentang Organisasi Dan Tatakerdja Di Propinsi Bali Dan Propinsi Nusa Tenggara Timur*. Djakarta: Departemen Dalam Negeri.
Cockcroft, James D. 1998. *Mexico's Hope: An Encounter with Politics and History*. New York, N.Y.: Monthly Review Press.
Cohen, Matthew Isaac. 2006. *The Komedie Stamboel: Popular Theater in Colonial Indonesia, 1891–1903*. Leiden KITLV Press.
Collier, William L., and Suhud Tjakrawerdaja. 1974. *Problems and Prospects of Increasing Cattle Exports from Nusa Tenggara Timur Province, Agro Economic Survey*.
Colombijn, Freek. 1994. *Patches of Padang: The History of an Indonesian Town in the Twentieth Century and the Use of Urban Space*. Leiden: Research School CNWS.
——. 2010. *Under Construction: The Politics of Urban Space and Housing During the Decolonization of Indonesia, 1930–1960*. Leiden: KITLV Press.
Conkling, Robert. 1975. *Bureaucracy in Makassar, Indonesia: The Political Anthropology of a Complex Organization*. PhD, Department of Anthropology, University of Chicago, Chicago.
——. 1979. "Authority and Change in the Indonesian Bureaucracy." *American Ethnologist* 6 (3):543–54.
——. 1984. "Power and Change in an Indonesian Government Office." *American Ethnologist* 11 (2):259–74.
Cooley, Frank L. 1976. *Memperkenalkan Gereja Masehi Injili Timor, Benih Yang Tumbuh, Xi*. Jakarta: Lembaga Penelitian dan Studi Dewan Gereja-gereja di Indonesia.
Coppel, Charles A. 1983. *Indonesian Chinese in Crisis*. Kuala Lumpur: Oxford University Press.
Coser, Lewis A. 1956. *The Functions of Social Conflict*. Glencoe, Ill.: Free Press.
Costello, Michael A., Thomas R. Leinbach, and Richard Ulack. 1987. *Mobility and Employment in Urban Southeast Asia: Examples from Indonesia and the Philippines, International Studies in Migration*. Boulder, Colo.: Westview Press.
Cribb, Robert. 2000. *Historical Atlas of Indonesia*. Surrey, UK: Curzon.
——. 2010. *Digital Atlas of Indonesian History*. 2 ed. Copenhagen: Nias Press.
Crouch, Harold. 1979. "Patrimonialism and Military Rule in Indonesia." *World Politics* 31 (4):571–87.
——. 1988. *The Army and Politics in Indonesia*. rev. ed. Ithaca, NY: Cornell University Press.
Cunningham, Clark E. 1962. *People of the Dry Land: A Study of the Social Organisation of an Indonesian People*. D.Phil., Faculty of Anthropology and Geography, University of Oxford, Oxford.
Dagang, Thomas Didimus. 2004. *Netralitas Birokrasi Pemerintah: Studi Tentang Pengaruh Etnisitas Dalam Birokrasi Pemerintah Di Kota Kupang*. MA, Program Pasca Sarjana Program Studi Magister Politik Lokal dan Otonomi Daerah, Universitas Gadjah Mada, Yogyakarta.
Dahl, Robert A. 1967. "The City in the Future of Democracy." *American Political Science Review* 61 953–70.
Datta, Satya, ed. 1990. *Third World Urbanisation: Reappraisals and New Perspectives*. Stockholm: Swedish Council for Research in the Humanities and Social Sciences (HSFR).
Davis, Diane E. 1999. "The Power of Distance: Re-Theorizing Social Movements in Latin America." *Theory and Society* 28 (4):585–638.
Davis, Mike. 2004. "Planet of Slums: Urban Involution and the Informal Proletariat." *New Left Review* 26:5–34.
Departement van Economische Zaken. 1936. *Volkstelling 1930*. 8 vols. Vol. VIII. Overzicht voor Nederlandsch-Indië. Batavia: Landsdrukkerij.
Deutsch, Karl W. . 1961. "Social Mobilization and Political Development." *American Political Science Review* 55 (3):493–514.
Dick, Howard. 1985. "The Rise of a Middle Class and the Changing Concept of Equity in Indonesia: An Interpretation." *Indonesia* 39:71–92.

——. 1986. *The Indonesian Interisland Shipping Industry: An Analysis of Competition and Regulation*. Singapore: Institute of Southeast Asian Studies, Asean Economic Research Unit.
——. 2002. *Surabaya, City of Work: A Socioeconomic History, 1900–2000, Southeast Asia Series No.106*. Athens, Ohio: Ohio University Center for International Studies.
Dick, Howard, and P.J. Rimmer. 1998. "Beyond the Third World City: The New Urban Geography of Southeast Asia." *Urban Studies* 35 (12):2303–21.
Dick, Howard, and Peter J. Rimmer. 2003. *Cities, Transport and Communications: The Integration of Southeast Asia since 1850*. Houndmills: Palgrave Macmillan.
Dick, Howard, Vincent J.H. Houben, J. Thomas Lindblad, and Thee Kian Wie, eds. 2002. *The Emergence of a National Economy: An Economic History of Indonesia, 1800–2000, Southeast Asia Publications*. Leiden: KITLV Press.
Dicker, Gordon. 1959. *The Proclamation of the Gospel in Timor: A Study of the Evangelical Church of Timor in Relation to Its Historical Antecedents*. MTh, Melbourne College of Divinity, Melbourne.
——. 2007. *Our Life and Work in Timor*. [Sydney]: [Self-published].
Diessen, J.R. van, and R.P.G.A. Voskuil. 1998. *Stedenatlas Nederlands-Indië*. Purmerend: Asia Maior.
Dietrich, Stefan. 1989. *Kolonialismus Und Mission Auf Flores (Ca. 1900–1942), Münchener Beiträge Zur Süd- Südostasienkunde; Bd. 1*. Hohenschäftlarn: Renner.
Diprose, Rachael. 2002. *Putra Daerah: Identity, Grievances, and Collective Action*. BA Honours, Modern Languages, Arts Faculty, University of New South Wales, Sydney.
Direktorat Agraria NTT. 1973. Pelaksanaan Tugas-Tugas Keagrariaan Di Daerah Propinsi Nusa Tenggara Timur. [Kupang]: Direktorat Agraria, Propinsi Nusa Tenggara Timur.
Direktorat Pemerintahan. 1973. Proyek Pelita: Bahan-Bahan Pelajaran; Pendidikan Pejabat Pamong Praja, Propinsi Nusa Tenggara Timur, 1973/74. Kupang: Direktorat Pemerintahan pada Kantor Gubernur Kepala Daerah Propinisi Nusa Tenggara Timur.
Djeki, J.J. 1980. *Sejarah Revolusi Kemerdekaan (1945 S/D 1949) Daerah Nusa Tenggara Timur*. [Kupang]: Departemen Pendidikan dan Kebudayaan, Proyek Inventarisasi dan Dokumentasi Daerah Nusa Tenggara Timur.
Doko, I.H. 1975. *Nusa Tenggara Timur Dalam Kancah Perjuangan Kemerdekaan Indonesia: Beberapa Catatan Ungkapan Kenang-Kenangan Pribadi*. Bandung: Masa Baru.
——. 1981a. *Pahlawan-Pahlawan Suku Timor*. Jakarta: Balai Pustaka.
——. 1981b. *Perjuangan Kemerdekaan Indonesia Di Nusa Tenggara Timur*. Jakarta: Balai Pustaka.
——. 1982. *Timor, Pulau Gunung Fatuleu, "Batu Keramat"*. Jakarta: Balai Pustaka.
Drake, Christine. 1989. *National Integration in Indonesia: Patterns and Policies*. Honolulu: University of Hawai'i Press.
Dürr, Heiner. 1982. "Raumentwicklung Im Dilemma Zwischen Wachstums- Und Gleichheitzeilen, Indonesien Als Beispiel." *Geographische Rundschau* 34 (2):49–57.
Elson, Robert E. 2008. *The Idea of Indonesia: A History*: Cambridge University Press.
Emerson, Rupert. 1979 [1937]. *Malaysia: A Study in Direct and Indirect Rule*. Kuala Lumpur: University of Malaya Press.
Emmerson, Donald K. 1978. "The Bureaucracy in Context: Weakness in Strength." In *Political Power and Communications in Indonesia*, edited by Karl D. Jackson and Lucian W. Pye, 82–136. Berkeley: University of California Press.
End, Th. van den, ed. 1987. *Gereformeerde Zending Op Sumba, 1859–1972: Een Bronnen-publicatie, Project Kerkhistorische Uitgaven Indonesië; 2*. [Oegstgeest]: Raad voor de Zending der Ned. Hervormde Kerk.
Evers, Hans-Dieter. 1972. Urban Involution: The Social Development of Southeast Asian Towns. *Working Paper No. 2*. Singapore: Dept. of Sociology, University of Singapore.
——. 1987. "The Bureaucratization of Southeast Asia." *Comparative Studies in Society and History* 29 (4):666–85.
——. 2007. "The End of Urban Involution and the Cultural Construction of Urbanism in Indonesia." *Internationales Asien-Forum* 38 (1–2):51–65.

Evers, Hans-Dieter, and Solvay Gerke. 1994. Social Mobility and the Transformation of Indonesian Society. *Working Paper no.202*. Bielefeld: University of Bielefeld Sociology of Development Research Centre.
Fagg, Donald R. 1958. *Authority and Social Structure: A Study in Javanese Bureaucracy*. PhD, Department of Social Relations, Harvard University, Cambridge, US.
Farram, Steven. 2002. "Revolution, Religion and Magic: The Pki in West Timor, 1924–1966." *Bijdragen tot de Taal-, Land- en Volkenkunde (BKI)* 158 (1):21–48.
——. 2004. *From "Timor Koepang" to "Timor Ntt": The Political History of West Timor 1901–1967*. PhD, Law, Business and Arts, Northern Territory University, Darwin.
Feith, Herbert. 1957. *The Indonesian Elections of 1955, Interim Reports Series; 6* Ithaca, NY: Modern Indonesia Project, Southeast Asia Program, Department of Far Eastern Studies, Cornell University.
——. 1958. *The Wilopo Cabinet, 1952–1953; a Turning Point in Post-Revolutionary Indonesia, Monograph Series*. Ithaca, NY: Modern Indonesia Project, Cornell University.
——. 1964. "President Soekarno, the Army and the Communists: The Triangle Changes Shape." *Asian Survey* 4 (8):969–80.
——. 2007 [1962]. *The Decline of Constitutional Democracy in Indonesia*. Jakarta: Equinox.
Firman, Tommy. 2004. "Demographic and Spatial Patterns of Indonesia's Recent Urbanisation." *Population, space and place* 10:421–34.
Forth, Gregory. 2009. "Heads under Bridges or in Mud: Reflections on a Southeast Asian 'Diving Rumour'." *Anthropology Today* 25 (6):3–6.
Fox, James J. 1977. *Harvest of the Palm: Ecological Change in Eastern Indonesia*. Cambridge, Mass.: Harvard University Press.
——. 1980. "The Movement of the Spirit in the Timor Area: Christian Traditions and Ethnic Identities." In *Indonesia: The Making of a Culture*, edited by James J. Fox, 235–46. Canberra Research School of Pacific Studies, The Australian National University.
——. 2000. "Tracing the Path, Recounting the Past: Historical Perspectives on Timor." In *Out of the Ashes: Destruction and Reconstruction of East Timor*, edited by James J. Fox and Dionisio Babo Soares, 1–27. Canberra: ANU E Press.
Francillon, Gérard. 1967. *Some Matriarchic Aspects of the Social Structure of the Southern Tetun of Middle Timor*. PhD, Australian National University, Canberra.
Franck, Manuelle. 1993. *Quand La Riziere Rencontre L'asphalte…: Semis Urbain Et Processus D'urbanisation a Java-Est, Etudes Insulindiennes / Archipel No.10*. Paris: Editions de l'Ecole des Hautes Etudes en Sciences Sociale,.
Friend, Theodore. 2003. *Indonesian Destinies*. Cambridge, MA: Belknap Press of Harvard University Press.
Geertz, Clifford. 1956. *The Social Context of Economic Change: An Indonesian Case Study*. Cambridge, Mass.: Center for International Studies, MIT.
——. 1963a. *Agricultural Involution: The Processes of Ecological Change in Indonesia*. Berkeley and Los Angeles, Cal.: University of California Press.
——. 1963b. "The Integrative Revolution: Primordial Sentiments and Civil Politics in the New States." In *Old Societies and New States*, edited by Clifford Geertz, 105–157. New York: Free Press.
——. 1963c. *Peddlers and Princes: Social Development and Economic Change in Two Indonesian Towns*. Chicago: University of Chicago Press.
——. 1965. *The Social History of an Indonesian Town*. Cambridge, Mass.: The M.I.T. Press.
Geertz, Hildred. 1963. "Indonesian Cultures and Communities." In *Indonesia*, edited by Ruth T. McVey, 24–96. New Haven: Human Relations Area Files.
Gottdiener, M., and Joe R. Feagin. 1988. "The Paradigm Shift in Urban Sociology." *Urban Affairs Quarterly* 24 (2):163–87.
Gould, Roger V., and Roberto M. Fernandez. 1989. "Structures of Mediation: A Formal Approach to Brokerage in Transaction Networks." *Sociological Methodology* 19:89–126.
Granovetter, Mark. 1973. "The Strength of Weak Ties." *The American Journal of Sociology* 78 (6):1360–80.

Gray, Clive. 1979. "Civil Service Compensation in Indonesia." *Bulletin of Indonesian Economic Studies* 15 (1):85 - 113.
Gubernur NTT. 1970. Keterangan Pemerintah Propinsi Nusa Tenggara Timur Dimuka Dewan Perwakilan Rakjat Daerah Gotong Rojong Propinsi Nusa Tenggara Timur Dalam Sidang Ke Iii Tahun 1970/1971. Kupang: Biro Administrasi Umum, Kantor Gubernur Kepala Daerah Propinsi Nusa Tenggara Timur.
Hadiz, Vedi R., and Daniel Dhakidae, eds. 2005. *Social Science and Power in Indonesia.* Jakarta: Equinox.
Hägerdal, Hans. 2012. *Lords of the Land, Lords of the Sea: Conflict and Adaptation in Early Colonial Timor, 1600–1800, Verhandelingen Van Koninklijk Instituut Voor Taal-, Land- En Volkenkunde; 273.* Leiden: KITLV Press.
Hall, Peter A., and Rosemary C.R. Taylor. 1996. "Political Science and the Three New Institutionalisms." *Political Studies* 44 (5):936–57.
Halsema, W.B. van. 1995. "Van Zending Naar Oecumenische Samenwerking: De Periode 1947–1992." In *De Zending Voorbij: Terugblik Op De Relatie Tussen De Gereformeerde Kerken in Nederland En De Christelijke Kerk Van Sumba 1942–1992*, edited by W.B. van Halsema, P.N. Holtrop, H. Reenders and J.A.C. Vel, 61–99. Kampen: Kok.
Hardjoprakoso, Mastini. 1977. *Koleksi Surat Kabar Perpustakaan Museum Pusat 1810–1977.* Jakarta: Perpustakaan Museum Pusat.
Hardoy, Jorge E., and David Satterthwaite, eds. 1986. *Small and Intermediate Urban Centres: Their Role in Regional and National Development in the Third World.* London: Hodder and Stoughton.
Harriss-White, Barbara. 2003. *India Working: Essays on Society and Economy, Contemporary South Asia ; 8.* Cambridge: Cambridge University Press.
Hart, Gillian Patricia. 2002. *Disabling Globalization: Places of Power in Post-Apartheid South Africa.* Berkeley: University of California Press.
Harvey, Barbara S. 1977. *Permesta: Half a Rebellion.* Ithaca, NY: Cornell University Modern Indonesia Project.
Hedman, Eva-Lotta E. 2006. *In the Name of Civil Society: From Free Election Movements to People Power in the Philippines.* Hawai'i: University of Hawai'i Press.
Henley, David. 2012. "Agrarian Roots of Industrial Growth: Rural Development in Southeast Asia and Sub-Saharan Africa." *Development Policy Review* 30 (Supplement):25–47.
Heo, W. Dimoe. 1972. *Monograpi Wilajah Koperasi Kabupaten Kupang.* Kupang: Kantor Koperasi kabupaten Kupang.
Herbst, Jeffrey. 2000. *States and Power in Africa: Comparative Lessons in Authority and Control.* Princeton, NJ: Princeton University Press.
Hermanus, Th. M. 1985. *Ikhtisar Perkembangan Pemerintahan Di Daerah Nusa Tenggara Timur.* 3 vols. Kupang: typed manuscript.
Honna, Jun. 2006. "Local Civil-Military Relations During the First Phase of Democratic Transition, 1999–2004: A Comparison of West, Central and East Java." *Indonesia* 82:75–96.
Hugo, Graeme. 1996. "Urbanization in Indonesia: City and Countryside Linked." In *The Urban Transformation of the Developing World*, edited by Josef Gugler, 133–83. Oxford: Oxford University Press.
Hugo, Graeme J., Terence H. Hull, Valerie J. Hull, and Gavin Jones. 1987. *The Demographic Dimension in Indonesian Development, East Asian Social Science Monographs.* Singapore: Oxford University Press.
Huizer, Gerrit. 1974. "Peasant Mobilisation and Land Reform in Indonesia." *Review of Indonesian and Malayan affairs* 8 (1):81–138.
Jackson, Karl D. 1980. *Traditional Authority, Islam and Rebellion: A Study of Indonesian Political Behavior.* Berkeley and Los Angeles: University of California Press.
Jeffrey, Craig. 2010. "Timepass: Youth, Class, and Time among Unemployed Young Men in India." *American Ethnologist* 37 (3):465–81.
Jones, Gavin W. 1988. "Urbanization Trends in Southeast Asia: Some Issues for Policy." *Journal of Southeast Asian Studies* 19 (1):137–54.

Jong, Chr. G.F. de, ed. 2006. *Als Hunner Één: Brieven Van Piet En Jet Middelkoop, West-Timor, 1922–1942, Uitgaven Van De Werkgroep Voor De Geschiedenis Van De Nederlandse Zending En Overzeese Kerken. Kleine Reeks; 12*. Zoetermeer: Boekencentrum.

Kahin, Audrey R., ed. 1985. *Regional Dynamics of the Indonesian Revolution: Unity from Diversity*. Honolulu: University of Hawaii Press.

Kalecki, Michal. 1972. "Social and Economic Aspects of 'Intermediate Regimes'." In *Selected Essays on the Economic Growth of the Socialist and the Mixed Economy*, edited by Michal Kalecki, 162–9. New York: Cambridge University Press.

Kammen, Douglas, and Katharine McGregor, eds. 2012. *The Contours of Mass Violence in Indonesia, 1965–1968*. Singapore: NUS Press for the Asian Studies Association of Australia.

Kana, Christoffel. 1969. *Sedjarah Perkembangan Pemerintahan Di Timor Sampai Indonesia Merdeka*. Sardjana Muda, Pendidikan, Universitas Negeri Nusa Tjendana, Kupang.

Kantor Sensus NTT. 1971. Laporan Penjelenggaraan Persiapan Sensus Penduduk 1971 Didalam Propinsi Nusa Tenggara Timur. Kupang: Kantor Sensus dan Statistik, Propinsi Nusa Tenggara Timur.

Kato, Tsuyoshi. 2003. "Images of Colonial Cities in Early Indonesian Novels." In *Southeast Asia over Three Generations: Essays Presented to Benedict R. O'g. Anderson*, edited by James T. Siegel and Audrey R. Kahin, 91–123. Ithaca, NY: Cornell University Press.

Kawuryan, Anna Maria Siti. 1998. Educational Achievement and Sectoral Transition in the Indonesian Labor Force. *Bulletin Number 98-3*. Minneapolis: Economic Development Center, University of Minnesota.

Kementerian Penerangan Sunda Ketjil. 1953. *Republik Indonesia: Propinsi Sunda Ketjil*. Djakarta: Kementerian Penerangan, Indonesia.

Khan, Mushtaq H. 2000. "Rents, Efficiency and Growth." In *Rents, Rent-Seeking and Economic Development: Theory and Evidence in Asia*, edited by Mushtaq. H. Khan and Jomo K.S., 21–69. Cambridge, U.K.: Cambridge University Press.

Khan, Mushtaq H., and Jomo K.S., eds. 2000. *Rents, Rent-Seeking and Economic Development: Theory and Evidence in Asia*. Cambridge, U.K.: Cambridge University Press.

King, Dwight Y. 1982. "Indonesia's New Order as a Bureaucratic Polity, a Neopatrimonial Regime or a Bureaucratic-Authoritarian Regime - What Difference Does It Make?" In *Interpreting Indonesian Politics: Thirteen Contributions to the Debate*, edited by Benedict R. O'G. Anderson and Audrey Kahin, 104–16. Ithaca, N.Y.: Cornell University Press.

King, Seth S. 1966. "The Great Purge in Indonesia." *New York Times Magazine*, 8 May, 4.

Kleden, Tony, Maria Matildis Banda, and Dion D.B. Putra, eds. 2007. *15 Tahun Pos Kupang Suara Nusa Tenggara Timur*. Kupang: Timor Media Grafika.

Klinken, Gerry van. 2007. *Communal Violence and Democratization in Indonesia: Small Town Wars, Routledge Contemporary Southeast Asia Series; 15*. London: Routledge.

——. 2008. "Blood, Timber, and the State in West Kalimantan, Indonesia." *Asia Pacific Viewpoint* 49 (1):35–47.

——. 2009a. "Decolonization and the Making of Middle Indonesia." *Urban Geography* 30 (8):879–97.

——. 2009b. "Patronage Democracy in Provincial Indonesia." In *Rethinking Popular Representation*, edited by Olle Törnquist, Neil Webster and Kristian Stokke, 141–59. Basingstoke: Palgrave Macmillan.

——. 2012. "'Don't Write This': Researching Provincial Biographies in Indonesia." In *Locating Life Stories: Beyond East-West Binaries in (Auto)Biographical Studies*, edited by Maureen Perkins, 169–92. Honolulu: Biographical Research Center, University of Hawai'i Press.

——. 2013a. "Brokerage and the Making of Middle Indonesia." *City & Society* 25 (1):135–55.

——. 2013b. Murder in Maumere: Postcolonial Citizenship. *Oratie*. Amsterdam: University of Amsterdam.

Klinken, Gerry van, and Joshua Barker, eds. 2009. *State of Authority: The State in Society in Indonesia*. Ithaca, NY: Cornell University Southeast Asia Program.

Klinken, Gerry van, and Ward Berenschot, eds. 2014. *In Search of Middle Indonesia: Middle Classes in Provincial Towns*. Leiden: Brill.

Klinkert, H.C. 1913. *Bloemlezing Uit De Maleische Geschriften, Ten Behoeve Van De Gouvernements Inlandsche Scholen En Van Hen, Die Het Maleisch Met Latijnsch Karakter Beoefenen*. 3 ed. Leiden: E. J. Brill.

Koch, Kurt. 1971. *Revival in Indonesia*. Grand Rapids: Kregel.

Koehuan, M., B.K. Kotten, and H. Bunga. 1982. *Sejarah Perlawanan Terhadap Imperialisme Dan Kolonialisme Di Nusa Tenggara Timur*. Jakarta: Proyek Inventarisasi dan Dokumentasi Sejarah Nasional, Direktorat Sejarah dan Nilai Tradisional, Departemen Pendidikan dan Kebudayaan.

Kolimon, Mery, and Lilya Wetangterah, eds. 2012. *Memori-Memori Terlarang: Perempuan Korban & Penyintas Tragedi '65 Di Nusa Tenggara Timur*. Kupang: Yayasan Bonet Pinggupir.

Kopkamtib. 1968. *Bahan-Bahan Pokok G.30.S / P.K.I & Penghantjurannja*. 3 vols: Komando Operasi Pemulihan Keamanan dan Ketertiban.

——. 1969. Laporan Kopkamtib Pada Sidang Paripurna Kabinet Pembangunan Tgl 12 Agustus 1968: Rahasia. Jakarta: Sekretaris Kopkamtib (Komando Operasi Pemulihan Keamanan dan Ketertiban).

Kopkamtibda Nusra. 1975a. Jawaban Masalah Penting Laksus Pangkopkamtib Daerah Nusa Dalam Rangka Rapat Kerja Kodam Xvi/ Ud Tahun 1975: Rahasia. Denpasar: Komando Operasi Pemulihan Keamanan dan Ketertiban Daerah Nusatenggara.

——. 1975b. Program Kerja Laksus Pangkopkamtib Daerah Nusra Tahun 1975/ 1976: Rahasia. [Denpasar]: Komando Operasi Pemulihan Keamanan dan Ketertiban Daerah Nusatenggara.

Kopong, Elias, A.Z. Soh, Ch. Kana [et al.]. 1981. *Permainan Rakyat Daerah Nusa Tenggara Timur*. Kupang Proyek Inventarisasi dan Dokumentasi Kebudayaan Daerah Nusa Tenggara Timur, Pusat Penelitian Sejarah dan Budaya, Departemen Pendidikan dan Kebudayaan.

Kwantes, R.C., ed. 1975–82. *De Ontwikkeling Van De Nationalistische Beweging in Nederlandsch-Indië*. 4 vols. Groningen: J.B. Wolters.

Lalamentik, W.J. 1961. *Information About Nusa Tenggara Timur*. Kupang.

Lay, Cornelis. 2014. "Growing up in Kupang." Pp 146–68 in *In Search of Middle Indonesia: Middle Classes in Provincial Towns*, edited by Gerry van Klinken and Ward Berenschot. Leiden: Brill.

Legge, J.D. 1961. *Central Authority and Regional Autonomy in Indonesia: A Study in Local Administration, 1950–1960*. Ithaca, New York: Cornell University Press.

Leirissa, R.Z., Kuntowidjojo, and M. Soenjata Kartadarmadja, eds. 1984. *Sejarah Sosial Kota Kupang Daerah Nusa Tenggara Timur 1945–1980*. Jakarta: Proyek Inventarisasi dan Dokumentasi Sejarah Nasional, Departemen Pendidikan dan Kebudayaan.

Lerner, Daniel. 1964. *The Passing of Traditional Society: Modernizing the Middle East*. London: Collier.

Lev, Daniel S. 1966. *The Transition to Guided Democracy: Indonesian Politics, 1957–1959*. Ithaca, N.Y.: Department of Asian Studies. Southeast Asia Program.

Li, Tania Murray. 2009. "To Make Live or Let Die? Rural Dispossession and the Protection of Surplus Populations." *Antipode* 41 (S1):66–93.

Liliweri, Alo, Egi Didoek, and Ignas Kulas, eds. 1984. *25 Tahun Ntt, Apa Kata Mereka? (Sebuah Bunga Rampai)*. Kupang: DPD I KNPI NTT.

Lipton, Michael. 1977. *Why Poor People Stay Poor: A Study of Urban Bias in World Development*. London: Temple Smith.

Locher, G.W. 1945. Security-Onderzoek Van I.H. Doko, Lid Van De Raad Van De Soenda-Eilanden, Opgesteld Door G.W. Locher, Adviseur Conica. 1945. Doorslag. KITLV.

Logemann, J.A.H. 1953. "The Characteristics of Urban Centers in the East." In *Eastern and Western World: Selected Readings*, edited by Netherlands Universities Foundation for International Cooperation, 85–104. The Hague/ Bandung: Van Hoeve.

Logsdon, Martha G. 1998. "Development of Indonesia's Civil Service 1974–1994." *Journal of Political and Military Sociology* 26 (Summer):3–22.
Lonsdale, John, and Bruce Berman. 1979. "Coping with Contradictions: The Development of the Colonial State in Africa." *Journal of African History* 20:487–506.
Lubis, Mochtar. 1963. *Twilight in Jakarta*: Hutchinson & Co.
Lucas, Anton E. 1991. *One Soul One Struggle: Region and Revolution in Indonesia*. Sydney: Asian Studies Association of Australia in association with Allen and Unwin.
Lynd, Robert S., and Helen Merrell Lynd. 1929. *Middletown: A Study in Contemporary American Culture*. New York: Harcourt, Brace and Co.
Lynd, Robert S., and Helen Merrell Lynd. 1937. *Middletown in Transition: A Study in Cultural Conflicts*. New York: Harcourt, Brace and Co.
Mackie, J.A.C. 1967. *Problems of the Indonesian Inflation*. Ithaca, N.Y.: Cornell University, Department of Asian Studies.
——. 1971. "The Indonesian Economy, 1950–1963." In *The Economy of Indonesia: Selected Readings*, edited by Bruce Glassburner, 16–69. Ithaca, NY: Cornell University Press.
Mackie, J.A.C., C.A. Coppel, K.D. Thomas, Y. Panglaykim, and W. Gungwu. 1976. *The Chinese in Indonesia: Five Essays*. Melbourne: Thomas Nelson.
Magenda, Burhan. 1991. *East Kalimantan: The Decline of a Commercial Aristocracy*. Ithaca: Cornell University Press.
Malehere, Adhie, and Wolas Krenak. 2006. "Pahlawan Nasional Kebanggaan Ntt." *Suara Pembaruan*, 10 November.
Manafe, Aco. 2009. *I H Doko: Berjuang Hingga Akhir*. Kupang: Artha Wacana Press.
Mann, Michael. 1993. *The Sources of Social Power*. 3 vols. Vol. 2. Cambridge: Cambridge University Press.
Manusama, A. Th. 1917. *Stephan De Lima De Amboneesche Toovenaar: Een Verhaal Uit Oud-Batavia*. Weltevreden Visser & Co.
Marquez, Gabriel Garcia. 1970 [orig. Spanish 1967]. *A Hundred Years of Solitude*. London: Penguin.
Marsden, Peter V. 1982. "Brokerage Behavior in Restricted Exchange Networks." In *Social Structure and Network Analysis*, edited by P.V. Marsden and N. Lin, 201–18. Beverly Hills, CA: Sage.
Maryanov, Gerald S. 1959. *The Establishment of Regional Government in the Republic of Indonesia*. PhD, Department of Government, Indiana University, Bloomington.
Mboi, Ben, and edited by Basri K. 2009. *Sekelumit "Sejarah" Terbentuknya Provinsi Nusa Tenggara Timur*. Kupang: Undana Press.
McGee, T.G. 1991. "The Emergence of Desakota Regions in Asia: Expanding a Hypothesis." In *The Extended Metropolis: Settlement Transition in Asia*, edited by Northon Ginsburg, Bruce Koppell and T.G. McGee, 3–25. Honolulu: University of Hawai'i Press.
McKinnon, Malcolm. 2011. *Asian Cities: Globalization, Urbanization and Nation-Building, Nias Monographs 120*. Copenhagen: NIAS Press.
McTaggart, W. Donald. 1982. "Land Use in Sukabumi, West Java: Persistence and Change." *Bijdragen tot de taal-, land- en volkenkunde* 138 (2–3):295–316.
McWilliam, Andrew R. 1999. "From Lord of the Earth to Village Head: Adapting to the Nation-State in West Timor." *Bijdragen tot de Taal-, Land- en Volkenkunde* 155 (1):121–44.
Mellor, John. 1976. *The New Economics of Growth: A Strategy for India and the Developing World*. Ithaca: Cornell University Press.
Merton, Robert K. 1968. *Social Theory and Social Structure*. New York: The Free Press.
Migdal, Joel S. 2001. *State in Society: Studying How States and Societies Transform and Constitute One Another, Cambridge Studies in Comparative Politics*. Cambridge: Cambridge University Press.
Miles, Douglas. 1976. *Cutlass and Crescent Moon: A Case Study of Social and Political Change in Outer Indonesia*. Sydney: Center for Asian Studies, University of Sydney.
Miller, Michelle Ann. 2013. "Decentralizing Indonesian City Spaces as New 'Centers'." *International Journal of Urban and Regional Research* 37 (3):834–48.

Milone, Pauline Dublin. 1966. *Urban Areas in Indonesia: Administrative and Census Concepts, Research Series / University of California. Institute of International Studies; No 10*. Berkeley, Cal.: Institute of International Studies, University of California.
Mishra, Pankaj. 2006. *Butter Chicken in Ludhiana: Travels in Small Town India*. Chicago: Pan Macmillan.
Mortimer, Rex. 1974. *Indonesian Communism under Sukarno: Ideology and Politics, 1959–1965*. Ithaca, N.Y.: Cornell University Press.
Mrázek, Rudolf. 2010. *A Certain Age: Colonial Jakarta through the Memories of Its Intellectuals*. Durham: Duke University Press.
Myrdal, Gunnar. 1968. *Asian Drama: An Inquiry into the Poverty of Nations*. 3 vols. New York: Pantheon.
Nahak, Servinus, et al, eds. 2009. *50 Thn Ntt, Seri Buku Vox No.53/01/2009*. Maumere: Seminari Tinggi St Paulus Ledalero.
Napitupulu, B. 1968. "Hunger in Indonesia." *Bulletin of Indonesian Economic Studies* 4 (9):60–70.
Nas, Peter J.M. 1981. *Indonesian Cities: A Typology of Kotamadya'S, Working Paper; No. 3*. Leiden: Leiden University.
——. ed. 1986. *The Indonesian City: Studies in Urban Development and Planning*. Dordrecht: Foris.
Netti, A.G. Hadzarmawit, and Hans Itta. 1997. *Kupang Dari Masa Ke Masa*. Kupang: Pemerintah Kabupaten Daerah Tingkat II Kupang.
Niel, Robert Van. 1960. *The Emergence of the Modern Indonesian Elite*. The Hague: Van Hoeve.
Niessen, Nicole. 1999. *Municipal Government in Indonesia: Policy, Law, and Practice of Decentralization and Urban Spatial Planning*. Leiden: Universiteit Leiden. School of Asian, African, and American Studies. Research School CNWS.
Noach, M.A. 1972. *Langkah Pertama: Suatu Tinjauan Terhadap Periode 25 Tahun Gmit: 31 Oktober 1947 - 31 Oktober 1971*. Kupang: Majelis Harian Sinode.
NUDS. 1985. Laporan Akhir Nuds: Laporan Utama, September 1985. [Jakarta]: Proyek Strategi Nasional Pengembangan Perkotaan (NUDS) - Direktorat Tata Kota dan Tata Daerah; United Nations Development Program (UNDP); United Nations Centre for Human Settlements (UNCHS).
Onvlee, Louis. 1953–55. 1 Kitlv-Inventaris 94 Or. 635 Collectie Louis Onvlee (1893–1986), Zendeling Op Sumba En Hoogleraar Culturele Antropologie Aan De Vrije Universiteit; Met Teksten Van Zijn Medewerkers Op Sumba En Verzamelde Documenten. 1871–1912, 1926–1984.
Oostingh, Roelof van Zeeveld. 1970. *The Pegawai Negeri of Bandung: Structure and Process in Indonesia*. PhD, Sociology and Anthropology, University of Virginia, Charlottesville.
Ormeling, F.J. 1956. *The Timor Problem: A Geographical Interpretation of an Underdeveloped Island*. Groningen: Wolters.
Paauw, Douglas S. 1960. *Financing Economic Development: The Indonesian Case*. Glencoe, Ill.: Free Press of Glencoe.
Panitya. 1972. *Kesimpulan Hasil Symposium Terbatas Persoalan Tanah Suku Daerah Propinsi Nusa Tenggara Timur Tanggal 15 Mei S.D. 20 Mei 1972 Di Kupang*. [Kupang]: Panitya Symposium Terbatas Persoalan Tanah Suku Daerah Propinsi Nusa Tenggara Timur.
Parera, A.D.M. 1969. *Portugis Dan Belanda Di Kota Kupang*. [Kupang]: [n.p.].
Passar, Kanis, ed. 2005. *Ensiklopedi: Mereka & Karya, Untuk Generasi Berlanjut Ntt*. Kupang: Yayasan Cinta Flobamora Abdi.
Pauker, Guy J. 1958. "The Role of Political Organizations in Indonesia." *Far Eastern Survey* 27 (9):129–42.
Pauker, Guy J. 1964. *Communist Prospects in Indonesia*. Santa Monica, Calif.: Rand Corporation.
PD Tjendana. 1970. Berkas Rapat Pemegang Saham Tahun Buku 1969–1970. Kupang: Perusahaan Daerah "Tjendana" Kabupaten Kupang.
——. 1971. Berkas Rapat Pemegang Saham Tahun Buku 1970–1971. Kupang: Perusahaan Daerah Kabupaten Kupang "Tjendana" Kupang.

Pemda NTT. 1966. *Monografi Propinsi Nusa Tenggara Timur: Menurut Keadaan Sampai Tanggal 31 Desember 1966*. [Kupang]: Pemerintah Daerah Propinsi Nusa Tenggara.
——. 1972. Gagasan Dasar Menyongsong Penyusunan Repelita Ii Di Daerah Propinsi Nusa Tenggara Timur. Kupang: Pemerintah Daerah Propinsi Nusa Tenggara Timur.
——. 1973. Pola Umum Rencana Pembangunan 25 Tahun Daerah Propinsi Nusa Tenggara Timur. [Kupang]: Pemerintah Daerah Propinsi Nusa Tenggara Timur.
Perdagangan, Departement. 1971. Ichtisar Perkembangan Harga-Harga Dan Data Statistik Perdagangan: Periode - Oktober 1971. [Jakarta]: Departemen Perdagangan.
Peters, George W. 1973. *Indonesia Revival: Focus on Timor*. Grand Rapids, Michigan: Zondervan.
Pinches, Michael, ed. 1999. *Culture and Privilege in Capitalist Asia*. Edited by Richard Robison, *The New Rich in Asia*. London/ New York: Routledge.
Portes, Alejandro, Manuel Castells, and Lauren A. Benton, eds. 1989. *The Informal Economy: Studies in Advanced and Less Developed Countries*. Baltimore, MD: Johns Hopkins University Press.
Post, Peter, William H. Frederick, Iris Heidebrink, Shigeru Sato, William Bradley Horton, and Didi Kwartanada, eds. 2010. *The Encyclopedia of Indonesia in the Pacific War, Handbook of Oriental Studies. Section 3 Southeast Asia, 19*. Leiden: Brill; In cooperation with the Netherlands Institute for War Documentation.
Prior, John Mansfield. 2011. "The Silent Scream of a Silenced History." *Exchange* 40:117–43, 311–21.
Purdey, Jemma. 2006. *Anti-Chinese Violence in Indonesia, 1996–1999*. Singapore: Singapore University Press.
Ravallion, Martin. 1988. "Inpres and Inequality: A Distributional Perspective on the Centre's Regional Disbursements." *Bulletin of Indonesian Economic Studies* 24 (3):53–71.
Redfield, Robert, and Milton B. Singer. 1954. "The Cultural Role of Cities." *Economic Development and Cultural Change* 3 (1):53–73.
Reid, A.J.S. 1980. "The Structure of Cities in Southeast Asia, Fifteenth to Seventeenth Centuries." *Journal of Southeast Asian Studies* 11 (2):235–50.
Reid, Anthony. 1974. *The Indonesian National Revolution 1945–1950*. Hawthorne: Longman.
Reksodihardjo, Sarimin. 1957. *Memori Penjerahan Gubernur Kepala Daerah Propinsi Nusa Tenggara: 1–4-1952 - 30–3-1957*. 3 vols. Singaradja: Pemerintah Daerah Propinsi Nusa Tenggara.
——. 1960 [1957]. *Report on the Lesser Sunda, Indonesia, 1952–1957: Memori Penjerahan Gubernur, Kepala Daerah Propinsi Nusa Tenggara*. 2 vols. New York: CCM Information Corporation.
Reno, William. 1995. *Corruption and State Politics in Sierra Leone*. Cambridge, UK: Cambridge University Press.
Ricklefs, M.C. 2008. *A History of Modern Indonesia since C.1200*. 4 ed. Basingstoke: Palgrave Macmillan.
Rietveld, Piet. 1988. "Urban Development Patterns in Indonesia." *Bulletin of Indonesian economic studies* 24 (1):73–95.
Riggs, Fred W. 1964. *Administration in Developing Countries: The Theory of Prismatic Society*. Boston: Houghton Mifflin.
——. 1966. *Thailand, the Modernization of a Bureaucratic Polity*. Honolulu: East-West Center Press.
Robinson, Geoffrey. 1995. *The Dark Side of Paradise: Political Violence in Bali*. Ithaca: Cornell University Press.
Robison, Richard. 1978. "Toward a Class Analysis of the Indonesian Military Bureaucratic State." *Indonesia* 25:17–39.
Rocamora, Jose Eliseo. 1974. *Nationalism in Search of Ideology: The Indonesian Nationalist Party, 1946–1965*. PhD, Cornell University, Ithaca NY.
Roeder, O.G. 1971. *Who's Who in Indonesia: Biographies of Prominent Indonesian Personalities in All Fields*. Djakarta: Gunung Agung.

Rondinelli, Dennis A. 1983. *Secondary Cities in Developing Countries: Policies for Diffusing Urbanization, Sage Library of Social Research; 145*. Beverly Hills London: Sage Publications.

Rutz, Werner. 1987. *Cities and Towns in Indonesia: Their Development, Current Positions and Functions with Regard to Administration and Regional Economy*. Berlin: Borntraeger.

Samiarsa, Indra, et al. 1969. *Rentjana Kota Kupang*. 2 vols. Djakarta: Direktorat Tata Kota dan Daerah, Direktorat Djendral Tjipta Karya, Departemen Pekerdjaan Umum dan Tenaga Listrik.

Santoso, Wartini, ed. 1984. *Katalogus Surat Kabar 1810–1984*. Jakarta: Perpustakaan Nasional.

Savage, Mike, Alan Warde, and Kevin Ward. 2003. *Urban Sociology, Capitalism and Modernity*. 2 ed. London: Palgrave Macmillan.

Schmitt, Hans O. 1962. "Foreign Capital and Social Conflict in Indonesia 1950–58." *Economic Development and Cultural Change* 10 (3):284–93.

Schoggen, Phil. 1989. *Behavior Settings: A Revision and Extension of Roger G. Barker's Ecological Psychology*. Stanford, Calif.: Stanford University Press.

Schulte Nordholt, H.G. 1971. *The Political System of the Atoni of Timor, Verhandelingen Van Het Koninklijk Instituut Voor Taal-, Land- En Volkenkunde; 60*. The Hague: Nijhoff.

Schulte Nordholt, Henk. 2011. "Modernity and Cultural Citizenship in the Netherlands Indies: An Illustrated Hypothesis." *Journal of Southeast Asian Studies* 42 (3):435–57.

Schulte Nordholt, Henk, and Gerry van Klinken, eds. 2007. *Renegotiating Boundaries: Local Politics in Post-Suharto Indonesia*. Leiden: KITLV.

Scott, James. 1998. *Seeing Like a State: How Certain Schemes to Improve the Human Condition Have Failed*. New Haven: Yale University Press.

Scott, Peter Dale. 1985. "The United States and the Overthrow of Sukarno, 1965–1967." *Pacific Affairs* 58 (2):239–64.

Sekda TTS. [1978]. *Memori Bupati Kepala Daerah Tingkat Ii Timor Tengah Selatan Tahun 1973–1978*. [Soë]: Sekretariat Wilayah Daerah Tingkat II Timor Tengah Selatan.

Setwilda. 1978. Riwayat Hidup Pj Gubernur Kepala Daerah Tingkat I Nusa Tenggara Timur Bapak Brigjen Tni El Tari. Kupang: Setwilda Tingkat I NTT.

Shiraishi, Saya S. 1997. *Young Heroes: The Indonesian Family in Politics*. Ithaca, New York: Cornell Southeast Asia Program Publications.

Sidik, Mohd. Danung, et al. 1968. Laporan Inventarisasi Land Use Tahun 1967 Propinsi Nusa Tenggara. Kupang: Kantor Inspeksi Land Use Nusa Tenggara Timur.

Sidik, Muh. Danung. 1973. Kota Kupang Dalam Peta. Kupang: [n.p.].

Siegel, James T. 1979. *Shadow and Sound: The Historical Thought of a Sumatran People*. Chicago: The University of Chicago Press.

Simandjuntak, Deasy. 2010. *Who Shall Be Raja? Patronage Democracy in North Sumatra, Indonesia*. PhD, University of Amsterdam, Amsterdam.

Slater, Dan. 2011. *Ordering Power: Contentious Politics and Authoritarian Leviathans in Southeast Asia*: Cambridge University Press.

Smail, John R.W. 1964. *Bandung in the Early Revolution, 1945–1946: A Study in the Social History of the Indonesian Revolution*. Ithaca: Southeast Asia Program, Cornell University.

Smail, John R. W. 1968. "The Military Politics of Northern Sumatra: December 1956-October 1957." *Indonesia* 6 (October):128–87.

Soedarma, M. Hatin, F. Gunarwan Suratmo, and Mursidin. 1968. *Masalah Penghidjauan Propinsi Nusa Tenggara Timur*. Djakarta: Direktorat Penggunaan Tanah, Direktorat Djenderal Kehutanan, Departemen Pertanian.

Soh, Andre Z., and Maria N.D.K. Indrayana. 2008. *Timor Kupang Dahulu Dan Sekarang*. Jakarta: Kelopak.

Sørensen, Aage B. 2000. "Toward a Sounder Basis for Class Analysis." *American Journal of Sociology* 105 (6):1523–58.

Stoler, Ann Laura. 2009. *Along the Archival Grain: Epistemic Anxieties and Colonial Common Sense*. Princeton, N.J.: Princeton University Press.

Sulistyo, Hermawan. 2000. *Palu Arit Di Ladang Tebu: Sejarah Pembantaian Yang Terlupakan 1965–1966*. Jakarta: Kepustakaan Gramedia Populer.
Sumarto, Hadi. 1962. *Nusa Tenggara Timur: 20 Desember 1958–20 Desember 1962*. Kupang: Djapen Daerah Tk I NTT.
Sundhaussen, Ulf. 1982. *The Road to Power: Indonesian Military Politics, 1945–1967*. Kuala Lumpur: Oxford University Press.
Sutherland, Heather. 1979. *The Making of a Bureaucratic Elite: The Colonial Transformation of the Javanese Priyayi*. Singapore: Heinemann.
Sutter, John Orval. 1959. *Indonesianisasi: Politics in a Changing Economy, 1940–55*. 4 vols, *Data Paper No. 36*. Ithaca, N.Y.: Department of Far Eastern Studies, Cornell University.
Tanter, Richard. 1990. "The Totalitarian Ambition: Intelligence and Security Agencies in Indonesia." In *State and Civil Society in Indonesia*, edited by Arief Budiman, 215–88. Clayton, Vic.: Monash University, Centre of Southeast Asian Studies.
Tanter, Richard, and Ken Young, eds. 1990. *The Politics of Middle Class Indonesia*. Clayton, Vic: Monash University CSEAS.
Tari, El. 1969. *Laporan Umum Gubernur Kepala Daerah Propinsi Nusa Tenggara Timur Pada Konperensi Gubernur Kepala Daerah Se-Indonesia Di Djakarta Oktober 1969*. Kupang: Pemerintah Daerah propinsi Nusa Tenggara Timur, Sekretariat.
——. 1972. *Memori Gubernur Kepala Daerah Propinsi Nusa Tenggara Timur Tahun 1958–1972*. 3 vols. Kupang: Biro Administrasi Umum, Kantor Gubernur Kepala Daerah Propinsi NTT.
Taylor, Jean Gelman. 2003. *Indonesia: Peoples and Histories*. New Haven/ London: Yale University Press.
The Siauw Giap. 1959. "Urbanisatieproblemen in Indonesië." *Bijdragen tot de Taal-, Land- en Volkenkunde (BKI)* 115 (3):249–76.
Tidey, Sylvia. 2012. *State, Society and Reciprocal Obligations in Kupang, Eastern Indonesia*. PhD, University of Amsterdam, Amsterdam.
Tim Penyusun Repelita ke II NTT. 1972. Pendapatan Regional Propinsi Nusa Tenggara Timur 1967–1971. Kupang: Pemerintah Daerah Propinsi Nusa Tenggara Timor dan Kantor Sensus & Statistik Propinsi Nusa Tenggara Timur.
Timmer, C.P. 2004. "The Road to Pro-Poor Growth: The Indonesian Experience in Regional Perspective." *Bulletin of Indonesian Economic Studies* 40 (2):177–207.
Titus, Milan, and Alet van der Wouden. 1998. "Town and Hinterland in Central Java, Indonesia." In *Town and Hinterland in Developing Countries: Perspectives on Rural-Urban Interaction and Regional Development*, edited by Milan Titus and Jan Hinderink, 143–78. Amsterdam: Thela-Thesis.
UNFPA. 2007. Unleashing the Potential of Urban Growth. *state of world population 2007*. New York: United Nations Population Fund.
Utrecht, E. 1969. "Land Reform in Indonesia." *Bulletin of Indonesian Economic Studies* 5 (3):71 – 88.
Vel, Jacqueline. 2007. "Campaigning for a New District in West Sumba." In *Renegotiating Boundaries*, edited by Henk Schulte Nordholt and Gerry van Klinken, 91–119. Leiden: KITLV Press.
Versluys, Mick. [n.d. - circa 1960]. *Njonja Aspiran: Lief En Leed in De Residentie 'Timor En Onderhorigheden'*. n.p.
Vickers, Adrian. 2005. *A History of Modern Indonesia*. Cambridge, UK: Cambridge University Press.
Vidich, Arthur J., and Joseph Bensman. 2000 [1958]. *Small Town in Mass Society: Class, Power and Religion in a Rural Community*. Revised ed. Urbana and Chicago: University of Illinois Press.
Wal, S.L. van der, ed. 1982. *Officiële Bescheiden Betreffende De Nederlands-Indonesische Betrekkingen, 1945–1950*. 20 vols. 's-Gravenhage: Instituut voor Nederlandse Geschiedenis.
Warren, Carol. 1993. *Adat and Dinas: Balinese Communities in the Indonesian State*. Kuala Lumpur: Oxford University Press.

Washbrook, David A. 1976. *The Emergence of Provincial Politics: The Madras Presidency 1870–1920*. Cambridge: Cambridge University Press.
Wawa, Jannes Eudes, ed. 2004. *Kanis Pari: Jangan Takut Berpolitik*. Jakarta: Bank Naskah Gramedia; Pusat Edukasi dan Kajian Masyarakat.
Webb, R. A. F. Paul. 1986. "The Sickle and the Cross: Christians and Communists in Bali, Flores, Sumba and Timor, 1965–67." *Journal of Southeast Asian Studies* 17 (1):94–112.
Wertheim, W.F. 1959. *Indonesian Society in Transition: A Study of Social Change*. 2 ed. The Hague: Van Hoeve.
——. 1964. "Betting on the Strong?" In *East-West Parallels: Sociological Approaches to Modern Asia*, 259–77. The Hague: Van Hoeve.
——. 1987. "Colonial and Post-Colonial Cities as Arenas of Conflict." *Bijdragen tot de Taal-, Land- en Volkenkunde* 143 (4):539–544.
——. 1955. "Changes in Indonesia's Social Stratification." *Pacific Affairs* 28 (1):41–52.
Wessel, Margit van. 2001. *Modernity and Identity: An Ethnography of Moral Ambiguity and Negotiations in an Indian Middle Class*. PhD, University of Amsterdam, Amsterdam.
WFP. 2009. *A Food Insecurity and Vulnerability Atlas of Indonesia 2009*. Rome: Food Security Council, Department of Agriculture, World Food Programme.
White, Ben. 2005. "Between Apologia and Critical Discourse: Agrarian Transitions and Scholarly Engagement in Indonesia." In *Social Science and Power in Indonesia*, edited by Vedi Hadiz and Daniel Dhakidae, 107–141. Jakarta and Singapore: Equinox and ISEAS.
Widiyatmika, Munandjar. 1983. *Sejarah Sosial Kota Kupang 1653–1980*. Kupang: Pusat Penelitian Universitas Nusa Cendana.
——. 2007. *Lintasan Sejarah Bumi Cendana*. Kupang: Pusat Pengembangan Madrasah.
Wirth, Louis. 1938. "Urbanism as a Way of Life." *American Journal of Sociology* 44 (1):3–24.
Wisseman Christie, Jan. 1991. "States without Cities: Demographic Trends in Early Java." *Indonesia* 52:23–40.
Wolf, Eric. 1956. "Aspects of Group Relations in a Complex Society: Mexico." *American Anthropologist, New Series* 58 (6):1065–78.
Wolters, O.W. 1982. *History, Culture, and Region in Southeast Asian Perspectives*. Singapore: Institute of Southeast Asian Studies.
——, ed. 1999. *History, Culture and Region in Southeast Asian Perspectives*. 2 ed. Ithaca, NY: Southeast Asia Program Publications, Cornell University.
Wouden, Alette Auguste van der. 1997. *Three Small Towns in Central Java: A Comparative Study of Their Economic Structure and Regional Importance*. PhD, Faculteit Ruimtelijke Wetenschappen, Universiteit Utrecht, Utrecht.
Yong Mun Cheong. 1982. *H. J. Van Mook and Indonesian Independence: A Study of His Role in Dutch-Indonesian Relations, 1945–48*. The Hague: Martinus Nijhoff.
Zanden, Jan Luiten van, and Daan Marks. 2012. *An Economic History of Indonesia 1800–2010, Routledge Studies in the Growth Economies of Asia*. London: Routledge.
Zed, Mestika. 1991. *Kepialangan, Politik Dan Revolusi: Palembang 1900–1950*. PhD, Faculteit der Sociaal-Culturele Wetenschappen, Vrije Universiteit, Amsterdam.

INDEX OF PERSONAL NAMES

www.ingramcontent.com/pod-product-compliance
Ingram Content Group UK Ltd.
Pitfield, Milton Keynes, MK11 3LW, UK
UKHW022209051026
15624UKWH00001B/71

9 789004 265080